Teacher Education and Practice

The Journal of the Texas Association
of Colleges of Teacher Education

EDITORIAL POLICY

Teacher Education and Practice, a peer-refereed journal, is dedicated to the encouragement and the dissemination of research and scholarship related to professional education. The journal is concerned, in the broadest sense, with teacher preparation, practice and policy issues related to the teaching profession, and learning in the school setting. The journal also serves as a forum for the exchange of diverse ideas and points of view within these purposes. As a forum, the journal offers a public space in which to critically examine current discourse and practice and engage in generative dialogue. Alternative forms of inquiry and representation are invited, and authors from a variety of backgrounds and diverse perspectives are encouraged to contribute.

The journal spans the boundaries of professional education in conventional and unconventional ways to offer multiple perspectives of teacher education and practice that seek to move beyond more traditional views of professional education. The journal is interested in manuscripts that explore the relationship between professional education and

- social justice, equity, caring, and democracy;
- challenges of teaching in preK–12 schools—public and private;
- state and federal policy;
- growing diversity—racial, ethnic, linguistic, and cultural;
- sociohistorical, sociocultural, and sociopolitical contexts of teaching;
- changing role of professional education in the larger context of a changing society;
- innovative and compelling ideas related to preparation and practice; and
- alternative approaches to the inquiry and understanding of how teachers learn.

Relatedly, manuscript submissions that *Teacher Education and Practice* accepts may include

- expositions;
- research reports—applied and basic research studies;
- policy position statements as well as analyses of the implications of existing policy;
- conversations or interviews—solicited and invited;
- creative writings that illuminate important innovative issues through alternative approaches; and
- book reviews and review essays—single-book reviews and multiple-book review essays.

PERMISSION TO PHOTOCOPY—POLICY STATEMENT

For copying rights to the articles within this journal, beyond those permitted by Sections 107 and 108 of the U.S. Copyright Law, please contact the Copyright Clearance Center, Inc., 222 Rosewood Drive, Danvers, MA 01923, or by e-mail at info@copyright.com.

TEACHER EDUCATION AND PRACTICE (ISSN 0890-6459)—Published quarterly—Winter, Spring, Summer, and Fall, one volume per year, by Rowman & Littlefield Education, 4501 Forbes Boulevard, Suite 200, Lanham, MD 20706. Postage paid at Blue Ridge Summit, PA 17214. POSTMASTER: Please send address changes to *TEP* Subscriptions, 4501 Forbes Boulevard, Suite 200, Lanham, MD 20706. Phone: 1-800-273-2223. Fax: (717) 794-3852. E-mail: journals@rowman.com.

Subscription rates:

Annual institutional: $170 domestic/$195 international
Annual individual: $66 domestic (TACTE member discount $56)/$106 international

PUBLISHING AND BUSINESS OFFICES

Rowman & Littlefield Education, 4501 Forbes Boulevard, Suite 200, Lanham, MD 20706. (301) 459-3366.

REPRINT CORRESPONDENCE—Write to Reprint Department, Rowman & Littlefield Education, 4501 Forbes Boulevard, Suite 200, Lanham, MD 20706.

GENERAL—*Teacher Education and Practice* is not responsible for the views expressed by individual contributors in articles published in the journal.

A Rowman & Littlefield Education journal published in partnership with the Texas Association of Colleges of Teacher Education (TACTE).

Contents

TEACHER EDUCATION AND PRACTICE

The editorial staff of *Teacher Education and Practice*, a journal originally founded by the Texas Association of Colleges of Teacher Education (TACTE), shares a professional commitment with its editorial advisory board and editorial reviewers to publish a high-quality journal.

EDITOR

Patrick M. Jenlink
Department of Secondary Education and Educational Leadership, McKibben 404j
Stephen F. Austin State University, P.O. Box 13018-SFA, Nacogdoches, Texas
75962-3018
Tel.: 936-468-2908   FAX: 936-468-1573   E-mail: pjenlink@sfasu.edu

ASSOCIATE EDITOR

Karen Embry Jenlink
Department of Secondary Education and Educational Leadership
Stephen F. Austin State University

MANAGING EDITOR

Carlie Wall
Rowman & Littlefield

PRODUCTION EDITOR

Darren Williams
Rowman & Littlefield

Editorial

Teacher Education, Democracy, and the Social Imaginary of Accountability

Patrick M. Jenlink

Preparing teachers for schools is a function of furthering the democratic ideals that guide a society in its continual progress toward realizing democracy. Realization of the democratic society the United States aspires to be, through its public education system, requires that teacher education take responsibility for the "development of more democratic forms of professionalism in teaching and teacher education" (Zeichner, 2010, p. 1550). However, in contrast, historically, teacher education has often not been concerned, albeit not by choice, with furthering democratic ideals. The audit culture[1] that has evolved over the past several decades in U.S. public education (P–16) has construed teachers as compliant technicians,[2] enacting predefined "best practices" with a predefined curriculum measured against external tests, a situation for which skill, not intelligence, is required (Giroux, 2012).

In the predawn era of neoliberalism, the "political climate of public education was seen as a public good, a value to the state by producing a society that could maintain and defend democratic ideals" (Bylsma, 2015, p. 4). However, as public education entered the neoliberal era, the perception of higher education—and therein teacher education—"shifted from a public good to a private asset, [and] the field has become increasingly privatized" (p. 4), and teacher education has become a commodity redefining universities as centers of production that yield products and services, diminishing the value of the teacher's role in achieving the social and democratic purposes of education.

Sleeter (2008), in examining the neoliberal assaults on teacher education, noted that neoliberalism's agenda is undermining equity and democracy. Neoliberalism has asserted pressures, counterintuitive to equity and democracy, that direct teacher education away from explicit equity-oriented teacher preparation and toward preparing teachers as technicians, away from defining teacher quality in terms of professional knowledge and toward defining it in terms of testable content knowledge, and toward shortening university-based teacher education or bypassing it altogether. In her examination, Sleeter emphasized the importance of collaborating with diverse, often underserved communities as a way of pushing back against neoliberalism. The effect of these pressures is deleterious to equity in our educational systems and to the efficacy of democracy as a way of life in our society.

Weiner (2007) has argued, rightly so, that neoliberalism opposes social cohesion and seeks to redirect education's social purposes. The neoliberal agenda is to reduce education's political and social (in contrast to its preferred economic) responsibilities, valorize individual competition, and enforce meritocratic outcomes, reducing social cohesion. Anton, Fisk, and Holmstrom (2000) have argued that the task of social cohesion is reasserting education's character as a "public good." As a goal of teacher education, social cohesion addresses the need for education as a social institution and for teacher education as the responsible agency for preparing teachers to "promote social attitudes such as acceptance of ethnic and religious differences, and as social justice and equality of opportunity" (Weiner, 2007, p. 281).

Public education in general and teacher education in particular, have, in most instances, been reshaped to become the arm of neoliberal economic policy, "defined both as the problem (in failing to provide a multi-skilled flexible workforce) and the solution (by upgrading skills and creating a source of national export earnings" (Blackmore, 2000, p. 134). Teacher education is facing the emergence and evolution of the neoliberal social imaginary,[3] which, through the use of standards, assessments, and accountability, aims to restrict educators to particular kinds of thinking that conceptualize education in terms of producing individuals who are economically productive; the individual becomes an economic product.

The Social Imaginary of Accountability

Public education, defined through a neoliberal social imaginary, is increasingly less concerned with its role in preparing civic-minded citizens to populate democratic publics (Weiner, 2007). A social imaginary is a way of thinking shared in a society by ordinary people, the common understandings that make everyday practices possible, giving them sense and legitimacy. It is largely implicit, embedded in ideas and practices, carrying within it deeper normative notions and images constitutive of a society. It involves, as Taylor (2004) explained, a representation of "the ways in which people imagine their social existence . . . the expectations that are normally met, and the deeper normative notions and images that underlie these expectations" (p. 23).

Writing on cultures of democracy, Taylor (2007) further explained that a social imaginary provides a set of common understandings that are tightly "interwoven with an idea of how [things] ought to go" (p. 120). In this sense, a social imaginary, through its manifestation in society, confirms certain ideas and practices as legitimate. Therefore, a social imaginary is socially constructed and broadly shared and has a tremendous pedagogical effect on populations in legitimating what is regarded as normal, natural, and appropriate. A social imaginary influences how people—the public—think about government and being governed and about social institutions such as education and about accountability of social institutions. In this sense, the social imaginary[4] is "largely implicit, embedded in ideas and practices, carrying within it deeper normative notions and images, constitutive of society" (Rizvi & Lingard, 2010, p. 34).

The social imaginary of accountability—a system of standards, assessments, and accountability measures—is a complex concept the meaning of which, when understood through the neoliberal lens of "new public manageralism" (Hill, 2006),[5] has a very different meaning than when understood through the lens of democracy. Ranson (2003), in explaining accountability in terms of public accountability in a social institution such as education, argued that to be accountable is to be "'*held to account*,' defining a relationship of formal control between parties, one of whom is mandatorily held to account to the other for the exercise of roles and stewardship of public resources" (p. 460; emphasis in the original). When standards and assessment and accountability mechanisms are designed to diminish professionalism—professional accountability to one's profession—in favor of a regime of neoliberal managerial accountability,[6] the governance of education shifts the emphasis to the public as consumer at the expense of the professional as provider. Regarding the public's belief in "trusting the professional, authoritative judgement has been replaced by trust in mechanisms of explicit, transparent, systematic public accountability that seeks to secure regulatory compliance of professional practice" (p. 468). The erosion of public trust in the institution of education and the demise of professional accountability work hand in hand to erode ideals integral to democratic society and the educational system necessary to ensure a democratic citizenry.[7]

The argument has been made (Giroux, 2012, 2013, 2014; Gunzenhauser, 2013; Helsby, 1999; Lipman, 2011, 2013; Rizvi & Lingard, 2010) that the "social imaginary of accountability" as part of the neoliberal agenda is a market-driven illusion intended to create mystification in the public with respect to education/educational institutions; such imaginaries are structured around tendentially empty and essentially ambiguous signifiers. The "neoliberal social imaginary" is seen as the effect of transforming particular elitist and political economic interests into what is put forth as a universal interest (a form of "common sense") to the public—the mystification of education achieved through a neoliberal agenda. In the end, as Apple (2007) explained, the "issue is not whether or not we need accountability, but the logics of accountability that tend now to guide the process of higher education" (p. 15).

The Social Imaginary of Accountability for Democracy

Many if not most of the pressures on teacher education today are a result of the embedding of neoliberal ideas and policies about markets, privatization, deregulation, and the private versus public good (Apple, 2007; Ball, 2004;

Hursh, 2006; Kumashiro, 2010; Zeichner, 2010, 2012). Necessary to a strong, well-supported system of public education and the realization of the ideals of a democratic American society is a social imaginary of democratic account-ability.

A social imaginary of democratic accountability in public education might best be understood as a dynamic system of democratic mechanisms and measures intrinsically interdependent and intertwined—a system con-cerned explicitly with preparing teachers as agents of democracy who will enter classrooms in schools and prepare students as democratic citizens necessary for the future well-being of society. This system of measures, as Levinson (2011) explains, has a role "to play in public education within a democracy for two reasons. First, they are necessary to advance the public good. Second, they have the potential to enable specifically democratic goods" (p. 128).

However, fostering and sustaining a social imaginary of democratic ac-countability will not be easy, nor will it be without challenges from the domi-nant neoliberal discourses that currently exercise decided control of educa-tion and much of society. Standards, assessments, and accountability measures typically end up promoting compliance; these mechanisms "skew teachers' instructional efforts toward the narrower content range and even the format and other essentially arbitrary features of the test itself, rather than toward the full range of educational standards or (most importantly) toward student learning" (Levinson, 2011, p. 133). Standardized tests and learning outcomes are examples of artificial quantification of learning designed to meet expecta-tions of efficiency and accountability—mechanisms designed for purposes of control and commodification.

A system of standards, assessment, and accountability measures is ill suited to the work of fostering a social imaginary of democratic accountability nec-essary to public education and to teacher education. Two reasons stand out. First, standardized goals, content, and assessments are uniform and static, whereas empowering teacher education is particular, context specific, and dynamic. Second, standards, assessments, and accountability mechanisms that are dominated by the "new public managerialism" of people or groups outside education are imposed on public education and teacher education, undermining a democratizing education system by removing the locus of control from educators who need to model empowered democratic civic ac-tion and students who need to practice it (Levinson, 2011).

A social imaginary of democratic accountability must necessarily involve communication and negotiation between teacher educators and the public[8]—between teachers and other constituencies of schools—including (perhaps especially) students. As Sleeter (2008) argued, communication and "collabora-tion means strengthening emphasis on democracy as a central education value" (p. 1955). This is the first step to a re-creating a bond of "trust" between the public and its educational system, a bond that has been steadily eroded by the neoliberal agenda of commodifying education. Importantly, while it is not possible to return to the predawn era before the neoliberal agenda was unleashed on education, it is possible to recognize the deleterious nature of the neoliberal agenda and, in so doing, take a step forward in reclaiming the function of public education in the democratization of our society.

Replacing the neoliberal imaginary of a managerial accountability with a social imaginary of democratic accountability is critical to the future of public education as a function of democratizing society. In society and in public education, this form of democratization must involve processes for the recognition of difference (including differences in power) and for dealing with conflict in constructive ways. In this sense, a democratic accountability, rather than focused extensively on a system of standards, assessment, and accountability mechanisms concerned with technical efficiency and the commodification of education, must provide opportunities for dialogue among those with opposing views. This dialogue of democratic accountability, as Ranson (2003) explains, "presupposes a public sphere informed by very different principles from the neoliberal polity: a sphere of public goods to be determined through participation in collective deliberation in the purposes and conditions of citizenship" (p. 471).

What public education in general and teacher education in particular is or can be—what the function of public education is in furthering democratic society—depends on creating a social imaginary of democratic accountability that the public shares and owns. It is, as Ranson (2003) explained, "the democratic institutions of the public sphere that constitute the conditions of trust and mutual accountability" (p. 471). Democratic accountability, in concert with recognizing public education's function in a democratic society, must be shared between local and national authorities to ensure that local needs are met and voices heard but also ensuring a consistency in democratic practices (Hursh, 2007).

Freedom in Democratic Accountability

Freedom in American society is a democratic ideal; it is both a right and a responsibility—a responsibility of each citizen to ensure that freedom is afforded to all. Freedom in public education is (or has been in the past) a condition of teaching and learning, freedom of "mind," and freedom of beliefs and values. However, in the decades since the dawn of neoliberalism's control in public education, freedom has been diminished for educators and students alike.

The neoliberal interpretation of the public as consumer connotes a form of consumer accountability wherein public trust "is secured by specifying performance and regulating compliance. It is this form of accountability, with its potentially punitive image, that has become anathema to professional communities who reject its instrumental rationale and techniques" (Ranson, 2003, p. 460). In essence, the true freedom is reduced and marginalized, and the public and its education system are victimized and villainized, respectively. The social imaginary of democratic accountability is concerned with discursive reason where "accounts of action make intelligible their intentions and the narrative histories we have authored and are responsible for" (p. 461).

Vassallo (2013) argues that education "either functions as an instrument which is used to facilitate integration of the younger generation into the logic of the present system and bring about conformity [a pedagogy of dehumanization]" (p. 34) or takes a more critical, democratic path and "becomes the practice of freedom, the means by which men and women deal critically and creatively with reality and discover how to participate in the transformation of their world" (p. 34). Vassallo's argument for freedom extends to teacher preparation, where the work of teacher educators is made increasingly problematic as they face conflicting pressures created by the logic of neoliberal accountability to, on one level, privilege some groups over others and, on another level, to ensure that disadvantaged groups have a voice in educational decision making—consumer accountability and the asymmetrical nature of power and purpose in relationships in contrast to the more symmetrical nature of power and purpose in relationships.

In determining democratic accountability as a social imaginary within and for public education, Levinson (2011) draws attention to the need to ask critical questions that go below the surface of what the public is told is good in terms of standards, assessments, and accountability mechanisms. Freedom is born not of silence but rather from giving voice. The dominant relations of accountability are not value neutral but rather reveal the practices, structures, and codes that shape the public imaginary of education. These forms of accountability express the public purposes that are valued, the knowledge claims that are regarded as authoritative, and whose authority acquires legitimacy. Accountability begins with difficult questions: What role should the standards, assessments, and accountability measures have in public education? What does the public believe and value about education? What do teachers represent to the public? What does the public trust or not trust in public education? What are the democratic implications of the standards, assessments, and accountability mechanisms in the contemporary educational landscape? What role does the public have in shaping a new social imaginary of accountability? What role does education have in shaping a new social imaginary of education? Answers to these questions in the public "define a conception of the public good underpinned by a structure of power and authority: accountability constitutes and evaluates the relationship of the public to the polity (Ranson, 2003, p. 470).

Final Reflections

Democratic accountability, in the sense of fostering a new social imaginary for society—the very language and discourse that construe the purposes and achievements of public education and therein teacher education—should reflect social and political processes representative of democratic ideals (Levinson, 2011; Ranson, 2003). To the extent that standards, assessment, and accountability mechanisms are now sorting students in public schools and commodifying teacher preparation programs, we should at least question the democratic implications of the position of these mechanisms in the contemporary educational landscape.

Importantly, as Weiner (2007) has argued, teacher educators as agents of democracy must give strong political argument about our society's need for education as a public good" (p. 283) and for "teacher education's value as a public good" (p. 283). We must reassert education's character as a "public good"; advancing the need for social cohesion in meeting education's purpose in democratic society is a necessary step forward. Equally important, teacher educators as agents of democracy must recognize that the work before them is difficult, challenging, and necessary if a democratic accountability mediated by relationships within the whole community of professional practice and the large community of parents and citizens is to be achieved. Mediating the impact of the tightly regulated deregulation of education amid a market-based economy of education and, at the same time, ensuring democracy will require an advocacy of standards of complexity and a concern for the public good. **TEP**

Notes

1. Michael Power's (1999) notion of the "audit society" symbolizes the transformative effect of accountability on society and its educational systems. The "audit culture," as a manifestation of neoliberal policies advocating extreme accountability in education, is represented by the advancement and fulfillment of checklists and criteria without fundamental reflection on how these mechanisms contribute to the social and intellectual enrichment of the students. The ultimate objective pleasing the students and parents—conceived as consumers in neoliberal ideology—gives priority to the most concrete, quantifiable results: employment supplants enlightenment. The university's mission narrows to job training rather than expanding the mind to explore possibilities, solve problems, and find creative expression (Schwartzman, 2013; Tuchman, 2009).
2. Zeichner (2012) has argued that in contrast to preparing teachers as professionals, which is viewed by neoliberals as too costly to build and "maintain a professional teaching force to teach everyone's children" (p. c), neoliberals have advocated preparing teachers "as technicians to implement the teaching scripts with which they are provided in the belief that the preparation these teachers receive and the subsequent scripting of instruction will lead to improvements in pupils' standardized test scores" (p. c). Zeichner noted Teach for America as an example of preparing teachers as technicians—temporary teachers in a system designed for teacher replacement every "few years by other narrowly trained teachers" (p. c).
3. Evans and Sewell (2013) explain that the neoliberal social imaginary extols entrepreneurship, self-reliance, and sturdy individualism; equates untrammeled pursuit of self-interest and consumer satisfaction with human freedom; glorifies personal wealth;

sees volunteerism as the appropriate way to solve social problems; and associates government programs with inefficiency, corruption, and incompetence. The neoliberal social imaginary shapes individual goals and behavior while simultaneously making neoliberal political ideology and policy paradigms seem "natural" (Somers, 2008).

4. Hill (2006) explains "new public managerialism" as the "importation into the old public services of the language and management style of private capital," which he rightly argues "has replaced the ethic, language and style of public service and duty" (p. 119). In the university, inclusive of teacher preparation programs, "the language of education has been very widely replaced by the language of the market, where lecturers 'deliver the product,' 'operationalize delivery,' and 'facilitate clients' learning' within a regime of 'quality management and enhancement,' where students have become 'customers' selecting 'modules' on a pick'n'mix basis, where 'skill development' at universities has surged in importance to the derogation of the development of critical thought" (pp. 119–120).

5. Jaramillo and McLaren (2009) are instructive in understanding the implication of the social imaginary in American society: "A central feature of the U.S. imaginary has historically been shaped by the notion that capitalism is compatible with democratic social formations. From the onset, schooling in the United States has served an important purpose in an evolving capitalist economy, supporting the values of individualism and 'merit' most closely aligned with fitting a populace to the demands of capitalist 'democracy'" (p. 13). Extrapolating this logic, the "neoliberal social imaginary" is concerned with the embedding of market logics into the standardization and determination/control of education. Accountability, standards, and assessment, in this sense a managerial system, culminate in a system of determination/control of education. In particular, there is an emphasis of "neoliberal rationality" that foregrounds the market and how it extends and disseminates market values to educational institutions and social action.

6. Accountability to one's profession under the historical bureaucratic model in contrast to accountability in terms of efficiency in a consumer model has very different implications for teacher education. Olsen and Peters (2005), in examining accountability in higher education, are instructive in distinguishing professional and managerial accountability:

- Bureaucratic: professional accountability, is ex-ante, where rules and regulations are specified in advance and accountability is measured in terms of process; formulated in terms of standards, based on expertise of those who work in a particular area.
- Consumer: managerial accountability, associated with market systems, based on price; which works in terms of contracts in which the performance is rewarded or punished according to the achievement of pre-set targets and externally imposed objectives. (p. 328)

7. A democratic society is founded on a set of ideals and beliefs and counter to a neoliberal agenda. Barber (1997) argues that attacking education and vilifying educators as an agenda to convince the public that the system is broken diminishes the foundation of our democratic society:

In attacking public education critics are attacking the very foundation of our democratic civic culture. Public schools are not merely schools for the public, but schools of publicness: institutions where we learn what it means to be a public and start down the road toward common national and civic identity. They are the forges of our citizenship and the bedrock of our democracy. Vilifying public school teachers and administrators and cutting public school budgets even as we subsidize private educational opportunity puts us in double jeopardy: for as we put our children at risk, we undermine our common future, at the same moment, in constraining the conditions of liberty for some, we undermine the future of democracy for all. (p. 22)

The neoliberal agenda is one of economics and commodification of education, in particular teacher education, which requires that the public believe the neoliberal imaginary of what constitutes a "good system" of education. The first step in drawing the public into the neoliberal imaginary is tell the public why democratic accountability is wrong, and the second step is to demonstrate that the education system is not meeting an economic metric while at the same time convincing the public that the metric is about quality and not about efficiency. Convincing the public that the neoliberal agenda is in the public's best interest is, as the old story goes about the devil, the greatest trick ever played on the public and its educational system.

8. Ranson (2003) explains the importance of the "public" in negotiating a social imaginary of democratic accountability:

The deep purpose of the public sphere is to constitute the social and political preconditions that make society possible, the agreements that enable social life to proceed: who is to be a member, what rights and duties are expected, and what will count as fair distribution of goods and opportunities. Such decisions will determine the basis of justice and well-being in society: they will remain essentially contested, only achieving legitimacy through democratic deliberation. (p. 473)

References

Anton, A., Fisk, M., & Holmstrom, N. (2000). Introduction. In A. Anton, M. Fisk, & N. Holmstrom (Eds.), *Not for sale: In defense of public goods* (pp. xv–xx). Boulder, CO: Westview Press.

Apple, M. W. (2007). Education, markets, and an audit culture. *International Journal of Educational Policies*, *1*(1), 4–19.

Ball, S. (2004, June). Everything for sale: The commodification of everything. Annual Education Lecture. London: London Institute of Education.

Barber, B. (1997). Public schooling: Education for democracy. In J. Goodlad & T. McMannon (Eds.), The public purpose of education and schooling (pp. 21–32). San Francisco: Jossey-Bass.

Blackmore, J. (2000). Globalization: A useful concept for feminists rethinking theory and strategies in education. In C. A. Torres and N. Burbules (Eds.), Globalization and education: Critical perspectives (pp. 133–155). New York: Routledge.

Bylsma, P. E. (2015). The teleological effect of neoliberalism on American higher education. College Student Affairs Leadership, 2(2). http://scholarworks.gvsu.edu/csal/vol2/iss2/3

Evans, P. B., & Sewell, W. H., Jr. (2013). The neoliberal era: Ideology, policy, and social effects. In P. A. Hall & M. Lamont (Eds.), Social resilience in the neoliberal era (pp. 35–68). New York: Cambridge University Press.

Giroux, H. A. (2012). *The neoliberal attack on education.* http://www.truthdig.com/report/item/can_democratic_education_survive_in_a_neoliberal_society_20121017

Giroux, H. A. (2013). Beyond dystopian education in a neoliberal society. http://www.uta.edu/huma/agger/fastcapitalism/10_1/giroux10_1.html

Giroux, H. A. (2014). Neoliberalism's war on higher education. Chicago: Haymarket Books.

Gunzenhauser, M. G. (2013). Ethics for the new political economy: What can it mean to be professionally responsible. Philosophical Studies in Education, 44, 10–28.

Helsby, G. (1999). Changing teacher's work. Buckingham: Open University Press.

Hill, D. (2006). Educational perversion and global neoliberalism. In E. W. Ross & R. Gibson (Eds.), Neoliberalism and educational reform (pp. 107–144). Cresskill, NJ: Hampton Press.

Hursh, D. W. (2006). Marketing education: The rise of standardized testing, accountability, competition, and markets in public education. In E. W. Ross & R. Gibson (Eds.), Neoliberalism and educational reform (pp. 15–34). Cresskill, NJ: Hampton Press.

Hursh, D. W. (2007). Assessing No Child Left Behind and the rise of neoliberal education policies. American Educational Research Journal, 44(3), 493–518.

Jaramillo, N. E., & McLaren, P. (2009). From the imaginary to the real: Towards a critical teacher education. International Journal of Educational Policies, 3(1), 5–19.

Kumashiro, K. (2010). Seeing the bigger picture: Troubling movements to end teacher education. Journal of Teacher Education, 61(1–2), 56–65.

Levinson, M. (2011). Democracy, accountability, and education. Theory and Research in Education, 9(2), 125–144.

Lipman, P. (2011). The new political economy of urban education: Neoliberalism, race, and the right to the city. New York: Routledge.

Lipman, P. (2013). Economic crisis, accountability, and the state's coercive assault on public education in the USA. Journal of Education Policy, 28(5), 557–573.

Olsen, M., & Peters, M. A. (2005). Neoliberalism, higher education and the knowledge economy: From the free market to knowledge capitalism. Journal of Educational Policy, 20(3), 313–345.

Power, M. (1999). The audit society: Rituals of verification. Oxford: Oxford University Press.

Ranson, S. (2003). Public accountability in the age of neo-liberal governance. Journal of Education Policy, 18(5), 459–480.

Rizvi, F., & Lingard, B. (2010). Globalizing education policy. New York: Routledge.

Schwartzman, R. (2013). Consequences of commodifying education. Academic Exchange Quarterly, 17(3), 1–7.

Sleeter, C. (2008). Equity, democracy, and neoliberal assaults on teacher education. Teaching and Teacher Education, 24(6), 1947–1957.

Somers, M. R. (2008). Genealogies of citizenship: Markets, statelessness, and the right to have rights. New York: Cambridge University Press.

Taylor, C. (2004). Modern social imaginaries. Durham, NC: Duke University Press.

Taylor, C. (2007). Cultures of democracy and citizen efficacy. Public Culture, 19(1), 117–150.

Tuchman, G. (2009). Wannabe u: Inside the corporate university. Chicago: University of Chicago Press.

Vassallo, S. (2013). Critical pedagogy and neoliberalism: Concerns with teaching self-regulated learning. *Studies in Philosophy and Education*, 32, 563–580.

Weiner, L. (2007). A lethal threat to U.S. teacher education. *Journal of Teacher Education*, 58(4), 274–286.

Zeichner, K. (2010). Competition, economic rationalization, increased surveillance, and attacks on diversity: Neo-liberalism and the transformation of teacher education in the U.S. Teacher and Teacher Education, 26, 1544–1552.

Zeichner, K. (2012). Two visions of teaching and teacher education for the twenty-first century. North Dartmouth: Center for Policy Analyses, University of Massachusetts Dartmouth.

The Importance and Clarity of the New Council for the Accreditation of Educator Preparation Principles and Standards

FRANK B. MURRAY

ABSTRACT: A convenience sample of leaders from 49 Teacher Education Accreditation Council–accredited programs rated the five new Council for the Accreditation of Educator Preparation standards as *important* (but not *essential*) for the purposes of documenting program quality, but they also rated the standards as only *mostly clear* rather than *sufficiently* or *very clear*. There were statistically significant differences between the mean ratings of the five standards, between the ratings of those who accepted and rejected some public reporting measures favored by policymakers, and between those who were willing or unwilling to have a "gold star" accreditation for allegedly superior programs. The survey results are discussed in the context of other surveys of teacher education accreditation standards and the national narrative about teacher education.

There is a long-standing narrative in the United States that teacher education is "broken" because teachers, now and in the past, have been so poorly prepared that the nation's schools are perpetually at risk (Aldeman, Carey, Dillon, Miller, & Silva, 2011; Conant, 1963; Crowe, 2010; Greenberg, Pomerance, & Walsh, 2011; Judge, Lemosse, Paine, & Sedlak, 1994; Kanstoroom & Finn, 1999; Koerner, 1963; Mitchell & Barth, 1999; Teacher's College, 2009; University of Virginia, 2009). Several recent reform-minded groups, such as the Project 30 Alliance, the Holmes Group (subsequently the Holmes Partnership), the Renaissance Group, Teachers for a New Era, the National Board for Professional Teaching Standards, and the National Commission on Teaching and America's Future, all sought to change this depressing narrative, but apparently none have succeeded, as the narrative continues (see Teacher's College, 2009; University of Virginia, 2009).

Hoping to finally change this prevailing narrative, the new Council for the Accreditation of Educator Preparation (CAEP) adopted five accreditation standards with 30 components (see http://caepsite.org). CAEP's theory of action was that if accreditation were mandated, as it is in most other professions, CAEP could eventually compel all education schools to do in fact what some had hoped they would do voluntarily in the prior national reform initiatives.

The CAEP Standards

The new standards require providers of educator preparation programs (EPPs) to have multiple forms of evidence about two areas of competence: (1) the program graduate's competence to teach effectively and (2) the faculty's competence to deliver quality programs. Specifically, these new standards required faculty to supply evidence that the educators who completed their programs were competent in their teaching subject matters, pedagogy, and teaching skills and that the faculty themselves were competent to use that evidence to systematically monitor and steadily enhance the quality of the programs they offer. Of particular note was that the bar for the evidence of the graduates' teaching skill now had been raised to include evidence that the students of the graduates learned what was taught to them by the recent EPP graduates. In other words, to be accredited, an EPP now had to show that, through its graduates, the EPP had a positive impact on K–12 learning and accomplishment.

Prior Surveys on Teacher Education Accreditation Standards

Before the CAEP Board of Directors adopted the new standards, McKinley Advisors in Washington, D.C., surveyed a convenience sample of national stakeholders in public education about the five CAEP standards. The educational faculty members in the sample (about 250 respondents) rated the five standards in the 2.00+ to 3.00+ ranges of 5-point scales with regard to (1) how appropriately challenging the standards were, (2) how completely they address educator's needs, and (3) how well the available evidence accurately demonstrates the standard (1 = not at all to 5 = completely).

Table 1 presents the mean ratings given in the McKinley report from the education faculty members.

In the McKinley survey, the lowest mean ratings were found for the "evidence available to demonstrate the standard." Of the 50 occasions a rating was made (five standards from the 10 groups), 33 out of 50 times the mean rating of available evidence was lower than the mean "challenging" rating, an event that would occur by chance only three in 100 times (by a binomial test).

Three groups of raters—the alternate route providers, education faculty members, and discipline faculty members—gave lower than the overall mean ratings to each question about a standard, while three other groups—policymakers, others, and P–12 staff—gave higher than the overall mean rating to each question for each standard. Evidently, the providers or those closest to accreditation were somewhat less impressed with the standards than those farther away from the actual delivery of educator preparation programs. CAEP standards 1 and 2 drew more support than the others insofar as 70%, more or less, gave them the top two ratings (4 or 5) on challenge and meeting

Table 1.   Mean Ratings (1–5) from Education Faculty Members in the McKinley Sample of the Five Proposed CAEP Standards on Their Challenge, Meeting Needs, and Accuracy of Evidence for Them[a]

	Proposed CAEP Standards				
Survey Topics	1	2	3	4	5
Appropriately challenging[b]	3.82	3.79	3.00	3.00	3.35
Meeting educator needs[b]	3.59	3.73	2.96	2.94	3.28
Evidence accurately demonstrates standards[c]	3.32	3.51	2.98	2.80	3.19

[a] The terms in the complete scale (1–5) were not revealed in the McKinley report, nor were the standard deviations of the ratings, tests of significant differences between the means, or correlations among the means presented.

[b] Scale: 1 = not at all to 5 = completely.

[c] Scale: 1 = not well at all to 5 = completely.

needs. Standards 3, 4, and 5 drew only 40+% to 50+% of this level of support by contrast.

A convenience sample of about 80 members of the TEAC, one of the two founding members of CAEP, had been surveyed on two prior occasions (2005 and 2007) about the TEAC accreditation principles and standards with regard to the value of the TEAC principles and standards for documenting and for improving program quality. On the whole, the members rated the TEAC principles in the 4.00 to 5.00 range on a 5-point scale of relative importance, which ran from (1) not needed to (2) marginal to (3) useful to (4) important to (5) essential for the value of the principle and standard in documenting program quality and for improving it. The magnitudes of these ratings are also in line with the ratings that faculty, students, and cooperating teachers in TEAC-accredited programs gave of students' accomplishments with regard to the same standards in other online TEAC surveys (Murray, 2011, 2013a, 2013b).

Results of the Survey of TEAC Members on CAEP Standards

In 2013, a convenience sample of 49 of TEAC's 200 members completed an online survey, managed by Zarca, about the new CAEP standards. The 49 respondents' ratings were, as in the earlier TEAC surveys, in the 4.00 to 5.00 range with regard to the importance of the proposed CAEP standards (and their 30 components). By a one-sample t test, their mean ratings (1–5) were significantly higher statistically than the McKinley sample's mean faculty ratings (1–5) of each of the standards.

While the survey questions differ between the McKinley and TEAC surveys, there is arguably some conceptual similarity between the question of "importance" of the standards and the questions about the standards being "challenging" and "meeting the needs of educators." If the standards are seen as challenging and meeting the needs of educators, they could be seen reasonably as important for documenting quality and improving it. Along the same lines, the question about whether the available evidence allows the standard to be demonstrated accurately could be seen as similar to the question with regard to the clarity of the standard.

The reliability of the TEAC survey results for the survey was acceptable with Cronbach's alphas of .91 for the 30 importance items and .96 for clarity for the 30 clarity items. Table 2 gives the means of the importance and clarity ratings for each proposed standard.

The differences between the mean *importance* and mean *clarity* ratings were also statistically significant for each standard in Table 2. The ratings of importance and clarity are also positively and significantly correlated for each standard (.45, .44, .56, .48, and .67, respectively). This would seem to indicate that while the standards are seen as more important than they are clear, those that are less important are also proportionately less clear with regard to how the EPP would support them.

It is also the case that all but two of the differences between the standards themselves are statistically significant. The exceptions are that standard 1 (content and pedagogy) and standard 2 (clinical partnerships) do not differ in importance, nor do standards 3 and 5. Clearly, in both surveys, standard 1 (content and pedagogy) and standard 2 (clinical partnerships) are seen as the most important of the standards. The three other standards are in a different category and are seen as useful but not essential and only *mostly clear* with regard to how they could be supported.

Table 2. TEAC Ratings (1–5) of the Components of the Five Proposed CAEP Standards with Regard to Their Importance and Clarity

Standards Topic (Number of Components); Importance & Clarity	n	Minimum	Maximum	M	SD
Standard 1: Content and Pedagogy (9)					
Importance	49	2.56	5.00	4.35	.56
Clarity	46	1.22	5.00	3.36	.75
Standard 2: Clinical Partnerships (3)					
Importance	49	2.00	5.00	4.13	.81
Clarity	49	1.00	5.00	2.89	1.05
Standard 3: Recruitment (8)					
Importance	47	1.13	5.00	3.63	.79
Clarity	44	1.00	5.00	3.07	.86
Standard 4: Impact on P–12 (4)					
Importance	47	1.25	4.50	3.34	.75
Clarity	48	1.00	5.00	2.76	.92
Standard 5: Quality Control (6)					
Importance	44	1.83	5.00	3.77	.75
Clarity	43	1.00	5.00	3.14	.88

On the whole, the correlations, all significantly positive, between the ratings of the standards on clarity are higher than they are for importance, which means that the respondents were in agreement more about the lack of clarity than on the importance of the standard themselves. It would seem, based on both the McKinley and the TEAC surveys, that the implementation of the CAEP standards will be dependent on greater clarification of how the standards can be met. The correlations also point to the fact that those satisfied with the importance or clarity of one standard are likely to be satisfied with the others and vice versa.

Given that the McKinley survey showed that the faculty groups were less enthusiastic about the standards than other groups, there remains the question of whether the relatively low McKinley ratings of some standards (3, 4, and 5 in particular) are attributable to the reluctance of faculty to do the extra work and accept the burdens entailed in the standard or whether it is that the faculty members genuinely think the standard is wrongheaded. It is possible to shed some light on this question by analyzing the differences in ratings given by those TEAC respondents who were willing to reveal publicly some straightforward and more or less enlightened facts about their EPP and those who were not willing to reveal these facts.

Gold Star Accreditation

The TEAC survey also asked members to rate several types of evidence for the award of an exemplary accreditation status (the gold star) and some consumer protection categories of evidence for posting on the EPP websites. Table 3 gives the percentages of respondents who favored using the following kinds of evidence as the basis for the award of gold star accreditation.

Relatively little confidence is shown in basing a gold star accreditation award on the percentage of graduates who were teachers of the year, but there seems to be considerably more support for the award if the program can show that the interpretations of its assessments are highly reliable and valid.

There are some revealing differences in the ratings of the standards between those who were in favor and those who were not in favor of disclosing the information or using it as a basis for the award of gold star accreditation. When raters, for example, were asked if increasing the reliability and validity of their local assessments would be an adequate basis for awarding a gold star to the EPP, those who thought so also rated 27 of the 30 components of the standards as clearer than those who were not willing to award the star on this basis (binomial, $p < .0001$). With regard to the importance of the standards for demonstrating quality, they rated 22 of 30 (binomial, $p < .01$) components higher. Only one other gold star candidate, the percentage of graduates who earned National Board for Professional Teaching Standards certification, had any similar impact on the ratings of the standards (binomial test, $p < .01$). Per-

Table 3.   Percentage in Favor of Potential Gold Star Markers of Quality

Potential Markers of Quality to Be Considered in Awarding a Gold Star Rating	*In Favor (%)*
Program assessments shown to be highly reliable and valid	55.1
High percentage of completers who were designated by their state as high-gain producing teachers	22.4
High percentage of completers who earned national board certification	20.4
High percentage of completers who were teachers of the year	16.3

centages of teachers of the year and value-added designees had only chance relationships with the 30 component ratings.

Consumer Protection

Accreditation has several functions, and the two most significant are the public assurance of quality and the improvement in the quality of accredited programs. Accreditation is also thought to better inform the public, particularly prospective students, about the value and features of the program in which they are considering enrolling. The survey asked TEAC members about 12 common lines of evidence that might be useful to prospective students as they consider where they might like to study. Table 4 gives the percentages of respondents who favored the disclosure of various kinds of evidence about the operation of an educator preparation program for the purposes of consumer protection.

On the whole, as Table 4 shows, there were clear differences in what the members thought should be disclosed, with the most acceptable levels being only in the 40% to 60% range of respondents' support and the least acceptable levels being in only the 4% to 5% range of respondents who would disclose some kinds of evidence to the public. It is fair to conclude that the majority of respondents would not be in favor of any of the last four items in Table 4 of consumer protection as a basis for accreditation or public disclosure.

Those who would disclose the percentage of program completers who found a teaching position, for example, rated the importance of each standard significantly higher than those who would not disclose the percentage. They also rated the importance of 28 of the 30 components of the standards higher than those who said they would not disclose the percentage (binomial, $p < .0001$).

Along these lines, those who would be willing to disclose the percentage of minority students in their program also rate the five standards significantly higher with regard to their importance for demonstrating a quality program. They also rated 29 of the 30 components of the five standards higher (binomial, $p < .0001$).

The same pattern was found with regard to those who would disclose the percentage of completers versus those who would not disclose the percentage

Table 4.   Percentage in Favor of 12 Potential Annual Reporting Markers

Potential Markers of Quality and Sound Operation for Annual Reporting to the Public	In Favor (%)
Percentage of admitted students who complete the program	62.0
Average GPA of students completing the program	61.2
Percentage of completers who seek a professional position who find one	55.1
Average SAT, ACT, or GRE scores of students admitted to the program	55.1
Percentage of courses taught by full-time faculty	55.0
Average number of years to completion	51.0
Average GPA of students admitted to the program	49.0
Percentage of completers who are still working in the field 5 years after completion	46.9
Percentage of courses taught by adjunct faculty	18.0
Percentage of students who pay back loans associated with the program	5.1
Percentage of minority students in the program	4.1
Percentage of students who take out loans associated with the program	4.1

with regard to their ratings of the standards. The patterns are also found for those who would report the years to completion, the standardized admission scores, the entry and exit grade-point index, the percentage of courses in the program taught by full-time faculty, the percentage who complete the program, and the percentages of those teaching 5 years after the program was completed.

When all 30 components of the standards are considered, the differences so overwhelmingly favor those who would make the disclosure or report as to be too unlikely to have occurred by chance (the binomial test). The individual mean differences between those who would and would not disclose a fact invariably favor those who would disclose or report a percentage, score, or practice of an EPP.

One interpretation of these findings is that the percentages of those unwilling to disclose an EPP fact can be attributed in most instances to an *unenlightened* view of accountability because the field generally accepts the view that such matters as hiring rates and completion rates are entirely relevant and appropriate facts for the "consumer" to know about an EPP. Thus, it would seem that those who share an *enlightened* view of public accountability also see the CAEP standards as significantly more important for accreditation than those who do not have this view.

An Exception

There was one standard component common to all the comparisons above that displayed an exception to the pattern. It was this: "CAEP Component 1.5—Candidates use research and evidence to continually evaluate and improve their practice, particularly the effects of their choices and actions on others, and they adapt their teaching to meet the needs of each learner." Those who said that they were not willing to disclose any of the consumer protection categories of information rated this component higher than those who said they would disclose the information. This is probably because they did not see these disclosures as only consumer protection themes and interpreted them as quality indicators and, of course, could think of no research evidence to support the claim that these indicators had anything to do with a quality program.

An Indication of Consistency

One sign, in addition to the Cronbach's alphas reported above, that the responders were consistent in their ratings was the fact that the 12 responders who would award a gold star based on the percentage of value-added state designees rated the value-added standard component higher (3.42 vs. 2.50) than the 39 who would not give a gold star on this basis, a difference that was statistically significant (t test). Otherwise, the differences in ratings between these 12 and 39 raters were chance differences on every other component rating.

Conclusion

Based on an assumption that there is a reasonable degree of comparability in the questions of the two surveys, the TEAC members who responded to the survey seem to show more support for the proposed CAEP standards than the faculty or field in general in the McKinley sample. Of course, there are undoubtedly TEAC faculty members in the McKinley survey sample, which may mean that the differences in survey outcomes may be greater than suggested here.

One interpretation of the relatively stronger support for the importance of the proposed standards by the TEAC members is that the CAEP standards align well with TEAC's quality principles and their exclusive reliance on evidence and outcomes. Along these lines, Farkas and Duffett (2010) found that 67% of teacher education faculty who were identified as reform-minded teacher educators sought higher standards (as opposed to only 4% who were satisfied with current practices). The relatively lower ratings for the clarity of the proposed standards also aligns with the freedom the TEAC system, now the *Inquiry Brief Pathway* in CAEP, and affords EPPs to make their case for accreditation with the evidence on which they truly rely to determine program quality—provided that it meets scholarly standards for evidence in the social sciences.

Whether there is comparability between the surveys, the TEAC survey respondents, like the McKinley respondents, find CAEP standards 1 and 2 to be important ways to document the quality of their EPP with relatively less but still substantial confidence in the other three standards. That the standards are rated lower in clarity than they are in importance points to the wisdom of the CAEP board's unanimous adoption of the standards with the understanding that there needs to be flexibility in their interpretation going forward. The evidence also points in the direction that those respondents who are forward thinking with regard to consumer protection issues and the lines of evidence that distinguish high-quality EPPs are more in favor of the standards and their components than are those who are less willing to disclose these kinds of facts about their programs.

There are some reasons to think CAEP accreditation will succeed in altering the narrative where others have largely failed despite the fact that the Holmes Group, to take one example, was founded in large measure over doubts about whether accreditation mattered at all (Lanier, 2007). Brabeck (2014), for example, has argued that the new CAEP standards provide a "historic consensus" (1) because their formulation was made by "deans, state policymakers, local superintendents, union leaders, teachers, P–12 student parents, alternative preparation programs, and even critics of educator preparation and accreditation"; (2) because accreditation by these new standards will be granted largely on the evidence that the program has had a positive impact on school learning and accomplishment; and (3) because of the leverage possible from the unprecedented potential scale of CAEP accreditation.

Previously, less than half the nation's providers were accredited, but now CAEP will accredit more than 60% of all the nation's providers, who account for nearly two-thirds of newly prepared teachers. Today, 23 states require accreditation for all public teacher education institutions, and 31 states require accreditation for the majority of their institutions (Brabeck, 2014). With the endorsement of the standards by the Council of Chief State School Officers (2012) and with the proposed 2014 federal rules for Titles II and IV of the Higher Education Act of 1965 (https://www.federalregister.gov/articles/2014/12/03/2014-28218/teacher-preparation-issues), there is the potential for a universal mandate for meeting these standards.

In addition, the field is now in a more credible position to implement the standards because, unlike earlier times, the field has newer technologies and methods for large-scale data management and linkages to impact (Worrell et al., 2014), has a new generation of standards-based assessments (e.g., edTPA; http://www.edtpa.com), has documented existence proofs of sustainable partnerships between universities and school districts (National Council for the Accreditation of Teacher Education, 2010), and has the conceptual work and track record of prior reform groups, providing a sounder theoretical grounding for the standards (e.g., the Holmes Partnership, the Teacher Education Accreditation Council, Project-30, the National Council on Teaching for America's Future, and Teachers for a New Era).

Finally, CAEP has "raised the bar" for the evidence it accepts that its standards have been met. The entire logic of new standards is that, over time, the field would have ever more persuasive evidence that the graduates of educator preparation programs were competent. At one time, the course syllabus was persuasive evidence of candidate competence, to take one example, but it is not any longer. The CAEP theory of action is that ever more persuasive evidence about the competence of tomorrow's educators will change the narrative. **TEP**

References

Aldeman, C., Carey, K., Dillon, E., Miller, B., & Silva, E. (2011). *A measured approach to improving teacher preparation.* Washington, DC: Education Sector.

Brabeck, M. (2014, March 25). *Teacher preparation: Ensuring a quality teacher in every classroom.* Testimony before the Senate Committee on Health, Education, Labor and Pensions.

Conant, J. B. (1963). *Education of American teachers.* New York: McGraw-Hill.

Council of Chief State School Officers. (2012). *Our responsibility, our promise: Transforming educator preparation and entry into the profession.* Washington, DC: Author.

Crowe, E. (2010). *Measuring what matters: A stronger accountability model for teacher education.* Washington, DC: Center for American Progress.

Farkas, S., & Duffett, A. (2010). *Cracks in the ivory tower?* Washington, DC: Thomas B. Fordham Institute.

Greenberg, J., Pomerance, L., & Walsh, K. (2011). *Student teaching in the United States.* Washington, DC: National Center on Teaching Quality.

Judge, H., Lemosse, M., Paine, M., & Sedlak, M. (1994). *The university and the teachers.* Wallingford, Oxfordshire, United Kingdom: Triangle Books.

Kanstoroom, M., & Finn, C. (1999). *Better teachers, better schools.* Washington, DC: Thomas Fordham Foundation.

Koerner, J. D. (1963). *The miseducation of American teachers.* Boston: Houghton Mifflin.

Lanier, J. (2007). Forward. In *The Holmes Partnership trilogy* (pp. xi–xxvii). New York: Peter Lang.

Mitchell, R., & Barth, P. (1999). How teacher licensing tests fall short. *Thinking K–16, 3*(1), 247–249.

Murray, F. (2011). Evidentiary standards for consensus standards in teacher education. *Teacher Education and Practice, 24*(4), 19–23.

Murray, F. B. (2013a). Cooperating teachers' evaluation of accredited teacher education programs. *Teacher Education and Practice, 26*(3), 542–553.

Murray, F. B. (2013b). Counter-intuitive findings from the Teacher Education Accreditation Council's surveys of candidates and faculty about candidate knowledge and skill. *Issues in Teacher Education, 22*(2), 7–16.

National Council for the Accreditation of Teacher Education. (2010). *Report of the blue ribbon panel on clinical preparation and partnerships for improved student learning.* Washington, DC: Author.

Teacher's College. (2009). *Teacher preparation: Reforming the uncertain profession.* http://www.edgovblogs.org/duncan/2009/10/a-call-to-teach

University of Virginia. (2009). *A call to teach.* http://www.tc.columbia.edu/news/article.htm?id=7179

Worrell, F., Brabeck, M., Dwyer, C., Geisinger, K., Marx, R., Noell, G., et al. (2014). *Assessing and evaluating teacher preparation programs.* Washington, DC: American Psychological Association.

Frank B. Murray is H. Rodney Sharp Professor Emeritus in the School of Education at the University of Delaware. He is a fellow in the American Psychological Association, the American Psychological Society, and the American Educational Research Association and was president of the Jean Piaget Society. He has been an active researcher, publishing over 200 articles and chapters in psychology and education, and has served on the editorial boards of the principal journals in his field. His areas of specialization are cognitive development, accreditation, and teacher education reform. He may be reached via e-mail at fmurray@udel.edu.

Powerful and Personal Professional Development

ANGELA FALTER THOMAS

ABSTRACT: This article examines professional development experiences from the National Board for the Professional Teaching Standards (NBPTS) in the United States. Ten National Board–certified teachers were interviewed on three separate occasions about their professional development from the NBPTS. The data analysis suggests that teachers who earn their National Board certification are empowered and actively involved in their profession. They self-report that the professional development from NBPTS has been engrained in them as a result of their participation, denoting that this professional development is ideal for teachers. With the recent focus on teacher performance and increased accountability, such examination provides an even deeper understanding of professional development for teacher educators through National Board certification.

The United States is in the midst of a vast and sweeping education reform. This reform has produced an environment in which the standards of accountability have been increased in the wake of policy initiatives such as the Common Core State Standards (National Governors Association Center for Best Practices and Council of State School Officers, 2010) and Race to the Top (U.S. Department of Education, 2009). This potent recipe for reform encompasses principal and teacher evaluations that will include student test scores, widespread adoption of rigorous academic content standards, and the development of high-stakes standardized tests that align with these new standards (Gulamhussein, 2013).

With the adoption of these new standards, teachers nationally, greater than ever before, are in need of effective and transformative professional development to meet these standards. Principals and administrators play a pivotal role in supporting teachers' professional development opportunities that help them effectively respond to these changing expectations (Mraz, Vintinner, & Vacca, 2014). Education reform relies on teachers learning to increase student learning (Desimone, 2011).

Yet a growing body of research is indicating that all too often, this professional development falls short of delivering that which it promises: enhanced student learning (Yoon, Duncan, Lee, Scarloss, & Shapley, 2007). This is often due to reliance on short-term, episodic, and disconnected professional learning provided by most school districts (Hill, 2009).

Not only have these traditional, one-size-fits-all workshop programs been proven ineffective, but teachers themselves deem them as useless (Darling-Hammond et al., 2009). Furthermore, schools have implemented professional learning not knowing exactly what they hope to accomplish. Without a specific purpose to guide their experiences, they often fall prey to clever consultants and adept entrepreneurs concerned more with what sells than with what works to improve student learning (Guskey, 2014). These clever consultants, or self-declared "experts," disregard the localized, individual needs of teachers and students.

Recent research (DeMonte, 2013) aimed at professional development policy recommendations conducted by the Center for American Progress found that features of professional learning linked to improvement include professional development opportunities that are intensive, sustained, and job embedded and that foster collaboration among teachers regarding improving teaching. According to the National Comprehensive Center for Teacher Quality, professional development is job embedded when it is "grounded in day-to-day teaching practice, and is designed to enhance teachers' instructional practices around content" (Croft, Coggshall, Dolan, & Powers, 2010, p. 2). Ultimately, sustained professional development can have a profound impact on teachers and the students they serve (Darling-Hammond & McLaughlin, 2011).

Researchers have also found evidence supporting the value of professional development that features reflection. Critical self-reflection is an essential part of transformative, powerful professional development. Such transformative professional development provides educators with a deeper personal experience that changes and influences them further to learn and grow (Beavers, 2011).

Professional development provides teachers with the opportunity to gain new knowledge and the option of implementing their new understanding(s) in a productive manner within a classroom environment. According to research by Ingvarson (1998), the best system for professional development is the National Board certification (NBC) available from the National Board for Professional Teaching Standards (NBPTS). Even more so, most teachers who have experienced National Board candidacy describe it as the best professional development they have ever experienced, even when they do not achieve the certification (Hunzicker, 2011). Many view the NBC process as a high-quality learning opportunity, holding the potential to impact candidates' knowledge, skills, and practices in ways that enhance their ability to improve student performance. According to Mistilin, Chung, and Darling-Hammond (2008), the process of NBC allows teachers to have a personal professional development process that capitalizes on reflective opportunities for teachers to hypothesize about what is working well in their daily work and what needs to be refined. The focus highlights teachers' own practices rather than being asked to focus on teaching disconnected from their daily work.

Research indicates that the NBC process develops teachers' practice and also provides high-quality professional development (Areglado, 1999; French, 1997). Lustick and Sykes (2006) conclude that when compared to other professional development options, such as graduate course work, NBC is a transformative experience for many teachers. Lustick and Sykes (2006) conclude that the NBC process itself improves teacher knowledge and skills in advancing and supporting student learning. NBPTS promotes its certification as a process that fosters collaboration, reflection, and recognition of effective teaching practices (NBPTS, 1991; Tracz, Daughtry, & Henderson-Sparks, 2005). NBPTS values and rewards excellence in teaching that directly reflects the impact of quality professional development on teachers' practices.

NBC in the United States

In the early 1980s, A Nation at Risk served as a catalyst for moving education from a social problem to a public policy issue (Fowler, 2004). As a result of the public awareness and focus on educational reform generated by that report, in 1986 A Nation Prepared: Teachers for the 21st Century was published. This called for the creation of the NBPTS, an independent, nonprofit, nonpartisan, and nongovernmental organization. The report also called for a restructuring of schools to provide a more professional environment for teachers, greater accountability for student progress, and incentives for teachers linked to student performance (Carnegie Task Force on Teaching as a Profession, 1986). The NBPTS was created to establish standards for high professional teaching competence and to issue certificates only to those who meet the highest of standards.

The NBPTS mission is to establish high and rigorous standards for what accomplished teachers should know and be able to do, to develop and operate a national voluntary system to assess and certify teachers who meet those standards, and to advance related education reforms for the purpose of improving student learning in American schools (NBPTS, 1991). The NBPTS hopes that teachers who score high enough to become National Board–certified teachers (NBCT) will be rewarded with higher income and more job prestige and given leadership roles in teacher preparation, support, and supervision (NBPTS, 2000).

Professional Development Through NBPTS

A model of continuous professional growth allows individual teachers to examine critically their own classroom performance and to discover ways to improve their practice. In the United States, the NBPTS has pioneered such a system of professional development tied to assessments for NBC. This system enables teachers to measure their performance against high standards developed by their peers. In an effort to raise the quality of teacher education across the country, school boards and administrators should look to the NBPTS's intensive standards-based teacher certification process as a guide for professional development.

Recent initiatives in teacher education have emphasized performance-based assessments (Liston, Borko, & Whitcomb, 2008). Certification by the NBPTS is a voluntary, performance-based teacher assessment process focused on a teacher's grade level and subject area. The average candidate for NBC reports spending hundreds of hours in preparation of their portfolio. Completing the portfolio is a demanding, rigorous, and tedious process embedded in the day-to-day work of teachers. In the portfolio, National Board candidates provide a written reflective commentary and analysis on each entry that contains additional pedagogical knowledge assessment. Inside the completed portfolio of each candidate are two videotapes or DVDs of the candidate teaching. The four entries make up the performance-based assessment portion of the NBC process, making up 60% of each candidate's score. The remaining 40% of the score is determined at an assessment center where candidates take exams on a computer.

The NBPTS provided a definite set of standards stating what accomplished teachers should know and be able to do as well as a way to measure who meets those standards. The certification earned by NBPTS is different from that of licensing, which occurs after teachers have graduated from an accredited institution. NBC is currently available in 25 different certificate areas that include 15 subject areas and that are classified into seven different student age categories.

To delve more deeply into this professional development available from the NBPTS, I turned to 10 experts on NBC: those educators who have endured the rigorous process themselves and who scored high enough to achieve the status of being a NBCT. In a qualitative research study, the 10 NBCTs were interviewed on three separate occasions. The NBCTs participating in this study were from all four regions of the United States and earned their certifications in a variety of subject areas and grade levels.

Methodology

Research Paradigm

This study was conducted from the perspective of interpretivist/constructivist research (Erickson, 1986). Interpretivist research is based on the interpretation of naturally occurring events and the representation of those events in the data. It is a reconstruction of the perspectives held by the participants. Merriam (1998) writes, "Reality is constructed by individuals interacting in their social worlds. Qualitative [interpretivist] researchers are interested in understanding the meaning people have constructed, that is, how they make sense of their world and the experiences they have in the world" (p. 6). Interpretivist research attempts to look at the data to uncover meaning and understand the deeper implications of people's actions in a qualitative manner (Somekh & Lewin, 2005).

Participant Selection

According to the U.S. Department of Education, in the 2007–2008 school year, there were 3,634,000 teachers teaching in the United States. As of November 2008, 63,879 teachers had achieved NBC. Nationwide, less than 2% of all teachers were NBCTs (NBPTS, 2007). By the 2014–2015 school year, there were 3.7 million teachers teaching in the United States. As of December 2014, more than 110,000 teachers had achieved NBC. Nationwide, less than 2% of all teachers are NBCTs (NBPTS, 2014). Between 1994 and 1998, 1,837 of America's teachers achieved NBC. In order to identify potential participants for this study—investigating the impact of the professional development on the NBCTs over time—the researcher obtained a list from the NBPTS of all NBCTs who achieved their certification between 1994 and 1998 and who agreed to release their names and school districts. There were 673 of these individuals.

These 673 potential participants were contacted for this investigation via the U.S. Postal Service. This initial mailing also included a demographic questionnaire and asked the volunteers to return their items to the researcher. Once selected, this group formed a unique population of teachers who went through the NBC process and achieved NBC in prior years.

Patton (1990) writes that a fundamental distinction between quantitative and qualitative studies is the use of sampling. For the purpose of this investigation, criterion sampling was employed. With criterion sampling, participants are selected for intense study due to some predetermined characteristics. The attributes, listed here in order of importance, were used to select the participants for this investigation in order to get a wide variety of NBCTs: length of time they had been a NBCT, whether they stayed in the classroom or went on to do other things, what their area of certification was, what type of school they were teaching in, and in what region of the country they taught. Ultimately, 10 NBCTs were selected. Tables 1 and 2 provide the demographics of the selected participants by whether they remained in the classroom or left to pursue areas outside of teaching. Table 3 contains the demographics of all study participants.

Table 1. NBCTs Who Remained in the Classroom

NBCT—Teaching	Current Career	NBC Area	Urban, Rural, or Suburban	Free Lunch	Region	Ethnicity	Education Level	Gender
"Betty" NBCT 1	First-grade teacher	EC-GEN	Rural	19%	South	Caucasian	Bachelor's	F
"Ellie" NBCT 2	Seventh-grade science and language arts	MC-GEN	Rural	26%	Midwest	Caucasian	Post-MA	F
"Karen" NBCT 3	11th- and 12th-grade math	AYA Math	Urban	80%	Midwest	African American	Doctorate	F
"Lydia" NBCT 4	Sixth-grade teacher	MC-GEN	Suburban	30%	West	Caucasian	Master's	F
"Brad" NBCT5	Third-grade teacher	MC-GEN	Suburban	2%	Northeast	Caucasian	Master's	M

Table 2. NBCTs Who Left the Classroom

NBCT—Left Teaching	Current Career	NBC Area	Urban, Rural, or Suburban	Free Lunch	Region	Ethnicity	Education Level	Gender
"Tina" NBCT 6	Principal	MC-GE	Suburban	51%	Midwest	Caucasian	Post-MA	F
"Julie" NBCT 7	Professional development provider	EA-GEN	Urban	52%	West	Asian	Doctorate	F
"Rachel" NBCT 8	Assistant superintendent	EA-EN	Suburban	6%	Northeast	Caucasian	Post-MA	F
"Jerry" NBCT 9	Supervisor of instruction	GE-MC	Suburban	4%	Northeast	Caucasian	Post-MA	M
"Kelsey" NBCT 10	Literacy coach	EC-GEN	Suburban	40%	South	Caucasian	Post-MA	F

Table 3. Demographics of Study Participants[a]

Demographics	Category	Percentage
Gender	Female	82%
	Male	18%
Career	Remained in the classroom	50%
	Left the classroom	50%
10-year certificate	Renewed	73%
	Did not renew	27%
Educational background	Bachelor's	9%
	Master's	18%
	Post-MA	55%
	Doctorate	18%
Free and reduced lunches	Low (0%–30% of school population)	45%
	Medium (31%–70% of school population)	45%
	High (71%–100% of school population)	9%
Region	Midwest	36%
	Northeast	27%
	South	18%
	West	18%
School type	Rural	27%
	Suburban	55%
	Urban	18%
Ethnicity	African American	9%
	Asian	9%
	Caucasian	82%
NBPTS certification area	EA/ELA	17%
	EA/GEN	8%
	EC/GEN	25%
	MC/GEN	42%
	AYA/MATH	8%

[a]Percentages may not equal 100% due to rounding of percentages and/or no responses. In the case of certification, the categories do not add up to 100% due to multiple certificates by one of the case studies. Regions were identified by the U.S. Census Bureau.

Data Collection

Qualitative methods offer a potentially powerful means of uncovering the complex experiences of participants in research studies. Qualitative research methods were utilized in this study in order to gain a more holistic picture of the professional development experiences of the NBCTs. Three separate interviews, approximately 1 hour in length, were conducted with each teacher. All teachers also completed a survey.

Interviews

Interviews were conducted as a way to obtain, supplement, and extend knowledge regarding the teachers' thoughts and interpretations of their professional development experience through the NBPTS. The semistructured interview format (Flick, 2014) was selected so that the teachers could provide more detailed information to set questions while also allowing for some spontaneous questions or comments. The author of this study conducted the study's interviews using a guided interview format. In this approach, the interviewer and the interviewee had a list of questions to be asked for each of the interviews. This type of interview allowed the researcher to probe for more in-depth responses.

All interviews were conducted via telephone and were digitally recorded live via an Internet website located at http://www.instantconference.com. The telephone interview was used as a strategy to obtain data, allowing interpersonal communication without a face-to-face meeting. The participants were sent each set of interview questions via e-mail approximately 1 week prior to the scheduled interview. Interviews offer insight into the respondents' memories and explanations of why things have come to be as well as give descriptions of current happenings. When a researcher asks about past events, the interviewees must rely on their memories. The human memory can be inaccurate; therefore, in order to make the interviews as fruitful as possible, the questions were sent prior to the interviews. This allowed the participants to be informed of the areas to be discussed, and it provided them with time to think and reflect on the questions. Following the telephone interview, both the researcher and the participant had access to the telephone playback of the interview in a digital file.

Surveys

The teachers also completed a survey featuring open-ended, descriptive questions regarding participating in the NBC process. Questions were designed in order to investigate the teachers' individual journeys throughout the certification process and beyond. According to Creswell (2015), open-ended questions do not constrain individual responses and are ideal for allowing participants to create responses based on their own experiences and not the researcher's.

Data Analysis

Thematic analysis is a qualitative descriptive approach described as "a method for identifying, analyzing and reporting patterns (themes) within data" (Braun & Clarke, 2006, p. 79). The main purpose of coding in thematic analysis is to make connections between different parts of the data (Alhoiailan, 2012). It involves the search for and identification of common threads that extend across an entire set of data (Flick, 2014). According to Braun and Clark (2006), it minimally organizes and describes the data set in detail.

Three researchers engaged the data of this project for an inductive thematic method of reading and rereading the transcribed interviews and the survey responses of the teachers. In an inductive approach, the themes are linked to the data (Alhoiailan, 2012). As such, the process of coding occurred without trying to fit the data into a preexisting model.

Using Braun and Clarke's (2006) suggestions for qualitative coding, the three researchers first worked independently, handling one set of data at a time. They first analyzed the interview transcripts and then the descriptive survey questions. They each followed the six phases of thematic analysis by initially familiarizing themselves with the data by reading and rereading the transcripts, making notes of their initial thoughts. Next, they generated initial codes by documenting where and how patterns occur in the data. Then they searched for themes among the codes by combining codes. For their fourth step, each researcher reviewed the themes and how they supported the data. Then the theme was defined and named. Finally, a meeting was conducted in which the researchers met to discuss and compare their findings.

Internal Validity

A number of factors were utilized in the study to enhance the internal validity, including member checks. According to Reilly (2013), member checks give participants opportunities to correct errors and challenge what they perceive as flawed interpretations. They allow participants to give additional or clarifying information that may be stimulated by reviewing their contributions and is a way to eliminate the possibility of misrepresentation and misinterpretation of the data. Participants should be provided with the opportunity to review the data, analysis, and final reports resulting from action research (Mills, 2013).

In the study, member checks were used so that input would be received from the teacher participants and that the analysis would be accurate. Following each interview, the digitally audio-recorded interviews were transcribed verbatim, and a copy was then given to each participant as a member check. Participants checked the transcripts for accuracy and were encouraged to provide any clarification or additional information. The teachers also read the final results of the study for verification that their beliefs, perspectives, and experiences were accurately represented. They were in agreement.

Rigor can be achieved by outlining the decisions made throughout the research process. This provides a justification for the methodological and interpretative judgments of the researcher (Houghton, Casey, Shaw, & Murphy 2013). While conducting the data analysis, three researchers separately coded the data by hand and ultimately determined themes. They followed Clarke and Braun's (2013) qualitative thematic coding suggestions, which include becoming familiar with the data, coding, searching for themes, reviewing themes, defining and naming themes, and writing up. They then met to discuss and compare findings.

Low-inference descriptors are the use of descriptive phrases very close to the participants' accounts (Flick, 2014). Quotes taken verbatim (i.e., direct quotations) are generally used as a type of low-inference descriptor. Because the findings are grounded in the data of the interviews and surveys, I used specific quotations from the participants in this article. Doing so permitted me to confirm that the reported findings are adequately supported by the participants' words.

Findings

A major purpose of this study was to determine whether the NBCTs believe that the professional development from the NBPTS is beneficial. The data analysis indicates that these NBCTs are changed as a result of their professional development experience. They are empowered and actively involved in their profession. They believe that the professional development experience they received from the NBPTS is ideal for teachers and that their experience has been engrained in them.

Forever Changed

"I'm forever changed as a teacher," declares Brad, a third-grade teacher. Brad does not stand alone; 9 of the 10 NBCTs believe that the standards of the NBPTS are instilled in them as a result of completing the certification process. Brad says, "It's a part of me. I now go through the essential elements, things required for good teaching, naturally." Lydia, who teaches sixth grade, says she is now more reflective and analytical in her work. She finds that she questions her teaching a lot since applying to be an NBCT. Lydia shares that going through the process caused her to really think deeply about what she does and why she does it, and that has continued in how she now teaches. Middle school teacher Ellie discovered that she now thinks, analyzes, and reviews lessons and data much more frequently than before her certification attempt. Julie earned her NBC as an early adolescent generalist. She believes that earning NBC impacted her by making her constantly reflect on her work. "No matter what you're teaching, if you're not thinking deeply about what you're teaching and why you're teaching it that way, you're not focused and doing the best job of serving your students."

Tina obtained her NBC as a middle childhood generalist. She believes that going through the National Board process made her a better teacher and that the principles of the National Board have been instilled in her and affect what she does every single day. Karen, a high school math teacher, says that becoming nationally certified upped her standards and made them higher. "I can never go back to being the kind of teacher I was before I went through National Board." Karen states that she uses the NBPTS standards in her work but not consciously because she has internalized them. "It's just a part of who I am now." Betty, who teaches first grade, believes that the most profound change in becoming an NBCT is in her daily teaching. She changed the way she assesses because of what she learned going through National Board. "I do real assessments now, and I assess to teach better. I didn't do that before National Board."

Actively Involved

Professional development is most effective when it is focused on active learning and specific teaching practices. In order for professional development to be successful, teachers must be engaged participants, not passive recipients. Kelsey, a former state teacher of the year, earned her NBC as an early childhood generalist. She says, "It was incredibly exhausting work, but it was so rewarding because I wasn't learning about someone else's teaching; I was analyzing my own teaching and learning how to do it better." Jerry earned his NBC as a middle childhood generalist. He shares, "Attempting National Board allowed me to have professional development for the first time that actually enhanced my teaching, established professional discourse, raised the standards for my teaching performances, and encouraged me to collaborate with other educators." Lydia says that the National Board "made me really dig in to my own teaching, to rip apart what I was doing, and to put it back together in a better, more meaningful way. I never had the opportunity to do anything like that before." These National Board participants attribute their increased professional development to the National Board process because it directly engages candidates in their own teaching and learning.

In order to have a substantial effect on teacher learning and to improve classroom practices, professional development should be focused on providing high-quality, hands-on experiences. Lydia believes that the professional development that National Board offers is unlike anything one could ever learn attending a workshop or taking a class. She reports that she had attended many "'sit and get' trainings before, but National Board isn't anything like that. You have to be totally involved and immersed in your teaching and in your students, not listening to someone tell you what to do."

With National Board, the focus is on the teachers' own practices rather than on teaching that is disconnected from their daily work. According to Mistilin et al. (2008), the process of NBC allows teachers to have individualized professional development, which capitalizes on reflective opportunities for them to hypothesize about what is working well in their daily work and what needs to be refined. Professional development focused on precise instructional practices increases teachers' use of those practices in their classrooms. Karen states, "After NBC, I became more conscious of looking at student work and looking at standards; therefore, I became more conscious of examining student work differently than I ever did before." She believes that going through the NBC process was a rigorous and incredibly gratifying experience, forcing her to pay attention to outcomes and intentions. As a result, she learned to pay closer attention to her students and their work and to deeply reflect. "Before going through National Board, I did not do the kind of evaluation or reflection of students' work that I do now."

Empowered Learners

Teachers must view attempts at professional development not as something being done to them but instead as something being done for and with them. A new image of professionalism shows teachers working creatively and collaboratively as members of learning communities and thinking systemically about their own practice in the context of educational research. NBC is an example of teacher-directed growth in which teachers choose to seek certification and study their own teaching to find ways they can improve. The existence of NBC changes the way professional development functions and raises the standards of quality for teacher professional development.

Additionally, teachers must believe that what they learn produces changes for their students and their classrooms. All 10 of the NBCTs in this research study agree that attempting NBC helps teachers make changes in their teaching that impact their students for the better. One of the main reasons Brad pursued NBC was because he thought it would be good professional development. "Attempting National Board opened my eyes and really got me thinking about my students." He found the process of earning national certification to be an invigorating and empowering professional development.

Lydia shares that she had to try NBC for herself: "It was my own hunt for professional development. My school district was not providing quality professional development. I did this solely on my own to make myself a better teacher, and without a doubt, it did! I learned so much about good teaching and how to teach better."

Professional development should no longer be viewed as an event that occurs on a particular day of the school year; rather, it must become integrated into the daily work of educators. Teachers need opportunities for reflection and analysis; however, few occasions and little support for that type of professional development appear to exist in teachers' environments. True professional development guides teachers to critical reflection, which is an examination of themselves as teachers, what they believe, and why they believe it. This process of self-reflection is the key to meaningful professional development (Smith, Gordon, Colby, & Wang, 2005).

Ideal Professional Development

NBC allows teachers to attempt certification from the NBPTS voluntarily. The NBC process is demanding and rigorous, requiring many hours to complete extensive reflection papers and to document instruction (Smith et al., 2005), but it is often perceived as a positive professional development experience for teachers (Lustick & Sykes 2006; Tracz et al., 2005). Rachel earned her

NBC for early adolescent English language arts. She believes that attempting NBC helps teachers obtain the ability to plan sound instruction and to deliver high-quality learning experiences for students. "Going through the NBPTS process is where I really learned about teaching and learning." Lydia adds, "Having gone through the process and through many other professional development experiences during my career, I believe the best system for professional development is National Board. I view it as a high-quality learning opportunity, holding the potential to affect the candidates' knowledge, skills, and practices in ways that help them improve student performance for a very long time to come."

Tina believes that NBC is the best possible professional development that exists for teachers. "Being an NBCT instilled in me a love of professional development." Kelsey thinks that going through the NBC process was professional development like she had never experienced before and was something for which she had been wanting so long. She believes that NBC is focused solely on growing and learning as a teacher. "I have to say that the year I attempted National Board was the year I learned the most about myself as a teacher." She also describes that year as one of the best years she has ever had in teaching.

Teachers rarely have opportunities to determine their own professional development. Unlike traditional professional development, NBC candidates determine the specifics they will incorporate into their portfolio submissions. In this study, the NBCTs provided powerful testimonials about the impact that the process has had on them. These 10 NBCTs agree that the process was a dynamic professional development experience that improved their teaching and their students' learning.

Tina became intrigued by NBC as a way to keep current and fresh with her teaching. It was something she could do right in her own classroom. She shares,

> Without a doubt, going through the NBC process taught me so much about good teaching, and it really improved my practice. What I learned going through the NBC process is obviously an integral part of who I am and what I do as a teacher. I don't know how someone can go through such an intense yearlong process and not be forever changed. How can one watching video after video of their teaching and not make improvements? How can one write approximately 100 pages of their teaching and their students' work and not be a better teacher?

The professional development offered through the NBPTS is unquantifiable according to those interviewed; the opportunities for growth do not cease with certification. At a time when professional development is lacking for so many teachers, NBC provides a refreshing alternative and a guide for professional development.

Implications

NBC allows teachers to attempt certification from the NBPTS voluntarily. The NBC process is demanding and rigorous, requiring many hours to complete extensive reflection papers and to document instruction, but it is often perceived as a positive professional development experience for teachers (Tracz et al., 2005). Rachel, from the Northeast, holds an NBC for early adolescent English language arts. She believes that attempting NBC helps teachers obtain the ability to plan sound instruction and to deliver high-quality learning experiences for students. "Going through the NBPTS process is where I really learned about teaching and learning. I view it as a high-quality learning opportunity, holding the potential to affect the candidates' knowledge, skills, and practices in ways that help them improve student performance for a very long time to come."

Tina believes that NBC is the best possible professional development that exists for teachers. "Being an NBCT instilled in me a love of professional development." Kelsey thinks that going through the NBC process was professional development like she had never experienced before and like she had been wanting for so long. She believes that NBC is focused solely on growing and learning as a teacher. "I have to say that the year I attempted National Board was the year I learned the most about myself as a teacher." She also describes that year as one of the best years she has ever had in teaching.

Teachers rarely have opportunities to determine their own professional development. Unlike traditional professional development, NBC candidates determine the specifics they will incorporate into their portfolio submissions. In this study, the NBCTs provided powerful testimonials about the impact that the process has had on them. These 10 NBCTs agree that the process was a dynamic professional development experience that improved their teaching and their students' learning.

Over the course of her career, Tina has seen big changes in professional development opportunities. "When I started teaching, we were funded to attend one teaching conference each year. As a new teacher, this was how I got my best teaching ideas." As budget cuts continued, attending conferences was cut from the budget. Tina longed to attend conferences because of the professional development it offered her, but it was no longer an option. Therefore, she became intrigued by NBC as a way to keep current and fresh with her teaching. It was something she could do right in her own classroom.

Tina shares, "Going through NBC was to me professionally like having a spa day for my soul." She states that NBC is the best possible professional development that exists for teachers. According to Jerry, there are not enough NBCTs, and if every teacher could become a master teacher, it would be better for all students. "It should be our goal for all of our teachers to be excellent, for all of our teachers to achieve the highest level of certification they can." Rachel says that unless one has actually attempted the NBC process oneself, one cannot ever really understand the intensity and the profound nature of this professional development.

The professional development offered through the NBPTS is unquantifiable according to those interviewed; the opportunities for growth do not cease with certification. At a time when professional development is lacking for so many great teachers, NBC provides a refreshing alternative. Even if school districts cannot encourage their teachers to pursue NBC, they can take the fundamental principles of this high-quality professional development and make certain that it exists for their teachers and ultimately the learners they serve.

Implications for Administrators

The primary role of administrators in the process of professional development is one of enabling teachers to discuss teaching openly and to build on their existing knowledge of teaching and learning in order to improve instructional outcomes. NBC is one avenue of professional development that administrators can confidently suggest to teachers that will not only help build their skills but also empower them throughout the process.

Although administrators are not required to be involved in the NBPTS process, administrators can support teachers throughout their certification process by offering to serve as a reference as teachers compile evidence of leadership and collaborative accomplishments. Administrators can create and develop support groups for teachers within their districts as they engage the NBPTS process and could consider having district-level coordinators to coordinate resources and support teachers. Providing this guidance and mentoring can help candidates understand the process and its requirements better (Mraz et al., 2014).

Conclusions

NBC is meant to complement the existing licensure procedures currently in existence in the United States. This voluntary process requires countless hours of deep analysis and reflection while stressing collaboration and consideration toward change and growth. Teachers who engage in this process are required to be thoughtful and analytical about their content, pedagogy, and assessment. NBCTs have provided information regarding the positive impact that the NBPTS process has had on their professional lives. In teaching, limited opportunities for high-quality professional development exist; however, utilizing a system in place such as NBC from the NBPTS, teachers could improve their teaching and ultimately improve their students' education. **TEP**

References

Alhoiailan, M. (2012). Thematic analysis: A critical review of its process and evaluation. *West East Journal of Social Sciences*, 1(1), 39–47.

Areglado, N. (1999). I became convinced. *Journal of Staff Development*, 20(1), 35–37.

Beavers, A. (2011). Teachers as learners: Implications of adult education for professional development. *Journal of College Teaching and Learning*, 6(7), 25–30.

Braun, V., & Clarke, V. (2006). Using thematic analysis in psychology. *Qualitative Research in Psychology*, 3, 77–101.

Carnegie Task Force on Teaching as a Profession. (1986). *A nation prepared: Teachers for the 21st century*. New York: Carnegie Forum on Education and the Economy.

Clarke, V., & Braun, V. (2013). *Successful qualitative research: A practical guide for beginners*. London: Sage.

Creswell, J. (2015). *Educational research: Planning, conducting, and evaluating quantitative and qualitative research* (5th ed.). Boston: Pearson.

Croft, A., Coggshall, J. G., Dolan, M., & Powers, E. (2010). *Job-embedded professional development: What it is, who is responsible, and how to get it done well*. Washington, DC: National Comprehensive Center for Teacher Quality.

Darling-Hammond, L., Wei, R. C., Andree, A., Richardson, N., & Orphanos, S. (2009). *Professional learning in the learning profession: A status report on teacher development in the United States and Abroad*. Dallas, TX: National Staff Development Council.

Darling-Hammond, L., & McLaughlin, M. (2011). Policies that support professional development in an era of reform. *Phi Delta Kappan*, 92(6), 81–92.

DeMonte, J. (2013). *High-quality professional development for teachers*. Washington, DC: Center for American Progress. http://www.americanprogress.org/issues/education/report/2013/07/15/69592;high-quality-professional-development-for-teachers

Desimone, L. M. (2011). A primer on effective professional development. *Phi Delta Kappan*, 92(6), 68–71.

Erickson, F. (1986). Qualitative methods in research on teaching. In M. C. Wittrock (Ed.), *Handbook of research on teaching* (3rd ed., pp. 119–159). New York: Macmillan.

Flick, U. (2014). *An introduction to qualitative research* (5th ed.). Thousand Oaks, CA: Sage.

Fowler, F. (2004). *Policy studies for educational leaders: An introduction* (2nd ed.). Upper Saddle River, NJ: Pearson Education.

French, V. (1997). Teachers must be learners, too: Professional development and national teaching standards. *NASSP Bulletin*, 81(585), 38–44.

Gulamhussein, A. (2013). Teaching the teachers: Effective professional development in an era of high stakes accountability. http://www.centerforpubliceduction.org/Main-Menu/Staffingstudents/Teaching-the-Teachers-Effective-Professional-Development-in-an-Era-of-High-Stakes-Accountability/Teaching-the-Teachers-Full-Report-pdf

Guskey, T. (2014). Planning professional learning. *Educational Leadership*, 71(8), 10–16.

Hill, H. C. (2009). Fixing teacher professional development. *Phi Delta Kappan*, 90(7), 470–476.

Houghton, C., Casey, D., Shaw, D., & Murphy, K. (2013). Rigor in qualitative case-study research. *Nurse Researcher*, 20, 12–17.

Hunzicker, J. (2011). Effective professional development for teachers: A checklist. *Professional Development Education*, 37(2), 177–179.

Ingvarson, L. (1998). Professional development as the pursuit of professional standards: The standards-based professional development system. *Teaching and Teacher Education*, 14(10), 127–140.

Liston, D., Borko, H., & Whitcomb, J. (2008). The teacher educator's role in enhancing teacher quality. *Journal of Teacher Education*, 59(2), 111–116.

Lustick, D., & Sykes, G. (2006). National Board Certification as professional development: What are teachers learning? *Education Policy Analysis Archives*, 14(5). http:// www.redalyc.org/html/2750/275020543005

Merriam, S. (1998). *Qualitative research and case study applications in education*. San Francisco: Jossey-Bass.

Mills, G. (2013). *Action research: A guide for the teacher researcher* (5th ed.). Boston: Pearson.

Mistilin, S., Chung, W., & Darling-Hammond, L. (2008). Improving teachers' assessment practices through professional development: The case of National Board Certification. *American Educational Research Journal*, 45(3), 669–700.

Mraz, M., Vintinner, J., & Vacca, J. (2014). Professional development. In S. Wepner, D. Strickland, & D. Quatroche (Eds.), *Administration and supervision of reading programs* (5th ed., pp. 124–134.) New York: Teachers College Press.

National Board for Professional Teaching Standards (NBPTS). (1991). *Toward high and rigorous standards for the teaching profession* (3rd ed.). Washington, DC: Author.

National Board for Professional Teaching Standards. (2000). *A distinction   that matters: Why national teacher certification makes a difference*. Washington, DC: Author.

National Board for Professional Teaching Standards. (2007). *55,000 reasons to believe: The impact of National Board Certification on teacher quality in America*. Arlington, VA: Author.

National Governors Association Center for Best Practices and Council of State School Officers. (2010). *Common Core State Standards for English language arts and literacy in history, social studies, science and technical studies*. Washington, DC: Author.

Patton, M. (1990). *Qualitative evaluation and research methods* (2nd ed.). Newbury Park, CA: Sage.

Reilly, R. (2013). Found poems, member checking and crises of representation. *The Qualitative Report*, 18, 1–18.

Smith, T. W., Gordon, B., Colby, S. A., Wang, J. (2005). *An examination of the relationship between depth of student learning and National Board certification status*. Boone, NC: Office for Research on Teaching, Appalachian State University.

Somekh, B., & Lewin, C. (2005). *Research methods in the social sciences*. Thousand Oaks, CA: Sage.

Tracz, S., Daughtry, J., & Henderson-Sparks, J. (2005). The impact of NBPTS participation on teacher practice: Learning from teacher perspectives. *Educational Research Quarterly*, 28(3), 36–50.

U.S. Department of Education. (2009). *Race to the Top program executive summary*. http://www.ed.gove/programs/racetothetop/executivesummary.pdf

Yoon, K. S., Duncan, T., Lee, S. W. Y., Scarloss, B., & Shapley, K. L. (2007). Reviewing the evidence on how teacher professional development affects student achievement. Issues & answers. REL 2007-No. 033. Washington, DC: U.S. Department of Education, Institute of Education Sciences, National Center for Education Evaluation and Regional Assistance, Regional Educational Laboratory Southwest.

Angela Falter Thomas joined the faculty of Bowling Green State University (BGSU) in 2009 as an assistant professor. Before joining the faculty at BGSU, Angela was a middle school reading and English teacher at Seneca East, located in Attica, Ohio, where she taught public school for 20 years. Her work has been published in Voices from the Middle, Middle Level Learning, Middle Ground, AMLE Magazine, *the* Journal of Instructional Pedagogies, California Reader, the Illinois Reading Council Journal, *and the* Journal of Ethnographic and Qualitative Research. *She may be reached via e-mail at AngThom@bgsu.edu.*

Preservice Teacher Supervision Within Field Experiences in a Decade of Reform

A Comprehensive Meta-Analysis of the Empirical Literature from 2001 to 2013[1]

REBECCA WEST BURNS, JENNIFER JACOBS, AND DIANE YENDOL-HOPPEY

ABSTRACT: In the past decade, as the clinical component of teacher education has gained increasing attention, it makes sense that the supervision of those field experiences should also garner attention. This comprehensive, qualitative meta-analysis used the findings from 69 studies published between 2001 and 2013 in the field of preservice teacher (PST) supervision as data to address the question, What can we learn about PST field supervision since the publication of the NCATE PDS Standards? Findings suggest that despite a lack of a common definition and a common conceptual framework, PST supervision within field experiences is expanding and becoming more sophisticated, indicating that perhaps the increased call for collaboration and school–university partnerships is contributing to this complexity. This warrants greater attention to, increased resources for, and common nomenclature in PST supervision.

Within the teacher education literature, student teaching, as the capstone clinical experience in teacher preparation, is often lauded as the most important aspect of professional preparation (Cuenca, 2012; Wideen, Mayer-Smith, & Moon, 1998; Wilson, Floden, & Ferrini-Mundy, 2001). The recent call from the National Council for Accreditation of Teacher Education (NCATE, 2010) Blue Ribbon Panel Report, the NCATE (2001) Professional Development School (PDS) Standards, the American Association of Colleges of Teacher Education (2010), and other national educational reform efforts have been loud and harmonious. They argue that more preservice teacher (PST) education must occur through clinical experiences and that pre-K–12 partners must be authentically involved in ensuring that these clinical experiences are of high quality. These documents suggest the need for more systematic and intentional school–university collaboration to accomplish these goals. This means that the role that school faculty, administrators, and university faculty play in PST preparation needs to be reconceptualized. Previously, the PST supervisor has often been the primary or the only link between the university and the field, shouldering much of the responsibility for supporting the PST (Slick, 1998) and building program coherence (Lee, 2011; McIntyre & Byrd, 1998). These complexities position the PST supervisor within teacher preparation as incredibly important to the professional preparation of teachers.

Unfortunately, clinical experiences in teacher preparation continue to be held in low regard (Beck & Kosnik, 2002; Hoover, O'Shea, & Carroll, 1988). This low regard for the clinical component of learning to teach is particularly evident in larger teacher preparation programs where the labor-intensive nature of supervision has been relegated to the work of new faculty, graduate students, adjunct faculty, and/or retired teachers (Slick, 1998) with little supervision offered by seasoned research faculty. Some evidence suggests that the move to enhance clinical preparation has resulted in increased attention to the mentoring offered by practicing teachers to support PST learning (Rodgers & Keil, 2007). Although veteran teachers and retired principals demonstrate excellence as educators, the problem with supervision being conducted primarily by these educators is that their work is often governed by strength of personality, relationship, and experience rather than by a shared sense of research, mission, theory, and practice (Burns & Badiali, 2015; Sergiovanni & Starratt, 2007). The lack of focus on research and systematic connections between theory and practice leads to less reform in the ways we conceive of high-quality, reform-oriented teacher education. This was evident in the review conducted by Guyton and McIntyre (1990) more than 20 years ago. They noted that "more student teaching innovations were reported in 1968 than in 1982" (p. 522).

Just prior to the release of the NCATE PDS Standards, Clift and Brady (2005) conducted a comprehensive literature review of methods course work and field experiences from 1995 to 2001. They found that research on PST supervision focused on the role of the supervisor and the evaluation of PSTs. They also found that the term "university supervisor" seemed to be commonly used and understood in the literature. However, when Clift and Brady conducted their literature review, school–university partnerships were just emerging in terms of applying the principles set forth by the Holmes Group (1986) and John Goodlad and the National Network for Educational Renewal (Rutter, 2011). This time period was evident in the literature review findings. Clift and Brady (2005) stated, "We have no insight into how PDS environments impact supervisors" (p. 329). Now, more than a decade later, the opportunity exists to analyze the literature related to PST supervision in our current era of reform. Perhaps now that school–university partnerships have had time to mature, there may be more insight into PST supervision. Therefore, we elected to engage in a qualitative meta-analysis of the empirical literature from the release of the NCATE PDS Standards in 2001 as data to generate new knowledge about PST supervision. This analysis will help the teacher education community better understand how supervision is or is not changing in light of the recent reform efforts.

The purposes of this meta-analysis are twofold: (1) to generate new knowledge about PST supervision within field experiences in an era of increased emphasis on clinical experiences through school–university collaboration and (2) to raise questions about how the identified empirical literature addresses the complexities, challenges, and successes associated with the PST supervision since the movement to enhanced collaboration with schools.

Methods

A qualitative meta-analysis is a distinct type of synthesis in which findings from completed empirical studies focused on a targeted area are intentionally combined (Sandelowski & Barroso, 2007). Paterson, Thorne, Canam, and Jillings (2001) suggest that "the raison d'etre of meta-study is to go beyond the aggregation of existing research but to follow a rigorous procedure, whereby new insights can be derived from the detailed analysis of a vast number of studies addressing the topic" (p. 184). By engaging in qualitative meta-analysis, we brought together a set of potentially underutilized empirical studies in a way that enhanced the utility and relevance of these smaller-scale studies. This process allowed us to pose new questions and obtain a more comprehensive representation of investigated phenomena by treating the findings of primarily qualitative studies as data (Timulak, 2007). The products of our meta-analysis utilize research findings to generate new knowledge (Scholes, 2003) for the field of PST supervision.

Selection and Organization of Studies

Although many different educators can assume the role of supervision, for this study we focused on the role and function of "university supervisor." By focusing on the university supervisor, we did not include collaborating teachers, instructors, and so on. We defined the function of supervision as promoting PST learning, which is inherently different from evaluation (Nolan, 1997; Nolan & Hoover, 2011). This theoretical orientation meant that we excluded the evaluation function that a supervisor sometimes assumes as a part of his or her responsibility.

The initial search team was comprised of three research faculty and six doctoral students. We set up a joint RefWorks account so that we did not duplicate our efforts and could easily import citations, organize them, and have a shared searchable database comprised of each identified article. Study selection for this meta-analysis included all peer-reviewed articles related to PST published between 2001 and 2013 that were identified within the ERIC, Education Full Text, and Google Scholar databases.

Our search began by identifying the descriptors that characterized the field of supervision. We believed the main concept was the action of the supervisor followed by the context of where the activity occurred. To organize the search, we created a search matrix (Table 1) using concept descriptors within each database.

This matrix included ERIC descriptors that attended to the concepts of (1) *time/context* (field experience, field experience programs, practicums, and

Table 1. Search Matrix With Concept Descriptors

Concept 1 – Time/Context	Concept 2 – Student	Concept 3 – Action	Concept 4 – Teacher Educator
Field Experience ERIC: Field experience (D) programs Practicums (D) Student Teaching (D)	Preservice Teacher Preservice teachers (D) Student teachers (D)	Supervision (D) Practicum supervision (D)	University Supervisor
Student Teaching (D)	Teacher Candidates	Coaching Coaching (Performance) (D) Facilitators (individuals) (D)	Field Adviser
Internship Preservice Teacher Education (D) Internship programs(D)	Prospective Teacher (ERIC: use Preservice teachers (D))	Evaluation/Evaluating Evaluation (D) Educational Assessment (D) Formative Evaluation (D) Program Evaluation(D)	
Professional Development School Professional Development Schools (D)		Observation Classroom observation School Visitation (D)	
Partnership Partnerships in education (D) Educational Cooperation (D) School community Relationship (D)			

student teaching), (2) *the student* (teacher candidate, PST, student teacher, and prospective teacher), (3) *the action* (supervision, practicum supervision, coaching, and classroom observation), and (4) *teacher educator* (university supervisor and field adviser). These descriptors allowed for powerful advanced searching.

After creating the search matrix, we divided up the cells of the matrix among eight researchers. We used two different databases (ERIC and Education Full Text) to explore each cell in the matrix and made note as to the number of "hits" that occurred in each cell. The next step included downloading all of the citations into a table organized with the following headings: APA Reference, theme related to supervision, keep/remove, and reason for removal. Google Scholar was used as a check and triangulation on the viability of the search approach. The resulting pool contained more than 800 articles that were then scrutinized through a series of reviews in order to select the appropriate studies. Table 2 provides a summary of the study selection process.

During the first review, the researchers reviewed the abstracts and eliminated 470 articles from the pool for one or more of the following reasons: not university PST supervision, not empirical, and/or not within date parameters. The elimination left 342 articles in the pool. During the second review, the full team once again reviewed the 342 remaining articles, but this time the article rather than the abstract was examined. This led to removing 234 additional articles that either could not be located, were not PST university supervision, or were not empirical. This level of review reduced the pool to

Table 2. Study Selection and Analysis Process

Round of Selection	Number of Articles Reviewed	Reduction/Sorting
Initial search—consisted of abstract review (full team review)	812	470 (not university supervision; 75 not empirical; 34 not empirical and not supervision; 13 not within date parameters; 3 no abstract found)
Second review—consisted of paper review/abstract review and requests for papers made at this point (full team review)	342	234 (could not locate, not university supervision; not research; initial coding)
Third review—consisted of reduction and sorting into themes (authors' review)	108	42 (not university supervision; not empirical)
Fourth review (conducted by authors)	68	Analysis of article contents by category and synthesis for each category developed. These categories became subquestions.
Fifth review (conducted by authors)	Varied by category	An individual meta-analysis was conducted for each subquestion.

108 remaining articles that met our criteria. For the third review, the research team was reduced to three research faculty who have expertise and knowledge of the field of instructional supervision. These three researchers read all 108 articles to ensure that the remaining articles still met the selection criteria and noted which of the identified thematic categories the remaining empirical PST articles represented. These criteria led to a final removal of 39 articles, leaving a total of 69 studies for review that reflect PST supervision between 2001 and 2013. When reviewing meta-analyses in a literature search, a typical number of studies included ranged from as few as eight articles to as many as 15 articles for one meta-analysis. Therefore, the unification of our individual meta-analyses for all 68 studies, as reported in this article, exists as quite a comprehensive meta-analysis.

Analysis of the Articles

Table 2 shows five reviews for the study selection and analysis. The fourth and fifth reviews were the actual analyses of the articles. As the three researchers read the articles, they identified a set of codes that described the main themes of each article. These codes were grouped to produce five categories that became subquestions of this analysis. They included the following:

1. What are the tasks a supervisor enacts?
2. How do supervisors engage in observation and feedback, and what are the outcomes?
3. What is the current role of technology in supervision?
4. What type of professional development is provided for PST field supervisors?
5. How do supervisors form relationships and build community?

For each subquestion, we looked across the studies and disaggregated them by qualitative, quantitative, and mixed methodologies. We also thought it would be important to note if articles were written by international authors. Table 3 shows the number of studies within each subquestion and the disaggregation by methodology.

As Table 3 indicates, each subquestion used data from as few as 10 to as many as 33 studies, meaning that each subquestion had an adequate number of studies to be its own meta-analysis. Table 4 lists all of the studies used in this meta-analysis. Thirty-two of the articles were used only once across categories, while 37 of the articles were used more than once across categories. In the fifth review, each sub question was analyzed as its own individual meta-analysis.

While findings from the individual subquestion meta-analyses have been shared (Burns, Jacobs, & Yendol-Hoppey, 2014, in press; Jacobs, Burns, & Yendol-Hoppey, 2014), the purpose of this article is to provide a summary of the new knowledge generated from across the sub–meta-analysis. Our article

Table 3. Articles Disaggregated by Category

Citation	Tasks	Observation/Feedback	Technology	Professional Development	Relationships
Akcan, S., & Tatar, S. (2010). An investigation of the nature of feedback given to pre-service English teachers during their practice teaching experience. *Teacher Development, 14*(2), 153–172.		X			X
Alger, C., & Kopcha, T. J. (2009). eSupervision: A technology framework for the 21st century field experience in teacher education. *Issues in Teacher Education, 18*(2), 31–46.			X		
Basmadjian, K. G. (2011). Learning to balance assistance with assessment: A scholarship of field instruction. *Teacher Educator, 46*(2), 98–125. doi:10.1080/08878730.2011.552845		X		X	
Bates, A. J., Ramirez, L., & Drits, D. (2009). Connecting university supervision and critical reflection: Mentoring and modeling. *Teacher Educator, 44*(2), 90–112. doi:10.1080/08878730902751993	X				
Bates, A. J., Drits, D., & Ramirez, L. A. (2011). Self-awareness and enactment of supervisory stance: Influences on responsiveness toward student teacher learning. *Teacher Education Quarterly, 38*(3), 69–87.	X				
Beck, C., & Kosnik, C. (2002). Professors and the practicum: Involvement of university faculty in preservice practicum supervision. *Journal of Teacher Education, 53*(1), 6–19.	X				
Bullock, S. M. (2012). Creating a space for the development of professional knowledge: A self-study of supervising teacher candidates during practicum placements. *Studying Teacher Education, 8*(2), 143–156.	X			X	X
Bullough, R. V., Jr., & Draper, R. J. (2004). Making sense of a failed triad: Mentors, university supervisors, and positioning theory. *Journal of Teacher Education, 55*(5), 407–420.	X				X
Caires, S., Almeida, L. S., & Martins, C. (2009). The socioemotional experiences of student teachers during practicum: A case of reality shock? *Journal of Educational Research, 103*(1), 17–27. doi:10.1080/00220670903228611	X	X			

Campbell, T., & Lott, K. (2010). Triad dynamics: Investigating social forces, roles, and storylines. *Teaching Education, 21*(4), 349–366. doi:10.1080/10476210903518396

Carter, D. (2005). Distributed practicum supervision in a managed learning environment (MLE). *Teachers and Teaching: Theory and Practice, 11*(5), 481–497.

Chaliès, S., Escalié, G., Bertone, S., & Clarke, A. (2012). Learning 'rules' of practice within the context of the practicum triad: A case study of learning to teach. *Canadian Journal of Education, 35*(2), 3–23.

Conderman, G., Morin, J., & Stephens, J. T. (2005). Special education student teaching practices. *Preventing School Failure, 49*(3), 5–10.

Coulon, S. C., & Lorenzo, D. C. (2003). The effects of supervisory task statements on preservice teachers' instructional behaviors during retaught lessons. *Education, 124*(1), 181–193.

Cuenca, A., Schmeichel, M., Butler, B. M., Dinkelman, T., & Nichols, J. R., Jr. (2011). Creating a "third space" in student teaching: Implications for the university supervisor's status as outsider. Teaching & Teacher Education, 27(7), 1068–1077.

Edwards, A., & Mutton, T. (2007). Looking forward: Rethinking professional learning through partnership arrangements in initial teacher education. *Oxford Review of Education, 33*(4), 503–519. doi:10.1080/03054980701450928

Falconer, K. B., & Lignugaris-Kraft, B. (2002). A qualitative analysis of the benefits and limitations of using two-way conferencing technology to supervise preservice teachers in remote locations. *Teacher Education and Special Education, 25*(4), 368–384. doi:10.1177/088840640202500406

Fenimore-Smith, J. (2004). Democratic practices and dialogic frameworks: Efforts toward transcending the cultural myths of teaching. *Journal of Teacher Education, 55*(3), 227–239. doi:10.1177/0022487104263679

(continued)

Table 3. (Continued)

Citation	Tasks	Observation/Feedback	Technology	Professional Development	Relationships
Gal, N. (2006). The role of practicum supervisors in behaviour management education. *Teaching & Teacher Education, 22*(3), 377–393. doi:10.1016/j.tate.2005.11.007	X				
Gimbert, B., & Nolan, J. F., Jr. (2003). The influence of the professional development school context on supervisory practice: A university supervisor's and interns' perspectives. *Journal of Curriculum & Supervision, 18*(4), 353–379.					X
Gronn, D., Romeo, G., McNamara, S., & Yjong, H. T. (2013). Web conferencing of pre-service teachers' practicum in remote schools. *Journal of Technology & Teacher Education, 21*(2), 247–271.			X		
Gwyn-Paquette, C., & Tochon, F. V. (2002). The role of reflective conversations and feedback in helping preservice teachers learn to use cooperative activities in their second language classrooms. *Modern Language Journal, 86*(2), 204–226. doi:10.1111/1540–4781.00145	X				
Haigh, M., & Ward, G. (2004). Problematising practicum relationships: Questioning the "taken for granted." *Australian Journal of Education, 48*(2), 134–148.					X
Hamel, C. (2012). Supervision of pre-service teacher: Using Internet collaborative tools to support their return to their region of origin. *Canadian Journal of Education, 35*(2), 141–154.		X	X		X
Haughton, N. A., & Keil, V. L. (2009). Engaging with faculty to develop, implement, and pilot electronic performance assessments of student teachers using mobile devices. *Teacher Educator, 44*(4), 275–284. doi:10.1080/08878730903180218		X	X		
Hertzog, H. S., & O'Rode, N. (2011). Improving the quality of elementary mathematics student teaching: Using field support materials to develop reflective practice in student teachers. *Teacher Education Quarterly, 38*(3), 89–111.		X			

Jacobs, J., & Yendol-Hoppey, D. (2010). Supervisor transformation with in a professional learning community. *Teacher Education Quarterly, 37*(2), 97–114.

Johnson, I. L., & Napper-Owen, G. (2011). The importance of role perceptions in the student teaching triad. *Physical Educator, 68*(1), 44–56.

Knapczyk, D. R., Hew, K. F., & Frey, T. J. (2005). Evaluation of online mentoring of practicum for limited licensed teachers. *Teacher Education & Special Education, 28*(3), 207–220. doi:10.1177/088840640502800407

Koerner, M., Rust, F. O., & Baumgartner, F. (2002). Exploring roles in student teaching placements. *Teacher Education Quarterly, 29*(2), 35–58.

Kopcha, T. J., & Alger, C. (2011). The impact of technology-enhanced student teacher supervision on student teacher knowledge, performance, and self-efficacy during the field experience. *Journal of Educational Computing Research, 45*(1), 49–73.

Lee, Y. A. (2011). Self-study of cross-cultural supervision of teacher candidates for social justice. *Studying Teacher Education, 7*(1), 3–18.

Levine, T. H. (2011). Features and strategies of supervisor professional community as a means of improving the supervision of preservice teachers. *Teaching and Teacher Education, 27*(5), 930–941.

Long, J. J., van Es, Elizabeth A., & Black, R. W. (2013). Supervisor–student teacher interactions: The role of conversational frames in developing a vision of ambitious teaching. *Linguistics & Education, 24*(2), 179–196. doi:10.1016/j.linged.2013.02.002

Lopez-Real, F., Stimpson, P., & Bunton, D. (2001). Supervisory conferences: An exploration of some difficult topics. *Journal of Education for Teaching, 27*(2), 161–73.

Martel, J. (2012). Looking across contexts in foreign language student teacher supervision: A self-study. *New Educator, 8*(3), 243–257.

Meijer, P. C., Korthagen, F. A. J., & Vasalos, A. (2009). Supporting presence in teacher education: The connection between the personal and professional aspects of teaching. *Teaching and Teacher Education, 25*(2), 297–308.

(continued)

Table 3. (Continued)

Citation	Tasks	Observation/ Feedback	Technology	Professional Development	Relationships
Mevorach, M., & Strauss, S. (2012). Teacher educators' in-action mental models in different teaching situations. *Teachers and Teaching: Theory and Practice, 18*(1), 25–41.		X			
Miller, M. J., & Carney, J. (2009). Lost in translation: Using video annotation software to examine how a clinical supervisor interprets and applies a state-mandated teacher assessment instrument. *Teacher Educator, 44*(4), 217–231.		X	X		
Montecinos, C., Cnudde, V., Ow, M., Solis, M. C., Emy, S., & Riveros, M. (2002). Relearning the meaning and practice of student teacher supervision through collaborative self-study. *Teaching and Teacher Education, 18*(7), 781–793.	X			X	
Moore, R. (2003). Reexamining the field experiences of preservice teachers. *Journal of Teacher Education, 54*(1), 31–42. doi:10.1177 /0022487102238656	X				
Murray-Harvey, R. (2001). How teacher education students cope with practicum concerns. *Teacher Educator, 37*(2), 117–132. doi:10.1080/08878730109555286	X				
Nguyen, H. T. (2009). An inquiry-based practicum model: What knowledge, practices, and relationships typify empowering teaching and learning experiences for student teachers, cooperating teachers and college supervisors? *Teaching & Teacher Education, 25*(5), 655–662. doi:10.1016/j.tate.2008.10.001	X				X
Ochieng' Ong'ondo, C., & Borg, S. (2011). "We teach plastic lessons to please them": The influence of supervision on the practice of English language student teachers in Kenya. *Language Teaching Research, 15*(4), 509–528.	X	X			
Peña, C. M. (2007). Asking the right questions: Online mentoring of student teachers. *International Journal of Instructional Media, 34*(1), 105–113.		X	X		X

Reference	1	2	3	4	5
Prater, M. A., & Sileo, T. W. (2002). School-university partnerships in special education field experiences. *Remedial & Special Education, 23*(6), 325–348. doi:10.1177/07419325020230060301	X				X
Prater, M. A., & Sileo, T. W. (2004). Fieldwork requirements in special education preparation: A national study. *Teacher Education & Special Education, 27*(3), 251–263. doi:10.1177/088840640402700305					X
Rathel, J. M., Drasgow, E., & Christle, C. C. (2008). Effects of supervisor performance feedback on increasing preservice teachers' positive communication behaviors with students with emotional and behavioral disorders. *Journal of Emotional & Behavioral Disorders, 16*(2), 67–77. doi:10.1177/1063426607312537				X	X
Rock, M., Gregg, M., Gable, R., Zigmond, N., Blanks, B., Howard, P., & Bullock, L. (2012). Time after time online: An extended study of virtual coaching during distant clinical practice. *Journal of Technology and Teacher Education, 20*(3), 277–304.		X		X	
Rodgers, A., & Keil, V. L. (2007). Restructuring a traditional student teacher supervision model: Fostering enhanced professional development and mentoring within a professional development school context. *Teaching & Teacher Education, 23*(1), 63–80.				X	X
Scheeler, M. C., McAfee, J. K., Ruhl, K. L., & Lee, D. L. (2006). Effects of corrective feedback delivered via wireless technology on preservice teacher performance and student behavior. *Teacher Education and Special Education, 29*(1), 12–25.			X	X	X
Scherff, L., & Singer, N. R. (2012). The preservice teachers are watching: Framing and reframing the field experience. *Teaching & Teacher Education, 28*(2), 263–272.					X
Sewall, M. (2009). Transforming supervision: Using video elicitation to support preservice teacher-directed reflective conversations. *Issues in Teacher Education, 18*(2), 11–30.			X	X	X
Sherry, L., & Chiero, R. (2004). Project TALENT: Infusing technology in K–12 field placements through a learning community model. *Journal of Technology & Teacher Education, 12*(2), 265–297.	X	X		X	

(continued)

Table 3. *(Continued)*

Citation	Tasks	Observation/ Feedback	Technology	Professional Development	Relationships
Singer, N. R., & Zeni, J. (2004). Building bridges: Creating an online conversation community for preservice teachers. *English Education, 37*(1), 30–49.	X	X	X	X	X
Soslau, E. (2012). Opportunities to develop adaptive teaching expertise during supervisory conferences. *Teaching and Teacher Education, 28*(5), 768–779. doi:10.1016/j.tate.2012.02.009	X				
Tang, S. Y. F. (2003). Challenge and support: The dynamics of student teachers' professional learning in the field experience. *Teaching & Teacher Education, 19*(5), 483–498. doi:10.1016/S0742-051X(03)00047-7	X	X			
Tang, S. Y. F., & Chow, A. W. K. (2007). Communicating feedback in teaching practice supervision in a learning-oriented field experience assessment framework. *Teaching and Teacher Education, 23*(7), 1066–1085.		X			
Tate, P., Pyke, C., Kortecamp, K., & Muskin, C. (2005). Developing an ethical orientation toward supervisory practice through collaborative case writing. *Action in Teacher Education, 27*(3), 13–25.	X			X	
Tillema, H. H. (2009). Assessment for learning to teach: Appraisal of practice teaching lessons by mentors, supervisors, and student teachers. *Journal of Teacher Education, 60*(2), 155–167. doi:10.1177/0022487108330551		X			
Turunen, T. A., & Tuovila, S. (2012). Mind the gap: Combining theory and practice in a field experience. *Teaching Education, 23*(2), 115–130.	X				

Valencia, S. W., Martin, S. D., Place, N. A., & Grossman, P. (2009). Complex interactions in student teaching: Lost opportunities for learning. *Journal of Teacher Education, 60*(3), 304–322. doi:10.1177/0022487109336543

Ward, C. J., Nolen, S. B., & Horn, I. S. (2011). Productive friction: How conflict in student teaching creates opportunities for learning at the boundary. *International Journal of Educational Research, 50*(1), 14–20. doi:10.1016/j.ijer.2011.04.004

White, S. (2007). Investigating effective feedback practices for pre-service teacher education students on practicum. *Teaching Education, 18*(4), 299–311. doi:10.1080/10476210701687591

Williams, M., & Watson, A. (2004). Post-lesson debriefing: Delayed or immediate? An investigation of student teacher talk. *Journal of Education for Teaching: International Research and Pedagogy, 30*(2), 85–96.

Wilson, E. K. (2006). The impact of an alternative model of student teacher supervision: Views of the participants. *Teaching & Teacher Education, 22*(1), 22–31.

Yusko, B. P. (2004). Caring communities as tools for learner-centered supervision. *Teacher Education Quarterly, 31*(3), 53–72.

Zellermayer, M., & Margolin, I. (2005). Teacher educators' professional learning described through the lens of complexity theory. *Teachers College Record, 107*(6), 1275–1304. doi:10.1111/j.1467–9620.2005.00513.x

Table 4.   Subquestions Disaggregated by Methodology

Categories	Total Articles	Qualitative	Quantitative	Mixed	International
Tasks	32	25	2	5	9
Observation and feedback	33	20	7	6	11
Technology	11	7	1	3	2
Professional development	10	9	0	1	3
Relationships and community	23	17	0	6	6

responds to the overall main question—What can we learn from PST field supervision since the publication of the NCATE PDS Standards?—by providing summaries of each of the subquestions.

Findings

To summarize the findings of this comprehensive meta-analysis, the findings from each subquestion are used as topic headings in this section. The results of this study identify tasks and practices of PST supervision; define PST supervision and the PST supervisor; describe approaches, tools, and outcomes related to observation and feedback; describe how technology has enhanced and disrupted PST supervision; explain approaches to supervisor professional development; and reveal critical knowledge, characteristics, and skills to foster relationships in PST supervision.

The Tasks of PST Supervision

The sub–meta-analysis on supervisory tasks focused on the question, What are the tasks in which a supervisor engages? Initial analysis revealed a lack of conceptual frameworks and common terminology for various aspects of PST supervision, which meant that understanding tasks became increasingly difficult. However, we were able to glean five tasks and 12 practices from the studies. Tasks were defined as critical areas required to create the clinical context for meeting PST learning needs. Practices were defined as the pedagogical strategies supervisors used to actualize a task. The five tasks included (1) targeted assistance, (2) individual support, (3) collaboration and community, (4) curriculum support, and (5) research for innovation. Each of the five tasks identifies initial practices.

Supervisors engage in the task of targeted assistance to provide instructional support to change PSTs' practices. Instructional support occurs through the practices of providing targeted instructional feedback (Coulon & Lorenzo, 2003; Ochieng' Ong'ondo & Borg, 2011; Rock et al., 2009;

Scheeler, McAfee, Ruhl, & Lee, 2006) and fostering critical reflection (Bates, Ramirez, & Drits, 2009; Meijer, Korthagen, & Vasalos, 2009; Montecinos et al., 2002; Scherff & Singer, 2012; Sewall, 2009; Soslau, 2012).

Supervisors engage in the task of individual support because learning to teach in the clinical context can be physically, emotionally, and psychologically demanding. Individual support occurs through the practices of balancing challenge and support (Beck & Kosnik, 2002; Bullock, 2012; Tang, 2003) and helping PSTs cope with stress (Caires, Almeida, & Martins, 2009; Murray-Harvey, 2001).

Supervisors engage in the task of collaboration and community because supporting PST learning requires the collaborative efforts of multiple stakeholders. Collaboration and community occurs through the practices of developing quality placements (Beck & Kosnik, 2002; Bullock, 2012; Campbell & Lott, 2010; Moore, 2003; Murray-Harvey, 2010; Tang, 2003), maintaining triad relationships (Bullough & Draper, 2004; Campbell & Lott, 2010; Koerner, Rust, & Baumgartner, 2002; Rodgers & Keil, 2007; Sherry & Chiero, 2004; Wilson, 2006), and creating learner-centered PST communities (Cuenca, Schmeichel, Butler, Dinkleman, & Nichols, 2011; Nguyen, 2009; Yusko, 2004).

Supervisors engage in the task of curriculum support to ensure that the teacher preparation curriculum reflects shared understandings of a meaningful, relevant, and coherent pre-K–12 curriculum. Curriculum support occurs through the practices of fostering theory (Beck & Kosnik, 2002; Hertzog & O'Rode, 2011; Moore, 2003; Valencia, Martin, Place, & Grossman, 2009; Ward, Nolen, & Horn, 2011) and practice connections and strengthening curriculum planning (Turunen & Tuovila, 2012).

Supervisors engage in the task of research for innovation to continually enhance the teaching and learning processes. Research for innovation occurs through the practices of engaging in inquiry or self-study (Bullock, 2012; Bullough & Draper, 2004; Tate, Pyke, Kortecamp, & Muskin, 2012; Montecinos et al., 2002) and innovating to enhance supervision (Sewall, 2009; Sherry & Chiero, 2004; Singer & Zeni, 2004).

The identification of tasks and practices are by no means exhaustive; rather, they are a beginning identification for developing a common understanding of PST supervision. What was universal across these tasks and practices was that the end goal was to foster PST learning. This led to the realization that PST supervision and the PST supervisor are separate entities, resulting in two separate definitions. PST supervision became defined as the enactment of tasks and practices aimed at developing the PST's improvement of practice, while PST supervisors became defined as individuals who enact the function of PST supervision. These individuals may or may not be in formalized supervisory roles, but they are the individuals who perform the function of PST supervision, thus showing the distinction between the person and the process.

Observation, Feedback, and Outcomes

The sub–meta-analysis on observation and feedback attended to four questions: (1) What tools do supervisors use to give feedback?, (2) What is the content of supervisory feedback?, (3) How do supervisors provide feedback?, and
(4) What are the outcomes of observation and feedback on PST learning? The
meta-analysis begins to point to the need for a balanced approach to feedback.

Observation Tools

Within the research on observation and feedback, observation tools were
often not at the forefront of research studies unless connected to the use of
technology. The observation tools within empirical articles seemed to move
to the background as a source of data rather than the focus of the study. Only
two articles specifically studied the use of observations notes as a format to
capture data (Hertzog and O'Rode, 2011; Tillema, 2009). There were various examples of technology as an alternative to paper-and-pencil observation
instruments (Haughton & Keil, 2009; Sewall, 2009). Technological tools were
also described within the empirical literature as a method to support providing
feedback (Carter, 2005; Hamel, 2012; Pena & Almaguer, 2007; Rock et al., 2009;
Scheeler, McKinnon, & Stout, 2012; Singer & Zeni, 2004). These included Bug
in Ear (BIE) wireless technology (Rock et al., 2009; Scheeler et al., 2012); Skype
(Hamel, 2012); instructional management information systems (Carter, 2005);
online forums, listservs, or discussion boards (Pena & Almaguer, 2007; Singer &
Zeni, 2004); and e-mail (Rathel, Drasgow, & Christle, 2008).

Content of Feedback

In the empirical literature, findings from studies revealed that the content
of supervisory feedback was found to be more general in nature rather than
subject specific. The majority of feedback studied focused on general topics,
such as classroom management, lesson planning, student engagement, assessment, and professionalism rather than content-specific dialogue (Hertzog &
O'Rode, 2011; Tang & Chow, 2007; Valencia et al., 2009). The implications
of several of these studies were focused on how to bring greater content-specific dialogue to feedback (Hertzog & O'Rode, 2011; Martel, 2012; Valencia
et al., 2009). The meta-analysis also revealed that the content of supervisory
feedback could be influenced by the observation tool (Hertzog & O'Rode,
2011), beliefs or frame of the supervisor (Martel, 2012; Valencia et al., 2009),
the supervisor's knowledge base (Ochieng' Ong'ondo & Borg, 2011), and
roles within the triad (Akcan & Tatar, 2010).

Approaches to Feedback

The empirical literature illustrated that supervisors often differ in their approach to providing feedback. The articles could often be sorted into direct,

reflective, and more supportive approaches to feedback. The outcomes for PSTs often were discussed in connection to the development of instructional practices as well as increased depth or sophistication of reflection.

A *direct* approach to feedback was often characterized as immediate, corrective, telling, and often specific (Rathel et al., 2008; Rock et al., 2009; Scheeler et al., 2012). Often through tools such as BIE technology, the university supervisor provided immediate corrective feedback that targeted specific teaching behaviors (Rock et al., 2009; Scheeler et al., 2012). Many articles focused on these direct, immediate approaches and described the outcome of positive learning for PSTs in regard to enacting instructional practices (Rathel et al., 2008; Rock et al., 2009; Scheeler et al., 2012). The articles reviewed for this meta-analysis revealed that these direct approaches often led to positive results in relation to specific or what some may call more technical teaching behaviors (i.e., increased positive communication, choral response, and three timed trials). Many of these articles were found in the special education literature.

The sub–meta-analysis also revealed supervisory approaches to feedback that could be thought of as more *reflective*. Supervisors used strategies to promote reflection, such as questioning (Akcan & Tatar, 2010; Basmadjian, 2011; Mevorach & Strauss, 2012; Pena & Almaguer, 2007), promoting PST ownership and voice (Akcan & Tatar, 2010; Mevorach & Strauss, 2012; Sewall, 2009; Singer & Zeni, 2004), brokering theory-to-practice connections (Hamel, 2012; Mevorach & Strauss, 2012; Tang, 2003; Ward et al., 2011), and depersonalizing (Basmadjian 2011; Lopez-Real, Stimpson, & Bunton, 2001). With a reflective approach, outcomes of feedback included more sophisticated or deeper reflection through the development of adaptive expertise (Soslau, 2012), critical reflection (Bates et al., 2009; Meijer et al., 2009; Montecinos et al., 2002; Scherff & Singer, 2012; Sewall, 2009; Soslau, 2012), and more thoughtful discussion of practices (Long, van Es, & Black, 2013). While these studies discussed increased depth of reflection as an outcome, they could not necessarily make the connection to changes in PST instructional practice as influenced by these reflective approaches.

The Role of Technology

The sub–meta-analysis on technology in PST supervision addressed the question, What is the current role of technology in supervision? The research on technology and PST supervision revealed that tools could serve as technological innovations to solve issues in PST supervision. Those researched tools included video (Falconer & Lingnugaris-Kraft, 2002; Hamel, 2012; Miller & Carney, 2009; Sewall, 2009), social media tools (Babiuk, Mweti, & Yoon, 2004; Knapczyk, Hew, & Frey, 2005; Pena & Almaguer, 2007; Scherff & Singer, 2012; Singer & Zeni, 2004), mobile/wireless devices (Haughton & Keil, 2009; Rock et al., 2009; Scheeler et al., 2012), and course management systems (Carter, 2005). Some of these tools were also used in tandem, such as videoconferencing and mobile technology (Scheeler et al., 2012) and videoconferencing and social media (Alger & Kopcha, 2009; Falconer & Lignugaris-Kraft, 2002; Kopcha & Alger, 2011). The data revealed that technology in PST supervision is being used to enhance and sometimes disrupt previous conceptions of PST supervision.

Technology has enhanced PST supervision by using technological tools or combinations of technological tools to improve supervisors' ability to observe and give feedback (Falconer & Lignugaris-Kraft, 2002; Hamel, 2012; Haughton & Keil, 2009; Rock et al., 2009; Scheeler et al., 2012), improve communication (Alger & Kopcha, 2009; Knapczyk et al., 2005; Kopcha & Alger, 2011; Pena & Almaguer, 2007; Scherff & Singer, 2012; Singer & Zeni, 2004), combat the resource-intensive nature of PST supervision in remote locations (Carter, 2005; Falconer & Lignugaris-Kraft, 2002; Hamel, 2012; Rock et al., 2009), build stronger relationships (Alger & Kopcha, 2009; Carter, 2005; Falconer & Lignugaris-Kraft, 2002; Hamel, 2012; Knapczyk et al., 2005; Kopcha & Alger, 2011; Singer & Zeni, 2004), better elicit teacher candidate thinking, and empower teacher candidates (Alger & Kopcha, 2009; Knapczyk et al., 2005; Kopcha & Alger, 2011; Pena & Almaguer, 2007; Scherff & Singer, 2012), specifically to have ownership over the postobservation conference (Sewall, 2009). Technology has added an additional layer of support for teacher candidates (Alger & Kopcha, 2009; Kopcha & Alger, 2011; Singer & Zeni, 2004) and also for cooperating teachers (Alger & Kopcha, 2009; Kopcha & Alger, 2011).

Technology has disrupted previous notions of PST supervision by extending the work of supervisors beyond the scope of teacher candidates (Alger & Kopcha, 2009; Babiuk et al., 2004; Scheeler et al., 2012; Singer & Zeni, 2004), expanded the ways in which practical ideas were or could be exchanged (Alger & Kopcha, 2009; Pena & Almaguer, 2007; Singer & Zeni, 2004), and shifted traditional roles and responsibilities for supervisors and cooperating teachers (Alger & Kopcha, 2009; Falconer & Lignugaris-Kraft, 2002; Hamel, 2012; Knapczyk et al., 2005). Research sought to understand how technology could improve outcomes of PST supervision, such as improving PSTs' ability to observe classroom spaces (Pena & Almaguer, 2007; Scherff & Singer, 2012) and deepening PSTs' ability to reflect on their practice (Sewall, 2009).

Integrating technology into PST supervision was not a seamless endeavor; rather, it was wrought with technical challenges (Babiuk et al., 2004; Falconer & Lignugaris-Kraft, 2002; Haughton & Keil, 2009) and human-use challenges (Babiuk et al., 2004; Falconer & Lignugaris, 2002; Haughton & Keil, 2009; Rock et al., 2009). To tackle these challenges, the research suggested that professional development for integrating technology into PST supervision was needed (Babiuk et al., 2004; Haughton & Keil, 2009; Miller & Carney, 2009).

Professional Development for Supervisors

The sub–meta-analysis on professional development focused on the question, What type of professional development is provided for PST supervisors? We found that research about how supervisors engage in professional development to grow and develop is sparse. Across the articles found, the focus for supervisor professional development included creating a context for supervision (Bullock, 2012), technology integration (Sherry & Chiero, 2004), issues of social justice (Jacobs & Yendol-Hoppey, 2010), ethics (Tate, Pyke, Kortekamp, & Muskin, 2005), curricular change (Zellermayer & Margolin, 2005), online discussions (Singer & Zeni, 2004), balancing assessment and assistance (Basmadijian, 2011), and supporting PST reflection (Bullock, 2012; Montencinos et al., 2002).

Within the limited empirical articles written, professional learning communities and supervisor inquiry or self-study emerged as the two main structures for supervisor professional development. At times, these structures overlapped, as in a learning community of supervisors engaging in collaborative inquiry. Across both these structures for professional development, there was a common theme that professional development for supervisors included the element of deprivatizing practice (Basmadijian, 2011; Jacobs & Yendol-Hoppey, 2010; Levine, 2011; Montencinos et al., 2002; Singer & Zeni, 2004; Tate et al., 2005; Zellermayer & Margolin, 2005). Professional development involved making supervision practices and beliefs public either to a group of other supervisors (i.e., professional learning community) or to oneself (i.e., self-study). Another theme within the empirical articles illustrated that when supervisors made their practice public, they began to engage in critical reflection about their own beliefs as well as their practice of supervision (Bullock, 2012; Jacobs & Yendol-Hoppey, 2010; Tate et al., 2005; Zellmayer & Margolin, 2005).

Drawing from the empirical literature, the data indicated that specific activities occurred within professional development for supervisors within the contexts of professional learning communities and/or self-study. Within self-study, supervisors engaged in activities that included asking questions about practice, engaging in reflective writing, audiotaping/videotaping and transcribing conferences with PSTs, highlighting tensions between espoused platform and platform in use, reflecting on personal biography (i.e., past experiences, culture, and so on), identifying patterns in supervisory beliefs and practices, and presenting self-study findings with other supervisors. Within the practice of engaging in learning within a professional learning community, activities included writing cases, using dialogic tools to promote learning within community (modeling, probing, and reframing), reflecting on assumptions and beliefs about supervision, sharing problems of practice/dilemmas, sharing resources and practices, using protocols to structure conversation, and engaging in collaborative inquiry.

Building Relationships

The sub–meta-analysis on building relationships and community addressed the question, How do supervisors form relationships and build community? The research on building relationships in PST supervision continues to report on key aspects for successful relationships. The empirical literature identifies important characteristics that individuals must have in order to build successful relationships, key characteristics of the supervisory environment needed to build successful relationships, and critical knowledge that supervisors must have in order to build successful relationships. New knowledge generated from the meta-analysis identified practices and activities for building relationships in PST supervision.

Building successful relationships, especially in robust school–university partnerships such as professional development schools, requires vulnerability and a sense of humility (Gimbert & Nolan, 2003), communication (Hamel, 2012; Johnson & Napper-Owen, 2011; Lee, 2011; Nguyen, 2009; Pena & Almageur, 2007), and open-mindedness, flexibility, and dedication (Nguyen, 2009). Building successful relationships occurs within a supervisory environment. Trust and time continue to be essential features of a supervisory environment conducive to relationships and relationship building (Campbell & Lott, 2010; Chaliès, Escalié, Bertone, & Clarke, 2012; Gimbert & Nolan, 2003; Johnson & Napper-Owen, 2011; Koerner et al., 2002; Lee, 2011; Levine, 2011; Lopez-Real et al., 2001). Other characteristics of supervisory environments that are conducive to building successful relationships include a common project (Campbell & Lott, 2010; Gimbert & Nolan, 2003), collaborative problem solving (Lee, 2011), a shared purpose of pre-K–12 student learning (Gimbert & Nolan, 2003), and understanding power and positionality (Bullough and Draper, 2004; Campbell & Lott, 2010; Gimbert & Nolan, 2003; Johnson & Napper-Owen, 2011; Lee, 2011).

Building successful relationships requires skill and an extensive knowledge base. Overwhelmingly, the literature pointed to a need for supervisors to have contextual knowledge about the K–12 students (Gimbert & Nolan, 2003), PSTs (Gimbert & Nolan, 2003; Johnson & Napper-Owen, 2011; Knapczyk et al., 2005; Lee, 2011; Pena & Almaguer, 2007), teachers (Johnson & Napper-Owen, 2011; Knapczyk et al., 2005), the classroom context (Gimbert & Nolan, 2003), the school context (Hamel, 2012), the community context (Hamel, 2012), and the university context (Lopez-Real et al., 2001). Knowing how to work with children can be a successful strategy for building relationships with PSTs and mentor teachers (Gimbert & Nolan, 2003). Knowing about oneself (Lee, 2011), knowing when to intervene and support relationships (Johnson & Napper-Owen, 2011), and knowing interpersonality (Levine, 2011) are also essential knowledge for supervisors in order to build successful relationships in PST supervision. Having these types of knowledge permits supervisors to ask deeper questions about pedagogy and student learning (Gimbert & Nolan, 2003).

Drawing from the empirical literature, the data indicated that specific practices and activities can be used to build relationships. These practices included (1) establishing a readiness for analyzing practice, (2) developing interpersonal familiarity with all stakeholders, (3) creating a culture of trust and collegiality, and (4) modeling caring and fidelity. This meta-analysis also found that activities were not necessarily specific to one practice, meaning that some activities may address more than one practice. And in some cases, a practice was an activity of another practice, indicating that perhaps practices were nestled within practices. For example, modeling caring and fidelity is itself a practice but it can also be an activity that creates a culture of trust and collegiality. This nestling indicates that building relationships in an era of increased school–university partnerships is complex and requires a more extensive knowledge base and skill set.

Discussion and Implications

In the past decade, reform agendas have called for an increased focus on the clinical experience through collaboration between schools and universities to actualize high-quality PST education (NCATE, 2001, 2010). Researchers have identified the importance of program coherence as one element of high-quality teacher education (Grossman, McDonald, Hammerness, & Ronfeldt, 2008; Hammerness, 2006). Program coherence refers to the link between fieldwork and teacher education course work as essential for PST development. This type of coherence requires collaboration between those who serve as supervisors in pre-K–12 education as well as those who serve as supervisors for PST education. Supervisors fulfill a critical role in addressing these issues, as they are uniquely situated in spaces where they can help PSTs and school-based partners commingle theory and practice as they learn about teaching. Balancing approaches in supervisory feedback is necessary in order to foster increased reflective thinking, preservice emotional well-being, and changes in instructional practices. Supervisors also need to take into consideration the needs of the PST in order to provide a balanced approach.

What we learn from this comprehensive meta-analysis is that PST supervision is expanding, becoming more sophisticated and increasingly complex. The identification of tasks and practices is an indication that PST supervision is expanding beyond observation and feedback. Supervisors are being asked to work with more individuals, such as mentor teachers and pre-K–12 students, and enact additional tasks and practices that build relationships and community between and among a variety of individuals, expanding their role. Technological tools were not only focused on PSTs but also used as support systems for mentor teachers; this also shows that PST supervision extends beyond PSTs. Technology also expanded who had access to resources and practical ideas.

The increased push for school–university collaboration for increased clinical education is influencing the complexity of PST supervision. As supervisors are being asked to deepen PST reflection, work with more individuals, and perform a variety of tasks, PST supervision can no longer be conceived of and enacted simplistically through a few sporadic classroom observations. Rather, as the outcomes for PST supervision expand and focus on pre-K–12 student learning, PST supervision must become more sophisticated and therefore requires strategies for developing sophisticated knowledge bases and skill sets of PST supervisors. Previously, training for supervisors existed as the main form of professional development for supervisors (Areglado, 1998). Yet the increased attention to more sophisticated forms of professional development for PST supervisors, such as professional learning communities, practitioner inquiry, and self-study, indicates that PST supervision is becoming more complex. "Sit and gets" will no longer suffice for fostering the extensive knowledge and skills needed to enact PST supervision in an era of increased clinical education and school–university collaboration.

While previous reviews have noted a commonality in terminology but an indeterminate understanding of the role of school–university collaboration on PST supervision (Clift & Brady, 2005), this comprehensive meta-analysis is significant because it offers such insight. Increased collaboration has actually created a lack of common nomenclature in defining the role of the PST supervisor and the function of PST supervision. The use of multiple terms to define roles and explain functions of PST supervision is evidence of the increased complexity of PST supervision. Understanding who engages in formal supervisory roles and what tasks and practices are performed in these roles has complicated our understanding of PST supervision.

Despite confusion over terminology, increased collaboration has actually expanded the tasks of PST supervision, increasing the sophistication and complexity of PST supervision. These complexities position the PST supervisor within teacher education as incredibly important to the professional preparation of teachers, unlike prior critiques of the university supervisor (Morris, 1974; Sandgren & Schmidt, 1956; Schueler, Gold, & Mitzel, 1962). Perhaps the sophisticated nature and complexity of PST supervision in the current decade of reform may require the role of the "university supervisor" to be reconceptualized. Increased complexity of task means increased complexity of support, which may require the combination of technological tools and sophisticated and interrelated supervisory practices as innovations. These findings suggest that the expansive nature of PST supervision may require multiple individuals engaging in a variety of supervisory roles and enacting various tasks of PST supervision as opposed to previous notions of the university supervisor shouldering this burden. This means that the role of the university supervisor requires a shift. No longer can supervisors exist as marginalized triad members. Rather, PST supervisors in an era of increased clinical education and school–university collaboration require a shift in functions from supervisors *of* learning to liaisons *for* learning. As this role shifts, PST supervision will continue to require increased attention and support. A lack of understanding about the role of the PST supervisor and the function of PST supervision is likely to create many complexities that could thwart important teacher education reform efforts. The field of teacher education would benefit from a common nomenclature and a coherent conceptual framework that recognizes the complexity of PST supervision in an era of increased clinical education and school–university collaboration. **TEP**

Note

1. We would like to thank our doctoral student research team, Katie Arndt, Vanessa Casciola, Monica Gonzales, Rebecca Powell, Lori Rakes, Jennifer Ward, and Sarah Pennington, for their collaboration and support on this project.

References

Akcan, S., & Tatar, S. (2010). An investigation of the nature of feedback given to pre-service English teachers during their practice teaching experience. *Teacher Development, 14*(2), 153–172.

Alger, C., & Kopcha, T. J. (2009). eSupervision: A technology framework for the 21st century field experience in teacher education. *Issues in Teacher Education, 18*(2), 31–46.

American Association of Colleges of Teacher Education. (2010). *The clinical preparation of teachers: A policy brief.* http://edwebsfiles.ed.uiuc.edu/transitions/AACTE-Policy-Brief-March-2010.pdf

Areglado, R. J. (1998). Supervision in elementary schools. In G. R. Firth & E. F. Pajak (Eds.), *Handbook of research on school supervision* (pp. 591–600). New York: Macmillan.

Babiuk, G., Mweti, C., & Yoon, J. (2004). Effects of using a chat room during pre-service teachers' practicum. *Journal of Interactive Instruction Development, 16*(4), 11–17.

Basmadjian, K. G. (2011). Learning to balance assistance with assessment: A scholarship of field instruction. *Teacher Educator, 46*(2), 98–125. doi:10.1080/08878730.2011.552845

Bates, A. J., Ramirez, L., & Drits, D. (2009). Connecting university supervision and critical reflection: Mentoring and modeling. *Teacher Educator, 44*(2), 90–112. doi:10.1080/08878730902751993

Beck, C., & Kosnik, C. (2002). Professors and the practicum: Involvement of university faculty in preservice practicum supervision. *Journal of Teacher Education, 53*(1), 6–19.

Bullock, S. M. (2012). Creating a space for the development of professional knowledge: A self-study of supervising teacher candidates during practicum placements. *Studying Teacher Education, 8*(2), 143–156.

Bullough, R. V., Jr., & Draper, R. J. (2004). Making sense of a failed triad: Mentors, university supervisors, and positioning theory. *Journal of Teacher Education, 55*(5), 407–420.

Burns, R. W., & Badiali, B. (2015). When supervision is conflated with evaluation: Teacher candidates' perceptions of novice supervision. *Action in Teacher Education, 37*(4), 418–437. doi:10.1080/01626620.2015.1078757

Burns, R. W., Jacobs, J., & Yendol-Hoppey, D. (2014, October). *What do we continue to learn about preservice teacher supervision since the release of the NCATE PDS Stan-*

dards and Blue Ribbon Report? Part two of a qualitative meta-analysis. Paper presented at the annual meeting of the Council of Professors of Instructional Supervision, Atlanta.

Burns, R. W., Jacobs, J., & Yendol-Hoppey, D. (in press). The changing nature of the role of the university supervisor and the function of preservice teacher supervision in an era of increased school-university collaboration. *Action in Teacher Education.*

Caires, S., Almeida, L. S., & Martins, C. (2009). The socioemotional experiences of student teachers during practicum: A case of reality shock? *Journal of Educational Research, 103*(1), 17–27. doi:10.1080/00220670903228611

Campbell, T., & Lott, K. (2010). Triad dynamics: Investigating social forces, roles, and storylines. *Teaching Education, 21*(4), 349–366. doi:10.1080/10476210903518396

Carter, D. (2005). Distributed practicum supervision in a managed learning environment (MLE). *Teachers and Teaching: Theory and Practice, 11*(5), 481–497.

Chaliès, S., Escalié, G., Bertone, S., & Clarke, A. (2012). Learning "rules" of practice within the context of the practicum triad: A case study of learning to teach. *Canadian Journal of Education, 35*(2), 3–23.

Clift, R. T., & Brady, P. (2005). Research on methods courses and field experiences. In M. Cochran-Smith & K. M. Zeichner (Eds.), *Studying teacher education: The report of the AERA panel on research and teacher education* (pp. 309–424). Mahwah, NJ: Lawrence Erlbaum Associates.

Coulon, S. C., & Lorenzo, D. C. (2003). The effects of supervisory task statements on preservice teachers' instructional behaviors during retaught lessons. *Education, 124*(1), 181–193.

Cuenca, A. (2012). *Supervising student teachers: Issues, perspectives and future directions.* St. Louis, MO: Sense Publishers.

Cuenca, A., Schmeichel, M., Butler, B. M., Dinkelman, T., & Nichols, J. R., Jr. (2011). Creating a "third space" in student teaching: Implications for the university supervisor's status as outsider. *Teaching and Teacher Education, 27*(7), 1068–1077.

Falconer, K. B., & Lignugaris-Kraft, B. (2002). A qualitative analysis of the benefits and limitations of using two-way conferencing technology to supervise preservice teachers in remote locations. *Teacher Education and Special Education, 25*(4), 368–384. doi:10.1177/088840640202500406

Gimbert, B., & Nolan, J. F., Jr. (2003). The influence of the professional development school context on supervisory practice: A university supervisor's and interns' perspectives. *Journal of Curriculum and Supervision, 18*(4), 353–379.

Grossman, P., McDonald, M., Hammerness, K., & Ronfeldt, M. (2008). Constructing coherence: Structural predictors of perceptions of coherence in NYC teacher education programs. *Journal of Teacher Education, 59*(4), 273–287.

Guyton, E., & McIntyre, D. (1990). Student teaching and school experiences. In W. R. Houston (Ed.), *Handbook of research on teacher education* (pp. 514–534). New York: Macmillan.

Hamel, C. (2012). Supervision of pre-service teacher: Using Internet collaborative tools to support their return to their region of origin. *Canadian Journal of Education, 35*(2), 141–154.

Hammerness, K. (2006). From coherence in theory to coherence in practice. *Teachers College Record, 108*(7), 1241–1265.

Haughton, N. A., & Keil, V. L. (2009). Engaging with faculty to develop, implement, and pilot electronic performance assessments of student teachers using mobile devices. *Teacher Educator, 44*(4), 275–284. doi:10.1080/08878730903180218

Hertzog, H. S., & O'Rode, N. (2011). Improving the quality of elementary mathematics student teaching: Using field support materials to develop reflective practice in student teachers. *Teacher Education Quarterly, 38*(3), 89–111.

Holmes Group. (1986). *Tomorrow's teachers: A report of the Holmes Group.* Lansing, MI: Author.

Hoover, N. L., O'Shea, L. J., & Carroll, R. G. (1988). The supervisor-intern relationship and effective interpersonal communication skills. *Journal of Teacher Education, 39*(2), 22–27.

Jacobs, J., Burns, R. W., & Yendol-Hoppey, D. (2014, April). *The state of preservice teacher supervision in a decade of reform: A literature review.* Paper presented at the annual meeting of the American Educational Research Association, Philadelphia.

Jacobs, J., & Yendol-Hoppey, D. (2010). Supervisor transformation with in a professional learning community. *Teacher Education Quarterly, 37*(2), 97–114.

Johnson, I. L., & Napper-Owen, G. (2011). The importance of role perceptions in the student teaching triad. *Physical Educator, 68*(1), 44–56.

Knapczyk, D. R., Hew, K. F., & Frey, T. J. (2005). Evaluation of online mentoring of practicum for limited licensed teachers. *Teacher Education and Special Education, 28*(3), 207–220. doi:10.1177/088840640502800407

Koerner, M., Rust, F. O., & Baumgartner, F. (2002). Exploring roles in student teaching placements. *Teacher Education Quarterly, 29*(2), 35–58.

Kopcha, T. J., & Alger, C. (2011). The impact of technology-enhanced student teacher supervision on student teacher knowledge, performance, and self-efficacy during the field experience. *Journal of Educational Computing Research, 45*(1), 49–73.

Lee, Y. A. (2011). Self-study of cross-cultural supervision of teacher candidates for social justice. *Studying Teacher Education, 7*(1), 3–18.

Levine, T. H. (2011). Features and strategies of supervisor professional community as a means of improving the supervision of preservice teachers. *Teaching and Teacher Education: An International Journal of Research and Studies, 27*(5), 930–941.

Long, J. J., van Es, E. A., & Black, R. W. (2013). Supervisor–student teacher interactions: The role of conversational frames in developing a vision of ambitious teaching. *Linguistics and Education, 24*(2), 179–196. doi:10.1016/j.linged.2013.02.002

Lopez-Real, F., Stimpson, P., & Bunton, D. (2001). Supervisory conferences: An exploration of some difficult topics. *Journal of Education for Teaching, 27*(2), 161–173.

Martel, J. (2012). Looking across contexts in foreign language student teacher supervision: A self-study. *New Educator, 8*(3), 243–257.

McIntyre, D. J., & Byrd, D. M. (1998). Supervision in teacher education. In G. R. Firth & E. F. Pajak (Eds.), *Handbook of research on school supervision* (pp. 409–427). New York: Simon & Schuster Macmillan.

Meijer, P. C., Korthagen, F. A. J., & Vasalos, A. (2009). Supporting presence in teacher education: The connection between the personal and professional aspects of teaching. *Teaching and Teacher Education: An International Journal of Research and Studies, 25*(2), 297–308.

Mevorach, M., & Strauss, S. (2012). Teacher educators' in-action mental models in different teaching situations. *Teachers and Teaching: Theory and Practice, 18*(1), 25–41.

Miller, M. J., & Carney, J. (2009). Lost in translation: Using video annotation software to examine how a clinical supervisor interprets and applies a state-mandated teacher assessment instrument. *Teacher Educator, 44*(4), 217–231.

Montecinos, C., Cnudde, V., Ow, M., Solis, M. C., Emy, S., & Riveros, M. (2002). Relearning the meaning and practice of student teacher supervision through collaborative self-study. *Teaching and Teacher Education, 18*(7), 781–793.

Moore, R. (2003). Reexamining the field experiences of preservice teachers. *Journal of Teacher Education, 54*(1), 31–42. doi:10.1177/0022487102238656

Morris, J. E. (1974). The effects of the university supervisor on the performance and adjustment of student teachers. *Journal of Educational Research, 67*(8), 358–362.

Murray-Harvey, R. (2001). How teacher education students cope with practicum concerns. *Teacher Educator, 37*(2), 117–132. doi:10.1080/08878730109555286

National Council for the Accreditation of Teacher Education. (2001). *Standards for professional development schools*. Washington, DC: Author.

National Council for the Accreditation of Teacher Education. (2010). *Transforming teacher education through clinical practice: A national strategy to prepare effective teachers. A report of the Blue Ribbon Panel on Clinical Preparation and Partnership for Improved Student Learning*. Washington, DC: Author.

Nguyen, H. T. (2009). An inquiry-based practicum model: What knowledge, practices, and relationships typify empowering teaching and learning experiences for student teachers, cooperating teachers and college supervisors? *Teaching and Teacher Education, 25*(5), 655–662. doi:10.1016/j.tate.2008.10.001

Nolan, J. F. (1997). Can a supervisor be a coach? No. In J. Glanz & R. F. Neville (Eds.), *Educational supervision: Perspectives, issues, and controversies* (pp. 100–108). Norwood, MA: Christopher-Gordon.

Nolan, J., & Hoover, L. A. (2011). *Teacher supervision and evaluation: Theory into practice* (3rd ed.). Hoboken, NJ: Wiley.

Ochieng' Ong'ondo, C., & Borg, S. (2011). "We teach plastic lessons to please them": The influence of supervision on the practice of English language student teachers in Kenya. *Language Teaching Research, 15*(4), 509–528.

Paterson, B. L., Thorne, S. E., Canam, C., & Jillings, C. (2001). *Meta-study of qualitative health research: A practical guide to meta-analysis and meta-synthesis*. Thousand Oaks, CA: Sage.

Peña, C. M., & Almaguer, I. (2007). Asking the right questions: Online mentoring of student teachers. *International Journal of Instructional Media, 34*(1), 105–113.

Rathel, J. M., Drasgow, E., & Christle, C. C. (2008). Effects of supervisor performance feedback on increasing preservice teachers' positive communication behaviors with students with emotional and behavioral disorders. *Journal of Emotional and Behavioral Disorders, 16*(2), 67–77. doi:10.1177/1063426607312537

Rock, M., Gregg, M., Gable, R., Zigmond, N., Blanks, B., Howard, P., et al. (2012). Time after time online: An extended study of virtual coaching during distant clinical practice. *Journal of Technology and Teacher Education, 20*(3), 277–304.

Rodgers, A., & Keil, V. L. (2007). Restructuring a traditional student teacher supervision model: Fostering enhanced professional development and mentoring within a professional development school context. *Teaching and Teacher Education: An International Journal of Research and Studies, 23*(1), 63–80.

Rutter, A. (2011). Purpose and vision in professional development schools. *Yearbook for the National Society of the Study of Education, 110*(2), 289–305.

Sandelowski, M., & Barroso, J. (2007). *Handbook for synthesizing qualitative research.* New York: Springer.

Sandgren, D. L., & Schmidt, D. (1956). Does practice teaching change attitudes toward teaching? *Journal of Educational Research, 50*(8), 673–680.

Scheeler, M. C., McAfee, J. K., Ruhl, K. L., & Lee, D. L. (2006). Effects of corrective feedback delivered via wireless technology on preservice teacher performance and student behavior. *Teacher Education and Special Education, 29*(1), 12–25.

Scheeler, M. C., McKinnon, K., & Stout, J. (2012). Effects of immediate feedback delivered via webcam and bug-in-ear technology on preservice teacher performance. *Teacher Education and Special Education, 35*(1), 77–90.

Scherff, L., & Singer, N. R. (2012). The preservice teachers are watching: Framing and reframing the field experience. *Teaching and Teacher Education, 28*(2), 263–272.

Scholes, J. (2003). Meta-study of qualitative health research: A practical guide to meta-analysis and meta-synthesis. *Nursing in Critical Care, 8*(4), 184.

Schueler, R., Gold, B., & Mitzel, H. (1962). *Improvement of student teaching.* New York: City University of New York.

Sergiovanni, T. J., & Starratt, R. J. (2007). *Supervision: A redefinition* (8th ed.). New York: McGraw-Hill.

Sewall, M. (2009). Transforming supervision: Using video elicitation to support preservice teacher-directed reflective conversations. *Issues in Teacher Education, 18*(2), 11–30.

Sherry, L., & Chiero, R. (2004). Project TALENT: Infusing technology in K–12 field placements through a learning community model. *Journal of Technology and Teacher Education, 12*(2), 265–297.

Singer, N. R., & Zeni, J. (2004). Building bridges: Creating an online conversation community for preservice teachers. *English Education, 37*(1), 30–49.

Slick, S. K. (1998). The university supervisor: A disenfranchised outsider. *Teaching and Teacher Education, 14*(8), 821–834.

Soslau, E. (2012). Opportunities to develop adaptive teaching expertise during supervisory conferences. *Teaching and Teacher Education, 28*(5), 768–779. doi:10.1016/j.tate.2012.02.009

Tang, S. Y. F. (2003). Challenge and support: The dynamics of student teachers' professional learning in the field experience. *Teaching and Teacher Education, 19*(5), 483–498. doi:10.1016/S0742-051X(03)00047-7

Tang, S. Y. F., & Chow, A. W. K. (2007). Communicating feedback in teaching practice supervision in a learning-oriented field experience assessment framework. *Teaching and Teacher Education: An International Journal of Research and Studies, 23*(7), 1066–1085.

Tate, P., Pyke, C., Kortecamp, K., & Muskin, C. (2005). Developing an ethical orientation toward supervisory practice through collaborative case writing. *Action in Teacher Education, 27*(3), 13–25.

Tillema, H. H. (2009). Assessment for learning to teach: Appraisal of practice teaching lessons by mentors, supervisors, and student teachers. *Journal of Teacher Education, 60*(2), 155–167. doi:10.1177/0022487108330551

Timulak, L. (2007). Identifying core categories of client identified impact of helpful events in psychotherapy: A qualitative meta-analysis. *Psychotherapy Research, 17,* 305–314.

Turunen, T. A., & Tuovila, S. (2012). Mind the gap: Combining theory and practice in a field experience. *Teaching Education, 23*(2), 115–130.

Valencia, S. W., Martin, S. D., Place, N. A., & Grossman, P. (2009). Complex interactions in student teaching: Lost opportunities for learning. *Journal of Teacher Education, 60*(3), 304–322. doi:10.1177/0022487109336543

Ward, C. J., Nolen, S. B., & Horn, I. S. (2011). Productive friction: How conflict in student teaching creates opportunities for learning at the boundary. *International Journal of Educational Research, 50*(1), 14–20. doi:10.1016/j.ijer.2011.04.004

Wideen, M., Mayer-Smith, J., & Moon, B. (1998). A critical analysis of the research on learning to teach: Making the case for an ecological perspective on inquiry. *Review of Educational Research, 68*(2), 130–178.

Wilson, E. K. (2006). The impact of an alternative model of student teacher supervision: Views of the participants. *Teaching and Teacher Education: An International Journal of Research and Studies, 22*(1), 22–31.

Wilson, S. M., Floden, R. E., & Ferrini-Mundy, J. (2001). *Teacher preparation research: Current knowledge, gaps, and recommendations.* Washington, DC: Center for the Study of Teaching and Policy.

Yusko, B. P. (2004). Caring communities as tools for learner-centered supervision. *Teacher Education Quarterly, 31*(3), 53–72.

Zellermayer, M., & Margolin, I. (2005). Teacher educators' professional learning described through the lens of complexity theory. *Teachers College Record, 107*(6), 1275–1304. doi:10.1111/j.1467-9620.2005.00513.x

Rebecca West Burns is an assistant professor of elementary education at the University of South Florida. Her research agenda lies at the intersection of supervision, clinically rich teacher education, and school–university partnerships. She coordinates the Teacher Leadership Graduate Certificate and co-coordinates the undergraduate elementary education program. She cocreated the Mort Teacher Leader Academy, a unique clinically centered program designed to develop teacher leaders for urban schools. In 2013, she was awarded the Penn State University Alumni Association Early Career Achievement Award. She may be reached via e-mail at rebeccaburns@usf.edu.

Jennifer Jacobs is an assistant professor at the University of South Florida. She serves as coordinator of the elementary education doctoral program and co-coordinator of the undergraduate elementary cohort program. Her research centers on teacher professional learning and specifically a focus on equity. Within this overarching research focus, she looks at vehicles for professional learning that include field supervision/field experiences in clinically rich teacher education, teacher inquiry/action research, and teacher leadership. She may be reached via e-mail at jjacobs8@usf.edu.

Diane Yendol-Hoppey is a professor and the associate dean of education preparation and partnerships. She serves as the director of the David C. Anchin Center. Her research specifically focuses on understanding clinically rich teacher education, pre-service and in-service job-embedded teacher learning, and teacher leadership. Her leadership related to working with schools has helped develop and sustain multiple nationally recognized school–university partnerships. She has coauthored four books and published more than 50 articles that have appeared in such journals as Educational Researcher, *the* Teachers College Record, *and the* Journal of Teacher Education. *She spent 13 years teaching public school. She may be reached via e-mail at dyhoppey@usf.edu.*

One Mission, Two Systems, and a Big Gap

The Interaction of K–12 and Postsecondary Educators to Support the Common Core State Standards

Louis S. Nadelson and Suzanne H. Jones

ABSTRACT: Major K–12 education reform initiatives, such as the Common Core State Standards (CCSS), require extensive shifts in curricular and instructional approaches. Preparing for and engaging in the successful implementation of education reform endeavors must include extensive K–12 educator professional development. We posited that college of education faculty members in institutions of higher education (HE) were likely to play a major role in providing information and professional development for K–12 educators as they prepare for implementing the CCSS. We surveyed a sample of K–12 educators and HE faculty members to determine how they were interacting to support the CCSS and their emotions in relation to the standards. We found multiple gaps in support, leadership, and barriers and challenges between the perspectives and actions of the two groups of educators. We follow our presentation of results with possible explanations for the gaps, implications, and possible directions for future research.

The adoption of reform in K–12 education is a complex and effortful process (Cohen & Hill, 2001; Roehrig & Kruse, 2005; Somekh, 2008) that typically requires change in the mind-sets and practices of a wide range of stakeholders (Maton, 2008; Nadelson et al., 2012; Warren, 2005). Often, the biggest change expected in K–12 educational reform efforts are at the classroom level with shifts in curriculum and instruction (Bereiter & Scardamalia, 2006; Elmore, 2007) that require teachers to consider what and how to teach. Frequently, the same initiatives that influence K–12 schools are also influential on colleges of education that prepare K–12 teachers (King, 2011).

The nature of many education reform initiatives suggests that there is likely to be considerable overlap between the needs of K–12 preservice teachers and K–12 in-service teacher preparation to effectively the endeavors. However, the preparation of the preservice teachers to implement education reform efforts is primarily the responsibility of the college of education faculty members (Cochran-Smith, 2005; Darling-Hammond, 2010; Harvey, Yssel, Bauserman, & Merbler, 2008), which is not the case with the reform effort preparation of in-service teachers. Regardless, assuming the responsibility of preparing preservice teachers to implement reform efforts suggests that college of education faculty members need to have both the knowledge of the reform initiatives and the capacity to prepare others to implement the efforts. Given college of education faculty members' knowledge in reform initiatives and capacity to prepare others to implement reform efforts, it would seem the faculty members would be well positioned to lead reform-focused professional development and provide implementation support for in-service K–12 educators.

Given the alignment between the knowledge, capacity, and leadership position of college of education faculty members and the needs of K–12 educators with respect to education reform efforts, it would seem that collaborations between the institutions would be natural and occur frequently. The potential for collaborations between higher education (HE) faculty members and K–12 educators prompted us to wonder to what extent collaborations are taking place and what the nature of the collaborations is. Of particular interest was the communication and collaboration that was taking place in support of the implementation of the Common Core State Standards (CSSS). In addition, we were curious to learn more about how emotions were related to knowledge of and time spent learning about the standards and whether the relationships differed between the two groups of educators.

The goal of our research was determine how the two groups of educators perceived and interacted on issues of leadership, challenges and barriers, and support with respect to preparing for and implementing the CCSS. We contend that the interactions between K–12 faculty and HE faculty members in the context of the CCSS is a proxy for their interactions in relation to educational reform efforts in general.

Framework: Change and the Adoption of Innovation

The success of most education reform initiatives requires the involved K–12 educators to actively engage in a change process that results in their adopting and internalizing the education innovation (Ertmer & Ottenbreit-Leftwich, 2010). Engaging in a process of change and the adoption of innovation is a multifaceted process that typically involves acquisition of knowledge (Haney, Lumpe, Czerniak, & Egan, 2002), development of skills (Ertmer & Ottenbreit-Leftwich, 2010), maintaining an openness to change (Stanovich & West, 1997), association with a culture of support for change (Wandersman, Chien, & Katz, 2012), perceiving value in the innovation (Wozney, Venkatesh, & Abrami, 2006), and alignment with personal expectations for the innovation (Fenn & Raskino, 2008). Given the multifaceted nature of innovation adoption, there is justification for considering K–12 educators' effective implementation of education reform initiatives to be a rather complex and challenging process.

We argue the challenges associated with the complex and multifaceted nature of K–12 teacher innovation adoption may be catalyzed through HE faculty members who support the transition process. Further, we maintain that, when supported, teacher change and innovation adoption have a greater likelihood of being sustained. Thus, there is justification for our research on college of education faculty members' involvement with preparing and supporting K–12 educators' adoption and implementation of CCSS-aligned curriculum and instruction.

Educational Reform Efforts and the CSSS

Standards for K–12 student learning became widely recognized, formalized, standardized, and assessed with the adoption of the No Child Left Behind (NCLB) education reform initiative in association with the Elementary and Secondary Education Act (Hursh, 2007). Much of the development and adoption of the student learning standards associated with the NCLB initiative occurred at the state level (e.g., Mead & Mates, 2009). Some efforts were made to develop frameworks or standards at the national level that were frequently considered in the development of learning standards at the state level (e.g., Principles and Standards for School Mathematics of the National Council of Teachers of Mathematics and the Atlas of Science Literacy of the American Association for the Advancement of Science). Even with document generation at the national level to guide learning standard development and adoption, many state government and education stakeholders persisted in creating standards based on their knowledge, experiences, and culture. Thus, while there may be substantial overlap in the learning standards among states historically, there has been a lack of continuity of learning standards implementation and assessments nationally (National Center for Education Statistics, 2009).

In recognition of the potential ramifications of incomplete curricula, issues with students moving between states, and a desire for national standards (as many countries have; American Institutes for Research, 2015), representatives from the National Governors Association Center for Best Practices (2015) and the Council of Chief State School Officers developed and have promoted the CCSS (Common Core State Standards Initiative, 2015). The intention of the CCSS initiative was to create practice and content standards for K–12 mathematics and English language arts that states would adopt and implement. A major motivation for the standards was to ensure that students completed their K–12 education "college and career ready" (Common Core State Standards Initiative, 2015).

As with many prior and present educational reform efforts, there have been challenges with the levels of K–12 educators' knowledge accuracy and perceptions of the CCSS (Nadelson, Pluska, Moorcroft, Jeffrey, & Woodard, 2014). While professional development may help overcome the challenges associated with educational reform efforts (Kratochwill, Volpiansky, Clements, & Ball, 2007), there is also a need for a culture of change and general agreement in the larger educational community that there are benefits to adopting and implementing education initiatives (Kozma, 2005).

While the plans for state adoption of the CCSS were expected to take place with little opposition and embraced without challenge, the climate of change has shifted to that of resistance and in some cases hostility (Karp, 2013). The acrimony associated with CCSS adoption may be considered somewhat ironic given the alignment to many currently adopted and implemented standards (e.g., see the Crosswalk of Learning Standards and the Common Core State Standards of the American Association of School Librarians). Regardless, many states have adopted and are implementing the CCSS (Common Core State Standards Initiative, 2015). There are aspects of the CCSS that may be considered new to education (e.g., the practices and the integration across the curriculum) and therefore are likely to require K–12 teachers to shift their math and English language arts curricular choices and instructional approaches. The successful implementation of the practices and curriculum integration associated with the CCSS have required significant investment in the time of K–12 educators to adjust their instruction, modify their curriculum, and become educated to effectively teach aligned to the standards. We maintain that the shift in curricular choices and instructional approaches associated with the CCSS is likely to take place much more quickly and be more stable if the transition is supported by the larger educational community.

In-Service Teacher Preparation for Reform Through Professional Development

The effective implementation of complex reform initiatives requires high levels of teacher knowledge and skill (Van Driel, Beijaard, & Verloop, 2001). While there is potential for teachers to have acquired the knowledge and developed the necessary skills over time, there is a greater potential that teachers are in need of professional development to prepare and support their involvement in initiative implementation (Borko, 2004). One potential source of the professional development for K–12 educators comes from the faculty members in colleges of education in institutions of higher education (Borko, 2004). Faculty members in colleges of education commonly design, offer, and evaluate K–12 teacher professional development (Garet, Porter, Desimone, Birman, & Yoon, 2001). However, we argue that the needs of K–12 educators and interest and knowledge of college of education faculty members may not be aligned, and, therefore, college of education faculty members may not be working directly with K–12 educators or may be providing professional development that does not meet the needs of K–12 educators. The potential for misalignment between college of education faculty foci for providing professional development and K–12 educator needs provides justification for our research.

Emotions and Educational Reform

Educational reform may trigger strong emotional reactions from K–12 teachers, college of education faculty members, and the public at large. Strong emotional reactions are likely associated with educational reform efforts, particularly those that are considered to be controversial, such as the racial desegregation movement in U.S. schools during the 1950s and 1960s (Henry & Sears, 2002). The adoption of the CCSS has also sparked strong emotions from teachers, students, and parents (Strauss, 2014), including attitudes of resistance toward implementing the CCSS. For example, several states, including Texas, Nebraska, and Virginia, have passed legislation refusing to adopt the CCSS in part because of the outrage and frustration expressed by lawmakers, parents, and educators (Bidwell, 2014).

The relationship between educational reform and emotions is a burgeoning area of research among educational and cognitive psychologists. A seminal study conducted by Gregoire (2003) was an initial effort to understand why practicing teachers were resistant to adopting reform-oriented mathematics curricula that conflicted with their prior pedagogical beliefs. Gregoire developed the Cognitive-Affective Model of Conceptual Change (CAMCC) based on the results of her study. According to the CAMCC, emotional responses occur prior to processing the message and "as part of the appraisal process, serve as additional information for individuals as they interact with a complex, stressful message" (Gregoire, 2003, p. 168).

Gregoire's (2003) findings suggest that emotional responses to messages direct the level of engagement the individual has with the message. Positive and neutral emotions typically lead to heuristic processing of the message. In contrast, negative emotions, such as fear and anxiety, may promote deeper, systematic processing of the message. Gregoire (2003) argues that negative emotions, such as stress, can lead to acceptance and change if the individual perceives the learning context as a challenge. However, if the individual perceives the message as a threat, he or she will likely engage in avoidance behaviors.

The daily operations of school place a number of demands on K–12 educators that have been associated with emotions (Chang, 2009). Given that education reform initiatives may be part of the daily operation demands on K–12 educators, they are likely to experience a range of emotions associated with the efforts.

Of interest to us were K–12 and HE faculty members' emotions related to the CCSS, as we contend that the emotions are proxies for their perceptions of the value of and their competency in attending to the CCSS and likely influential on the educational community members' openness to change and support for the initiative. Although Gregoire (2003) has addressed elements of K–12 teachers' emotions toward educational reform, we have not been able to locate any reports of empirical studies of HE faculty emotions toward K–12 educational initiatives.

Method

Research Questions

The goal of our research was to determine the interaction between K–12 educators and college of education faculty members with regard to learning more about teaching and learning aligned with the CCSS. We also were interested in their perceptions and emotions toward the standards, as these variables are proxies for their levels of expectation and perhaps levels of interest in learning more about and supporting CCSS. The research questions guiding our research are the following:

- ➤ What are K–12 and HE faculty members' support needs and activities with respect to CCSS implementation?
- ➤ What are K–12 and HE faculty members' perceptions of the challenges and barriers of CCSS implementation?
- ➤ What are K–12 and HE faculty members' leadership perceptions and activities with respect to CCSS implementation?
- ➤ What are K–12 and HE faculty members' emotions toward the CCSS, and how are they related to their CCSS knowledge and communication comfort levels?

We hypothesize that the K–12 and HE faculty members would share similar passions and support for the standards and therefore would have similar emotions toward the CCSS. We also hypothesized that there would be moderate to extensive interactions between the K–12 and HE faculty members due to the K–12 educators' needs and the HE educators' expertise and leadership.

Participants

The participants in our research were 22 K–12 teachers and 58 HE faculty members who completed our study. It is important to note that we struggled to gain the participation of both K–12 teacher and HE faculty members. We solicited multiple school districts to gain permission to distribute our survey to the district teachers, and we were denied access; thus, our data collection of K–12 teachers was statewide and based on a publicly available mailing list of educators. The response to our request to participate was much less than we anticipated, with only 22 teachers completing our survey. However, the responses of the 22 K–12 teachers were very consistent, indicating that we were likely to gather similar data from other teachers, and thus we moved forward with our analysis. We recruited 58 HE faculty from an invitation e-mail distributed by a division of the American Educational Research Association to the membership. Although we received multiple responses from faculty indicating that they were interested in our research, they did not work with K–12 teachers.

Of the 22 K–12 teachers, 18 were female, and 4 were male. They were an average of 48.59 years old (SD = 11.84). These participants were 96% Caucasian, while the remaining 4% refused to answer. Three-quarters of the K–12 teachers where primarily responsible for teaching mathematics, and a quarter responded that their primary teaching responsibility was literacy. On a 10-point scale, the K–12 teachers indicated an average level knowledge of the CCSS as 7.45 (SD = 1.50) and an average level of comfort discussing the CCSS as 7.64 (SD = 1.68).

Of the 58 HE faculty members that completed our surveys, we had 36 who worked directly with teachers. Of the 36 participants, 26 were female, and 10 were male. They were an average of 47.14 years old (SD = 12.61). These participants were 86% Caucasian, 8% Asian, 6% African American, and 3% Native American, and 3% refused to answer. About half (54%) of the faculty indicated that they taught undergraduates, 40% at the master's level, and 19% at the doctoral level, and 19% indicted "other," reflecting that the faculty were likely to be teaching multiple levels of students. On a 10-point scale, the HE faculty indicated an average level knowledge of the CCSS as 6.86 (SD = 2.18) and an average level of comfort discussing the CCSS as 7.44 (SD = 2.31).

CCSS Interactions

To gather the data that we needed to answer our research questions associated with the support and interactions associated with the CCSS, we developed two parallel surveys: one for the K–12 educators and a second for the HE educators. The focus of the items for the survey was on needs, engagement with others, leadership, sources of information, barriers, and challenges to implementing the CCSS (see Table 1).

Emotions Toward CCSS

To gather our emotions toward the CCSS data, we modified the survey that was previously used in studies of emotions toward genetically modified foods (Broughton & Nadelson, 2012), Pluto's reclassification to a dwarf planet (Broughton, Sinatra, & Nussbaum, 2013), and students' emotions toward topics in science (Broughton, Pekrun, & Sinatra, 2012). We maintained the item list of emotions and the format of the survey but exchanged the context

Table 1. The CCSS Needs, Engagement, Barriers, and Challenges Items for K–12 and HE Educators

Faculty: HE	Faculty: K–12
What do you need to be more effective at helping K–12 teachers implement the CCSS?	What do you need to effectively implement the CCSS?
What sources do you rely on for information related to the CCSS?	What sources do you rely on for information related to the CCSS?
What CCSS professional development are you providing for local K–12 teachers?	How are you engaging with faculty in colleges of higher education for CCSS professional development?
What leadership do you provide to help local K–12 teachers implement the CCSS?	Describe the leadership that the faculty in your local college of education is providing to help you implement the CCSS.
Describe the support you are providing to local K–12 teachers to implement the CCSS.	Describe the support that the faculty in your local college of education is providing you to implement the CCSS.
How are you communicating with local K–12 teachers to provide information about the CCSS?	How is the faculty in your local college of education reaching out to the K–12 teachers in your area to provide information about the CCSS?
Describe the role that faculty in your college of education play in helping area K–12 teachers learn more about the CCSS.	Describe the role that faculty in your local College of Education play in helping you learn more about the CCSS.
Describe some of the barriers that faculty in colleges of education face in relation to helping K–12 teachers implement the CCSS.	Describe some of the barriers that K–12 teachers face in relation to implementing the CCSS.
Describe some of the challenges that college of education faculty face in relation to helping K–12 teachers implement the CCSS.	Describe some of the barriers that K–12 teachers face in relation to working with college of education faculty to implement the CCSS.

of genetically modified foods for the CCSS. The emotions survey has established validity and has been modified and effectively used in studies where emotions may be significant variables associated with learning (Broughton et al., 2011, 2012). The reliability analysis of our survey resulted in a Cronbach's alpha of .91, indicating a good level of internal consistency.

Qualitative Data Analysis Process

We conducted similar content analyses on the K–12 and the HE educators' responses to the nine open-ended items of our CCSS Needs, Engagement, Barriers, and Challenges surveys. Through our content analysis, we discovered three general themes across the participants' responses in each of the two groups: (1) support, (2) barriers and challenges, and (3) leadership.

We noted subcategories within each of the three general themes. For example, for our general theme of support, we noted subcategories of support for implementation, sources of information, and professional development. The subcategories for barriers and challenges we noted were barriers with implementing and challenges with HE support for K–12 educators. For the general theme of leadership, we uncovered subcategories of HE leadership provided to K–12 educators, HE support to K–12 educators to implement the CCSS, communication between HE and K–12 educators, and support from colleges of education for K–12 educators learning CCSS. Our third level of content analysis revealed additional categories within each of the subcategories, which we address in the "Results" section.

We developed a series of a priori codes to use in our analysis. However, we remained open to the emersion of additional trends in the data and responded with the development of post hoc codes when appropriate.

Results

Support

Our first guiding research question asked, What are K–12 and HE faculty members' support needs and activities with respect to CCSS implementation? To answer this question, we examined the responses to our items that prompted the participants to communicate what they perceive they need to be effective with implementing the CCSS, sources of information they rely on, and engagement in professional development. In Table 2, we share the themes and subthemes related to support, our codes, the frequency of responses, and representative statements.

Support for Implementation

Time for planning and thinking as well as professional development were reported most frequently across both groups of educators. Specifically, HE faculty indicated time (19%), with K–12 faculty reporting time for planning (36%). The need for additional professional development related to CCSS appeared in 30% of the HE faculty responses and in 23% of the K–12 faculty responses. These results suggest that those involved with implementing the CCSS in our schools would like more time to learn about the standards and how to effectively incorporate them.

We identified two differences in the responses for support for implementation. First, HE faculty responded that they would like to have more knowledge on the CCSS, such as an executive summary. None of the K–12 faculty specifically addressed more knowledge of the CCSS but rather focused on knowledge for implementation. We interpret the first finding to suggest that

Table 2. Support for Implementation, Codes, Frequency, and Representative Statements

Theme	Code	HE Occurrences of Total	HE Representative Statement	K-12 Occurrences of Total	K-12 Representative Statement
Support for implementation	Knowledge of CCSS	27%	It would be helpful to have an executive summary of CCSS with key information	0%	
	Time	19%	Time to plan, experiment, reflect	36%	Thinking and planning time; training time
	Teacher professional development	30%	Workshops that include specific examples in practice, not more information about the standards themselves	23%	Additional professional development; professional development in strategies for implementation
	Instructional materials	0%		27%	
Sources of information	Websites	43%	State website; http://www.corestandards.org	68%	http://www.corestandards.org
	State level	24%	State meetings	27%	State meetings
	District level	0%		27%	District information
	Individual level	0%		14%	Colleagues
Professional development provided	University support	27%	Preservice elementary teacher methods courses	0%	
	None	27%		45%	Informal
	Indirect	16%	Informal and usually in connection with questions asked as I supervise preservice teacher program	0%	

HE faculty members may not have a working grasp of the CCSS and are therefore interested in learning more about the standards. In contrast, K–12 faculty members are likely to have foundational knowledge of the CCSS and are more focused on professional development that would increase their capacity to implement the standards in their teaching. Along these lines, K–12 faculty members also responded that they would like to have access to instructional materials aligned with the CCSS, which was not a position shared by the HE faculty members. We also found that K–12 faculty members frequently shared that the lack of materials was a barrier to implementing the CCSS (as documented in Table 3).

Sources of Information

The primary source of CCSS information most frequently reported by both the HE and the K–12 groups was the Common Core State Standards Initiative website. Both HE faculty and K–12 faculty indicated that they also acquired information at the state level. We exposed a notable discrepancy between HE faculty and K–12 faculty for seeking information at the district level as well as at the colleague level. None of the HE faculty reported using the district level as a source of information for the CCSS. In contrast, a moderate amount of –12 faculty reported seeking information from the district level. We found a similar trend for the colleague level for CCSS information.

Professional Development

The responses of the HE faculty and K–12 faculty revealed contrasting views between the groups in relation to professional development as an avenue of support for implementing CCSS. The HE faculty indicated that they provided support for preservice teachers during methods courses as well as informally when the topic arises during preservice teacher supervision. In contrast, K–12 faculty most frequently reported having received no professional development. None of the K–12 faculty reported having received university support, either formally or informally. These findings suggest that K–12 faculty have not received professional development on the CCSS from institutions of higher education, while HE faculty shared a perception of supporting K–12 implementation.

Barriers and Challenges

Our second guiding research question was, What are K–12 and HE faculty members' perceptions of the challenges and barriers of CCSS implementation? To answer this question, we examined the responses to our items that encouraged participants to share what they perceived as challenges and barriers to effectively implement the CCSS. In Table 3, we provide the themes and subthemes related to barriers and challenges.

Table 3. Barriers and Challenges for Implementation, Codes, Frequency, and Representative Statements

Theme	Code	HE Occurrences of Total	HE Representative Statement	K-12 Occurrences of Total	K-12 Representative Statement
Barriers with implementing	Lack of knowledge	22%	I believe that most of the college of education faculty have not been taught the CCSS, and it is very different		
	Time	19%	Our plates are full with our responsibilities to our preservice teachers	36%	Time to incorporate into existing curriculum
	Lack of partnerships	11%	Lack of college/school partnerships		
	Lack of (student) materials			27%	No textbook; lack of materials aligned to the CCSS
	Lack of professional development			23%	Funding appropriated for professional development is far too little to keep teachers' own skills aligned
	Uninformed public			18%	Backlash from public has made it hard to get parental involvement
Challenges with HE support to K-12	No contact with colleges of education			41%	There are currently no partnerships of which I am aware
	Time	14%		14%	Many teachers simply do not have time to work with HE faculty
	Not applicable	14%			

Barriers with Implementing

The analyses revealed one common barrier, time, shared across both groups: HE (19%) and K–12 (36%). The focus on the barrier of time was comparable for the HE participants and the K–12 participants. HE participants noted that their responsibilities toward their preservice teachers did not allow time for teaching about the CCSS. Similarly, K–12 participants commonly noted that they lacked time to incorporate the CCSS into the existing curriculum.

HE participants also reported a lack of knowledge of the CCSS as well as a lack of college/school partnerships as barriers with implementing the CCSS. No additional barriers were reported by the HE participants. In contrast, the K–12 participants (27%) indicated a lack of instructional materials, such as textbooks and student learning materials, as barriers to implementation.

Leadership

Our third guiding research question was, What are K–12 and HE faculty members' leadership perceptions and activities with respect to CCSS implementation? To answer this question, we examined the participants' responses to our items for references to leadership and taking responsibility. The results are shown in Table 4. The response for taking leadership that was most frequently given by both HE (27%) and K–12 faculty (68%) was "None" in relation to HE taking a lead role in supporting K–12 faculty preparation to implement the CCSS. Similarly, HE faculty (22%) and K–12 faculty (55%) reported "None" in relation to HE faculty asserting or offering support for K–12 educator implementation of the CCSS. Also worth noting is the substantial gap related to communication between HE and K–12 faculty regarding the CCSS. While about a quarter of the HE faculty reported informal communication with K–12 educators (27%), none of the K–12 faculty reported informal communication with HE faculty members (0%). We found that 45% of the K–12 faculty reported "None" with respect to college of education faculty taking the lead in providing CCSS support to the K–12 community. Similarly, 45% of the HE faculty reported "None" with respect to leadership activities associated with supporting K–12 implementation of the CCSS.

Emotions

Our final guiding research question was, What are K–12 and HE faculty members' emotions toward the CCSS, and how are they related to their CCSS knowledge and communication comfort levels? We began our analysis by forming an overall positive emotion composite score by averaging the responses to our positive emotion items. We repeated the procedure

Table 4. Leadership of HE to K–12, Codes, Frequency, and Representative Statements

Theme	Code	HE Occurrences of Total	HE Representative Statement	K–12 Occurrences of Total	K–12 Representative Statement
HE leadership provided to K–12	None	22%		55%	No support provided
	Not applicable	16%		18%	
	Informal conversations	16%	If it comes up in discussion, I try to share my understanding and ideas		
	Develop curriculum	11%	Develop curriculum that is consistent with the CCSS		
HE support to K–12 to implement	None	27%		68%	None
	Not applicable	16%		.09%	
	Informal	16%	Any professional development is informal and usually in connection with questions asked as I supervise practicum experiences		
	Professional development	16%	Professional development and tools for task analysis and curriculum customization	.09%	
Communication between HE and K–12	Informal	27%	In-person communication during practicum supervision		
	None	.03%		45%	None
	Not applicable	16%		.09%	
	Courses	16%			
	Have no idea			18%	
College of education support for K–12 teachers learning the CCSS	None	45%		45%	None
	Not applicable	24%		.05%	
	Not sure	18%		18%	
	Professional development	.09%		.09%	

with our negative emotion items. Our comparison of composite scores between K–12 and HE faculty members resulted in a nonsignificant difference for both positive ($t = 1.05$, $p > .05$) and negative ($t = .68$, $p > .05$) emotions. Our results suggest that the overall positive and negative emotions associated with the CCSS are not significantly different for K–12 educators and HE faculty members. We also found that the K–12 educators and HE faculty members did not significantly differ in their levels of comfort discussing the CCSS and their perceived levels of knowledge of the CCSS.

Emotions and Level of CCSS Knowledge

We continued our analysis by examining the correlations between participants' self-rated level of CCSS knowledge and their positive emotions and found a positive relationship ($r = .45$, $p < .01$) such that as emotions become more positive, the level of perceived CCSS knowledge is rated higher (see Table 5). We found an analogous negative relationship between negative emotions associated with the standards and self-rated level of CCSS knowledge ($r = -.48$, $p < .01$) such that as negative emotions increased, the perceived CCSS knowledge level decreased. The relationship between emotions and perceived level of CCSS knowledge were similar for the K–12 educators and the HE faculty members.

Our correlation analysis also revealed a significant positive relationship between knowledge of the CCSS and the level of comfort talking about the CCSS ($r = .85$, $p < .01$). Similarly, we found that hours spent reviewing the CCSS was positively associated with both the level of comfort discussing the CCSS ($r = .31$, $p < .05$) and perceived knowledge of the CCSS ($r = .31$, $p < .05$). Similar to what we found with emotions and perceived knowledge of the CCSS, we found significant positive relationships with levels of comfort talking about the CCSS and positive emotions ($r = .51$, $p < .01$) and a negative correlation between negative emotions and level of comfort talking about the CCSS ($r = .51$, $p < .01$). We did not find any relationships between emotions and the hours spent reviewing the CCSS.

Differences in Emotions

As we looked at the graphic display of HE and K–12 faculty members' reported levels of emotion to our specific items (see Figure 1), we then explored the potential for significant differences in three emotions: overwhelmed, happy, and optimistic. Our analysis revealed a significant differences between K–12 and HE faculty members' for overwhelmed ($t = 2.59$, $p = .012$; HE: $M = 2.28$, $SD = 1.13$; K–12: $M = 3.14$, $SD = 1.36$) and for happy ($t = 2.20$, $p = .032$; HE: $M = 2.72$, $SD = .94$; K–12: $M = 3.32$, $SD = 1.09$), but we did not find the levels of optimism to be significantly different.

Table 5. Correlations Between Perceived CCSS Knowledge, Comfort Discussing the CCSS, Hours Spent Learning About the CCSS, and Emotions Toward the CCSS

	Knowledge of the CCSS	Comfort Level	Hours Spent Reviewing the CCSS Last Year	Positive Emotions	Negative Emotions	Overwhelmed	Hopeful	Happy	Optimistic
Knowledge of CCSS		.85**		.45**	-.48**	-.33*	.29*	.31*	.33*
Comfort level			.31*	.51**	-.52**	-.40**	.41**	.33*	.36**
Hours spent reviewing the CCSS last year				.14	-.04	.12	.12	.16	.14
Positive emotions					-.47**	-.30*	.77**	.74**	.82**
Negative emotions						.78**	-.40**	-.23	-.38**
Overwhelmed							-.22	-.16	-.13
Hopeful								.54**	.68**
Happy									.70**
Optimistic									

* Correlation is significant at the 0.05 level (two-tailed).

** Correlation is significant at the 0.01 level (two-tailed).

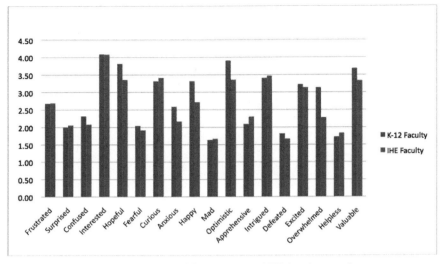

Figure 1.   Emotions toward the CCSS for K–12 and HE faculty members.

Discussion and Implications

We set out to determine how K–12 educators and HE faculty members were working together to prepare and implement the CCSS. The myths and perceptions surrounding the CCSS suggest that there is a need for a strong partnership between K–12 and HE faculty members for successful educational community implementation of the standards. We examined several facets of the collaboration between K–12 and HE faculty members and studied their emotions associated with the CCSS. Our results suggest that there is a big gap between the goal of the CCSS and the two educational systems.

In our examination of support, we found that HE faculty members perceived that they were providing adequate professional development and building the knowledge of K–12 educators. However, the K–12 educators perceived little or no support and no professional development, suggesting a gap in perceived delivery and received support. We speculate that the HE faculty perceive that the inclusion of the CCSS in preservice teacher courses may be adequate preparation and a substantial form of professional development being offered to K–12 educators.

We found that HE faculty members, while self-rating their knowledge of the CCSS the same as the K–12 educators, indicated more frequently a need for more knowledge of the standards. We reason that the lack of sufficient knowledge of the standards may limit HE faculty members' willingness to engage in providing support and professional development opportunities to in-service K–12 educators. Consequently, constrained knowledge may be leading the K–12 teachers and HE faculty members to frequently rely on websites as primary sources of CCSS information. Constrained knowledge could also explain why the two groups of educators tend not to communicate with each other to collectively develop knowledge of the standards and strategies for CCSS implementation. A more in-depth exploration of how knowledge of reform efforts influences K–12 and HE collaboration may be an important direction for future research.

When considering the barriers and challenges, it is apparent that both the K–12 educators and the HE faculty members perceived that time was an issue in relationship to implementing the CCSS. However, how the two groups of educators would spend time in association with the CCSS is likely to be different. We speculate that HE faculty members would be likely to use time to gain more knowledge of the standards and forming partnerships. In contrast, we speculate that K–12 educators would use the time to implement the standards. Thus, if time were provided, there would likely be a gap in how the K–12 educators and HE faculty members would use the time.

The K–12 educators shared that instructional materials and funding for professional development were needed to implement the standards, while these were not mentioned by the HE faculty members. We speculate that the gap reflects the difference in priorities and needs between those who are preparing people to implement an educational reform initiative (HE faculty members) and those responsible for the actual implementation (K–12 educators). Thus, it appears that K–12 educators are focused on classroom realities, something that was not shared by the HE faculty members.

One of the largest gaps we found was the large lack of awareness by K–12 educators of partnerships with colleges of education for CCSS support. While the partnerships may be assumed by the college of education faculty members, the relationships are not apparent to the K–12 educators, who are likely to benefit most from the support that the HE faculty members might provide. Without awareness of the partnerships, it is likely that K–12 educators will not consider HE faculty members as resources or support for their implementation of education reform efforts. Further, HE faculty members may need to put greater effort toward forming relationships with K–12 educators and making their partnerships visible. How partnerships develop and are fostered between college of education faculty members and K–12 educators to support reform efforts is likely to be a fruitful direction for future investigation.

We found a notable gap in the levels of assumed leadership by HE faculty members and the perceived levels of support for K–12 educators associated with the CCSS implementation. It may be that the professional development provided by HE faculty members is not perceived by the K–12 educators as a form of leadership. However, the K–12 educators also shared the lack of professional development opportunities coming from colleges of education, and this may explain the dearth of perceived leadership by HE faculty members. We also found that HE faculty members consider their work in schools supervising student teachers to be a form of leadership, which may be true on some level, but the role is not explicitly associated with reform implementation and supporting in-service K–12 educators. Our future research on K–12 and HE collaboration will include studies of leadership activities and roles.

The relationship between perceived knowledge of the CCSS, level of comfort discussing the CCSS, and emotions toward the CCSS suggests that the more that people know about the reform initiative, the more they tend to be more positive about the standards and feel more comfortable discussing the standards. We speculate that deeper knowledge of the CCSS allows people to understand how to achieve the potential benefits and outcomes, which are being "college and career ready." On the other hand, the lack of knowledge in association with negative emotions toward the standards suggests that constrained understanding accompanies fear, anger, and hopelessness. Thus, a gap in understanding and the associated negative emotions may hinder pursuit of knowledge and consideration of the potential benefits of the standards and raise the level of discomfort discussing the standards. Negative emotions may be used to justify the lack of K–12 educators' effective classroom implementation of the standards as well as the constrained levels of HE faculty member CCSS-related support to K–12 teachers. Our finding of the relationship between knowledge of the CCSS and emotions is aligned with the work of Gregoire-Gill (2003). Exploring how emotions are associated with learning more about and engaging in supporting implementation of reform initiatives is a valuable direction for future research.

Limitations

The first limitation of our research is the sample size. While we made concerted efforts to gather data from the broader K–12 community, we encountered substantial resistance and a lack of desire to participate. However, the trends in our data were pronounced, suggesting consistency in the responses of our K–12 participants with the broader K–12 community. We encourage other researchers to build on our research with a larger sample of K–12 educators.

The second limitation of our research was the lack ability to member check our results. Because we conducted our research online and anonymously, we were not able to follow up with participants with clarifying questions. However, as mentioned previously, we noted strong and consistent trends in responses that suggest consistency in our interpretation of the data. Future research may benefit from focus groups of interviews to gain deeper insights into perceptions and emotions toward the CCSS.

A final limitation of our research is related to the exploratory nature of our study. We limited the scope of the study because we were not sure what we were going to find. Thus, we focused primarily on the relationships between K–12 and HE faculty in relation to the CCSS. However, the responses indicated that the participants were thinking about and shared a much broader diversity of issues related to reform initiative implementation than we intended to explore. Again, focus groups and interviews may allow for greater clarification of and concentration on specific issues of K–12 educators' engagement in reform implementation.

Conclusion

The implementation of major educational reform initiatives is a complex process. The collaboration between K–12 educators and HE faculty members is critical to meeting the needs of many reform efforts. However, the gaps in knowledge, priorities, and perceptions of the key education community stakeholders may pose a significant barrier to effective program adoption and integration. Through our research, we exposed a number of critical gaps between K–12 educators and HE faculty members in association with the CCSS. In addition, we revealed an association between emotions toward and knowledge of the standards that may contribute to gaps in implementation. We maintain that recognizing, addressing, and overcoming such gaps is vital to institutionalizing education reform initiatives. **TEP**

References

American Institutes for Research. (2015). *International education standards and assessment.* http://www.air.org/page/international-education-standards-and-assessment

Bereiter, C., & Scardamalia, M. (2006). Education for the knowledge age: Design-centered models of teaching and instruction. In P. A. Alexander & P. H. Winne (Eds.), *Handbook of educational psychology* (2nd ed., pp. 695–713). Mahwah, NJ: Lawrence Erlbaum Associates.

Bidwell, A. (2014, August 20). Common core support in freefall. *US News and World Report.* http://www.usnews.com

Borko, H. (2004). Professional development and teacher learning: Mapping the terrain. *Educational Researcher, 33*(8), 3–15.

Broughton, S. H., & Nadelson, L. S. (2012). *Food for thought: Pre-service teachers' knowledge, emotions, and attitudes toward genetically modified foods.* Paper presented at the annual meeting of the American Educational Researchers Association, National Conference, Vancouver.

Broughton, S. H., Pekrun, R., & Sinatra, G. M. (2012). *Climate change, genetically modified foods, airport body scanners: investigating students' emotions related to science topics.* Paper presented at the annual meeting of the American Educational Researchers Association, National Conference, Vancouver.

Broughton, S. H., Sinatra, G. M., & Nussbaum, E. M. (2013). "Pluto has been a planet my whole life!" Emotions, attitudes, and conceptual change in elementary students learning about Pluto's reclassification. *Research in Science Education, 43*(2), 529–550.

Chang, M. L. (2009). An appraisal perspective of teacher burnout: Examining the emotional work of teachers. *Educational Psychology Review, 21*(3), 193–218.

Cochran-Smith, M. (2005). The new teacher education: For better or for worse? *Educational Researcher, 34*(7), 3–17.

Cohen, D. K., & Hill, H. C. (2001). *Learning policy: When state education reform works.* New Haven, CT: Yale University Press.

Common Core State Standards Initiative. (2015). *Standards in your state.* http://www.corestandards.org/standards-in-your-state

Darling-Hammond, L. (2010). Teacher education and the American future. *Journal of Teacher Education, 61*(1–2), 35–47.

Elmore, R. F. (2007). *School reform from the inside out: Policy, practice, and performance.* Cambridge, MA: Harvard Education Press.

Ertmer, P. A., & Ottenbreit-Leftwich, A. T. (2010). Teacher technology change: How knowledge, confidence, beliefs, and culture intersect. *Journal of Research on Technology in Education, 42*(3), 255–284.

Fenn, J., & Raskino, M. (2008). *Mastering the hype cycle: How to choose the right innovation at the right time.* Cambridge, MA: Harvard Business Press.

Garet, M. S., Porter, A. C., Desimone, L., Birman, B. F., & Yoon, K. S. (2001). What makes professional development effective? Results from a national sample of teachers. *American Educational Research Journal, 38*(4), 915–945.

Gregoire, M. (2003). Is it a challenge or a threat? A dual-process model of teachers' cognition and appraisal processes during conceptual change. *Educational Psychology Review, 15*(2), 147–179.

Haney, J. J., Lumpe, A. T., Czerniak, C. M., & Egan, V. (2002). From beliefs to actions: The beliefs and actions of teachers implementing change. *Journal of Science Teacher Education, 13*(3), 171–187.

Harvey, M. W., Yssel, N., Bauserman, A. D., & Merbler, J. B. (2008). Preservice teacher preparation for inclusion: An exploration of higher education teacher-training institutions. *Remedial and Special Education, 20*(10), 1–10.

Henry, P. J., & Sears, D. O. (2002). The symbolic racism 2000 scale. *Political Psychology, 23*(2), 253–283.

Hursh, D. (2007). Assessing No Child Left Behind and the rise of neoliberal education policies. *American Educational Research Journal, 44*(3), 493–518.

Karp, S. (2013). The problems with the common core. *Rethinking Schools, 28*(2), 10–17.

King, J. (2011). *Implementing the common core state standards: An action agenda for higher education.* http://www.acenet.edu/AM/Template.cfm?Section=Home&CONTENTID=39580&TEMPLATE=/CM/ContentDisplay.cfm

Kozma, R. B. (2005). National policies that connect ICT-based education reform to economic and social development. *Human Technology: An Interdisciplinary Journal on Humans in ICT Environments, 1*(2), 117–156.

Kratochwill, T. R., Volpiansky, P., Clements, M., & Ball, C. (2007). Professional development in implementing and sustaining multitier prevention models: Implications for response to intervention. *School Psychology Review, 36*(4), 618–631.

Maton, K. I. (2008). Empowering community settings: Agents of individual development, community betterment, and positive social change. *American Journal of Community Psychology, 41*(1–2), 4–21.

Mead, L. S., & Mates, A. (2009). Why science standards are important to a strong science curriculum and how states measure up. *Evolution: Education and Outreach, 2*(3), 359–371.

Nadelson, L. S., Fuller, M., Briggs, P., Hammons, D., Bubak, K., & Sass, M. (2012). The tension between teacher accountability and flexibility: The paradox of standards-based reform. *Teacher Education and Practice, 25*(2), 196–220.

Nadelson, L. S., Pluska, H., Moorcroft, S. Jeffery, A. & Woodard, S. (2014). Educators' perceptions and knowledge of the Common Core State Standards. *Issues in Teacher Education, 23*(2), 47–66.

National Center for Education Statistics. (2009) *Mapping state proficiency standards onto the NAEP scales: Variation and change in state standards for reading and mathematics, 2005–2009.* http://nces.ed.gov/nationsreportcard/pdf/studies/2011458.pdf

National Governors Association Center for Best Practices. (2015). *Common Core State Standards.* http://www.corestandards.org/about-the-standards/frequently-asked-questions.

Roehrig, G. H., & Kruse, R. A. (2005). The role of teachers' beliefs and knowledge in the adoption of a Reform-Based curriculum. *School Science and Mathematics, 105*(8), 412–422.

Somekh, B. (2008). Factors affecting teachers' pedagogical adoption of ICT. In J. Voogt & G. Knezek (Eds.), *International handbook of information technology in primary and secondary education* (pp. 449–460). New York: Springer.

Stanovich, K. E., & West, R. F. (1997). Reasoning independently of prior belief and individual differences in actively open-minded thinking. *Journal of Educational Psychology, 89*(2), 342–357.

Strauss, V. (2014, June 5). Two more states pull out of common core. *Washington Post.* http://www.washingtonpost.com

Van Driel, J. H., Beijaard, D., & Verloop, N. (2001). Professional development and reform in science education: The role of teachers' practical knowledge. *Journal of Research in Science Teaching, 38*(2), 137–158.

Wandersman, A., Chien, V. H., & Katz, J. (2012). Toward an evidence-based system for innovation support for implementing innovations with quality: Tools, training, technical assistance, and quality assurance/quality improvement. *American Journal of Community Psychology, 50*(3–4), 445–459.

Warren, M. (2005). Communities and schools: A new view of urban education reform. *Harvard Educational Review, 75*(2), 133–173.

Wozney, L., Venkatesh, V., & Abrami, P. (2006). Implementing computer technologies: Teachers' perceptions and practices. *Journal of Technology and Teacher Education, 14*(1), 173–207.

Louis S. Nadelson is an associate professor and director for the Center for the School of the Future in the Emma Eccles Jones College of Education at Utah State University. He has a BS from Colorado State University, a BA from Evergreen State College, an MEd from Western Washington University, and a PhD in educational psychology from the University of Nevada, Las Vegas. His scholarly interests include all areas of STEM teaching and learning, in-service and preservice teacher professional development, program evaluation, multidisciplinary research, and conceptual change. He uses his more than 20 years of high school and college math, science, computer science, and engineering teaching to frame his research on STEM teaching and learning. He brings a unique perspective of research, bridging experience with practice and theory to explore a range of interests in STEM teaching and learning. He may be reached via e-mail at Louis.nadelson@usu.edu.

Suzanne H. Jones is an assistant professor in the Emma Eccles Jones College of Education at Utah State University. Her research program investigates the role of emotions on conceptual change, belief change, and attitude change. Her research also includes investigations in the area of reading comprehension that focus on text structure and interventions, such as small-group discussions and argumentation. Her research program also explores the development of collective classroom efficacy as an avenue to enhancing student achievement. Her research has been published in Contemporary Educational Psychology, Learning and Instruction, Reading Research Quarterly, *and the* Journal of Teacher Education. *She may be reached via e-mail at suzanne.jones@usu.edu.*

Professional Literacy Publications and Their Role at Informing Policymakers About the Common Core Writing Reforms

Peter McDermott and Kelley Lassman

ABSTRACT: We examined the extent to which professional literacy journals might have informed policymakers about the writing reforms appearing in the Common Core State Standards (CCSS). Using content analysis of journals published by the International Reading Association, the National Council of Teachers of English, and the Council for Learning Disabilities between 2007 and 2013, we discovered five articles about teaching information and argument writing in the 3 years preceding the publication of the CCSS and 16 articles afterward. These findings suggest that the professional literature and the organizations publishing the journals exerted a weak voice at informing policymakers about the new writing standards. We argue that policymakers did not follow what they preached about the importance of using scientific evidence to inform school reform and that professional organizations must become more proactive in advocating for quality literacy education than they have as seen in the development of the CCSS.

Teacher knowledge is central to the success of all school reform (Carpenter, Fennema, Peterson, Chiang, & Loef, 1989; Darling-Hammond, 2006; Kirp, 2013; Schulman, 1987). For most of us, knowledge about teaching first occurs through our personal experiences when we were students in school. Later, we typically learn about teaching through formal study and classroom experiences in teacher preparation programs. Throughout our careers, most teachers work to remain current with new educational theories and teaching methods by attending professional conferences, joining teacher-inquiry groups, and participating in various other kinds of professional development activities. Central to all of our efforts is the role that professional publications have at informing us about new and evolving theories and practices for teaching reading and writing. In this study, we examined the role of professional literacy publications at informing the designers of the Common Core writing standards (National Governors Association Center for Best Practices & Council of Chief State Officers, 2010b).

There are many organizations promoting literacy education in our schools. Two that are widely recognized are the International Literacy Association (ILA) and the National Council of Teachers of English (NCTE). In addition, the Council for Learning Disabilities (CLD) provides a prominent voice for advocating for inclusive education of all children, and its journal manuscripts often examine strategies for improving the writing of students with disabilities in general education classrooms. These three organizations offer extensive resources for informing its members about current theories and practices for teaching writing, and their publications are widely read in literacy education. In this inquiry, we focused on the role that ILA, NCTE, and CLD journals might have had in sharing theories and practices about information and argument writing in K–12 settings. We selected informational and argument writing as the topics of this study because these forms of composition represent an important instructional shift of the Common Core State Standards (CCSS) (EngageNY, 2012). That is, practitioners using the CCSS to guide their instruction are to plan writing instruction that focuses on argument and information writing rather than the personal response and narrative that have been widely used for many years.

Methods for teaching writing, as other subject areas, have changed throughout the decades. The earliest method of teaching writing focused on penmanship (Hawkins & Razali, 2012), and many of our grandparents and great grandparents would attest to the time and effort that was placed on proper letter formation when they were in school. Later, writing instruction focused on spelling, punctuation and grammar (Hawkins & Razali, 2012) with the emphasis of instruction on the structure and forms of writing rather than the meaning inherent in it. In the 1980s, researchers, including Calkins (1986), Graves (1983), and Hansen (1987), among others, introduced "process writing"; an assumption of process writing was that the more students wrote, the better they would became at it. Recently, however, writing theorists have argued that extended practice with writing, as reflected in process writing, is insufficient for developing students' composing skills and argue that most students require explicit instruction in how rhetorical structure and purpose influence the expression of ideas (Graff, 2003; Graff & Birkenstein, 2009). The best-known teaching method of this kind is found in the work Graff and Birkenstein (2009), who offer templates for students to use when composing informational and argument writing. Finally, given the increasing presence of technology in everyday life, many teachers are now instructing their students in strategies for composing with digital devices (National Writing Project, 2010).

The CCSS

The recent reforms of the CCSS (National Governors Association Center for Best Practices & Council of Chief State Officers, 2010b) are now driving much of the writing instruction that occurs in today's schools in both general and inclusive classroom settings. Argument and information writing are represented in the first two anchor standards of the CCSS:

Anchor Standard #1: Write arguments to support claims in an analysis of substantive topics or texts, using valid reasoning and relevant and sufficient evidence. (National Governors Association Center for Best Practices & Council of Chief State Officers, 2010b, pp. 18, 41)

Anchor Standard #2: Write informative/explanatory texts to examine and convey complex ideas and information clearly and accurately through the effective selection, organization, and analysis of content. (National Governors Association Center for Best Practices & Council of Chief State Officers, 2010b, pp. 18, 41)

Argument and information writing are further seen in "Shift 5" of the CCSS, in which "writing emphasizes use of evidence from sources to inform and make arguments" (EngageNY, 2012).

Theoretical Framework

In the past 15 years, the federal government and critics of education have argued that decisions about classroom practices should be based on scientifically based research (No Child Left Behind Act, 2002; Educational Science Reform Act, 2002). Educational critics used medicine, with its reliance on scientific evidence to inform physicians' practices, as their model for how decisions about educational curriculum and instruction should be based. That is, policy decisions about curriculum and instruction should be based on scientific evidence. This was a major criticism made by the Bush presidency, and it remains today with the Obama administration, as seen in its emphasis on data to document school effectiveness. The assumption of the critics and policymakers has been that school reform lacked a research base and that it suffered from undue influence of anecdotal information, fads, and trends.

The importance of using empirical evidence to reform classroom practice has been an ongoing position that is readily found in the professional literature. Slavin (2008), for example, argued that research should inform policy and practice. He likened the state of educational research to that of medicine of 100 years ago, arguing that during the 20th century, medicine progressed tremendously by using the results of widespread clinical trials to inform its clinical practices. Importantly, he argued that education should similarly use evidence-based research to inform policymakers in identifying instructional programs and practices for classrooms. Duke and Martin (2011) explained that research should serve as a guide for policy and practice. Similarly, Sleeter (2014) wrote, "Evidence, to the extent it is available, should guide decisions about policy and practice" (p. 146).

There are counterarguments about the use of research evidence for informing classroom practice. Some educators distrust it because it is felt that one can find research evidence to support just about any practice (Nelson, Leffler, & Hansen, 2009). Others argue that education research is inherently more difficult to conduct than is research in the natural sciences because the independent variables of teaching and learning, particularly those related to social context, cannot be easily controlled (Berliner, 2002; Hostetler, 2005). Some critics claim that educational research is too theoretical, having little application to classroom practice and the improvement of student achievement (Sleeter, 2014).

Pearson (2013) discussed the role of research at informing the CCSS in reading. He wrote that a specific research base did not exist for the reading standards. Instead, the CCSS reading standards represented a "professional consensus" position by experts in literacy education. He explained that this consensus, in which he played a part, represented their collective wisdom that was derived from three sources: related research, professional experience, and best practices in literacy education. Pearson further explained that other educational reforms preceding the CCSS similarly used consensus to generate standards of learning performance and that consensus was not a radical position.

Appendix A of the CCSS indicated that the resources informing the writing standards were the following:

> *Writing arguments and writing informational/explanatory texts are priorities.* The Standards follow international models by making writing arguments and writing informational/explanatory texts the dominant modes of writing in high school to demonstrate readiness for college and career. (National Governors Association Center for Best Practices & Council of Chief State Officers 2010b, p. 41, emphasis in the original)

Appendix A further lists nine sources pertaining to the teaching writing of which the ideas of Graff (2003), Graff and Birkenstein (2009), and Postman (1997) are prominent. Much of the CCSS's rationale for its emphasis on argument and information writing are found in those three sources as well as in research from postsecondary education proponents, such as the College Board, calling for this kind of writing in K–12 classrooms (see National Governors Association Center for Best Practices & & Chief State School Officers, 2010a, Appendix A, pp. 23–25). Yet we found it interesting that the professional literacy journals were not cited as one of the resources for informing the standards in writing.

The theoretical perspective of this current study rested on what we felt was a reasonable question about the role of research and scientific evidence regarding writing instruction. We assumed that research published in major literacy journals would be used to either inform or guide new public policies and standards or that, if it were not used, the rationale for its omission would be explained.

Purpose of the Study

Given the public arguments of using empirical research for informing educational practice and reform, we wondered what role research served the CCSS policymakers in designing the writing standards. We questioned whether the writing standards were supported with a research base in the professional journals or whether Pearson's (2013) explanation about a "professional consensus" regarding the reading standards was also evident in the development of the writing standards. Surely, we assumed there must have been a research base for informing the policymakers about the shift from narrative and personal response to information and argument writing that the CCSS now requires. As a result of these issues, we examined the following questions:

> ➤ What was the frequency of manuscripts pertaining to argument and information writing appearing in ILA, NCTE, and CLD journals before and after the publication of the CCSS?
> ➤ What teaching strategies are recommended in ILA, NCTE, and CLD journals about teaching argument and information writing?
> ➤ What instructional patterns and trends about argument and information writing appeared in the ILA, NCTE, and CLD journals?

Method

This study consisted of content analyses of the major journals published by the ILA, NCTE, and CLD. Content analysis (Krippendorff, 2013; Weber, 1990) served as our research method because of its appropriateness for answering our research questions and because it has been shown to offer a systematic and replicable method for examining texts (Stemler, 2001).

Data Collection Procedures

We restricted our search to journals published by ILA, NCTE, and CLD because they are widely distributed and read by classroom and specialist teachers throughout the United States and elsewhere. From ILA, we examined the Journal of Adolescent and Adult Literacy, The Reading Teacher, and Reading Research Quarterly. Our review of the NCTE journals included Language Arts, the English Journal, and Research in the Teaching of English. We examined the Journal of Learning Disabilities and Learning Disabilities Quarterly because these two journals focus on research and practices for helping students with mild disabilities who are often placed in inclusive classrooms. Our literature searches did not include the ILA/NCTE collaborative website (http://www.readwritethink.org), nor did it include their other publications, such as Reading Today (ILA), the Council Chronicle (NCTE), book publications, or program listings from their annual conventions.

We limited our literature search to articles about composing only and thereby excluded articles about reading of information and argument texts. We developed a selection rule in which the words "expository," "information/informational," "argument," or "persuasive" writing must have been included in the manuscript's title or abstract to be included in our analyses. This selection rule (see Figure 1) and its rationale are made transparent so that readers

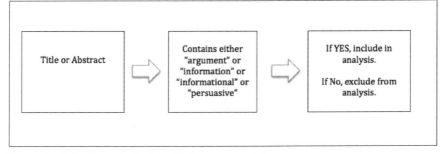

Figure 1. Selection rule for identifying manuscripts.

are able to independently decide about the accuracy of our findings. The purpose of the analysis was to collect evidence for determining the extent to which the professional literature about expository, informational, and argument writing might have contributed to policymakers' discussions about writing as it now appears in the CCSS.

This selection rule was the result of our need for a constant measure for analyzing the contents of these journals. We did not want one that allowed for variability in our decision making as to whether a journal article should be included in this analysis. This manuscript reports our analysis of those articles that fully fit this selection rule.

Our university library's search engines were used (ERIC, ProQuest, and Professional Development Collection) for identifying manuscripts in these journals. Using the Advanced Search feature of the databases, we consecutively used "writing" with "expository," "information," "informational," "persuasive," or "argument" and the journal's name. These terms captured the central focus of articles written about argument and information writing.

We further limited the literature search to the years 2007–2013. In our view, these years provided a reasonable band for the study in which the quantity of articles about information and argument writing would be compared and contrasted. This allowed a 3-year time period before and after the CCSS were first published.

Data Analysis and Representation

The final list of identified manuscripts pertained to research and/or the teaching of expository, informational, argument, and persuasive writing. After independently reading the identified manuscripts, we shared our analyses of their content until agreeing about their central meaning and focus. We then decided to represent our analyses in chart and table forms. We believed that a chart and table would be effective for visually identifying each manuscript's year of publication, author and manuscript title, journal title, central focus, and strategies/implications for teaching. The table proved to be especially helpful in our own analyses as we discussed the manuscripts and reached agreement on their meaning and focus

Results

We identified 21 articles about information or argument/persuasive writing appearing in ILA/NCTE/CLD journals between the years 2007 and 2013. These results further indicate that, not unexpectedly, there were many more manuscripts about information and argument writing (n = 16) in 2010 and afterward than before (n = 5). Eleven of the articles appeared in the NCTE publications, nine appeared in the ILA journals, and only one appeared in the CLD journals. An annotated listing of these articles is presented in Table 1.

Articles Published Before and After the CCSS

Five articles about information or argument/persuasive writing appeared between the years 2007 and 2009. During 2010, there were nine articles published about information or argument/persuasive writing. Seven articles appeared between 2011 and 2013. More specifically, four articles appeared in 2007, one appeared in 2008, and there were no published articles in 2009 in these eight journals. Eight articles appeared in 2010, two in 2011, two in 2012, and three in 2013. Figure 2 provides a visual display of the number of articles appearing each year about information and argument/persuasive writing between the years 2007 and 2013.

Teaching Strategies Recommended in These Manuscripts

The five articles appearing before publication of the CCSS discussed argument and/or persuasive writing. Mayer's (2007) article described how active learning can be generated in 11th-grade English classrooms by requiring students to participate in symposia about issues they care about (e.g., abortion, death penalty, teen pregnancy, human trafficking, and so on) and then writing persuasive essays representing their positions about the topics; Mayer's piece focused on active student discussion and participation with composing constituting a closing activity. Gebhard, Harman, and Seger (2007) presented a case study of how urban second-language learners learned to compose argument essays (essays to the principal about the loss of morning recess); she taught students organizational structure of argument and linguistic features of its genre (grammar, vocabulary, and rhetoric). Montelongo and Hernandez (2007) described how sentence frames could be effectively used in intermediate grades to teach information writing. Englert, Zhao, Dunsmore, Collings, and Wolbers (2007) examined the efficacy of teaching learning-disabled children how to use Internet sources when composing informational writing.

Table 1. Articles Relating to Argument and/or Informational Writing in Selected CLD, ILA, and NCTE Journals Between 2007 and 2013

Year	Author/Title	Journal	Focus	Teaching Strategies
2007	Mayer, J. Persuasive writing and student-run symposium	*English Journal, 96*(4), 39–46	Persuasive writing	Integrating persuasive speaking with writing
2007	Gebhard, M., Harman, R., & Seger, W. Reclaiming recess: Learning the language of persuasion	*Language Arts, 84*(5), 419–430	Difference between everyday language and academic language	Strategies for teaching academic language, particularly persuasion
2007	Montelongo, J., & Hernandez, A. Reinforcing expository reading and writing skills: A more versatile sentence completion task.	*The Reading Teacher, 60*(6), 538–546	Expository writing	Sentence completion tasks—sentence frames
2007	Englert, C., Zhao, Y., Dunsmore, K., Collings, N., & Wolbers, K. Scaffolding the writing of students with disabilities through procedural facilitation: Using an Internet-based technology to improve performance	*Learning Disability Quarterly, 30*(1), 9–29	Expository writing	Using Internet-based research vs. traditional sources for expository writing
2008	Anderson, D. The elementary persuasive letter: Two cases of situated competence, strategy, and agency	*Research in the Teaching of English, 42*(3), 270–314	Persuasive letter writing (argument)	Scaffolding persuasive writing with classroom talk, explicit forms, and topic choice
2010	Klein, P., & Rose, M. Teaching argument and explanation to prepare junior students for writing to learn.	*Reading Research Quarterly, 45*(4), 433–461	Argument writing/literature review	Critical discourse analysis
2010	McCann, T. Gateways to writing arguments	*English Journal, 99*(6), 33–39	Argument writing	Strategies for developing effective assignments in argument writing
2010	Heller, S. What it is, what it's not, and what's related: Exploring Plato's *Meno*	*English Journal, 99*(6), 51–55	Argument writing	Focus on persuasive writing by composing dialogue similar to Plato's in *Meno*

Year	Reference	Journal	Category	Description
2010	Hillocks, G. Teaching argument for critical thinking and writing: An introduction	*English Journal, 99*(6), 24–32	Argument writing	Teaching use of evidence and warrants
2010	Carbone, P. Using commonplace books to help students develop multiple perspectives	*English Journal, 99*(6), 63–69	Argument writing	Commonplace argument strategy
2010	Warren, J. Taming the warrant in Toulmin's model of argument	*English Journal, 99*(6), 41–46	Argument writing—use of warrants	Examines warrant writing and its misuses in textbooks
2010	Carbone, P., & Orellana, M. F. Developing academic identities: Persuasive writing as a tool to strengthen emergent academic identities	*Research in the Teaching of English, 44*(3), 492–516	Persuasive writing—rhetorical choices and voice	Writing to familiar/unfamiliar audiences (two voices)/ building on communicative competence rather than skill deficits
2010	Bradley, L., & Donovan, C. Information book read-alouds as models for second-grade authors	*The Reading Teacher, 64*(4), 246–260	Reading/writing connections	Use of information books in science and teaching writing
2010	Montelongo, J., Herter, R., Ansaldo, R., & Hatter, N. A lesson cycle for teaching expository reading and writing	*Journal of Adolescent and Adult Literacy, 53*(8), 656–666	Reading/writing connections	Teaching text structure, signal words. and using graphic organizers
2011	Newell, G., Beach, R., Smith, S., & VanDerHeide, J. Teaching and learning argumentative reading and writing: A Review of research	*Reading Research Quarterly, 46*(3), 273–304.	Argument writing/literature review	Cognitive and social perspectives
2011	Donovan, C., & Smolkin, L. Supporting informational writing in the elementary grades	*The Reading Teacher, 64*(6), 406–416	Informational writing	Teaching labels, facts, collections, and paragraphs in informational writing

(continued)

Table 1. (Continued)

Year	Author/Title	Journal	Focus	Teaching Strategies
2012	Coleman, J. M., Bradley, L., & Donovan, C. Visual representations in second graders' information book compositions	The Reading Teacher, 66(1), 31–45	Informational writing	Use of visuals in books and writing to support students thinking about science
2012	Cummins, S., & Quiroa, R. Teaching for writing expository responses to narrative texts	The Reading Teacher, 66(6), 381–386	Informational writing	Using interactive discussions, text structure. and front-loading activities with English language learners
2013	Maloch, B., & Bomer, R. Teaching about and with informational texts: What does research teach us?	Language Arts, 90(6), 441–451	Reading informational texts	Reading/writing connections
2013	Maloch, B., & Bomer, R. Informational texts and the Common Core Standards: What are we talking about, anyway?	Language Arts, 90(3), 205–213	Distinguishes between nonfiction and informational texts	Distinctive features of nonfiction/informational texts
2013	Monahan, M. B. Writing voiced arguments about science topics	Journal of Adolescent and Adult Literacy, 57(1), 31–40	Writing arguments and informational texts	Teach students how to use voice in writing science arguments

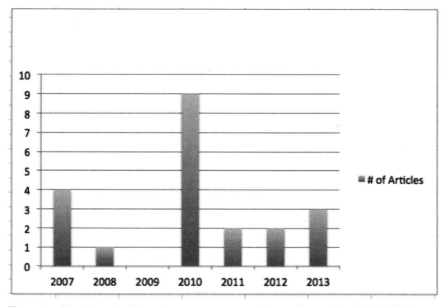

Figure 2.   Number of articles about argument or information writing: 2007–2013.

Anderson (2008) challenged conventional notions that elementary children were developmentally unprepared to write persuasive essays; using case studies, she described and explained how children can learn to write effective persuasive letters when topic choice and models with explicit forms of expression are taught to them. Anderson further argued that given the prominence of persuasive writing in high-stakes testing in the secondary grades, instruction for composing such essays must also occur in the earlier grades.

There were three articles appearing in the ILA's and NCTE's research journals (*Reading Research Quarterly* and *Research in the Teaching of English*, respectively) between 2010 and 2013. Klein and Rose (2010) examined the instructional features and framework for using writing to learn in the content areas, specifically the effects of various instructional features, including cognitive strategy instruction, on students' abilities to improve their ability to write arguments and improve their learning in the content areas. Carbone and Orellana (2010) examined the persuasive writing of sixth-grade bilingual students to determine the extent to which their voices and identities emerged; they document that when students have a choice in topic and audience, their writers' voices and identities are more likely to emerge. Newell, Beach, Smith, and VanDerHeide (2011) conducted an analytic review of research about argument writing in K–12 classrooms; they argue that cognitive and social perspectives of analysis should be combined in examining argument writing so that clear recommendations for classroom practice can be realized.

The intended audience of *The Reading Teacher* and *Language Arts* is elementary teachers. These two journals contained six articles about information and argument/persuasive writing during the years 2010–2013. Bradley and Donovan (2010) described how informational texts can be successfully used as mentor texts when second graders compose informational pieces. Donovan and Smolkin (2011) provided a developmental continuum of growth when elementary writers compose informational texts ranging from pictorial representation to captions to diagrams; they offer instruction for moving children from one stage of writing development to the next. Coleman, Bradley, and Donovan (2012) investigated how children can effectively use visual models from illustrated books in their own science writing; they argued that illustrated science books serve as models for children's own science writing. Cummins and Quiroa (2012) described ways teachers could use interactive discussions and text structures when teaching English language learners to write information texts. Maloch and Boomer (2013a) examined the various definitions of informational texts used by experts and the CCSS, and Maloch and Boomer (2013b) discussed the interrelationships between reading and writing and the strategies that can be used to teach informational writing to children.

The *English Journal*, an NCTE publication focusing on teachers of adolescents, contained five articles about argument/persuasive writing since 2010. McCann (2010) discussed "gateway" activities (prewriting) that help middle school and secondary students produce clear, logical arguments; he argues that critical thinking, rather than templates, are the key features of effective argument writing. Heller (2010) discussed how Plato's *Meno* could be used as a model text to help secondary students write logical arguments that are devoid of fallacy statements. Hillocks (2010) provided specific organizational strategies to help students think critically and compose clear, cogent argument essays. Carbone (2010) described how "commonplace books" (a classic form of journaling) could be effectively used to teach secondary students to use multiple perspectives and critical thinking when composing arguments. Warren (2010) explained how Toulmin's warrants are often omitted in discussions about argument writing; Warren argues that the strategies for composing arguments must be explicit in order for students to use them successfully.

Only two articles about informational/argument writing appeared in the ILA's *Journal of Adolescent and Adult Literacy* during this entire period (2007–2010). Montelongo, Herter, Ansaldo, and Hatter (2010) discussed how text structures, signal words, and graphic organizers could be used to improve adolescents' writing of informational texts. Monahan (2013) provides several strategies for helping adolescents compose effective argument essays, including problem-based essays, use of mentor texts, teaching structural features of arguments, and having content area teachers collaborate with language arts teachers.

Discussion

The premise of this study was that the professional literature about teaching writing will have played a role in informing or guiding policymakers in their decision making about developing the CCSS in writing. Basically, this had been the argument of national policymakers—that school curricula and classroom practice must be based on evidence, just as medicine used research. Our findings indicate that this was far from the case, at least as evidenced by the paucity of articles published about information and argument writing in major literacy journals prior to publication of the CCSS. There were far more articles about informational and argument writing after the CCSS (n = 16) than before (n = 5).

Education is a profession that endures endless reforms. During the Bush era, critics said that education too easily changed because of trends and fads within the profession and not from legitimate research data. Our analyses suggest that forces and pressures outside the profession contributed to the policy changes that are now evidenced in the CCSS in writing. Results of our study further indicate that major educational publications did not offer a body of empirical work for informing policymakers about information and argument writing; at least this work did not appear in their journals in the 3 years preceding publication of the CCSS. It was only after CCSS were adopted that articles about the shifts in literacy education appeared in sufficient numbers to suggest that the journals are contributing to the discourse about the policy changes.

In most respects, professional teaching organizations, as evidenced by the number of manuscripts appearing in their journals about information and argument writing, carried little weight in policy discussions about the writing standards. One conclusion to be drawn from the content analyses of this study is that professional teaching organizations must become more proactive and stronger in advocating for quality literacy education than they have in the recent past. Without doing so, literacy education will suffer from the interests and motivations of policymakers who are more likely to be uninformed about the research and practice of writing instruction than are the professional associations and members themselves. **TEP**

References

Anderson, D. (2008). The elementary persuasive letter: Two cases of situated competence, strategy, and agency. *Research in the Teaching of English*, 42(3), 270–314.

Berliner, D. (2002). Educational research: The hardest science of all. *Educational Researcher*, *31*, 18–20.

Bradley, L., & Donovan, C. (2010). Information book read-alouds as models for second-grade authors. *The Reading Teacher, 64*(4), 246–260.

Calkins, L. (1986). *The art of teaching writing.* Portsmouth, NH: Heinemann.

Carbone, P. (2010). Using commonplace books to help students develop multiple perspectives. *English Journal, 99*(6), 63–69.

Carbone, P., & Orellana, M. F. (2010). Developing academic identities: Persuasive writing as a tool to strengthen emergent academic identities. *Research in the Teaching of English, 44*(3), 492–516.

Carpenter, T. P., Fennema, E., Peterson, P. L., Chiang, C. P., & Loef, M. (1989). Using knowledge of children's mathematics thinking in classroom teaching: An experimental study. *American Educational Research Journal, 26*(4), 499–531.

Coleman, J. M., Bradley, L., & Donovan, C. (2012). Visual representations in second graders' information book compositions. *The Reading Teacher, 66*(1), 31–45.

Cummins, S., & Quiroa, R. (2012). Teaching for writing expository responses to narrative texts. *The Reading Teacher, 66*(6), 381–386.

Darling-Hammond, L. (2006). Securing the right to learn: Policy and practice for powerful teaching and learning. *Educational Researcher, 35*(7), 13–24.

Donovan, C., & Smolkin, L. (2011). Supporting informational writing in the elementary grades. *The Reading Teacher, 64*(6), 406–416.

Duke, N., & Martin, N. (2011). 10 things every literacy educator should know about research. *The Reading Teacher, 65*(1), 9–22.

Educational Science Reform Act. (2002). Public Law 107-279, 116 Stat. 1940.

EngageNY. (2012). *Common core shifts.* http://www.engageny.org/resource/common-core-shifts

Englert, C., Zhao, Y., Dunsmore, K, Collings, N., & Wolbers, K. (2007). Scaffolding the writing of students with disabilities through procedural facilitation: Using an Internet-based technology to improve performance. *Learning Disability Quarterly, 30*(1), 9–29.

Gebhard, M., Harman, R., & Seger, W. (2007). Reclaiming recess: Learning the language of persuasion. *Language Arts, 85*(5), 419–430.

Graff, G. (2003). *Clueless in academe.* New Haven, CT: Yale University Press.

Graff, G., & Birkenstein, C. (2009). *They say, I say: Moves that matter in academic writing* (2nd ed.). New York: Norton.

Graves, D. (1983). *Writing: Teachers and children at work.* Portsmouth, NH: Heinemann.

Hansen, J. (1987). *When writers read.* Portsmouth, NH: Heinemann.

Hawkins, L., & Razali, A. B. (2012). A tale of 3 P's—Penmanship, product, and process: 100 years of elementary writing instruction. *Language Arts, 89*(5), 305–317.

Heller, S. (2010). What it is, what it's not, and what's related: Exploring Plato's *Meno. English Journal, 99*(6), 51–55.

Hillocks, G. (2010). Teaching argument for critical thinking and writing: An introduction. *English Journal, 99*(6), 24–32.

Hostetler, K. (2005). What is "good" educational research? *Educational Researcher, 34,* 16–21.

Kirp, D. (2013). *The secret to fixing bad schools.* http://www.nytimes.com/2013/02/10/opinion/sunday/the-secret-to-fixing-bad-schools.html?pagewanted=all&_r=0

Klein, P., & Rose, M. (2010). Teaching argument and explanation to prepare junior students for writing to learn. *Reading Research Quarterly, 45*(4), 433–461.

Krippendorff, K. (2013). *Content analysis: An introduction to its methodology.* Thousand Oaks, CA: Sage.

Maloch, B., & Bomer, R. (2013a). Informational texts and the Common Core Standards: What are we talking about, anyway? *Language Arts*, 90(3), 205–213.

Maloch, B., & Bomer, R. (2013b). Teaching about and with informational texts: What does research teach us? *Language Arts*, *90*(6), 441–451.

Mayer, J. (2007). Persuasive writing and student-run symposium. *English Journal*, *96*(4), 39–46.

McCann, T. (2010). Gateways to writing arguments. *English Journal*, *99*(6), 33–39.

Monahan, M. B. (2013). Writing voiced arguments about science topics. *Journal of Adolescent and Adult Literacy*, *57*(1), 31–40.

Montelongo, J., & Hernandez, A. (2007). Reinforcing expository reading and writing skills: A more versatile sentence completion task. *The Reading Teacher*, *60*(6), 538–546.

Montelongo, J., Herter, R., Ansaldo, R., & Hatter, N. (2010). A lesson cycle for teaching expository reading and writing. *Journal of Adolescent and Adult Literacy*, *53*(8), 656–666.

National Governors Association Center for Best Practices & Council of Chief State School Officers. (2010a). *Common Core State Standards. Appendix A: Research supporting key elements of the standards.* http://www.corestandards.org/assets/Appendix_A .pdf

National Governors Association Center for Best Practices & Council of Chief State School Officers. (2010b). *Common Core State Standards for English language arts and literacy in history/social studies, science, and technical subjects.* http://www.corestandards. org/ELA-Literacy

National Writing Project. (2010). *Because digital writing matters: Improving student writing in online and multimedia environments.* San Francisco: Jossey-Bass.

Nelson, S. R., Leffler, J. C., & Hansen, B. A. (2009). *Toward a research agenda for understanding and improving the use of research evidence.* Portland, OR: Northwest Regional Educational Laboratory.

Newell, G., Beach, R., Smith, S., & VanDerHeide, J. (2011). Teaching and learning argumentative reading and writing: A review of research. *Reading Research Quarterly*, *46*(3), 273–304.

No Child Left Behind Act. (2002). Public Law 107-110, 1-1076, 115 Stat. 1425.

Pearson, P. D. (2013). Research foundations for the Common Core State Standards in English language arts. In S. Neuman & L. Gambrell (Eds.), *Reading instruction in the age of Common Core State Standards* (pp. 237–262). Newark, DE: International Reading Association.

Postman, N. (1997). *The end of education.* New York: Knopf.

Shulman, L. S. (1987). Knowledge and teaching: Foundations of the new reform. *Harvard Educational Review*, *57*(1), 1–22.

Sleeter, C. (2014). Towards teacher education research that informs policy. *Educational Researcher*, 43(3), 146–153.

Slavin, R. (2008). Evidence-based reform in education: What will it take? *European Educational Research Journal*, 7(1), 124–128.

Stemler, S. (2001). An overview of content analysis. *Practical Assessment, Research and Evaluation*, 7(17). http://pareonline.net/getvn.asp?v=7&n=17

Warren, J. (2010). Taming the warrant in Toulmin's model of argument. *English Journal, 99*(6),41–46.

Weber, R. P. (1990). *Basic content analysis* (2nd ed.). Newbury Park, CA: Sage.

Peter McDermott is a professor of education in the School of Education, Pace University. His research interests are in urban education, the new digital literacies, and international literacy education. He has published in these interest areas, and he regularly presents at the American Educational Research Association, the New England Educational Research Organization, the Northeastern Education Research Association, and New York's state reading conference. He may be reached via e-mail at pmcdermott@pace.edu.

Kelley Lassman is an assistant professor in the School of Education, Pace University. Her research interests include studying how adolescents with emotional/behavior disorders and those with language disorders can best learn in our secondary schools. She is particularly interested in refining teacher skills and instructional ability to meet these students' needs. A related research interest is teacher training and professional development of school personnel. She may be reached via e-mail at klassman@pace.edu.

Preparedness of Exemplary Early Career Teachers

CHRISTIE L. BLEDSOE, JUDY TROTTI,
KARI J. HODGE, AND TONY TALBERT

ABSTRACT: Using an explanatory sequential mixed-methods design, researchers explored the perceptions of early career teachers regarding their educator preparation programs. The participants ($n = 57$) were teachers with 3 years or less of teaching experience who graduated from one of the institutions affiliated with the Texas Association of Colleges of Teacher Education (TACTE). Teacher perceptions of preparedness were measured according to seven competencies established by TACTE. Teachers reported strong preparation across all seven competencies (especially instruction for diverse learners, content knowledge, and lifelong learning) but revealed interactions with parents and colleagues as an area in which they felt less prepared. In focus groups, participants ($n = 13$) provided recommendations for improving teacher education based on their first years of teaching experience.

Teacher preparation programs are under statewide and national scrutiny to determine if certain preparation programs impact new teachers more or less favorably when they become teachers. The National Council on Teacher Quality (NCTQ, 2014) reported that only 107 preparation programs out of 1,668 in the United States received high-quality rankings. Furthermore, the *Huffington Post* (Resmovits, 2014) shares the NCTQ study with the alarming headline, "How Teacher Prep Programs Are Failing New Teachers—And Your Kids."

Education Secretary Duncan has been called on by President Obama to overhaul how teacher preparation programs are evaluated. The administration asserts that few data are available for evaluating how programs are preparing teachers. Duncan suggests that most teachers admit that they were not adequately prepared to be teachers (Madhani, 2014).

Theoretical Framework

This project developed as an initiative from the Texas Association of Colleges for Teacher Education (TACTE, 2011) to engage in statewide research that identifies the primary elements that impact teacher quality. Therefore, the focus of this research was to design and implement a mixed-methods research plan that provided a depth and breadth of data addressing the TACTE "Vision for University-Based Teacher Preparation in Texas." The purpose of the research was to collect information concerning the applicability and impact of the TACTE-IHE early career exemplar teachers' preparation toward the seven TACTE competencies.

This study is framed around education competencies represented as knowledge, skills, and abilities necessary to effectively accomplish a task (Lombardo & Eichinger, 2004). At the center of the education competencies are six categories of qualities that individuals need in order to help school districts succeed in the 21st century. These qualities are individual excellence, organizational skills, courage, results, strategic skills, and operating skills. Seven specific competencies within those categories were developed by the AACTE state affiliate to be addressed in this study.

Explanatory Sequential Mixed Methods

This explanatory sequential mixed-methods study addressed exemplar early career teachers' perceptions of their teacher preparation program with respect to the seven TACTE competencies. There were two phases, starting with a quantitative phase and followed by a qualitative phase (Creswell & Plano-Clark, 2010). Phase 1 included the administration of a questionnaire comprised of Likert scaled items and open-ended items. Phase 2 consisted of focus group interviews in order to obtain qualitative data to confirm and extend the responses provided by participants in the questionnaire phase of the study (see Figure 1). The reason for using an explanatory sequential design was to collect complementary data to describe the perceptions of early career teachers regarding applicability of their preparation program to in-service teaching.

Research Questions

The following research questions served as the foundational points of inquiry for the study:

1. What is the perceived preparedness of exemplar early career teachers regarding the seven competencies of the TACTE vision for university-based teacher preparation in Texas?
2. What is the applicability and impact of a statewide framework for TACTE-IHE early career exemplar teachers' preparation as it relates to the seven competencies?

Instruments

Researchers who were also teacher educators developed data collection instruments structured on the theoretical framework of the seven elements

Phase	Procedures	Product

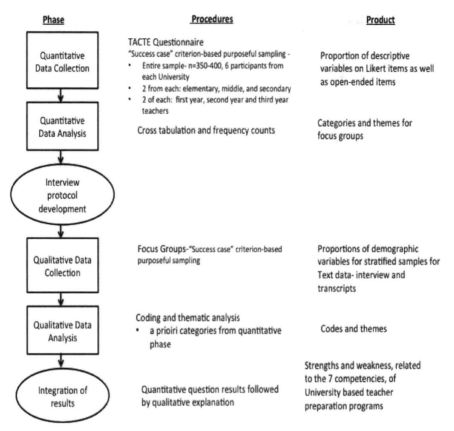

Figure 1. Diagram of the explanatory sequential design.

making up the "TACTE Vision for University-Based Teacher Preparation in Texas." The online survey was comprised of 14 questions with two questions relating to a set of competencies (see Appendix A). Participants responded to a Likert scale of 1 to 6 (strongly agree, agree, somewhat agree, somewhat disagree, disagree, and strongly disagree). One question for each of the following competencies was phrased negatively to improve validity:

1. Appropriate content knowledge
2. Skills to teach content knowledge and critical thinking
3. Continuous assessment of student learning
4. Use of data to make instructional decisions
5. Instruction that addresses the needs of diverse learners
6. Effective interactions with students, peers, and parents
7. Commitment to lifelong learning and professional development

Additionally, participants provided qualitative data in text boxes with seven open-ended questions addressing each of the competencies.

Focus group interviews were conducted with a semistructured approach. The questions related to the seven competencies in order to obtain more information about the early career teachers' perspectives regarding their preparation programs (see Appendix B).

Data Collection

Success case criterion-based purposeful sampling was used to investigate early career exemplar teacher's self-perception related to the seven TACTE competencies. In phase 1, deans of each TACTE institution had the opportunity to nominate up to six early career teachers as exemplars of their teacher preparation programs. The nominations could include two first-year teachers, two second-year teachers, and two third-year teachers. Nominees could represent any certification program or grade level. Each TACTE member institution determined the criteria for exemplar teachers that represent their institution and participates in the TACTE Early Career Teacher Research project. The nominees received multiple e-mails with the Web link to the online survey.

Phase 2 of data collection involved semistructured focus groups to extend the discussion and feedback of the data collected regarding the seven elements making up the TACTE "Vision for University-Based Teacher Preparation in Texas" (see Appendix B). The purpose of the focus group phase of the study was to confirm and extend the responses provided by participants in the questionnaire phase of the study. All nominees, including those who completed the online survey, received invitations for the focus groups at three locations in the state. Each of the three focus groups were 60 to 90 minutes in length. Focus group discussions were recorded and transcribed.

TACTE supported the project with financial support for a graduate assistant. Additional funds acquired through an American Association of Colleges of Teacher Education grant were used to enable travel for researchers to facilitate the focus groups. Additionally, each focus group participant received a $50 gift card for participating.

Data Analysis

Analysis of the quantitative data included descriptive frequency tables and cross tabulations. Variables for data disaggregation were (1) years of teaching experience, (2) level of certification, and (3) type of degree pursued (bachelor's, postbaccalaureate, or master's with teacher certification). The findings in this report reflect the data of the sample. The majority of the participants earned bachelor's degrees during their pursuit of teacher certification, so it was not possible to disaggregate the data according to type of degree.

In phase 2, a pattern-matching and constant comparative qualitative data analysis process was implemented for the focus group interviews. The qualitative analysis involved a two-level approach, including within-participant and across-participant theme development. After independently coding the data through a deductive process using the seven TACTE competencies as a framework, two researchers collaborated as coraters to develop the themes.

Participants

Faculty from TACTE institutions nominated graduates as early career exemplar teachers. Fifty-seven teachers completed the online survey representing 23 institutions. Each participant was also invited to participate in one of three focus groups at different locations in the state. The 13 focus group participants represented eight institutions.

For the quantitative questionnaire, participants' ages ranged from 20 to 54 years, with 23 (38%) between 20 and 24 years of age and 19 (32%) between 25 and 29 years of age. There were 3 (5%) males and 55 (95%) females. Seventeen (28%) participants identified themselves as white; 24 (41%) as white, non-Hispanic; 7 (11%) as African American; and 10 (16%) as Hispanic. The sample consisted of 23 (39%) first-year teachers, 21 (36%) second-year teachers, and 15 (25%) third-year teachers. Thirty-eight (63%) teachers were certified as early childhood to grade 6 (EC–6); 5 (8%) were middle school, grades 4 to 8; 9 (15%) were secondary, grades 8 to 12; and 8 (13%) were certified all-level (EC–12).

Focus group participants' ages ranged from 21 to 42 years or older, with 7 (54%) who were 21 to 25 years of age. There were 3 (23%) teachers from 26 to 30 years of age, 1 (8%) teacher from 31 to 35 years of age, 1 teacher from 39 to 42 years of age, and 1 teacher over 42 years of age. All (n = 13) participants were female. The sample consisted of 5 (38%) first-year teachers, 2 (15%) second-year teachers, and 6 (47%) third-year teachers. Among the 13 teachers in the focus groups, 19 certifications were represented. One teacher was certified to teach pre-K to grade 5 music, 7 (54%) to teach EC to grade 6, 4 (31%) to teach grades 4 to 8, 1 to teach EC to grade 12, 2 to teach EC to grade 12, 1 to teach Spanish, 1 to teach grades 8 to 12 bilingual, 1 to teach special education, and 1 to teach science. White teachers represented 70% of the focus group. African Americans were represented as 15%, and Hispanic teachers were represented with 15% of the total participants.

Findings

The quantitative data described the perceived preparedness of early career exemplars in TACTE competencies. Participants felt well prepared in all seven competencies; however, the data are more varied with lower perceptions of preparation for (Competency 4) using data for making instructional decisions and (Competency 6) effective interactions with students, peer, and parents.

Appropriate Content Knowledge

Through the quantitative questionnaire, a majority of early career teacher participants reported that they felt well prepared with appropriate content knowledge. Table 1 represents the levels of perceived preparedness.

In the focus groups, participants also expressed positive perceptions about preparedness regarding content knowledge. Most did report feeling well prepared to teach English language arts. However, the teachers associated their comments with pedagogy rather than content knowledge. They valued specific strategies and activities from their programs that transferred to use in the classroom. Both elementary and middle school math teachers felt less confident about teaching math. One participant said, "I know how to multiply, but teaching a fourth grader to multiply is a different thing." A secondary English teacher said, "I could have used more strategies for teaching writing."

Skills to Teach Content Knowledge and Critical Thinking

The second competency was preparing teaching with skills to teach content knowledge and critical thinking. As shown in Table 2, many participants (n = 45) felt well prepared to guide students to think critically regarding academic content. However, 9 participants selected somewhat agree, and 6 reported unfavorably about their preparation. In response to the negatively worded question (5), 4 graduates indicated that they were not provided with sufficient methods and strategies compared to 54 who felt prepared.

In the focus groups, participants struggled to answer this question confidently. Some expressed that professors had modeled critical thinking and engaged them in critical thinking as students, but some of the early career teachers did not feel prepared in developing critical thinking in their own students. Those who were confident in their ability mentioned Bloom's taxonomy. Two participants mentioned using open-ended questions as a way to promote higher-order thinking. One participant said it was difficult to implement critical thinking across age-groups, as the tasks would look quite different. One participant mentioned three specific courses at her university in which professors directly addressed higher-order thinking. This participant mentioned the use of verbs referring to academic skills that could frame questions to promote critical thinking. Teachers seemed more confident about teaching content knowledge but less confident about critical thinking.

Continuous Assessment of Student Learning

Early career teachers felt well prepared to conduct continuous assessment of student learning (see Table 3). Continuous assessment included progress monitoring as well as an emphasis on summative and formative assessments.

Table 1. Content Knowledge

Survey Question	Strongly Disagree	Disagree	Somewhat Disagree	Somewhat Agree	Agree	Strongly Agree	Total
1. Provided me with appropriate content knowledge	0	0	2	3	27	26	58

Survey Question	Strongly Agree	Agree	Somewhat Agree	Somewhat Disagree	Disagree	Strongly Disagree	Total
13. Did not equip me with sufficient knowledge appropriate to my subject area	1	2	4	16	35	0	58

Table 2. Content Knowledge and Critical Thinking

Survey Question	Strongly Disagree	Disagree	Somewhat Disagree	Somewhat Agree	Agree	Strongly Agree	Total
14. Prepared me to guide students to think critically regarding academic content	2	2	2	9	21	24	58

Survey Question	Strongly Agree	Agree	Somewhat Agree	Somewhat Disagree	Disagree	Strongly Disagree	Total
5. Did not provide me with sufficient methods and strategies to teach content knowledge and critical thinking	0	3	1	20	34	0	58

Table 3. Assessment

Survey Question	Strongly Disagree	Disagree	Somewhat Disagree	Somewhat Agree	Agree	Strongly Agree	Total
11. Taught me how to continually monitor student progress	0	2	2	5	22	27	58

Survey Question	Strongly Agree	Agree	Somewhat Agree	Somewhat Disagree	Disagree	Strongly Disagree	Total
6. Did not emphasize the use of both summative and formative assessments	0	0	3	16	39	0	58

Focus group participants referenced specific strategies for formative assessment they learned in college courses. Professors modeled these strategies and taught strategies explicitly. As preservice teachers, they observed these strategies in field-based courses and implemented them in internships or student teaching. One participant indicated strong preparation in summative assessments, such as end-of-unit testing, but indicated a need for more instruction about formative assessments. For example, she wondered if her students were learning to take notes, and she desired specific techniques to measure progress in learning that skill. A second participant in the same group mentioned that her school district spent an entire semester discussing the implementation of formative assessments and that her college preparation had provided the foundation for understanding formative assessments in her job. In a different focus group, a teacher applied knowledge obtained in her preparation program by assessing students before instruction and continually reminding herself to do so. She learned that in college classes, but sometimes she starts instruction without the initial assessment to guide instruction. A music teacher responded that using checklists with students was beneficial for her in using formative assessments.

Use of Data to Make Instructional Decisions

Although early career teachers indicated being prepared to use data to make instructional decisions, there were variations of preparedness represented in their responses. Many indicated *strongly agree* (n = 18) or *agree* (n = 20), but 15 indicated somewhat agree (see Table 4). When the data were disaggregated by years of experience, more first-year teachers chose *strongly agree* in comparison to the second- and third-year teachers. Responses to the negatively stated item (9) indicate that 15 students agree to some degree that they were not taught to collect and interpret data to guide instruction.

One participant mentioned a strong college emphasis on assessment, particularly using Response to Intervention data with one child; however, she mentioned the need for instruction in using data for a whole class. She got that opportunity in student teaching, but more emphasis was needed in college course work. Within that same group, a student mentioned she would like more information about grouping students and matching questions to the Texas Essential Knowledge and Skills (TEKS) to get a bigger picture of what students might not understand.

Instruction That Addresses the Needs of Diverse Learners

Overall, participants (n = 27) *agreed* that they were prepared to provide instruction for diverse learners. Similarly, some participants (n = 26) *strongly agreed* with their preparation to teach diverse learners.

Two participants noted that they felt well prepared to work with students who had varying learning styles. However, one participant noted the need

Table 4. Data-Driven Decision Making

Survey Question	Strongly Disagree	Disagree	Somewhat Disagree	Somewhat Agree	Agree	Strongly Agree	Total
3. Prepared me to differentiate instruction by analyzing student data	1	2	2	15	20	18	58

Survey Question	Strongly Agree	Agree	Somewhat Agree	Somewhat Disagree	Disagree	Strongly Disagree	Total
9. Did not teach me how to collect and interpret data to make instructional decisions	3	6	6	18	25	0	58

Table 5. Diverse Learners

Survey Question	Strongly Disagree	Disagree	Somewhat Disagree	Somewhat Agree	Agree	Strongly Agree	Total
10. Prepared me to provide instruction that meets the needs of diverse learners	0	1	0	4	27	26	58

Survey Question	Strongly Agree	Agree	Somewhat Agree	Somewhat Disagree	Disagree	Strongly Disagree	Total
4. Did not emphasize methods for teaching a diverse body of students	0	2	2	19	35	0	58

for greater preparation for working with English learners. Similarly, she felt that her preparation for modifying instruction for students with disabilities was lacking.

A second participant in the group mentioned that the population of English learners in her school spoke many different languages; for example, she taught students who came from Saudi Arabia and Egypt. She asked for help with using nonverbal cues. She was uncertain about where to go for help and what help might be available from administration for working with students who were emotionally disturbed. It was not until mid-semester that she began documenting classroom incidents relating to particular students.

A third member of that group mentioned how helpful using pictures and visuals is for English language learners. In a different focus group, a participant noted that taking English-as-a-second-language (ESL) courses in college was very helpful because her school is largely ESL with many different languages spoken in the classroom population.

A participant in one group mentioned taking one special needs course in college where she learned about the laws. She lamented a lack of preparation for working with students having severe disabilities. A participant in the same group noted finding help through her teaching team. One participant noted that in a class of 30 students, only three did not have a special need. Several students expressed being prepared to work with diverse students, but they were surprised by the number of students who had special needs or were English language learners. "Nine students speak no English; two are autistic. I don't know if they can prepare you for that (level of diversity) in college. If they had, I probably wouldn't have become a teacher."

Effective Interactions With Students, Peers, and Parents

Most early career teachers could at least *somewhat agree* about their ability to interact effectively with parents. However, this competency did not represent as much self-efficacy from teachers as most competencies in the study. For this competency, the fewest number of teachers (*n* = 14) chose *strongly agree* with their ability to effectively interact with parents.

Commitment to Lifelong Learning and Professional Development

Among the seven competencies explored in the study, lifelong learning and professional development were seen as areas of greatest preparation. Only two teachers indicated that this was an area of weakness in their preparation. One of the teachers who felt unprepared had been teaching 2 years, while the other had 3 years of experience.

One participant noted the need for more field experiences to have more practice with interactions. She indicated the lack of help she got from watching

Table 6. Interactions

Survey Question	Strongly Disagree	Disagree	Somewhat Disagree	Somewhat Agree	Agree	Strongly Agree	Total
2. Taught me how to interact with parents effectively	0	0	8	14	22	14	58

Survey Question	Strongly Agree	Agree	Somewhat Agree	Somewhat Disagree	Disagree	Strongly Disagree	Total
8. Did not prepare me to communicate effectively with other educators	0	0	2	24	32	0	58

Table 7. Lifelong Learning

Survey Question	Strongly Disagree	Disagree	Somewhat Disagree	Somewhat Agree	Agree	Strongly Agree	Total
7. Nurtured a desire to continue learning new content knowledge and teaching methods/strategies	0	2	0	1	15	40	58

Survey Question	Strongly Agree	Agree	Somewhat Agree	Somewhat Disagree	Disagree	Strongly Disagree	Total
12. Did not emphasize a commitment to lifelong learning and professional development	0	0	2	12	44	0	58

lessons on video recordings. She felt moderately prepared in working parents and moderately to less prepared in interacting with colleagues.

Most participants noted a lack of preparation for interacting with parents. "I wasn't ready for the hostility," said one. Another said, "It is difficult to get in touch with some parents who work five jobs." Another commented, "I would love to have been in parent conferences during student teaching."

All participants across the focus groups became aware of the need for professional development in their preparation programs. One participant said that professional development was modeled by her professor, who continues to study and further her own education as a professor. One participant noted that the preparation program provided her a volunteering opportunity with the Urban Educators Literacy Society, where she helped children with reading once a month. In a different focus group, a participant described her membership in a college campus group of Kappa Delta Pi and a Texas State Teachers Association campus organization as well. Participants in one group mentioned the need for continued development in the use of technology. "Collecting hours needs to be relevant to what you are doing. Emphasize something relevant to what you are doing," noted one participant.

Summary of Findings

Favorable responses about teacher preparation were compared across competencies in Table 8. Favorable responses are noted as *somewhat agree*, *agree*, and *strongly agree*. Early career teachers indicated preparedness most often ($n = 57$) in Competency 5: Instruction for Diverse Learners, while Competency 6: Interactions with Parents, Colleagues, and Students was an area in which teachers felt less prepared ($n = 50$). Table 9 represents comparisons of unfavorable responses as indicated by *strongly disagree*, *disagree*, and *somewhat disagree* and supports the findings of the favorable responses. Preparation regarding Competency 6: Interactions with Parents, Colleagues, and Students was perceived negatively most often.

Discussion

Findings from this study indicate that early career teacher exemplars viewed their teacher preparation as effective resulting in 380 (94.5%) responses ($n = 402$) as favorable to questions based on the seven TACTE competencies. Of this total, 175 (43%) *strongly agreed* that the competencies were adequately addressed in their teacher preparation programs. Competencies with most overall *favorable* responses are noted in descending order as follows:

Table 8.   Comparison of Favorable Responses About Preparation

Competency	Somewhat Agree	Agree	Strongly Agree	Total Favorable Responses
1. Content Knowledge	3	27	26	56
2. Content and Critical Thinking	9	21	24	54
3. Assessment	5	22	27	54
4. Use of Data for Instructional Decisions	15	20	18	53
5. Instruction for Diverse Learners	4	27	26	57
6. Interactions with Parents, Colleagues, and Students	14	22	14	50
7. Lifelong Learning	1	15	40	56
Totals	51	154	175	380

➤ Competency 5: Instruction for Diverse Learners ($n = 57$)
➤ Competency 1: Content Knowledge ($n = 56$) and Competency 7: Lifelong Learning ($n = 56$)
➤ Competency 2: Content Knowledge and Critical Thinking ($n = 54$) and Competency 3: Assessment ($n = 54$)
➤ Competency 4: Use of Data for Instructional Decisions ($n = 53$)
➤ Competency 6: Interactions with Parents, Students, and Colleagues ($n = 50$)

Only three participants *strongly disagree*d with effective teacher preparation in any of the seven competencies. Two of the three disagreements were represented by Competency 2: Content Knowledge and Critical Thinking. One respondent *strongly disagreed* with adequate preparation for Competency 4: Use of Data for Instructional Decisions. Total unfavorable responses ($n = 27$) represented only 7% of total responses ($n = 402$).

Table 9.   Comparison of Unfavorable Responses About Preparation

Competency	Strongly Disagree	Disagree	Somewhat Disagree	Total Unfavorable Responses
1. Content Knowledge	0	0	1	1
2. Content and Critical Thinking	2	2	2	6
3. Assessment	0	2	2	4
4. Use of Data for Instructional Decisions	1	2	2	5
5. Instruction for Diverse Learners	0	1	0	1
6. Interactions with Parents, Colleagues, and Students	0	0	8	8
7. Lifelong Learning	0	2	0	2
Totals	3	9	15	27

Competencies with most overall *unfavorable* responses are listed in descending order as follows:

> Competency 6: Interactions with Parents, Students, and Colleagues ($n = 8$)
> Competency 2: Content Knowledge and Critical Thinking ($n = 6$)
> Competency 4: Use of Data for Instructional Decisions ($n = 5$)
> Competency 3: Assessment ($n = 4$)
> Competency 7: Lifelong Learning ($n = 2$)
> Competency 5: Instruction for Diverse Learners ($n = 1$)
> Competency 1: Content Knowledge ($n = 1$)

Limitations and Conclusions

Some limitations were inherent to this study because of the size of institutions represented and/or number of participants. Similarly, a relatively small number participated in the focus groups. Limitations of the study and conclusions based on analyses of the data are provided.

Limitations

The TACTE member institution size is a variable that affected the representation of participants since each institution could have up to six nominees regardless of the number of graduates. However, by applying the seven TACTE competencies for all analyses, the variation in the program size of each TACTE member institution will be mitigated through the mixed-methods design focusing on a theoretical lens as the common denominator for analyses of all programs. In addition, designating first- through third-year teacher categories and two certificate ranges allowed for better organization of the data. It should be noted that middle school programs were represented in either the pre-K–6 or 7–12 certification designation.

The number of participants in the focus groups ($n = 13$) and the lack of diversity regarding ethnicity and/or gender could be a limitation of the study. A larger sample size in the focus groups might provide different results regarding teacher perceptions of their preparation. Variations in ethnicity might enrich the data beyond those recorded in this study. The presence of a male voice might provide a viewpoint not expressed by the females in the study.

Conclusions

TACTE institutions prepared exemplar teachers who feel well prepared to utilize the seven competencies as early career teachers. The quantitative data affirmed each competency as favorably addressed in TACTE-member teacher education preparation programs. Qualitative data supported and enriched findings with specific comments about preparation that were useful and necessary in supporting new teachers during the first 3 years of service.

TACTE member teacher preparation programs, as represented by participants in this study, provided new teachers (1) with tools to teach diverse learners, (2) with appropriate content knowledge, and (3) with awareness of the need to be lifelong learners. Early career exemplar teachers in this study also knew how to assess students using formative and summative assessments.

Responses concerning three particular competencies (6, 2, and 4) represented more than 70% of the unfavorable responses. In an effort to continue growth in teacher preparation effectiveness, TACTE-member preparation programs should address the following concerns of new teachers regarding their perceived ability (1) to effectively interact with parents (2) to provide opportunities for critical thinking within content areas and (3) to use data to guide classroom instruction.

Recommendations for Teacher Preparation Programs

This study provides support for several recommendations regarding the purpose set forth by the TACTE-member institutions regarding early career exemplar teachers' preparation toward the seven TACTE competencies. Competencies 6 and 4 received the fewest favorable responses, and Competencies 6, 2, and 4 received the most unfavorable responses. Recommendations are based on early career teachers' perceived needs for additional support in teacher education programs:

1. Introduce teacher candidates to family involvement theory and practice within courses. Several family involvement frameworks are available and could be used as supplemental course work. Use case studies to role-play specific family involvement scenarios within classes. Provide opportunities for interaction with parents through a course in which children are involved such as a tutoring setting.
2. Provide opportunities for teacher candidates to develop critical thinking opportunities for their future students within the course of lesson planning. Prompt candidates in writing questions and developing projects that require thoughts and actions that are beyond knowledge and comprehension.
3. Support teacher candidate efforts in becoming more expert at using data to drive decisions. Although early career teachers mentioned their perceived expertise with formative assessments and summative

assessments, to a lesser degree, they indicated a lapse in being able to use the data to make decisions. Analysis of formative assessment data could be a starting place for increasing efficacy in using data. Courses that require a field experience could provide opportunities for teacher candidates to analyze data with assessments they have performed with one (or more) student(s) during the field course. If these opportunities are not available, false data could be developed for practice purposes.

4. The final recommendations are provided based on comments of early career teachers outside the frame of the focus group questions and the online survey:

   a. Provide more observation time.
   a. Use videos of teaching to add authenticity.
   b. Use Eduphoria for planning, as it is widely used in practice.
   c. Show us how to use Gradebook software.
   d. Provide instruction using the 5E model for planning. **TEP**

Appendix A

Electronic Survey Open-Response Questions

1. What was especially effective in preparing you to teach the subject or grade(s) of your certification?
2. How could your preparation in content knowledge been improved?
3. What skills did you acquire that have enabled you to teach content knowledge effectively?
4. How were you prepared to engage students in critical thinking?
5. In what ways did your preparation program emphasize the importance of continuous assessment and progress monitoring?
6. How was this preparation of continuous assessment and progress monitoring applicable to your first year(s) of teaching?
7. In what ways were you prepared to make instructional decisions using student data?
8. How could your teacher preparation in making instructional decisions based on student data have been improved?
9. In what ways were you equipped to meet the instructional needs of diverse learners?
10. What were the strengths of your preparation program in preparing you to interact with colleagues and parents?
11. What were the strengths of your program in preparing you to interact with students?
12. How were you encouraged to continue learning and developing new skills for the duration of your career in education?

Appendix B

Focus Group Questions

Give feedback about your teacher preparation program as follows: well prepared, moderately prepared, not prepared:

1. How well did your teacher preparation program prepare you to teach the content in your subject area and/or grade level?
2. Describe specifically what you would have liked to have learned or experienced about different grade-level content areas in your program that you did not.
3. How well did your teacher preparation program prepare you to teach critical thinking skills to your students?
   a. Describe the learning experiences in your preparation program that contributed to your skills in this area.
   b. What impact have these experiences had on your performance in the classroom?
   c. Now having taught for at least a year, what would have been beneficial to you in teaching critical thinking skills?
4. In your teacher preparation program, how much importance was placed on continuous assessment of student learning?
   a. How well were you equipped to monitor student progress using various kinds of assessments?
   b. Name and describe some ways you were taught to assess student learning.
   c. Now having taught for at least a year, what would have been beneficial to you in assessing student learning?
5. How well did your teacher preparation program prepare you to use data to make instructional decisions?
   a. Describe the learning experiences that contributed to your skills to use data to make instructional decisions.
   b. Describe information that was lacking in your preparation program about using data to drive instruction.
   c. Now having taught for at least a year, what would have been beneficial to you in using data to drive instruction?
6. How well were you prepared to address the needs of diverse learners in your teacher preparation program? In what ways did your program equip or not equip you to meet the needs of a diverse group of students?
7. How well do you feel your teacher preparation program adequately prepared you to effectively interact with students, peers, and parents?
   a. Describe learning experiences that contributed to such interaction skills.
   b. After your first year(s) of teaching, in what ways are you better prepared to interact with students, peers, or parents?

8. How well did your teacher preparation program encourage you to continue learning?
    a. Describe continued professional development opportunities afforded to you in your program that leads you to a greater commitment to lifelong learning.
    b. Describe continued professional development opportunities that you wish you had had in your teacher preparation program that you now know would have been helpful.

References

Creswell, J., & Plano-Clark, V. (2010). *Designing and conducting mixed methods research* (2nd ed.). Los Angeles: Sage.

Lombardo, M. M., & Eichinger, R. W. (2004). *FYI: For your improvement, a guide for development and coaching* (4th ed.). Boston: Longmire.

Madhani, A. (2014, April 25). Obama wants better data on teacher preparation programs. *USA Today*, p. 1.

National Council on Teacher Quality. (2014). *Teacher prep review: National Council on Teacher Quality*. http://www.nctq.org/dmsView/Teacher_Prep_Review_2014_Report

Resmovits, J. (2014, June 17). How teacher prep programs are failing new teachers—and your kids. *Huffington Post*, p. 1.

Texas Association of Colleges for Teacher Education. (2011). http://atlantis.coe.uh.edu/tacte

Christie L. Bledsoe is an assistant professor at the University of Mary Hardin-Baylor, where she teaches graduate courses in research methods and design. Previously, she taught math and science in Texas public schools, and after earning a doctorate of education, she taught methods courses for preservice teachers. Her research interests include teacher preparation, math and science education, and technology. She is a sponsor of a chapter of Kappa Delta Pi honor society and currently serves at the second vice president of the Texas Association of Teacher Educators. She may be reached via e-mail at cbledsoe@umhb.edu.

Judy Trotti is an assistant professor at the University of Mary Hardin-Baylor, where she teaches literacy courses and pedagogy for teachers of English language learners. She taught both first and second grades in the public schools and gifted and talented students in grades K through 12 for nine years. She received a PhD in curriculum and instruction from the University of North Texas. Her research interests involve teacher preparation, literacy, and parent and family involvement. She may be reached via e-mail at jtrotti@umhb.edu.

Kari J. Hodge is currently a PhD candidate in educational psychology at Baylor University with a focus on measurement and quantitative methods. She holds an MA in education curriculum and instruction with a focus on teacher leadership and a BA in elementary education. She is currently an instructor for Baylor University, where she teaches instructional technology and teacher education courses and coteaches experimental design. Her research interests include cross-country studies in teacher education, technology implementation, assessment validity, and research methodology. She has published in the area of educational technology, gifted education, student success in higher education, and teacher effectiveness. She may be reached via e-mail at kari_hodge@baylor.edu.

Tony Talbert is a professor of social/cultural studies education and qualitative research in the School of Education at Baylor University. He refers to his field of research and teaching as "Education as Democracy," which integrates sociocultural and diversity education, socioeconomic justice education, and democracy education into a focused discipline of qualitative and ethnographic inquiry examining school and community stakeholder empowerment through activist engagement in political, economic, and social issues. His 29 years as an educator has included service to and consulting for public schools, universities, and governmental and corporate institutions. He may be reached via e-mail at tony_talbert@baylor.edu.

The Council for the Accreditation of Educator Preparation, *Techne*, and Curriculum

The Contraction of Teacher Education

GRETCHEN SCHWARZ

ABSTRACT: *Techne*, what Ellul defines as *technique* and Postman as *Technopoly*, dominates the Council for the Accreditation of Educator Preparation (CAEP), the current teacher education accreditation organization. Unfortunately, this worldview removes from teacher education moral/ethical and civic purposes and eliminates intellectual diversity, reducing teacher education to a test-addicted, by-the-numbers training agenda. The author asks the question whether it is too late to reclaim teacher education curriculum as a legitimate and fully human, intellectual and emotional, moral and civic mission of the university.

But lo! men have become the tools of their tools. (Thoreau, 1967, p. 1266)

The policies we have examined reveal a struggle for power over who will rule our nation's schools and colleges. If the forces of hyperrationalization are not checked, who will be the winners and losers in the struggle for power? (Wise, 1979, p. 212)

Teacher education in the nation's colleges and universities continues to be loudly criticized by politicians such as Arne Duncan, former secretary of education, as well as others. While much of this negativity can be traced to political agendas, probably few in teacher education do not also seek change and improvement. Scholars such as Darling-Hammond (2010), Co-chran-Smith, Ell, Ludlow, Grudnoff, and Aitken (2014), and Zeichner (2014) all call for rigorous and research-based reform in teacher education to meet diverse needs of P–12 students in changing times. At the same time, unfortunately, the large national teacher accreditation organization, the Council for the Accreditation of Educator Preparation (CAEP), has proceeded as if the one solution had arrived and all that is needed is the compliance of teacher education programs. CAEP offers some good ideas, and the students, the public, and professors themselves deserve a robust system for self-evaluation. However, CAEP threatens to reduce evaluation to a numbers game, limiting teaching to a matter of mere *techne*.

The warnings have appeared already. A few brave scholars have openly challenged the powerful national teacher accreditation behemoth, the National

Council for Accreditation of Teacher Education (NCATE), now known since 2013 as the Council for the Accreditation of Educator Preparation (CAEP). Richard Allington (2005), past president of the International Reading Association, gave a cogent argument for opposing NCATE for "undermining our efforts to develop thoughtful, autonomous, and effective teachers" (p. 199). Johnson, Johnson, Farenga, and Ness (2005), in their exposé of NCATE, urged institutions to do a cost–benefit analysis of the process; CAEP is expensive and time consuming.

Taubman (2009) argued how fear made so many deans of colleges of education subscribe to NCATE (now CAEP), explaining that teacher education has come to be ruled by the "audit culture." Taubman further explained, "It seemed as if valuable, although perhaps vulnerable, professional judgment and wisdom were being replaced by a measurable, defendable, and supposedly neutral process, in which educators and students were themselves reconstructed in terms of quantifiable outcomes" (p. 89).

Pinar (2004) noted early on that "NCATE is itself guilty of anti-intellectualism" (p. 214). Yet, overall, most college teacher education programs overseen by NCATE/CAEP and their education professors have simply gone along. Meanwhile, CAEP (2015) has legislated what may now become the national curriculum for teacher education. Not directly, of course, but the accreditation process laid out and available online (http://www.caep.org/caep-accreditation-standards) will determine the curriculum for teacher education in many colleges and universities. *Techne*, or what Ellul (1964) calls *technique* and Postman (1993) terms *Technopoly*, has largely taken over teacher education accreditation. The question remains whether it is too late to reclaim teacher education curriculum as a legitimate and fully human, intellectual and emotional, moral and civic mission of the university.

Techne Is All

The basic definition of *techne* is craft, skill, or the knowledge of how to do and make things through rational method. McCluskey and Winter (2012), in their examination of the digital university, trace *techne* to Aristotle, who placed *techne* at a lower status. "The physical labor involved for farming or mining was often performed by slaves. The name given to these routine forms of doing was *techne*" (p. 63). *Techne* in and of itself is not bad, of course; it is necessary to make societies run. Likewise, many of the items that CAEP demands are useful. However, when *techne*-knowing becomes the one way through which humans understand themselves and their world, human beings suffer, losing what makes them human—creativity, spirituality, and art, for example. In *The Technological Society*, French sociologist Jacques Ellul (1964) makes clear the future of society dominated by *techne* or *technique*. He states that *technique* does not mean just machines or technology but "the totality of methods rationally arrived at and having absolute efficiency . . . in every field of human activity" (p. xxv). *Technique* is a worldview, the lens through which all else is perceived. Ellul traces the history of *technique* and describes how it plays out in the economy, the state, sports, medicine, and education. Of education, Ellul says, it "will no longer be an unpredictable and exciting adventure in human enlightenment, but an exercise in conformity and an apprenticeship to whatever gadgetry is useful in a technical world" (p. 349). Children are educated not for their own distinct growth and liberation but rather for society's requirements; they must adapt. Instruction itself is technical. Says Ellul, "But the individual participates only to the degree that he is subordinate to the search for efficiency, to the degree that he resists all the currents today considered secondary, such as aesthetics, ethics, fantasy" (p. 74). Ellul adds that even "the human brain must be made to conform to much more advanced brain of the machine" (p. 349).

Moreover, language, too, is adapted to the needs of *technique*. Ellul (1990) claims that there exists a technological bluff, "the gigantic bluff in which discourse on techniques envelops us, making us believe anything . . . the bluff of politicians, the bluff of the media, the bluff of technicians when they talk about techniques" (p. xvi). Thus, hardly anyone even questions the jargon captured by Cochran-Smith (2005). She notes that teacher education language about "outcomes, and the language of 'results,' 'consequences,' 'effectiveness,' 'impact,' 'bottom lines,' and evidence' has been stitched into the logic of teacher education so seamlessly that it is now nearly imperceptible" (p. 411). *Technique* is autonomous, self-perpetuating, bureaucratic, and mechanistic—not a good fit for a profession many see as a calling. Ellul (1964) observes that "technology cannot put up with intuitions and 'literature.' It must necessarily don mathematical vestments. Everything in human life that does not lend itself to mathematical treatment must be excluded—because it is not a possible end for technique—and left in the sphere of dreams" (p. 431). CAEP is totally devoted to *technique*.

Neil Postman (1993), media and culture critic and educator, declares *Technopoly* to be "the submission of all forms of cultural life to the sovereignty of technique and technology" (p. 52). He adds, "*Technopoly* is a state of culture. It is also a state of mind. It consists in the deification of technology, which means the culture seeks its authorization in technology, and takes its orders from technology" (p. 71). Results of *Technopoly*, Postman's version of *techne*, include information glut, massive bureaucracy, belief in ongoing technical progress, the inability to offer moral guidance, and the belief that "technology can plainly reveal the true nature of some human condition . . . because the score, statistic, or taxonomy has given it technical form" (p. 90). Like Ellul (1964) with *technique*, Postman describes the historical rise of *technopoly* and then the religion or belief system that serves as its foundation—scientism, a kind of "hyperrationalization." Postman (1993) explains as follows:

This, then, is what I mean by Scientism. It is not merely the misapplication of techniques such as quantification to questions where numbers have nothing to say . . . not merely the claim of social researchers to be applying the aims and procedures of natural science to the human world. . . . It is the desperate hope, and wish, and ultimately the illusory belief that some standardized set of procedures called "science" can provide us with an unimpeachable source of moral authority, a suprahuman basis for answers to questions like . . . "What are good and evil ends?" "How ought we to think and feel and behave?" (pp. 161–162)

In addition, Postman notes, "Diversity, complexity, and ambiguity of human judgment are enemies of technique. They mock statistics and polls and standardized tests and bureaucracies" (p. 158).

A few scholars, drawing on the work of Ellul and Postman, among others, have noted the dangers of turning education itself into a technology (Johnson, 1995; Stivers, 2006; Stuchul, 1997). Stivers (2001) asserts that the entire university has been overtaken by *techne*. "We have unintentionally created a technological and magical world in which there is no room for reflection, normative reason, and moral judgement. . . . We are training students to be unreflective technicians" (p. 209). Bullough (2014) argues that scientism "and its supporting terministic screen . . . dominate discourse, constrain action, and narrow vision" within teacher education, under CAEP in particular (p. 8). How so?

On the surface, the teacher education curriculum is under no threat from CAEP. Standard 1 of CAEP enumerates the Teacher Education Accreditation Council standards, which include understanding of learner development, learning differences, learning environments, application of content, assessment, planning for instruction, instructional strategies, professional learning and ethical practice, and leadership and collaboration. These teaching basics do not excite argument; this list is useful. Thus, traditional teacher education courses, such as methods, child development, subject area instruction, classroom management, special education needs, and others, seem to lie in no immediate danger. However, CAEP, with absolute faith in *techne*, will affect teacher education curriculum in at least the following two ways:

1. Elimination of the moral, ethical, civic, and personal in teacher education. All purposes of education are reduced to one—economic—for society. All other human ethical values become the null curriculum.
2. Elimination of intellectual diversity from the teacher education enterprise. CAEP has found one way to do teacher education, one way to evaluate it, and everyone will be monitored for compliance.

The Null Curriculum

Competing values and beliefs about the purposes of American education have long led to uncomfortable contention. Some goals have been emphasized more than others at various periods, from the need to assimilate immigrants to the need to enable democratic citizens and from job training to encouraging personal and social growth. Fitting Americans into the world of business, however, has been policy since *A Nation at Risk* in 1983; the one and only aim of American education, as reflected in CAEP, at least, is economic—preparing people for work or college and then work. Therefore, in Standard 3: Candidate Quality, Recruitment, and Selectivity, teacher education is charged with demonstrating efforts to "know and address community, state, national, regional, or local needs for hard-to-staff schools and shortage fields, currently STEM, English-language learning, and students with disabilities" (CAEP, 2015, p. 4). Preparing teachers who care about students or who are devoted to social justice and equity is not a goal; putting teachers into the "right" job is. Also, the goal of preparing teachers who raise their students' scores is based on the economy and the idea, as Postman (1995) puts it, "that the vitality of any nation's economy rests on high standards of achievement and rigorous discipline in schools" (p. 28). Postman adds of this purpose, "Any education that is mainly about economic utility is far too limited to be useful, and in any case, so diminishes the world that it mocks one's humanity" (p. 31). What good is a "good job" if the society is unhealthy and the individual lost? CAEP closes off possibilities for teacher education to consider multiple goals.

The only evidence of success in all standards in CAEP is by the numbers, as listed in *Principles for Measures Used in the CAEP Accreditation Process* by Ewell (2013, pp. 4–5): examinations, surveys, observations (using a "well-developed observational protocol"), statistics, and curricular features, "such as the extent to which students are taught assessment methods," and, only if all else fails, case studies ("where quantitative measures are unavailable"). Moral and ethical principles cannot be demonstrated well on a Likert scale or multiple-choice standardized tests, so moral/ethical matters do not count. As Ellul (1964) states, "The technical phenomenon is the main preoccupation of our time. . . . It is really a question of finding the best means in an absolute sense, on the basis of numerical calculation" (p. 21). Although the ninth standard in CAEP Standard 1 is Professional Learning and Ethical Practice, the only vaguely moral part of the description refers to adapting practice "to meet the needs of the learner" (p. 4). Campbell (2013) suggests that this absence may result because "in the exhausting whirl of curricular and pedagogical training that occupies much of the technical focus on teacher education, ethics is regarded as a philosophical frill" (p. 428).

Sanger and Osguthorpe (2013) argue that there is actually a moral vacuum in teacher education. "Teacher education does not simply lack moral language—failing to develop intuitive moral understandings and motives of candidates—but actively (if unintentionally) suppresses that language and development through the employment of technical terms that obscure it" (p. 46). Not only the emphasis on quantitative measurement, but the language of CAEP itself is *technique* embodied. A teacher educator program in CAEP is a "provider," and the future teacher is a "candidate." The prose is littered with terms such as "exit criteria," "effective management," "high-performing organizations," and those favorites of statistics professors, "validity," reliability," and "verifiability." That teaching and teacher education remain uncertain undertakings that involve human relationships and judgments is not even considered, nor is the idea that teaching is difficult moral work. Not only do the language and the focus on numerical evidence that assume a direct correlation between what teachers teach and what students learn make the ethical aspects of schooling vanish, but such a focus ignores the many complex factors that influence schooling and students. As Cochran-Smith (2005) warns in an editorial from the *Journal of Teacher Education*, the focus on outcomes, defined mainly as test scores, "is a trap for teacher education that ignores the broader purposes of education in a democratic society and inappropriately places the onus for improving schools and schooling on teachers and teacher educators alone" (p. 411).

Postman (1993) notes, "The Technopoly story is without a moral center. It puts in its place efficiency, interest, and economic advance" (p. 179). The null curriculum in CAEP includes ethics, moral purpose, and ideals of education that transcend job training. Cochran-Smith (2003) observes, "At their very core, teaching and learning are matters of both head and heart, both reason and passion" (p. 374). Hansen (1995) maintains that the differences among teachers "have to do with the ethos of the person, his or her characteristic conduct when in the presence of students, his or her own reputation, expectations, hopes, fears, worries. The relationship between a teacher and students is invariably a moral one . . . for those qualities themselves constitute messages about how to interact with others" (p. 11). Teachers often enter teaching with the desire to serve others, and they deal daily with issues such as poverty, racism, and funding inequities. What do we do about these big-picture problems? Where do social justice and democracy come into the picture? Teacher education should also attend to daily concerns, ranging from the negativity of a colleague toward students to the bullying of a student outside class and from the question of how much to reveal about oneself online to the pressures that testing has put on students. Moreover, the ideals, the moral commitments, that bring teachers into schools can also sustain them. How do ethical concerns fit into ongoing professional development in an accreditation system focused on "high standards that rely on evidence-based measures of performance and continuous improvement" (CAEP Board of Directors, 2013)—numbers, since qualitative evidence does not meet "empirical evidence of each measure's psychometric and statistical soundness" (CAEP Board of Directors, 2013, p. 15)?[1] *Techne* at the heart of teacher accreditation replaces the ethical with the efficient, the moral and the meaningful with the measurable, the many aims of education, with just one—economic.

What does this mean for what remains in the teacher education curriculum? For one thing, foundations courses may soon disappear, particularly any that deal with social issues. Such courses have already begun to vanish in some universities. In a college curriculum in which there is a need to include more content and pedagogical knowledge courses and more *technique*, courses about ideas or ethics or the history and purposes of American education may seem unnecessary. There is little to no time for impractical or "theoretical" matters such as philosophy or history and certainly no place for the critique of current school policies. CAEP trains teachers for the status quo.

Moreover, "provider responsibilities" under Standard 1 (CAEP Board of Directors, 2013, p. 3) include all the Specialized Professional Associations (content area) standards and "skills and commitment that afford all P–12 students access to rigorous college- and career-ready standards" and "technology standards." Educational technology rates highly in CAEP. Standard 1.5 declares that "providers ensure that completers model and apply technology standards" (p. 3). Postman (1995) asserts that "nowhere do you find more enthusiasm for the god of Technology that among educators" (p. 38). Educational technology courses that *fail* to examine the social, ethical, personal, and educational effects of new technologies, positive and negative, are likely to increase.

In addition, since successful test taking is the final measure of success, certain models of teaching may well gain official approval, such as the "scientific" reading approaches endorsed under the No Child Left Behind Act. Because creativity, critical thinking, and questioning the status quo do not appear in CAEP along with career readiness and technology use, methods and curriculum courses may well need to narrow and focus their content to what is on the test. New ways of thinking? Teacher education to prepare the nation's children for democracy? Education for learning that transcends the Scantron tests? Much is absent in the CAEP curriculum.

Big Brother Knows Best

The accountability myth in teacher education purports to guarantee the public that tax or tuition money is well spent and that doubts about higher-education institutions can be laid to rest. Of course, teacher education programs should be able to give evidence of what they accomplish, although the notion that teacher education can itself ensure how new teachers perform is as absurd as the notion that what teachers do must result in uniformly high test scores among America's children. Do we jail parents for their children who engage in criminal behavior? Nevertheless, CAEP is all about mandating, measuring, and monitoring. For example, Standard 3: Candidate Quality, Recruitment, and Selectivity in CAEP Board of Directors (2013) sets grade-point average (GPA) and test score requirements for teacher candidates. "The provider ensures that the average GPA and assessment like ACT or GRE

➢ is in the top 50 percent from 2016–2017 . . . [and]
➢ is in the top 33 percent of the distribution by 2020" (pp. 8–9).

Evidence that higher test scores ensure better teachers is absent here, but if one wants teachers with higher grades or scores, just say it shall be so. The bureaucracy of *techne* relies on administrative technique, such as setting numerical goals. The bureaucracy sets uniform and inescapable expectations for all teacher education programs, no matter how much their size, organization, contexts, histories, aims, or students may differ.

"Value-added modeling" (supported by such groups as the Bill and Melinda Gates Foundation), public school student test scores, are included in the first measure under Standard 4: Program Impact. Moreover, the "provider" itself "maintains a quality assurance system comprised of valid data from multiple measures. . . . The provider supports continuous improvement that is sustained and evidence-based, and that evaluates the effectiveness of its completers" (p. 14). So states Standard 5 in CAEP Board of Directors (2013). CAEP measures many things—employer surveys, graduation rates, job placement rates, all kinds of test scores from licensure tests to P–12 test scores, and observations of preservice teachers—"using a well-developed observational protocol" (Ewell, 2013, p. 4). Some curricular features will be measured, such as "the extent to which students are taught assessment methods" (p. 4). Only numbers promise the certainty that CAEP claims for those who believe in scientism. Unfortunately, new ideas, life-changing class discussions, and the diverse stories that preservice teachers bring with them are not what CAEP values or counts.

To make all this work, of course, to "raise the bar in educator preparation," as the first goal in the CAEP (2014) *Strategic Plan*[2] states, requires the absolute power of CAEP and its constant monitoring. Thus, goals 4 and 5 of the *Strategic Plan* state "to increase accreditation's value" so that "more providers will participate and more states and districts will rely on accreditation for program approval, licensing, and hiring" and "to be a model accrediting body," in fact, the one and only model through which all providers (which need not be university or college programs by the way) must gain accreditation (pp. 2–3). Diversity among P–12 students is important, but diversity among teacher educators is clearly *not* a goal, intellectual freedom is *not* a value, and educating students for questioning or for divergent thinking and for democracy are *not* the aims. So what does this mean for the curriculum of teacher education? It means that individual teacher educators had better conform, in both the content of their teaching and even in the nature of their research. Perhaps the greatest threat of CAEP to teacher education curriculum is the narrow, instrumental, numbers-dominated view of what counts as educational research.

Just when it seemed safe for qualitative researchers to pursue their work in education, CAEP advocates the victory of the old behaviorist-positivist-business model. First, the CAEP Commission established its own standards supported by "research on effective management, and especially, by the Baldridge education award criteria, as well as recent trends and new approaches among accreditors" (CAEP Board of Directors, 2013, p. 2). Those "recent trends and new approaches" remain a mystery, but there is no mystery in management research or in Baldridge education award criteria. As Callahan's (1962) seminal book *Education and the Cult of Efficiency* made clear, a business model from "scientific management" and the Taylor system at the beginning of the 20th century to Total Quality Management near the end of 20th century and the "quality assurance system" demanded currently by CAEP has largely directed public schools and now teacher education. Callahan's (1962) words still capture the situation best:

> And when all the strands in the story are woven together, it is clear that the essence of the tragedy was in adopting values and practices indiscriminately and applying them with little or no consideration of educational values or purposes. It was not that some of the ideas from the business world might not have been used to advantage in educational administration, but that the wholesale adoption of the basic values, as well as the techniques of the business-industrial [today one might say business-digital] world, was a serious mistake in an institution whose primary purpose was the education of children. (p. 244)

Likewise, the Baldridge Program, part of the National Institute of Standards and Technology in the U.S. Department of Commerce, was first aimed at business but added education in 1998 according to the first page of its website (http://www.nist.gov/baldridge/about/what_we_do.cfm). Baldridge includes such aims as "help organizations achieve best-in-class levels of performance" and "identify and share best management practices, principles, and strategies." Malcolm Baldridge was a former secretary of commerce. The Baldridge National Quality Award in business and one in education are given annually. Bottom lines determine success for both.

Examining CAEP's own reference section supporting its claims to govern teacher education based on research, one finds the Educational Testing Service (2004), the Common Core Standards Initiative (2010), the Council of Chief State School Officers (2011), the National Center for Education Statistics (2011), the National Research Council (2010) (driven by the research models of science, engineering, and medicine available at http://www.nationalacademies.org/nrc), and, of course, NCATE (2010). The only often-quoted (more than once) and recognized scholars in teacher education include Lee Shulman and Linda Darling-Hammond. Most of the references, outside the clinical partnership section, come from polls, statistics, and organizations. Peter Ewell, who wrote the *Principles for Measures Used in the CAEP Accreditation Process*, is an expert in outcomes and assessment and vice president for the National Center for Higher Education Management Systems. He is not a teacher educator; CAEP is clearly uninterested in the research or ideas of various nationally respected teacher educators.

So where is a forum for educational qualitative researchers, for scholars of ideas, or for any researcher who dissents from the CAEP vision? Nowhere. This contraction of the definition of research poses the most damaging threat to the curriculum and the process of teacher education. Already, teacher research is being co-opted for CAEP within teacher education. At my own institution, in a CAEP preparation meeting, it was argued that student teachers or interns should do classroom research, proving the positive effect of the student teachers on their students' scores (with charts or graphs), or evidence for CAEP. Any other ideas for research that preservice teachers express would be ignored. Teacher research, then, is not seen as an emancipatory process in the service of social justice or other specific classroom needs as Cochran-Smith and Lytle (1992, 2006) have described. The teacher education program under CAEP needs "results," not thoughtful, autonomous new teachers. And what of the future for teacher education professors? Will tenure support any research not fitting into the positivist-business model? Will new courses be developed by active researchers to try out curriculum ideas such as media literacy education or some new integration of art and technology? Not if it is not on the test and cannot be measured by the numbers.

The role of teacher education has become to "train" new teachers to teach to the test and to focus educational research on the same goal. Stone (2006) critiques the preoccupation that already exists in graduate education with methods and methodology. Stone sees this trend aggravated by such mandates as No Child Left Behind and says that "how to do research" has turned into "valuing method as technology for its own sake and thus into technologization" (p. 527). She argues for "a start toward undermining the domination of from empirical research as the sole basis for educational and social change" (p. 543). Ewell's (2013) nine pages of *Principles for Measures Used in the CAEP Accreditation Process* leave little to no room for qualitative research or educational scholarship conceived of as the debate of ideas. CAEP's vision embraces the totalization of research, "technolization that limits research processes and potential results" (Stone, 2006, p. 527). The characteristics of such *technique* captured by Ellul (1964) are automatism, self-augmentation, monism, and universalism. Research is reduced to the one way, and such research will surely in turn limit the teacher education curriculum. Postman (1993) summarizes that under *Technopoly*, "the aim is not to reduce ignorance, superstition, and suffering, but to accommodate ourselves to the requirements of new technologies" (p. 70). Ironically, Art Wise (1979), the father of contemporary NCATE/CAEP, also declared, long ago, that "once the process of technocratic rationalization begins, there appears to be no limiting it" (p. 64). Teacher educators are commanded by CAEP to accommodate—"monitor" is a favorite word. The Panopticon rules many colleges and schools of teacher education but not yet all.

An Alternative?

Too many teacher educators have not connected the dots in the CAEP saga, and what Burns (2014) asserts seems true: "I can only conclude that, as the saying goes, we have met the enemy and it is us" (p. 2). No doubt, the current *techne*-driven model of CAEP appeals to many; it promises certainty, high standards, uniformity, accountability, and economic success in an anxious age. Such promises are a "bluff," according to Ellul (1990), who asks, "Are we then shut up, blocked, and chained by the inevitability of the technical system which is making us march like obedient automatons thanks to its bluff?" (p. 411). Of course, teacher education needs methods for ongoing assessment and inspiring and practical ideas for improvement. Curriculum change should be ongoing. No arguments there. However, NCATE, now CAEP, according to Bullough, Clark, and Paterson (2003), is characterized by "fear of diversity, distrust of teachers and teacher educators, a naïve faith in the ability and value of systems to control behavior and to assure quality performance, and narrow conceptions of teaching and learning" (p. 50). Is anything else possible besides the audit culture and the CAEP Big Brother?

What would happen to teacher education programs if teachers were seen as *intellectuals* (Giroux, 1988) with a *sense of vocation* (Hansen, 1995)? What if policymakers and teacher educators could admit that teaching is often an *uncertain* craft (McDonald, 1992)? What if teachers and teacher educators themselves were *brought back in* to educational reform, recognizing the *emotional work* of teaching in difficult times (Hargreaves & Evans, 1997)? What if *narrative as a way of knowing* and teacher lore were allowed a place in teacher education and development (Schubert & Ayers, 1992)? What if reformers and others could acknowledge that the *"roads to knowledge are many"* (Eisner, 1985, p. xi, emphasis added)? What if the teacher education self-study could be *exploratory, local, and contextual* (Cochran-Smith & the Boston College Evidence Team, 2009)? What if scholars and policymakers could welcome *multiple genres of research* in teacher education (Cochran-Smith et al., 2012)? Can teacher education build on the work of the many great teacher educator/scholars? Why not collect appropriate statistics, such as placement and graduation rates and test scores, but also add what each program deems important for its own aims and situation? Why not include interviews, focus groups, case studies on student attitudes, and reflections? Why not build an accreditation system that respects the humanity of teachers and the mystery of teaching and learning? Creating an alternative to CAEP would be difficult and time consuming in the current political climate, but it is not impossible. Such a development could allow the public to learn much more about teacher education programs as well. Does the profession have the will to do so in the face of considerable political pressure?

In Conclusion

The CAEP system "ensures" much, but it does not promise schooling that, as Postman (1995) says, "can be about how to make a life, which is quite different from how to make a living" (p. x). CAEP reforms do not offer lively course work/experiences in the moral/ethical aspects of teaching for preservice teachers. The accreditation machine does not ensure teacher education curricular concern with social justice, poverty, the information glut, engaging teacher voices in reform, engaging in democracy, or any of the larger social problems that impinge on education every day. Can we learn from Ellul, Postman, and the brave few who have spoken out in teacher education? Can a larger, less contracted and limited curriculum of teacher education, to say nothing of the governance and related research and teaching, still be salvaged from *techne* by its scholar/practitioners? The question lingers. **TEP**

Notes

1. The original 2013 version of the standards were used for this article. These were available for a while online at http://oldcaepnet.org. This site is now a "protected blog." The new version of the standards is available at http://caepnet.org. The differences would be worth further study if it were possible.
2. The original 2014 version of the strategic plan was used for this article. The URL is no longer accessible. The new version of the strategic plan is on the current website at http://www.caepnet.org. The differences would be worth further study if it were possible.

References

Allington, R. L. (2005). Ignoring the policy makers to improve teacher preparation. *Journal of Teacher Education, 56*(3), 199–204.

Bullough, R. V. (2014). Toward reconstructing the narrative of teacher education: A rhetorical analysis of "preparing teachers." *Journal of Teacher Education, 65*(3), 184–194.

Bullough, R. V., Clark, D. C., & Patterson, R. S. (2003). Getting in step: Accountability, accreditation and the standardization of teacher education in the United States. *Journal of Education for Teaching: International Research and Pedagogy, 29*(1), 35–51.

Burns, J. (2014). Our impoverished view of teacher education. *Teachers College Record.* http://www.tcrecord.org

Callahan, R. E. (1962). *Education and the cult of efficiency.* Chicago: University of Chicago Press.

Campbell, E. (2013). The virtuous, wise, and knowledgeable teacher: Living the good life as a professional practitioner. *Educational Theory, 63*(4), 413–430.

Cochran-Smith, M. (2003). Sometimes it's not about the money: Teaching and heart. *Journal of Teacher Education, 54*(5), 371–375.

Cochran-Smith, M. (2005). Teacher education and the outcomes trap. *Journal of Teacher Education, 56*(5), 411–417.

Cochran-Smith, M., & the Boston College Evidence Team. (2009). Re-culturing teacher education: Inquiry, evidence, and action. *Journal of Teacher Education, 60*(5), 458–468.

Cochran-Smith, M., Cannady, M., McEachern, K. P., Mitchell, K., Piazza, P., Power, C., et al. (2012). Teachers' education and outcomes: Mapping the research terrain. *Teachers College Record, 114*(10), 1–49.

Cochran-Smith, M., Ell, F., Ludlow, L., Grudnoff, L., & Aitken, G. (2014). The challenge and promise of complexity theory for teacher education research. *Teachers College Record, 116*(5), 1–38.

Cochran-Smith, M., & Lytle, S. (1992). *Inside/outside: Teacher research and knowledge.* New York: Teachers College Press.

Cochran-Smith, M., & Lytle, S. (2006). *Inquiry as stance.* New York: Teachers College Press.

Council for the Accreditation of Educator Preparation. (2014). *Strategic plan.* http://caepnet.org

Council for the Accreditation of Educator Preparation. (2015). *CAEP accreditation standards* (revised). http://caepnet.org/standards/introduction

Council for the Accreditation of Educator Preparation Board of Directors. (2013). *CAEP accreditation standards.* http://caepnet.org

Darling-Hammond, L. (2010). Teacher education and the American future. *Journal of Teacher Education, 61*(1–2), 35–47.

Eisner, E. (Ed.). (1985). *Learning and teaching the ways of knowing. The 84th yearbook of the National Society for the Study of Education* (Pt. 2). Chicago: University of Chicago Press.

Ellul, J. (1964). *The technological society.* New York: Vintage.

Ellul, J. (1990). *The technological bluff.* Grand Rapids, MI: Eerdmans.

Ewell, P. (2013). *Principles for measures used in the CAEP accreditation process.* http://caepnet.org

Giroux, H. A. (1988). *Teachers as intellectuals.* Granby, MA: Bergin & Garvey.

Hansen, D. T. (1995). *The call to teach.* New York: Teachers College Press.

Hargreaves, A., & Evans, R. (Eds.). (1997). *Beyond educational reform: Bringing teachers back in.* Buckingham: Open University Press.

Johnson, D. D., Johnson, B., Farenga, S. J., & Ness, D. (2005). *Trivializing teacher education: The accreditation squeeze.* Lanham, MD: Rowman & Littlefield.

Johnson, H. C. (1995). Education, technology, and human values: Ellul and construction of an ethic of resistance. *Bulletin of Science, Technology and Society, 15*(2–3), 87–91.

McCluskey, F. B., & Winter, M. L. (2012). *The idea of the digital university.* Washington, DC: Westphalia Press.

McDonald, J. P. (1992). *Teaching: Making sense of an uncertain craft.* New York: Teachers College Press.

Pinar, W. F. (2004). *What is curriculum theory?* Mahwah, NJ: Lawrence Erlbaum Associates.

Postman, N. (1993). *Technopoly.* New York: Vintage.

Postman, N. (1995). *The end of education.* New York: Knopf.

Sanger, M., & Osguthorpe, R. (2013). The moral vacuum in teacher education research and practice. In H. Sockett & R. Boostrom (Eds.), *A moral critique of contemporary education: The 112th yearbook of the National Society for the Study of Education* (Pt. 1, pp. 41–60). New York: Teachers College Press.

Schubert, W. H., & Ayers, W. C. (Eds.). (1992). *Teacher lore.* White Plains, NY: Longman.

Stivers, R. (2001). *Technology as magic.* New York: Continuum.

Stivers, R. (2006). The need for a "shadow" university. *Bulletin of Science, Technology and Society, 26*(3), 217–227.

Stone, L. (2006). From technologization to totalization in education research: US graduate training, methodology, and critique. *Journal of Philosophy of Education, 40*(4), 527–545.

Stuchul, D. L. (1997). Education as technology: The modern deception. *Bulletin of Science, Technology and Society, 17*(5–6), 291–296.

Taubman, P. M. (2009). *Teaching by numbers.* New York: Routledge.

Thoreau, H. (1967). Walden. In S. Bradley, R. C. Beatty, & E. Hudson Long (Eds.), *The American tradition in literature* (pp. 1242–1461). New York: Norton.

Wise, A. E. (1979). *Legislated learning.* Berkeley: University of California Press.

Zeichner, K. (2014). The struggle for the soul of teaching and teacher education in the USA. *Journal of Education for Teaching: International Research and Pedagogy, 40*(5), 551–568.

Gretchen Schwarz became a teacher educator at Oklahoma State University. She now teaches media literacy and various curriculum and teaching courses at her alma mater, Baylor University. Research interests include media literacy, graphic novels, teacher lore, and various curriculum issues. She may be reached via e-mail at Gretchen_Schwarz@baylor.edu.

How EdTPA May Help Preservice Teachers Understand Children

Thomas Huston

ABSTRACT: In conducting this study, I sought to contribute to the scholarly discourse of understanding how preservice student teachers experienced evaluation via teacher performance assessments. More specifically, to gain insight into Midwest University's teacher performance assessment process, I explored preservice student teachers' experiences completing the Educative Teacher Performance Assessment (EdTPA). Additionally, I examined informants' interpretations and impressions from their involvement in the EdTPA program. Through extensive interviews and thematic data analysis, this study generally supported the contention that the process of completing EdTPA deepened student teachers' understanding of their educational experience in a number of domains, in turn suggesting a broader awareness and appreciation of the complexities of learning to teach. Data indicated that identified "realms of understanding" fell into four areas of insight related to education: understanding children, understanding instructional strategies, understanding via collective learning, and understanding self as teacher. These findings lead to several practical ways in which teacher education might be improved, particularly in the area of better understanding children.

There has been a great demand for evidence for a better understanding of the assessment of teacher quality. This "culture of evidence" can be found in many proposals calling for evaluation data to inform policy and practice (Knapp, Copland, & Swinnerton, 2007). While there are currently initiatives to study the success and impact of teacher education programs via "evidence portfolios" that track graduates, there are also teacher performance assessments (TPAs) that measure if a teacher is "ready for the job" and if the teacher has an impact on student achievement (American Association of Colleges for Teacher Education [AACTE], 2013; Marshall, Beare, & Newell, 2012). In 2011, the U.S. Department of Education published a document titled *Our Future, Our Teachers*, and a plan of action for teacher education reform was initiated (Beare, Marshall, Torgerson, Tracz, & Chiero, 2012a; Beare, Torgerson, Marshall, Tracz, & Chiero, 2012b). In this report, the Obama administration recommended, among other ideas, that reforming teacher education would include "performance-based indicators of quality," also known as TPAs (Marshall et al., 2012). Now led by current Secretary of

Education Arne Duncan, the call for a countrywide reform in teacher education programs is well under way (Beare et al., 2012b).

Educative Teacher Performance Assessment (EdTPA) provided an attempt to offer a national test for new teachers entering the profession to showcase the real work of teaching. The EdTPA assessment aims to provide a platform for the learning of teaching and to also offer useful feedback in order to inform teacher education programs (Hochstetler, 2014). EdTPA's design was intended to articulate the notion that an assessment needs to be implemented to find out if new teachers are prepared for the job and if new teachers can demonstrate effective teaching of his or her subject to a broad range of learners (AACTE, 2013). The use of the EdTPA assessment has grown at a rapid pace. The people involved with EdTPA's design and implementation have included more than 1,000 teacher educators and P–12 elementary and secondary teachers and more than 450 institutions of higher learning ("Oregon," 2014). In 2012, EdTPA was piloted in field testing in 22 states and 160 higher-education institutions and with more than 9,000 teacher candidates (Darling-Hammond & Hyler, 2013). In the fall of 2013, after 2 years of field testing at 250 institutions and more than 12,000 teacher candidate submissions of the portfolio to train scorers and refine the test for validity, EdTPA was declared operational ("Oregon," 2014). As of March 2014, 34 states, as well as the District of Columbia, are now using EdTPA, and 20 of those states link EdTPA completion to state licensure (Hochstetler, 2014).

Due to the wide use of TPAs for teacher education programs, future employment, and/or tenure of preservice, in-service, and administrative staff, it was important to conduct research on how these instruments are used and the impact they have on the people taking them. Some of the major concerns surrounding TPAs included defining quality teaching or teaching in general, reliability of the assessments, costs, and the potential limitations the assessments impose on teacher education programs (Sandholtz & Shea, 2012).

A Brief History of TPAs

There has been a long tradition of trying to understand the performances of "good" teachers, or what makes an "effective" teacher. One of the first attempts at creating objectives that suggest what a teacher should know or do occurred in 1929. The Commonwealth Teacher-Training Study presented 1,001 characteristics of what makes "good" teachers. The study stated that a "radical reorganization of the curricula of teacher-training institutions is demanded" because, according to the preface of the study, "teacher training curricula . . . have been developed without clear definition of objectives and with no logical plan of procedure" (Charters & Waples, 1929, p. 5). The idea was that teacher education programs would teach these characteristics to prospective educators and that teachers would know that they are "good" if they possess these characteristics.

Since 1929, there have been a multitude of assessment methods disseminated to ensure that prospective teachers are ready for the classroom. There appears to be an endless debate, both public and private, as to the most effective means of measuring quality of teaching or if measuring the construct is even possible. Recently, traditional assessments of the competency of teachers have been denounced because they lack authenticity and validity. Traditional licensure tests, such as the Praxis II, still lack evidence that passing such tests indicates effective teachers or competent teaching (Torgerson, Macy, Beare, & Tanner, 2009). These traditional assessments for teacher licensure have been overshadowed because of accumulating evidence that TPAs are better at assessing instructional practice, as both the process and the product are evaluated (Torgerson et al., 2009). EdTPA has been the most recent addition of an assessment for teacher licensure. Some states require the assessment for licensure, while others have piloted a low-stakes version. According to the AACTE (2013), "Candidates who have completed the EdTPA report feeling better prepared for the realities of teaching (para. 8)," although there is no direct study attributed to the claim. The AACTE (2013) stated that teachers should be assessed on multiple measures and that EdTPA is showing enormous promise as one of those measures.

Through TPAs, teacher candidates' performance is measured on the basis of expected knowledge and skills, and these criteria are developed through standards. TPAs assess whether teacher candidates achieve the criteria of the standards being measured. Research has suggested that one positive attribute of TPAs is that there is a high level of agreement that the assessments' objectives successfully coincide with effective teaching (Sandholtz & Shea, 2012). Unlike traditional paper-and-pencil tests required for certification, the TPA provides evidence of candidates' knowledge of curriculum and skills in instruction because of the artifacts required by TPAs (e.g., lessons, student work, and videotaped instruction) (Mitchell, Robinson, Plake, & Knowles, 2001; Pecheone & Chung, 2006; Sandholtz & Shea, 2012). Research has also suggested that the method (performance assessment) in which TPAs collects data on teacher candidates forecasts teaching ability better than the paper-and-pencil tests (Sandholtz & Shea, 2012; Uhlenbeck, Verloop, & Beijaard, 2002). Paper-and-pencil tests emphasize a candidate's content knowledge rather than how the candidate implemented his or her knowledge and skills (Darling-Hammond & Snyder, 2000; Sandholtz & Shea, 2012).

Research has shown that teacher candidates learned a great deal about their own teaching because of TPAs (Bunch, Aquirre, & Tellez, 2009; Darling-Hammond & Snyder, 2000; Desimone, Porter, Garet, Kwang, Birman, 2012; Sandholtz & Shea, 2012). Teacher candidates have reported that participating in TPAs gave them a substantial understanding of their actions within classrooms and the behavior of students and the confidence that they can plan better instruction (Okhremtchouck et al., 2009; Sandholtz & Shea, 2012). With so much weight placed on TPAs for not only teacher credentialing but also informing the quality of teacher education programs, great concerns about TPAs exist in terms of fairness and validity (Sandholtz & Shea, 2012). Resources such as TPA graders and the money used for hiring and training them are also major concerns (Sandholtz & Shea, 2012).

For the purposes of this study, the three most recent assessment programs for teacher performance are briefly described to shed light on the origins of the only currently nationally endorsed TPA: EdTPA. The National Board for Professional Teaching Standards is discussed first; then the Performance Assessment of California Teachers (PACT), which is based on the National Board; and, finally, EdTPA, a national version of PACT. All three assessments require similar components, both written and videotaped, to capture a beginning teacher's planning, instruction, and assessment.

The National Board for Professional Teaching Standards

More than 20 years ago, the National Board for Professional Teaching Standards (NBPTS) was designed as an attempt to professionally position standards and generate assessments for teachers (Darling-Hammond & Hyer, 2013). The goal of the NBPTS written portfolio was for teachers to acknowledge and display the board's standards in their teaching in writing. The plan for the NBPTS was to use the exam results to stimulate a professional discourse regarding teacher education (Burroughs, 2000). The NBPTS provided a portfolio framework for teacher candidates to present videotapes of instruction, teacher reflective analyses to help construct specific needs of the students, information about the classroom and school, and other contextual information that offers an image of a teacher's practice and how particular student needs or demands shape it (Darling-Hammond & Hyer, 2013).

PACT

Another TPA initiative emerged in California, titled PACT. PACT was born in 2002 when the California state legislature required all teacher candidates to be licensed via performance assessment (Darling-Hammond & Hyer, 2013). The assessment included three units—teacher's planning, instruction, and assessment—plus a requirement that candidates demonstrate how they would modify plans for English language learners and students with disabilities. As the teaching develops, teachers are asked to write about the purpose behind their actions and what they would have changed in retrospect. Candidates also focus on the academic language in the discipline being taught and the proficiency of that language. Candidates include student work, student assessments, and a reflective piece on both. Finally, candidates also include a video clip of a short teaching lesson (Darling-Hammond & Hyer, 2013). In 2008, the AACTE took interest in a national version of PACT, and EdTPA was born.

EdTPA

Shortly after the AACTE took note of PACT, teachers and teacher educators from across the country, in collaboration with Stanford University, put forth a national version of PACT, and since that time it has been referred to as EdTPA (Darling-Hammond & Hyer, 2013). EdTPA is currently overseen by the Stanford Center for Assessment, Learning, and Equity (SCALE), and it provides training and resources to interested clients. Linda Darling-Hammond, an education professor at Stanford University, is one of the original developers of EdTPA, and the Stanford coalition maintains control over the direction of the assessment (Au, 2013).

Stanford sought proposals for an administrative partner in the development of the national version, and Pearson Education Publishing was selected because of its work on the earlier NBPTS version of the test (Darling-Hammond & Hyer, 2013). Evaluation Systems is a group at Pearson Education Publishing and is known as an "operational partner" with SCALE. Its role is to distribute portfolios and provide report results to both teacher candidates and teacher education programs ("Oregon," 2014). Pearson's main role includes decisions about refinement, the process for scoring, and the qualifications of potential scorers. Thus, expert teachers and teacher educators are being recruited to score the portfolios (Darling-Hammond & Hyer, 2013).

The EdTPA assessment portfolio is considered both predictive and educative; it furnishes evidence-based awareness about how a teacher candidate might perform as a classroom teacher and identifies what might need improvement (AACTE, 2013). EdTPA's primary goals for teacher candidates are to demonstrate that they can devise lessons for multiple learners, measure the effectiveness of their lessons, and identify strengths and weaknesses of their instruction (Roberts, 2012). The developers of EdTPA want the assessment to provide a "valid, reliable measure that would respect the complexity of teaching, and reflect the academic knowledge and intellectual abilities required to advance student learning" (Hochstetler, 2014, p. 11). The EdTPA assessment requires candidates to show skills in the following:

> ➤ Planning around student learning standards
> ➤ Adapting plans for students based on their specific needs
> ➤ Implementing and assessing instruction
> ➤ Developing academic language
> ➤ Evaluating student learning
> ➤ Reflecting on how to improve student outcomes by continuing to refine teaching plans and strategies (Hochstetler, 2014, p. 11)

Different states are currently deciding on how EdPTA fits into their programs. Teacher candidates at the University of Memphis must first pass the EdTPA in order to take the state's licensing exam (Roberts, 2012). In 2013, all Tennessee Board of Regents campuses adopted the EdTPA evaluation (Roberts, 2012). As of 2014, New York State and Washington State require all teacher candidates to pass the EdTPA as a condition for licensure and as a marker for graduation from their university program. In the fall of 2015, Illinois will require that to obtain licensure, teacher candidates will have to pass EdTPA. However, Illinois amended the mandate "to remove the graduation stipulation" (Hochstetler, 2014, p. 9). By 2015, seven states will link EdTPA to teacher certification or to review their teacher preparation programs (Sawchuck, 2014). Beginning in 2017, Oregon will require all teacher candidates to pass the EdTPA assessment before they can obtain a teaching license (Hochstetler, 2014; "Oregon," 2014). The main argument for this move, according to the executive director of the Oregon Teacher Standards and Practices Commission, is that EdTPA will provide strong, effective, and prepared teachers ("Oregon," 2014).

How Others Have Experienced EdTPA

Ashley DeBerry, an elementary teacher in Tennessee, completed her EdTPA portfolio in 2011. In 2012, Shelby County Schools named her teacher of the year. Ashley was quoted as saying that her beginning successes at teaching were due in part to the "rigor of the evaluation" that EdTPA requires (Roberts, 2012, p. 1A). Regarding EdTPA, DeBerry said, "A lot of tasks in the evaluation made you think deeper—how can I make accommodations for children with disabilities? How is my classroom set up?" (Roberts, 2012, p. 2A). Now a full-time teacher, DeBerry helps student teachers complete the EdTPA portfolio.

Jaclyn Midgette, an education graduate of East Carolina University, was quoted calling the EdTPA "stressful, drawn out, and exhausting," yet she stated the belief that the components measured in the test, particularly planning, instruction, and analytical skills, are prevalent in her current instruction as a full-time teacher (Sawchuk, 2014, p. 34). Midgette stated, "The reflection process they forced us to do is something I see myself doing daily. It's just not written out" (Sawchuk, 2014, p. 34). Alyssa Thompson, another first-year teacher and graduate from Illinois State University, took the EdTPA in 2012. Thompson said she believed that the exam was repetitive, but she was happy that the test focused on lesson planning and the assessment of students and believes that she now has an advantage of understanding her state's teacher evaluation system. She supports the idea that obtaining a license should require the demonstration of a skill and says of the EdTPA, "It's hard, but becoming a professional should be hard" (Sawchuck, 2014, p. 38).

Methodology

This study was conducted with the understanding that it would not "prove" anything. Informants were not representative of a generalized body of individuals. Instead, the purpose was to develop insight, to raise questions that have not yet been examined, to compare these ideas and questions with the existing literature, and to address new topics that have not appeared in the research thus far. Information derived from this study can inform scholars and teacher educators who are responsible for the preparation of future teachers.

Theoretical Perspective

The reasoning behind the choice of one methodology over another is linked to the nature of the subject studied and the fundamental goals of the research. Researchers gain insight into a given social phenomenon through their attempts to understand experiences of the social world. The goal of interpretive research is to explain other people's understandings of their own experience (Goodman, 1985). Thus, given the goals and interests of this researcher, the methodology used in this qualitative study fell within the tradition of interpretive ethnographic research (Glaser & Strauss, 1975; Spradley, 1979).

Access to the informants' own experiences cannot be achieved because an "experience" is an indeterminate "thing." Therefore, extensive interviews and thematic data analysis, allowed this research to discern informant experiences. As Blumer (1969) emphasized, this methodology allows the researcher to meet all the principal requirements of an empirical science: to come face-to-face with the social world being studied, to explore and advance abstract questions about this world, to find connections between categories of data, to devise ideas about these relations, and to arrange ideas into an analytical system that others can understand.

Setting

Midwest University is a major public research university located in a town of close to 80,000 people. Aside from the university, the town is arguably most noted for its college basketball programs, several famous musicians, and a popular annual bicycle race. The racial makeup of the city is 83% white, 4.6% African American, 8% Asian, and 3.5% Latino. The university has around 43,000 students, and the campus is often included in lists of the top 10 most beautiful universities. There are five academic departments in Midwest University's school of education, and all of them are typically ranked in the top 15 nationally.

Participants

The four participants in this study were between the ages of 20 and 25. All are white and appear to have comfortable backgrounds and lifestyles. Each stated that he or she is normally good at taking tests, had pleasant experiences in prior K–12 public education, and achieved high grade-point averages in high school. What follows is a brief portrait of each participant in the study (see Table 1 detailing each participant's grade and school).

Eric

Eric loves science. He calls himself a "science person." He is from a very small town, with only 112 students in his graduating class. While in college, he has worked hard to improve his writing. While in high school, he worked with children and knew then that he wanted to teach. He believes that the best teachers are caring ones.

Alexis

Alexis grew up near Chicago and stated that her high school was a top five school in the state. Her graduating class was around 600. She said she has known that she wanted to be a teacher since first grade. Alexis said she enjoys project-based assignments more than standardized tests. She feels that the best educators want students to succeed.

Chelsey

Chelsey did not know that she wanted to be teacher until she started college. She said her high school experience was full of extracurricular activities. She stated that she is not good at taking multiple-choice tests but excels at essays and believes that writing is one of her strong suits. All her favorite teachers in public education possessed an excitement for the profession.

Eleanor

Eleanor said she always wanted to be an educator because she enjoys the process of learning. She loved her experience in public education and was particularly

Table 1.   Grade and School Types of Study Participants

Name	Grade	School
Alexis	K	Suburban
Chelsey	5	Suburban
Eleanor	K	Rural
Eric	3	Suburban

fond of her years in elementary school. She has always been good at multiple-choice assessments and essay tests. She is not particularly fond of math.

Informant Compensation

The small number of informants who volunteered for this study was perhaps due to insufficient marketing of the piloting of the EdTPA program. More likely, it was because Midwest University's performance assessment program already required significant additional work, such as preservice teachers keeping extensive journals of their experiences, videotaping of their lessons, and writing essays based on observations and experiences, among other extra assignments. It is speculated that this limited the number of volunteers. Combining the extra work required by the EdTPA portfolio with the already rigorous requirements of student teaching was daunting. The researcher felt it was important to provide payment for the informants given the added stress of participating in this study, completing both the EdTPA and student teaching. After the institutional review board approved the proposed budget rationale, all four participants in the study received $150 as compensation for the extra time and energy they devoted to the study.

Procedures

Data Collection

The study used two main sources of data: interviews and written artifacts. More specific information about these methods and the instruments follows. First, an assistant dean of education at Midwest University compiled a list of every student teacher at Midwest University who volunteered to pilot the EdTPA assessment. Those people were contacted by e-mail and provided an institutional review board study information sheet that explained the study. They were invited to participate in this study based in part on their willingness to be candid about their experiences completing the EdTPA portfolio. Typically, depending on the topic of the study, when conducting ethnographic types of research, there are numerous informants from whom to choose. However, only five Midwest University students volunteered to participate in the voluntary EdTPA performance assessment pilot program, and four of those five agreed to take part in this study.

After recruitment, each informant participated in three to five in-depth, formal interviews (Bussis, Crittenden, & Amarel, 1976; Spradley, 1979), each lasting from 60 to 90 minutes. Interviews focused on emerging themes, were audiotaped, and were conducted over the course of a 5-month academic semester. Document review was another method for exploring data. Portions of the *EdTPA Handbook* were reviewed before, during, and after interviews to enhance the understanding of what informants were experiencing with particular vocabulary, instructions, rubrics, and so on. Although no other documents were reviewed, informants did read sections of their answers or questions prompted by EdTPA reflection documents. These reflection documents present information about how informants assessed their students, thought they performed during instruction, and accommodated different learners during both their planning and their assessment. EdTPA's *Elementary Education Handbook with Literacy and Math Components* was also used as a source for developing and structuring interview questions. Informants often struggled with instructions found in the *EdTPA Handbook*, and I would explicate the instructions along with the informant(s) so that I could understand what particular aspects of the vocabulary were confusing to them.

Participant Settings

Eleanor and Chelsey were student teaching more than 2 hours away from Midwest University, thus requiring that interviews be conducted via videoconferencing. Both Alexis and Eric were an hour away and were teaching in the same school district. Because Alexis and Eric lived on campus and both taught at nearby schools, Alexis drove Eric to every interview. As a result, Alexis and Eric were always interviewed together.

The first round of formal interviews occurred between August 28 and September 4, 2014; the second between September 16 and September 18, 2014; and the third between September 30 and October 30, 2014. Final interviews were conducted between October 28 and November 5, 2014. As time progressed, a small number of informal interviews or discussions occurred "naturally." This process of continued rapport with informants is important in conducting ethnographic interviews; too much formal interrogation will erode established rapport and might limit informant cooperation (Spradley, 1979). Interviews with Alexis and Eric were conducted together and in my office. I conducted the interviews with Chelsey and Eleanor separately in my home office via videoconferencing software.

Informants initially answered grand-tour questions (Spradley, 1979) designed to understand their backgrounds and decisions to volunteer for EdTPA. These included why they went into teaching, why they selected to participate in the EdTPA evaluation process, what they hoped to gain from the EdTPA experience, and how they experienced it at various points during the student teaching semester. The grand-tour questions served as a catalyst through which informants could "tell their story." Following the grand tour, formal interviews were structured around various areas of concern, such as the personal histories of informants, the social and educational values in relation to EdTPA's goals, informant perceptions and feelings toward themselves and each other, and informant perspectives toward specific events that occurred and ideas that were expressed during the school semester.

The formal interviews introduced what Spradley (1979) referred to as "ethnographic elements." The intent was to steadily develop rapport rather than engage in interrogation, and, as a result, meaningful responses from the informants are elicited (Spradley, 1979). Ethnographic elements included discussing the project's explicit purpose (e.g., the direction of where the interview is to go), ethnographic explanations (e.g., project explanations, recording explanations, native language explanations, and interview explanations), and, finally, ethnographic questions (e.g., descriptive, structured, and contrast questions) (Spradley, 1979). The structure for following Spradley's (1979) method for formulating ethnographic questions included descriptive and structured questions in an effort to draw meaning from each formal interview that can then be used for analysis.

Data Analysis

Rather than waiting until all data were collected, analysis began on completion of the first interview and was ongoing (Glaser & Strauss, 1975). This was a formal process during which I reviewed my notes from the interview and the audiotape. My goal was to record my initial impressions of the interview. Then, each week, I transcribed and coded interviews, reviewed applicable portions of the EdTPA Handbook and reviewed my notes, searched and updated my literature review, and examined other available texts. The goal was to prepare for subsequent interviews. I would normally transcribe the interview and make notes, underline certain areas for tentative coding, and highlight portions that I wanted to explore later. As these transcriptions were read, ideas that started becoming repetitive became initial organizing themes. For example, very early in the study, beginning early in September 2014, emerging themes from the data were tentatively organized and coded as "Assessment," "Feedback," "Instructions," "Learning Student Backgrounds," "Support Network," "Test Anxiety," "The Role of the University Supervisor and EdTPA," "Suggestions for Test Revisions," "Being a Good Writer and EdTPA," and "Video." I also prepared for subsequent interviews by highlighting certain topics from the most recent transcribed text in different colored fonts. As time went on, I created documents that were organized by themes. Each document contained excerpts from the various transcripts of each informant.

During the entire process of collecting data, I used the constant comparative analytic method (Glaser & Strauss, 1975) to find out if the emerging tentative themes would crystalize; that is, did emerging themes make sense, and were the data cohesive, or were tentative themes diverging? Qualitative research that is considered "good" can provide a deep understanding of a topic (Ellingson, 2008). The process of crystallization "seeks to produce knowledge about a particular phenomenon through generating a deepened, complex interpretation," and such depth is generated through many details that are put together by assembling separate items (Ellingson, 2008, p. 10). One principle of crystallization is to "offer deep, thickly described, complexly rendered interpretations of meanings about a phenomenon or group," as these powerful themes or patterns, sustained with illustrations, provide a spacious view of the environment or event (Ellingson, 2008, p. 10). Crystallized themes also begin to take a "hard" or "physical" form when it has become apparent, over time, that informant meaning is understood exactly as intended via the terms the informants were using.

A method I used to discover if I really understood emerging themes was a process of discrepant data (Glaser & Strauss, 1975). That is, I searched for data that might disprove themes or that suggested that a set of themes was not that important or that these themes, as first understood, needed to be altered. For example, the fact that video became so important prompted me to ask, "Why is video so important?" Informants said that working with video was important because it was beneficial, so in follow-up interviews, I wanted to find out why video was beneficial. I had not set out to answer those questions; rather, those questions guided future interviews (Glaser & Strauss, 1975). I could then ascertain if other informants were having similar experiences given the emerging themes. Then, only after this process, I would type the transcription of the newest interview; carefully read, highlight, and code for existing or new themes; and repeat the process.

This process was repeated throughout the study, and as time passed and more interviews were conducted, emerging tentative themes transitioned into crystallized themes. For example, by the beginning of October 2014, data showed that there was almost no discussion of the university supervisor's role (although the topic was explored, the supervisor's role was limited because of the nature of the findings from the pilot study). Early tentative themes generated from the data, such as video and kindergarten, began to emerge more than "Assessment," while "Feedback" and "Test Anxiety" slowly began to evolve into "Concept of Audience." As more data were collected and analyzed, I also began to see a connection to the existing literature. For example, as informants began expressing anxiety about the people who would be assessing their portfolios, I began to see connections to Burroughs's (2001) work on audience and the NBPTS. By the beginning of November 2014, I had accumulated nearly 350 pages of transcribed data. Some of the themes generated by these data are presented in the following sections.

Limitations

The sample size of this study was small, and, therefore the specific findings of this study are not representative or generalizable to a larger target population. However, this study was not intended to generalize to all student teachers; rather, the goal was to understand this set of participants' unique experiences and their interpretations of those experiences. It also was possible that, because this research involved a pilot study of the EdTPA program and was not assessed by external scorers (i.e., "low stakes"), informants did not take certain aspects of EdTPA as seriously as they would had it been a "high-stakes" evaluation. Additionally, because of the perhaps lower-stakes nature of the participants' portfolios, the concept of audience may have been impacted. In other words, instead of writing for external reviewers, student participants focused on an audience consisting of instructors and faculty whom they already knew and trusted. Finally, the group interviews may have created unintended power issues, with some respondents dominating the interview discussion (Spradley, 1979). However, every effort was made for a balanced conversation between participants so that no one dominated the discussion. In the case in which two participants were interviewed together, I regularly asked directly for the quieter informant to contribute to the conversation. During my review of the transcriptions, I checked this potential concern and believe I was successful in getting a similar amount of participation from both respondents. Finally, it is possible that the compensation provided to study informants may have biased the finding influencing who participated and why. Future research might address some of these limitations by conducting comparison studies with one or more of the U.S. states where EdTPA is mandated for educator licensure.

Findings: Potential Benefits of EdTPA

Research has stated that teacher candidates learn a great deal about their own teaching because of TPAs (Bunch, Aquirre, & Tellez, 2009; Darling-Hammond & Snyder, 2000; Sandholtz & Shea, 2012). The data from this study generally supported the contention that the process of completing EdTPA deepened students' understanding of their own teaching. Teacher candidates gained a deeper understanding of their educational experience in a number of realms. These realms of deeper understanding clearly implicated a broader awareness or appreciation of the complexities of learning to teach. The data indicated that these realms of understanding fell into four areas of insight related to education: understanding children, understanding instructional strategies, understanding via collective learning, and understanding self as teacher. The following section addresses how informants gained a broader awareness of understanding children.

Understanding Children

Perhaps one of the more important aspects to teaching is the idea that teachers should understand whom they are teaching. EdTPA requires student teachers to answer prompts that ask specific questions about the elementary students for which they will be teaching. The prompts are titled Elementary

Literacy Context for Learning Information and Elementary Mathematics Context for Learning Information (SCALE, 2013). These prompts ask informants to share information about the school in which they teach, the class featured in the assessment, and details about the students in the class. The last section of the prompt asks informants to "consider the variety of learners in your class who may require different strategies/supports or accommodations/modifications to instruction or assessment," including "English language learners, gifted students needing greater support or challenge, students with individualized education programs (IEPs) or 504 plans, struggling readers, and underperforming students or those with gaps in academic knowledge" (SCALE, 2013, pp. 49–51). The data suggested that the informants in this study thought more deeply about the makeup of their classroom because of the EdTPA Context for Learning prompts.

When informants were asked to provide details about their positive learning experiences with EdTPA, many responses suggested attention to details and accommodations for their elementary students that normally would not have occurred without the portfolio. It should be noted that many informants, such as Alexis, referred to the *Context for Learning* form as the "Cultural Section." Take, for example, the following:

> EdTPA made me think more about background and culture. We have parent teacher conferences in a few weeks and I feel like that's going to give me even more insight into these kids' backgrounds. I hadn't thought about student backgrounds until I started filling out the cultural section. Normally, I know if a student is high achieving or high ability, but now I was able to connect or ask why. I am thinking about their backgrounds a bit more. (Alexis, personal communication, September 2, 2014)

Above, Alexis stated that because of the *Context for Learning* portion of the portfolio assessment, she was better prepared for parent–teacher conferences because she gained more insight into particular student backgrounds. More importantly, she stated that she had not thought about the aspect of why a student's background might occur or develop and, as a result, thought more deeply on students and abilities as an attempt to understand why labels such as "high achieving" for children are generated. Finally, Alexis stated that she made connections with student backgrounds, and this could possibly affect her approach to instruction.

The *Context for Learning* section of the portfolio seemed to continuously generate deeper thoughts for each of the informants, and every informant responded positively to this new area of reflection. Other informants had similar responses regarding the *Context for Learning* section of the portfolio. For example, Chelsey and Eleanor stated,

> The cultural section helped my planning. I was the one-on-one person for a lot of the students with IEPs. I got to know them specifically, so I could make comments in my planning about what to do and what helps them. I've also gotten to know

what strategies are the best for them. (Chelsey, personal communication, September 4, 2014)

I think it's great that we had to do the context for learning because I know that in all of our reading classes, they say time and time again that you have to find out who you're teaching before you can teach. So I thought that was very helpful. It talked about "Did you engage everyone" and I think that's something I have to constantly ask myself because I have some diverse learners. (Eleanor, personal communication, August 28, 2014)

Chelsey's comment stated that her planning was directly affected by the information she gathered while completing the *Context for Learning* prompt. She thought more about approaches to planning by designing instructional strategies that are best suited for her students with IEPs. Eleanor referenced the emphasis placed on the importance of student background information within her teacher education courses. She stated that the *Context for Learning* prompts encouraged her to reflect on how to continuously engage all learners via understanding of her students.

Below, Chelsey discussed specific details of how she arranged her classroom and student partners because of gaining knowledge about her students:

The cultural section made me focus specifically where these students were going to be at this time and who they were going to partner with, etc. I designated the partners beforehand and we paired them high level with high level, medium with medium, and low with low. The partners that needed accommodations were partnered together, but they were partnered with my supervising teacher in the back. So that was kind of planned, based on the reading levels and other things that were discovered while completing the cultural section. (Chelsey, personal communication, September 18, 2014)

Chelsey's comments show how in depth she was reflecting on students' prior knowledge and backgrounds and as a result made adjustments to instruction. Chelsey then discussed how filling out the *Context for Learning* section of the portfolio affected one of her lessons:

After filling out the culture section, I discovered that we were focusing on a story that might be offensive to a few students because their backgrounds kind of related to it, and so I just made sure everything was natural, obviously because that's how you should be as a teacher. Those students were really interested in the story, and that was good because they provided some nice feedback. For example, the story took place in Africa, and I used a map to introduce the story. The students that had been to Africa before with their families stated things like, "Oh I've been here," and "This is what it's like now." It was nice because they helped the lesson a lot, and because students added their personal experiences. (Chelsey, personal communication, September 18, 2014)

Chelsey discussed how the notion of "audience" also played a role in informants examining their classroom makeup when it came to planning and instruction. Finally, the *Context for Learning* prompt encouraged Chelsey to examine how she might respond to those students who needed accommodations if she were teaching alone:

> The cultural section also made me focus on what I would do if was teaching alone. So that kind of was interesting that I learned some things about that in these documents. For example, my supervising teacher was in the back of the class working with some of the IEP students. In the document I added a paragraph or two discussing how if I didn't have any help or support, then I would put certain students all at the same table. That way, I could just be at one table and wouldn't have to walk around the classroom all at the same time by myself. It would eliminate trying to run back and forth to different students that needed help. (Chelsey, personal communication, October 30, 2014)

In the above exchange, Chelsey was conscious of the students in her classroom and was even extrapolating certain circumstances in order to define her role as a lead teacher in a future classroom. Chelsey also mentioned that an emphasis on student backgrounds existed in her teacher education course work. She stated that her attention to understanding students was more focused because of the portfolio's video requirement, and as a result she thought about her students more:

> Obviously throughout my undergraduate experience I focused on accommodations, but I don't think [the accommodations] would be as detailed as they are if I wasn't going to be in a videotape. It definitely made me think about it a little bit more. (Chelsey, personal communication, September 4, 2014)

The data in this study aligned with other research suggesting that EdTPA prompted deeper thoughts about understanding children's backgrounds (Roberts, 2012). As mentioned, Ashley DeBerry, an elementary teacher in Tennessee who completed her EdTPA portfolio in 2011, stated that because of the tasks in EdTPA, she thought more deeply about children with disabilities, how her classroom was set up, and how she can accommodate the needs of her students (Roberts, 2012, p. 2A).

By design, the EdTPA portfolio required a large amount of reflection on what occurs before, during, and after teaching. EdTPA also requires student teachers to provide answers to multiple commentaries on planning, instruction, assessment, and video. Through these commentaries, informants continued to think about their students and make appropriate changes to their instruction. As a result, those reflections on instruction resulted in a deeper understanding of both students and appropriate instructional strategies, as will be discussed below.

Discussion and Implications

The usefulness of any study is gauged not only by what the findings elucidate about particular phenomena but also by what such findings suggest about future practice. As a result of this study, some of the findings reported suggest a consideration of certain implications for overall teacher education. In particular, four themes worthy of further discussion emerged in the findings: effects of videotaping, the EdTPA Context for Learning Prompt, collective learning, and audience. The following section addresses practical implications related to EdTPA's Context for Learning prompt.

Implications for Teacher Education Curricula and for Further Educational Research

The findings that surfaced from this study provide some tangible revelations into the student teaching experience. Implications result from the findings that suggest practical ways in which teacher education might be improved on, particularly in regard to considerations for student teaching programs. This section presents a discussion and recommendations for teacher education curricula on the topics of the EdTPA Context for Learning prompt.

The EdTPA Context for Learning Prompt

Apart from analyzing the effects of EdTPA as a whole, it is equally important to examine certain parts of EdTPA that provided informants in this study profound insight into various educational realms. Teacher educators and educational institutions who may not be interested in using TPAs might still gain valuable information that would enhance their teacher education programs and ultimately its prospective educators. One component of EdTPA that could be utilized as a stand-alone assignment for educational course work and/or student teaching is the Context for Learning prompt.

The *Context for Learning* prompt found within the EdTPA assessment fostered deep reflection on classroom students' backgrounds, including information on language, culture, and learning. As previously discussed, in these sections, the informants were asked about the school where they were teaching, the class featured in the assessment, and the students in the class featured in the assessment. As mentioned previously, the prompt asked informants to "consider the variety of learners in your class who may require different strategies/supports or accommodations/modifications to instruction or assessment," including "English language learners, gifted students needing greater support or challenge, students with IEPs or 504 plans, struggling readers, and underperforming students or those with gaps in academic knowledge" (SCALE, 2013, pp. 49–51). As reported, informants provided many details on how this prompt engaged them in new ways that enhanced their planning, instruction, and assessment and ultimately led to a better understanding of children and of themselves.

EdTPA's *Context for Learning* prompt has not gone unnoticed. It has already been recognized at Midwest University as a useful tool apart from EdTPA. In the fall of 2014, the anchor program at Midwest University announced the adoption of a similar *Context for Learning Information* addendum to the anchor program's student teaching seminar in upcoming semesters. The purpose of the meeting was to collect feedback from university supervisors. Many of the supervisors were somewhat skeptical that student teachers would have the time to collect such information. Based on the informant responses in this study, it would appear that gathering this information is a wise addition to requirements because of its helpfulness with understanding children. It is equally important for teacher educators to examine a similar prompt even without implementing a TPA, especially in light of the desire for prospective educators to know and understand the growing array of diverse students.

The *Context for Learning* prompt provided by EdTPA is a prompt directly linked to EdTPA, and it helped informants understand their children better. Further research might explore if certain questions posed within the *Context for Learning* prompt fostered the crucial social dynamic that was needed for learning to occur (Sandholtz & Shea, 2012). The major activities of teaching take place in real time and include social and intellectual communication. The students in the environment form this communication, and therefore the task of teaching is considered very complex (Sandholtz & Shea, 2012). Teachers approach the context of the environment, and the students shape this context based on their cultural and linguistic backgrounds. Therefore, teachers have to implement expert judgment when approaching specific content and students, and because of this contextually specific dynamic that teaching requires, scenarios that arise are often not formulaic (Sandholtz & Shea, 2012). In the past, this nonsingular focus on the achievement of students becomes problematic when TPAs enter the context of teaching. How do EdTPA or TPAs play a role within these contextually specific dynamics?

One example could be found of how the *Context for Learning* prompt provided by EdTPA compelled informants to consistently analyze classroom students' cultural and linguistic backgrounds. Because of this prompt, the preservice teacher understood more about how students shape the context of the environment and therefore was able to implement better judgment when approaching specific content and students. Successful educators' teaching has been shown to encapsulate a socially constructed undertaking conditional on the components (physical, historical, and cultural) of the environment (Sandholtz & Shea, 2012). This idea suggests that educators might function successfully within a community on entering a mode of enculturation into that specific community's subjective point of view (Brown & Duguid, 1991). The *Context for Learning* prompt successfully initiated a mode of enculturation among informants. Without this prompt, informants may have been slower to function successfully within the classroom community. New research could examine how studying the context of students increases expert judgment, enculturation, and, ultimately, successful teaching.

The findings in this study supported previous and emerging research on TPAs. The developers of EdTPA wanted the assessment to provide a "valid, reliable measure that would respect the complexity of teaching, and reflect the academic knowledge and intellectual abilities required to advance student learning" (Hochstetler, 2014, p. 11). These findings suggested that TPAs provide student teachers with a considerable understanding of their actions within classrooms and of the behavior of students and with better planning of instruction (Okhremtchouck et al., 2009; Sandholtz & Shea, 2012). The results of this study also suggested that informants showed through product and process that they can devise lessons for multiple learners, measure the effectiveness of the lessons, and identify strengths and weaknesses of their instruction via reflection (Roberts, 2012). In addition, the results aligned with the 96% of teacher candidates who described their experience with EdTPA as an experience that facilitated learning, as in the study by Darling-Hammond and Hyler (2013). Those candidates felt that they became enlightened specifically on their own teaching practice and how students learn (Darling-Hammond & Hyer, 2013). Informants in this study gained a better understanding of children, instructional strategies, and educational topics via collective learning and gained insight about their developing teacher identity. **TEP**

References

American Association of Colleges of Teacher Education (AACTE). (2013). *The changing teacher preparation profession: A report for AACTE's professional education data system (PEDS)*. New York, NY: Author.

Au, W. (2013). What's a nice test like you doing in a place like this? The EdTPA and corporate education "reform." *Rethinking Schools*, *27*(4), 22–27.

Beare, P., Marshall, J. Torgerson, C., Tracz, S., & Chiero, R. (2012). Toward a culture of evidence: Factors affecting survey assessment of teacher preparation. *Teacher Education Quarterly*, *39*(1), 159–173.

Beare, P., Torgerson, C., Marshall, J., Tracz, S., & Chiero, R. (2012). Examination of alternative programs of teacher preparation on a single campus. *Teacher Education Quarterly*, *39*(4), 55–74.

Blumer, H. (1969). *Symbolic interactionism: Perspective and method*. Englewood Cliffs, NJ: Prentice-Hall.

Brown, J. S., & Duguid, P. (1991). Organizational learning and communities-of-practice: Toward a unified view of working, learning, and innovation. *Organization Science*, *2*(1), 40–57.

Bunch, G., Aguirre, J., & Téllez, K. (2009). Beyond the scores: Using candidate responses on high stakes performance testing to inform teacher preparation for English learners. *Issues in Teacher Education*, *18*(1), 103–128.

Burroughs, R. (2000). Community of practice and discourse communities: Negotiating boundaries in NBPTS certification. *Teachers College Record*, *102*(2), 344–374.

Burroughs, R. (2001). Composing standards and composing teachers: The problem of national board certification. *Journal of Teacher Education*, *52*(3), 223–232.

Bussis, A., Chittendem, E., & Amarel, M. (1976). *Beyond surface curriculum*. Boulder, CO: Westview Press.

Charters, W. W., & Waples, D. (1929). *The Commonwealth Teacher-Training Study*. Chicago: University of Chicago Press.

Darling-Hammond, L., & Snyder, J. (2000). Authentic assessment of teaching in context. *Teaching and Teacher Education, 15*(5–6), 523–545.

Darling-Hammond, L., & Hyler M. (2013). The role of performance assessment in developing teaching as a profession. *Rethinking Schools, 27*(4), 10–15.

Desimone, L., Porter, A., Garet, M., Kwang, S., & Birman, B. (2012). Effects of professional development on teachers' instruction: Results from a three-year longitudinal study. *Educational Evaluation and Policy Analysis, 24*(2), 81–112.

Ellingson, L. (2008). *Engaging crystallization in qualitative research: An introduction*. Los Angeles: Sage.

Glaser, G., & Strauss, A. (1975). *The discovery of the grounded theory: Strategies for qualitative research*. Chicago: Aldine.

Goodman, J. (1985). What students learn from early field experiences: A case study and critical analysis. *Journal of Teacher Education, 36*(6), 42–48.

Hochstetler, S. (2014). The critical role of dispositions: What's missing in measurements of English teacher candidate effectiveness. *The Clearing House: A Journal of Educational Strategies, Issues, and Ideas, 87*(1), 9–14.

Knapp, M., Copland, M., & Swinnerton, J. (2007). Understanding the promise and dynamics of data-informed leadership. In P. Moss (Ed.), *Evidence and decision making, the 106th yearbook of the National Society for the Study of Education* (pp. 74–104). Malden, MA: Blackwell.

Marshall, J., Beare, P., & Newell, P. (2012). U.S. Department of Education's teacher education reform: How does your program rate? *The Renaissance Group, 1*(1), 3–4.

Mitchell, K. J., Robinson, D. Z., Plake, B. S., & Knowles, K. T. (Eds.). (2001). *Testing teacher candidates: Licensure examines play limited role in boosting teacher quality*. Retrieved from: http://www8.nationalacademics.org/onpinews/nwsitem .aspx?RecordD=10090

Okhremtchouck, I., Seiki, S., Gilliland, B., Ateh, C., Wallace, M., & Kato, A. (2009). Voices of pre-service teachers: Perspectives on the performance assessment for California teachers (PACT). *Issues in Teacher Education, 18*(1), 18–62.

Oregon joins movement to assess skills of aspiring teachers. (2014, March 21). http:// www.prnewswire.com/news-releases/oregon-joins-movement-to-assess-skills-of-aspiring-teachers-251431121.html

Pecheone, R. L., & Chung, R. R. (January/February 2006). Evidence in teacher Education: The performance assessment for California teachers (PACT). *Journal of Teacher Education, 57*(1), 22–36.

Roberts, J. (2012, November 3). University of Memphis puts teeth in teacher training. *The Commercial Appeal*, pp. 1A, 2A.

Sandholtz, J. H., & Shea, L. M. (2012). Predicting performance: A comparison of university supervisors' predictions and teacher candidates' scores on a teaching performance assessment. *Journal of Teacher Education, 63*(1), 39–50.

Sawchuk, S. (2014). Performance-based test for teachers rolls out. *Education Week, 33*(3), 1–22.

Spradley, J. (1979). *The ethnographic interview*. New York: Rinehart & Winston.

Stanford Center for Assessment, Learning, and Equity. (2013). *EDTPA questions and answers about NCATE accreditation*. http://edtpa.aacte.org/wp-content/uploads/2013/01/edTPA-QA-about-NCATE-Accreditation-10-12-20121.pdf

Torgerson, C. W., Macy, S. R., Beare, P., & Tanner, D. E. (2009). Fresno assessment of student teachers: A teacher performance assessment that informs practice. *Issues in Teacher Education, 18*(1), 63–82.

Uhlenbeck, A. M., Verloop, N., & Beijaard, D. (2002). Requirements for an assessment procedure for beginning teachers: Implications for recent theories on teaching and learning. *Teaches College Record, 104*(2), 242–272.

U.S. Department of Education. (2011). *Our future, our teachers: The Obama administration's plan for teacher education reform and improvement.* http://www.2ed.gov/inits/ed/index/html

Thomas Huston has been working in the field of education since 1996. He received his MS and BA from Purdue University and taught at the secondary level for 3 years. He continued his education at Indiana University, Bloomington, where he received his PhD in curriculum and instruction, specializing in curriculum studies and social foundations of education. His teaching interests include English education, multicultural education, new media, and educational anthropology. His current research concentrates on the preparation and professional development of teachers, along with additional interests, including developing effective curricula for critical media literacy and the deliberative arts. He may be reached via e-mail at tphuston@indiana.edu.

Preservice Teacher Field Experience Learning Through Early Literacy Assessment

Documenting the Knowledge, Skills, and Dispositions

CAROL A. ZEHMS-ANGELL AND YUKO IWAI

ABSTRACT: This study explored 21 elementary school preservice teachers' learning experience on early literacy assessment. In particular, it focused on what knowledge and skills they perceived they gained after administrating Clay's Observation Survey with children in school. The participants received training on Clay's Observation Survey and administered it during their field experience. Data were collected from a questionnaire. Results showed that their confidence levels in administrating Clay's Observation Survey increased; they identified three early literacy skills (pictures, letter–sound relationship, and basic concepts of print) as the areas they learned the most; their comments on young children's literacy learning were general and did not provide any details.

Lawmakers, through federal legislation, require schools to hire highly qualified teachers (Individuals with Disabilities Education Improvement Act [IDEIA], 2004; No Child Left Behind [NCLB] Act, 2002). Highly qualified or well-prepared teachers must be able to monitor student progress and provide best-practice intervention in order to close the achievement gap that currently exists for young literacy learners. As a result, school of education faculty must ensure that their teacher candidates are well prepared. The International Reading Association (IRA, 2003) supports this when it states, "Only if teachers are well prepared to implement research-based practices and have the professional knowledge and skill to alter those practices when they are not appropriate for particular children will every child learn to read" (p. 3). Researchers and school professionals, then, cannot dispute the importance of preparing qualified literacy instructors.

School professionals are mandated to implement Response to Intervention (RtI) (IDEIA, 2004; NCLB, 2002). When implementing an RtI process, classroom teachers are required to monitor student progress through ongoing assessments and create effective instructional practices used with each child. Teachers must not only administer appropriate assessments but also analyze data and create appropriate instructional settings for children based on that data. Developers of the 10 Interstate New Teacher Assessment and Support Consortium (InTASC) Model Core Teaching Standards (Council of

Chief State School Officers, 2011, p. 15) concur with well-prepared teachers needing these skills when they state, "The teacher understands and uses multiple methods of assessment to engage learners in their own growth, to monitor learner progress, and to guide the teacher's and learner's decision making" (InTASC main principle 6).

Similarly, the assessment standard of the IRA (2010) states that teachers should "use a variety of assessment tools and practices to plan and evaluate effective reading and writing instruction" (element 3). To prepare highly qualified teacher candidates, teacher preparation faculty must ensure that the graduating candidates have an understanding of research-based instructional practices, assessment implementation, data analysis, and instructional planning. Well-prepared teachers, therefore, must be skilled in these essential skills for schools to focus on student success. Teacher preparation faculty use professional standards to guide teacher preparation programs and the legal mandates now placed on teacher candidates.

Assessment tools that can drive instruction and can help teachers know when to alter practices are essential to well-prepared teachers. Specifically, classroom literacy teachers must be able to "select, develop, administer, and interpret assessments, both traditional and electronic, for specific purposes" (IRA, 2010, Standard 3.2) and "use assessment data to evaluate students' responses to instruction and to develop relevant next steps for teaching" (IRA, 2010, Standard 3.3). Teacher observation and other assessment tools used within the classroom help teachers make informed decisions about children's instructional needs. Many (1999) states, "It is the act of . . . assessing, whether informally or through formal assessment techniques, that provides the insights to make . . . responsive teaching possible" (p. 572), which is a key to effective classroom instruction. This mirrors the requirements when implementing RtI and progress monitoring.

Preservice teachers require instructional assessment knowledge and skills to be well prepared when graduating. In particular, preservice teachers must have an understanding of literacy assessment tools, such as running records, miscue analysis, and Clay's Observation Survey (Clay, 1993, 2000), and how to collect data and use those data to guide instruction. If preservice teachers are to become responsive teachers as mandated, they need to be trained in the careful administration and use of observation techniques and literacy assessment tools, both formal and informal. Faculty should prepare preservice teachers to use assessment data to create instruction that is appropriate to facilitate student progress.

Campbell and Evans (2000) devised a study to see if 65 preservice teachers incorporated sound assessments into lesson plans during student teaching. After reviewing 309 lesson plans, these researchers found that the student teachers were not following recommended assessment practices despite extensive assessment training in their prior campus course work and called for further studies to investigate the link between assessment training and preservice teachers' application of such training. Volante and Fazio (2007) examined literacy assessment among 69 elementary/junior high preservice teachers. They found that the preservice teachers indicated lower self-efficacy about literacy assessment and expressed the need to improve their practical knowledge in this area. Bain, Brown, and Jordan (2009) noted that university instructors need to include more instructions about assessments and teach critical evaluation skills for future educators in their teacher education programs.

Researchers need to document preservice teacher perceptions as evidence when looking into effective literacy teacher education programs. Maloch et al. (2003) followed 101 novice teachers into their professional teaching experiences and asked for reflections on the teacher preparation programs. Study participants noted the value and variety of fieldwork experiences and student teaching placements. Preservice teachers perceived early fieldwork experiences allowing for development of expertise in more realistic classroom settings as more beneficial experiences. Preservice teachers in this study also commented on the value of one-on-one tutoring experiences and the opportunity to communicate with parents as part of their field experiences. Maloch et al. (2003) recommended that field experiences include careful supervision and reflective dialogue to lead preservice teachers to make instructional decisions and feel comfortable with their own teaching. Oboler and Gupta (2010) pointed out the important connection between practice and theory through the field experiences where teacher candidates would further strengthen their knowledge and practical skills though learning by doing.

Angell and Heiden (2004) demonstrated that preservice teachers who had received training in literacy were able to administer Clay's Observation Survey (Clay, 1993, 2000) and interpret the results of the literacy assessment tasks accurately. From this study, Angell and Heiden (2004) suggested that preservice teachers acquired a good deal of knowledge about the early literacy development of young children through their experience in administering the assessment to first graders in a school setting. Angell and Heiden (2006) investigated 19 preservice teachers' dispositions to document what they valued about practical field experiences and the usefulness of the early literacy assessment tools they had been taught to use. Overall, 96% of the preservice teachers stated that the field-based assessment experience helped them to understand literacy behaviors in young children. Preservice teachers reported feeling "confident" (57%) or "very confident" (39%) in being able to administer the assessment tasks. Similarly, 79% of the preservice teachers reported confidence in their ability to interpret the assessment results. The majority of preservice teachers (92%) reported that they would choose to administer "most" if not "all" of Clay's Observation Survey tasks if hired in a first-grade classroom in the future.

After considering this research, we were curious to know what knowledge the preservice teachers perceived they gained after implementing the informal early literacy assessments, specifically Clay's Observation Survey (Clay, 1993, 2000), in real-world settings after on-campus training in assessment and an off-campus field experience. The researchers proposed to document preservice teachers' perceived learning of early literacy development and assessment after completing an on-site administration and analysis of results of Clay's Observation Survey (Clay, 1993, 2000). Specifically, the researchers wanted to document specific skill areas that preservice teachers felt they learned about, including assessment administration and young children's literacy development.

Importance of the Study

Teacher education professionals are responsible for much of the published research that informs the field regarding effective literacy instruction methods, strategies, materials, and assessments. Little research exists on preservice teachers' perceptions of their own learning about assessment implementation and perceptions of young children's early literacy development through assessment. This study provides documentation within this field of literature. The researchers aim to provide a baseline of study results from which future researchers can begin to build in order to inform preservice teacher preparation programs regarding their growth in early literacy development and assessment concepts, especially as they relate to RtI and progress monitoring. Essentially, after preservice teachers are effectively trained to provide reliable early literacy assessment and use the data to monitor children's progress through stages in reading development (Angell & Heiden, 2004) and show value in such training (Angell & Heiden, 2006), teacher preparation faculty can begin to provide evidence of effective literacy assessment instruction and preservice teacher growth in required competencies.

Method

The setting for the study was an elementary-level reading methods course in an undergraduate teacher preparation program at a midwestern comprehensive university. Early literacy assessment training was part of the reading methods course. The participants were preservice students just admitted to the teacher education program and were concurrently enrolled in the first pre–student teaching field experience delivered in a professional development school model. Preservice teachers received university course instruction on-site at an elementary school and were assigned to an elementary classroom (grades 1 through 5) to complete a 50-hour field experience requirement in the same building. As part of the field experience, preservice teachers tutored a child from their respective field experience classroom. Classroom teachers chose the students to receive tutoring assistance. The course instructor taught the preservice teachers how to administer Clay's Observation

Survey to provide the preservice teachers with a tool to assess first graders in a school setting later in the semester. Training consisted of two 3-hour class periods to introduce and practice administering the assessment tasks and a 1-hour session on interpretation of assessment results and relating the results to stages of reading development (Leslie & Jett-Simpson, 1997). The assessment training included the administration of Clay's Observation Survey to all first-grade students within the building and interpretation of data for the five Clay's Observation Survey tasks, which included concepts about print, word reading, letter identification, vocabulary writing, and hearing and recording sounds in words (Clay, 1993, 2000).

Subjects

Twenty-one university students who were enrolled in the elementary reading methods course participated in the study. They were in the first professional field experience course sequence. As part of their experience, preservice teachers tutored a struggling reader from their assigned classroom. Following the field-based assessment experience, university students were asked to complete a survey, containing a four-level Likert scale and open-ended questions about the experience.

Data Collection

The survey measured preservice teachers' confidence level in administrating Clay's Observation Survey and consisted of two parts. Part A of the survey contained 23 four-level Likert scale items. It includes three subcategories: assessment administration (six questions), preservice teacher learning about young children's literacy (10 questions), and preservice teacher literacy learning (seven questions). The first 16 questions in the subcategories of assessment administration and preservice teacher learning about young children's literacy were formatted in a retrospective survey format (Gutek, 1978; Kindle & Colby, 2008) written in a then–now sequence. Questions asked students to compare and rate their learning on administration and literacy learning topics before they had the experience (then) and after the assessment experience (now) to document where the students perceived growth. Students responded to both "then" and "now" ratings after the literacy assessment training and implementation was completed. Part A survey items concluded with the third sub-category, pre-service teacher literacy learning, which included seven items written in a traditional four-level Likert scale questions format, using "none," "little," "moderate," and "high" as level descriptors. These seven items were designed to measure the perceived learning contribution the experience had on their learning about early literacy assessment and young children's learning (see Tables 1 to 3).

Part B of the survey asked students to respond to 17 open-ended questions about their literacy assessment learning and young children's literacy. It consisted of two subcategories: early literacy assessment administration (seven questions) and preservice teacher learning young children's literacy learning (10 questions). The questions in the early literacy assessment administration subcategory used the stem "What did you learn about . . . ?" and asked six assessment administration items, including administrating formal assessments, scoring formal assessments, interpreting data from formal assessment, the ways young children respond to formal assessment, instructional application through formal assessment administration, and the assessment environment. An additional question in this subcategory was related to any unforeseen problems the university students encountered during the administration.

In the second subcategory, preservice teachers were also asked 10 questions about their learning in regard to young children's literacy, including alphabet, sight words, pictures, letter–sound relationships, basic concepts of print, writing, learning differences, voice–print match, range of ability, and instructional needs. The open-ended stem "What did you learn about young children and . . . ?" was used. Open-ended questions mirrored those in the 16 retrospective questions in the first two subcategories asked in Part A of the survey.

Data Analysis and Results: Part A

Of the 21 surveys distributed to the preservice teachers, 21 surveys were returned (100%). The overall results show that students perceived that they learned about early literacy assessment and young children's literacy through a variety of instructional methods.

Survey results were tabulated to reflect the percentage of students responding to each comparison rating level for then–now ratings, respectively. As expected, preservice teachers tended to rate their previous knowledge (then) on each assessment topic lower than their current knowledge (now) on corresponding assessment-related topics after completing an early literacy assessment experience with young children.

Assessment-Related Preservice Learning

When asked to rate their level of learning on the assessment topics compared to their previous knowledge, the majority of students selected the moderate to high ratings to describe their learning growth. On assessment-related topics, preservice teachers tended to report an increase of two rating levels, from no knowledge to moderate knowledge, with the exception of their ratings learning about children's behavior during assessment and learning about the assessment environment, which increased only one rating level (see Table 1).

Table 1. Then–Now Survey Results for Assessment-Related Topics (Subcategory 1 in Part A)

Assessment Item	Then					Now				
Level	None	Little	Moderate	High	%	None	Little	Moderate	High	%
Administration of tasks	**71**	24	5	0	100	0	5	**57**	38	100
Scoring of tasks	**76**	24	0	0	100	0	5	**57**	38	100
Interpreting of tasks	**76**	24	0	0	100	0	5	**81**	14	100
Child behavior during assessment	48	**52**	0	0	100	0	5	**75**	20	100
Instructional application of outcomes	**76**	24	0	0	100	0	14	**62**	24	100
Assessment environment	43	**52**	5	0	100	0	5	**50**	45	100

Table 2. Then–Now Survey Results for Preservice Teacher Learning About Young Children's Literacy (Subcategory 2 in Part A)

Young Children's Learning Item	Then					Now				
	None	Little	Moderate	High	%	None	Little	Moderate	High	%
Alphabet	10	67	24	0	101*	0	5	52	43	100
Sight words	33	48	19	0	100	0		38	57	100
Pictures	14	43	38	5	100	0	10	29	62	101*
Letter–sound relationships	23	59	14	5	101*	0	9	36	55	100
Basic concepts of print	24	57	19	0	100	0	5	62	33	100
Writing	25	55	20	0	100	0	5	60	35	100
Learning differences	10	48	43	0	101*	0	5	52	43	100
Voice–print match	38	48	14	0	100	5	5	52	43	100
Range of ability	10	62	29	0	101*	0	11	67	22	100
Instructional needs	10	62	29	0	101*	0	9	55	36	100

Note. * = value higher than 100% due to rounding.

Young Children's Literacy Preservice Learning

When asked to rate their previous knowledge to their current knowledge regarding young children's learning topics after assessment instruction and administration, students again tended to rate their previous knowledge lower than their current knowledge. Interestingly, preservice teachers tended to say that they had a "little knowledge" regarding young children's literacy learning prior to the assessment instruction and administration experience. Students reported similar levels of growth on the assessment-related topics. For knowledge gained regarding young children's literacy, preservice teachers tended to report an increase of one rating level, with the exception of their knowledge of sight words, pictures, and letter–sound relationships. These three areas increased two rating levels (see Table 2).

Source of Preservice Teacher Learning

Preservice teachers rated the source of their learning of literacy assessment and young children's literacy. Overall, preservice teachers rated the literacy assessment instructional strategies received as "moderate-" to "high-"level sources for learning about literacy assessment and young children's learning. Only one (5%) preservice teacher rated viewing a video of the assessments being administered as contributing to their literacy assessment learning. Two instructional strategies that received the highest rating for being the best source of learning about literacy assessment and young children's learning were actually administering the assessment (67%) and observing children in the assessment session (57%). Instructional strategies that received an equal contribution (moderate to high contribution) ratings for learning about early literacy assessment included direct practice with peers (38%) and having the opportunity to assess multiple children (36%). Preservice teachers rated the face-to-face course instruction and self-study/review as instructional strategies that contributed moderately to their literacy assessment learning. Table 3 provides a listing of preservice learning sources and respective ratings.

Data Analysis and Results: Part B

Open-ended responses were read and coded by the two researchers and compared for interrater reliability. Any responses not coded the same way were discussed, and a code was agreed on by the researchers for 100% reliability. First, responses were read for the creation of comment categories. Each researcher read the comments and made a listing of common themes for categories. These categories were discussed and agreed on before actually coding individual comments. Second, comments for survey questions 1 to 3 and 5 and 6, focusing on assessment learning, were coded using the following

Table 3.   Sources of Preservice Teacher Literacy Learning (Subcategory 3 in Part A)

Source of Literacy Learning	Level				%
	None	Little	Moderate	High	
Actual assessment administration	0	5	29	**67**	101*
Course instruction on administration	0	5	**52**	**43**	100
Video within course on administration	5	0	0	0	5
Practice with peers	0	24	**38**	**38**	100
Studying/reviewing	5	16	**53**	26	100
Assessing multiple children	9	18	**36**	**36**	99*
Observation of children	0	10	33	**57**	100

Note. * = value higher or lower than 100% due to rounding.

five categories: "administrative learning," "assessment environment," "assessment application," "preservice teacher learning," and "other." All the question 4 comments related to "administrative learning"; therefore, the researchers further examined the comments and coded them separately, using eight categories: "different/varied responses," "nervous/anxious," "boring," "attention issues," "effort," "attitude toward testing," "general comments," and "other." Question 7 was coded separately using "student distractability," "student general behaviors," "teacher familiarity with assessments," and "other."

Third, comments for 10 survey questions in the second subcategory, focusing on young children's literacy learning, were coded separately based on responses given for each item. Items varied by topic, including "prereading concepts," "reading and writing concepts," "learning differences," and "abilities and instructional needs" (see Table 4).

Assessment Administration Open-Ended Comments

Based on the assessment administration open-ended responses in the first subcategory, preservice teachers commented on learning about assessment procedures for each question. For questions 1 to 5, preservice teachers commented on their "administrative learning" the most with respective question totals ranging from 31% to 100% of that question's total responses. They also commented that they "learned when administrating the actual survey, following the directions for each subset was very important" and "learned tips while administrating. For example, you aren't supposed to say 'good job,' rather don't compliment them [children], when they are taking the assessment." In terms of scoring, the preservice teachers shared that "it is important to keep in mind the individual student, the things noticed during assessment that aren't necessarily included in the assessment but have a significant impact on the scoring." They also commented on interpreting data: "sometimes the administrator of the assessment can influence the results by saying something

Table 4.   Preservice Teacher Responses of Young Children's Literacy Learning by Question (Subcategory 2 in Part B)

Young Children's Literacy Learning	Codes							Total Responses
Question 1 — Alphabet	Recognition 15% (4)	Relationship (Letter–Sound–Word) 4% (1)	Reversals 30% (8)	Learner Differences 0% (0)	Quantity 0% (0)	General 48% (13)	Other 4% (1)	100% (27)
Question 2	Recognition	Instruction	Number of sight words	Learner differences	Quantity	General	Other	
Question 3 — Sight words	Recognition 11% (3)	Text support 33% (9)	Text Distraction 26% (7)	Learner differences 4% (1)	Quantity 0% (0)	General 11% (3)	Other 15% (4)	100% (27)
Question 4 — Pictures	Recognition 16% (5)	Decoding 28% (9)	Reversals 22% (7)	Learner differences 0% (0)	Quantity 0% (0)	General 33% (11)	Other 0% (0)	99%* (32)
Question 5 — Letter–sound relationships	Directionality 7% (2)	Book handling 26% (7)	Phonemic awareness 0% (0)	Print construction 0% (0)	Quantity 4% (1)	General 37% (10)	Other 26% (7)	100% (27)
Question 6 — Basic concepts of print	Directionality 18% (5)	Spelling strategies 4% (1)	— 7% (2)	Learner differences 36% (10)	Quantity —	General 14% (4)	Other 21% (6)	100% (28)

(continued)

Table 4. (Continued)

Young Children's Literacy Learning

	Codes						
Question 7	Previous experience	Instruct ion	Learning style	—	General	Other	—
Learning differences	10% (3)	19% (6)	3% (1)	—	48% (15)	19% (6)	99%*(31)
Question 8	Previous experience	Instruction	Correspondence	—	General	Other	—
Voice–print match	9% (2)	22% (5)	39% (9)	—	9% (2)	22% (5)	101%* (23)
Question 9	Previous experience	Instruction	Grade–age correspondence	Writing–reading differences	General	Other	—
Range of ability	4% (1)	7% (2)	11% (3)	19% (5)	52% (14)	7% (2)	100% (27)
Question 10	Range of abilities	Child learning	Teacher delivery	—	General	Other	—
Instructional needs	20% (5)	16% (4)	40% (10)	—	12% (3)	12% (3)	100% (25)

Note. * = value higher or lower than 100% due to rounding.

they are not supposed to do trying to help students." Regarding instructional application through assessment administration, preservice teachers shared that "the results or observations made through the assessment allow insight into the child's strengths/weakness" and that "by doing an assessment, you can learn what a student struggles with or what a student excels in so a teacher may know how to approach them with learning and teaching." For question 6 on assessment environment, preservice teachers noted "children need to be in the same environment so they are under the same conditions as everyone else." Table 5 provides a summary of the response percentages within each question and accompanying raw scores.

As stated earlier, all the question 4 responses related to preservice teacher assessment tool administration learning. When looking further into the topics expressed within question 4 (33 total responses), preservice teachers noted they learned about the nervousness or anxiety the children experienced during the testing situation (24%) or about the child's attitude toward testing (15%) or made general comments about how children responded (25%). Some comments were the following: "They [children] all respond differently, some are more distractible than others, some are more hesitant and for some their success depends on the day," and "I learned that students are usually willing to participate in assessments if the person administering the test explains the process and the purpose of the test." In addition, preservice teachers commented on unforeseen problems they encountered during the administration (question 7), including "keeping track at the same time as giving my tutee devoted attention and genuine interest."

Young Children's Literacy Learning Open-Ended Comments

Because each question in this section of the survey was focused on a particular literacy learning topic, each question was analyzed separately and coded according to themes found within each question's responses. Of the 10 questions, preservice teachers responded the most to the "general" comment category of six questions (1, 3, 4, 6, 7, and 9) (with the highest frequency ratings, between 44% and 52%, for four out of six questions), meaning that almost half of the comments did not specifically address a topic related to the young children's learning as indicated in the prompt. For example, students wrote "by the end of first grade they know it [alphabet]" and "young children love pictures."

Preservice teachers were able to respond about young children's literacy learning (questions 1 to 6 and 8) but at lower frequencies (3% to 39%). They also noted their specific literacy observations for other questions (question 2: instruction; question 5: print construction; question 8: voice–print correspondence; and question 10: teacher delivery). Preservice teachers shared that "some sight words are harder than others, but the more you include them in

Table 5. Summary: Assessment Administration Open-Ended Comments (Subcategory 1 in Part B)

Codes	Question 1 Administration	Question 2 Scoring	Question 3 Interpreting Data	Question 4 Ways Children Respond	Question 5 Instructional Applications	Question 6 Assessment Environment
Administrative learning	63% (22)	48% (14)	31% (10)	100% (33)	37% (10)	3% (1)
Assessment environment	17% (6)	0% (0)	6% (2)	—	0% (0)	47% (14)
Assessment application	20% (7)	0% (0)	25% (8)	—	15% (4)	0% (0)
Preservice teacher learning	0 % (0)	48% (14)	31% (10)	—	41% (11)	50% (15)
Other	0% (0)	3% (1)	6% (2)	—	7% (2)	0% (0)
Total response	100% (35)	99%* (29)	99%* (32)	100% (33)	100% (27)	100% (30)

Note. () = raw number of responses; * = lower than 100% due to rounding.

everyday lessons, the more they will begin to put these words in their vocabulary" (question 2), "they [children] may not know what everything means but they know some words and they know the print contains a message" (question 5), "I learned that children write words the way they think they sound by the way they say the word" (question 8), and "some need explicit directions while others do not" (question 10).

Preservice teachers identified the following topics as their second most frequently occurring items they noticed about literacy learning for questions 1 to 10, respectively: reversals (30%), number of sight words (24%), text support (28%), decoding and other (26%), other (21%), spelling strategies (37%), instruction and other (19%), instruction and other (22%), writing–reading differences (19%), and range of abilities (20%) among students assessed (see Table 4 for the percentage of topic statements).

Discussion

In this study, we looked at preservice teachers' experiences and perceptions of preparing and administrating Clay's Observation Survey to provide preservice teacher preparation programs with insights about their growth in early literacy development and literacy assessment. Four significant conclusions were derived from this study. First, the preservice teachers perceived an increase in their confidence levels from "none" and/or "little to moderate" regarding how to prepare to implement the informal assessment tool and interpret data. This shows that they felt comfortable administering the assessment and/or at least felt prepared to conduct the assessment with better understanding of the instructional directions. The results are aligned with those of a previous study (Angell & Heiden, 2004) that found preservice teachers' understanding of the assessment tool with integrity and of how to interpret the results.

Second, while the preservice teachers acknowledged the importance and usefulness of using class instruction on campus, they valued actual assessment administration and observing children in the classrooms as the most effective in understanding how to prepare and administer the assessment tool. While there has not been much research on the effectiveness of preparing preservice teachers for Clay's Observation Survey, in particular, the results of this study showed the perceived value of administering and experiencing the assessment tool with actual children. To prepare preservice teachers, teacher educators should consider providing students with administrating assessment instruments authentically, meaning in the classrooms with appropriate grade-level children.

Third, while we found that the preservice teachers identified three early literacy skills—pictures, letter–sound relationships, and basic concepts about print—as the areas they learned the most about in their 4-point scale survey, they did not provide detailed or specific comments about what they learned in these areas in their open-ended questions. In fact, the preservice teachers provided general comments in their open-ended questions on the items for pictures and letter–sound relationships the most. This result indicates that much of what the preservice teachers commented on was not directly related to literacy learning of pre-K–12 students or that the preservice teachers were not able to articulate their literacy learning to be classified into a literacy-related topic heading. It implies that the preservice teachers may need to observe more children learning early literacy skills in the classrooms and to administer Clay's Observation Survey multiple times to gain in-depth insights about the children's early literacy trends and features.

Additionally, the preservice teachers provided general comments on other areas of young children's literacy learning, including alphabet, writing, learning differences, and range of abilities in their open-ended questions. This indicates that they shared general comments on 7 out of 10 early literacy skills. This may imply that the preservice teachers are still developing and learning about how to observe, analyze, and reflect on their experiences of assessment administration.

Recommendations

Based on the study, we have recommendations for future research, including extended experience in giving Clay's Observation Survey over multiple children over time as well as observing children in the assessment experience. This more intensive experience will allow preservice teachers the opportunity to document more specifically the concepts of early literacy. In addition, extended assessment experiences will allow preservice teachers an opportunity to reflect on the assessment experience itself, document assessment environment effects on children, and see growth in early literacy skills of young children. Preservice teachers may also require more instruction and modeling on observing literacy behavior, children's behavior and determining reasons for behaviors seen, and assessment result analysis. Future research conducted needs to specifically document a connection between what preservice teachers observe of their own learning and assessment result analysis as well as the literacy learning of young children.

Conclusion

This study looked at preservice teachers' experiences and reflections regarding preparing and administrating Clay's Observational Survey. The researchers aimed to provide insights about how they evaluated their experiences compared between before and after the assessment administration with young children in school. The survey results revealed that they felt prepared to administer the assessment tool with children. They found observation of children in school and actual administration of the assessment instrument the most useful and effective in order to develop their skills for conducting it and to understand what assessment looks like in the real setting.

Even though the results indicated that the preservice teachers rated three literacy skills (pictures, letter–sound relationships, and basic concepts of print) as "high" learning areas, they were not very specific when describing what they observed and learned about pictures and letter–sound relationships. Perhaps preservice teachers may need to analyze multiple data sets from children's early literacy assessments and discuss child characteristics, including trends, strengths, and weaknesses, for developing appropriate instruction. This may help preservice teachers understand various young children's literacy levels and develop their assessment, analyzing, and instructional design skills more appropriately and in depth. However, some of their comments showed their understandings and observations of children's early literacy skills, providing specific examples from their first assessment experience with young children (Angell & Heiden, 2004). These comments will help teacher education instructors understand what preservice teachers notice about and how they observe early literacy assessment and young children's literacy skills. This information will inform teacher educators about what areas preservice teachers need to focus on while preparing them to become highly qualified teachers.

There were some limitations in this study. The survey was based on the students' self-rated scores. Each individual evaluates his or her understanding differently; some may overestimate and others underestimate their understanding. Also, the results of this study may not be generalized to other settings due to a lower number of participants. **TEP**

References

Angell, C. A., & Heiden, D. E. (2004). The implementation integrity of early literacy assessment conducted by pre-service teachers. *Reading Professor, 44*, 97–121.

Angell, C. A., & Heiden, D. E. (2006). Valuing field experience training: Perceptions of pre-service teachers. *Reading Professor, 28*, 11–14.

Bain, S. K., Brown, K. S., & Jordan, K. R. (2009). Teacher candidates' accuracy of beliefs regarding childhood interventions. *Teacher Educator, 44*, 71–89. doi:10 .1080/08878730902755523

Campbell, C., & Evans, J. (2000). Investigation of pre-service teachers' classroom assessment practices during student teaching. *Journal of Educational Research, 93*(6), 350–356.

Clay, M. (1993). *An observation survey of early literacy achievement.* Portsmouth, NH: Heinemann.

Clay, M. (2000). *Concepts about print.* Portsmouth, NH: Heinemann.

Council of Chief State School Officers. (2011). *InTASC model core teaching standards: A resource for state dialogue.* Washington, DC: Interstate New Teacher Assessment and Support Consortium.

Gutek, B. A. (1978). On the accuracy of retrospective attitudinal data. *Public Opinion Quarterly*, 390–401.

Individuals with Disabilities Education Improvement Act. (2004). Public Law No. 108-446.

International Reading Association. (2003). *Investment in teacher preparation in the United States: A position statement*. Newark, DE: Author.

International Reading Association. (2010). *Standards for reading professionals: Revised 2010*. Newark, DE: Author. http://www.reading.org/General/CurrentResearch/Standards/ProfessionalStandards2010/ProfessionalStandards2010_Role6.aspx

Kindle, P. A., & Colby, I. (2008). School selection preferences of public and private university MSW students: A retrospective study. *Journal of Social Work Education*, *44*(3), 97–113.

Leslie, L., & Jett-Simpson, M. (1997). *Authentic literacy assessment: An ecological approach*. New York: Longman.

Maloch, B., Flint, A. S., Eldridge, D., Harmon, J., Loven, R., Fine, F.C., et al. (2003). Understanding, beliefs, and reported decision making of first-year teacher preparation programs. *Elementary School Journal*, *103*(5), 431–457.

Many, J. (1999). Assessment and instruction in a graduate literacy education class: Reflecting what I'm learning in what I do. *Journal of Adolescent and Adult Literacy*, *42*(7), 566–580.

No Child Left Behind Act. (2002). Public Law No. 107-110.

Oboler, E. S., & Gupta, A. (2010). Emerging theoretical models of reading through authentic assessments among preservice teachers: Two case studies. *Reading Matrix*, *10*(1), 79–95.

Volante, L., & Fazio, X. (2007). Exploring teacher candidates' assessment literacy: Implications for teacher education reform and professional development. *Canadian Journal of Education*, *30*(3), 749–770.

Carol A. Zehms-Angell is a full professor in the Department of Educational Studies at the University of Wisconsin, La Crosse. She teaches special education courses focusing on high-frequency disabilities and how to best serve those students in the general education setting. Her research interests include early literacy strategies and assessment, inclusive practices, and professional dispositions. She may be reached via e-mail at cangell@uwlax.edu.

Yuko Iwai is an associate professor in the Department of Educational Studies at the University of Wisconsin, La Crosse. She teaches literacy courses, such as literacy methods, foundations of literacy, and literacy for diverse learners courses, to undergraduate and graduate students. Her research interests include metacognitive reading, English language learners, multicultural children's literature, and literacy in teacher education. She may be reached via e-mail at yiwai@uwlax.edu.

Utility of the Multi-Tiered Instruction Self-Efficacy Scale in Assessing Needs and Short-Term Gains of Preservice Teachers for Multitiered Instruction

Susan Barnes and Melinda S. Burchard

ABSTRACT: Researchers demonstrated that the Multi-Tiered Instruction Self-Efficacy Scale works with a population of preservice teachers in assessment of self-efficacy for multitiered instruction. The scale demonstrated strong internal consistency (.94). With 148 participants, all juniors in a teacher preparation program, areas of greatest need for professional development included data-driven decision making and meeting the needs of English language learners. Significant short-term gains were made in overall self-efficacy for multitiered instruction as well as in the six subcomponents of finding and evaluating evidence-based solutions, collaboration, monitoring interventions, data-driven decision making, engaging learners, and meeting the needs of English language learners.

In an environment of accountability for high-quality instruction, how can we know if newly certified teachers are ready to teach all the students in their classrooms? Teacher preparation programs must prepare preservice teachers with knowledge and skills across numerous domains of practice to meet the needs of a very diverse population of students.

Background

Responsive instruction, required by the No Child Left Behind Act (2002), necessitates multitiered instruction, structuring levels of ever-increasing support for students who struggle with learning. Such a system emphasizes such actions as teaching with high-quality practices, teaming creatively, gathering meaningful data on the progress of students, and problem solving to meet needs of struggling small groups and individuals.

In order to assess the professional development needs of in-service teachers, researchers developed the Multi-Tiered Instruction Self-Efficacy Scale (MTISES). That scale worked to measure overall self-efficacy of teachers for implementing multitiered teaching. The MTISES also worked to assess professional development needs for the specific constructs of multitiered instruction (Barnes & Burchard, 2010, 2011). No such tool has been investigated for use with preservice teachers.

As teacher education programs prepare future teachers with high-quality skills, program instructors should model responsive instruction, adjusting to meet the unique needs of preservice teachers. Modeling good assessment practices includes assessment of needs and, importantly, accountability for learning outcomes of these postsecondary learners. Thus far, no system is established to assess the needs of preservice teachers or their perception of gains in their efficacy for providing multitiered instruction after receiving college course instruction and field placement experiences designed to improve their performance in this kind of differentiated instruction. The purpose of this study was to investigate the utility of the MTISES for use with preservice teachers and to assess gains over one intensive semester of specific course work and preservice field experiences addressing multitiered instruction or Response to Intervention approaches.

Research Questions

The questions addressed here are the following:

1. Does the MTISES work similarly in measuring self-efficacy using multitiered instructional approaches for preservice teachers as it does for in-service teachers?
2. What are the professional development needs of preservice teachers in using multitiered instructional approaches?
3. Are there gains in self-efficacy for multitiered instructional practices from the beginning to the end of the semester for preservice teachers?

This article addresses these questions using several methods, including descriptive and factor analyses.

Procedures

Participants

This study took place in the teacher preparation program of a small private mid-Atlantic college. Undergraduate enrollment is approximately 2,800 annually with approximately 10% underrepresented populations and approximately 60% females (Messiah College Offices of Institutional Research and Marketing and Communications, 2011–2012, 2013–2014). Participants were recruited from junior preservice teachers enrolled in concurrent courses in inclusion practices, an introductory course about teaching English language learners, and a course in instructional design and assessment. All were participants in pre–student teaching field placements, requiring application of skills learned in the classroom. Recruitment occurred during the fall of 2011 and again in the fall of 2013.

Instrumentation

During both pre- and posttest sessions, participants completed the MTISES (Appendix A). Using 28 Likert scale items, this instrument asks teachers to indicate how much professional development they need for various teaching actions of multitiered instruction. In measuring self-efficacy for teachers' use of multitiered instructional practices, researchers demonstrated that the MTISES worked. Examination of internal consistency for the overall scale as a measure of self-efficacy resulted in a Cronbach's alpha of .952. In other words, the MTISES items work together well as a measure of one construct: self-efficacy for multitiered instruction (Barnes & Burchard, 2011). Furthermore the instrument worked to measure professional development needs for six more specific constructs: collaborating with teams to use universal design for teaching and assessing learners, collaborating with other professionals, using evidence-based strategies, using data for decision making, implementing interventions, and meeting the needs of English language learners (Barnes & Burchard, 2011). This 28-item questionnaire takes approximately 10 minutes to complete. It is free and easy to use and can be helpful to those providing in-service to teachers and to those planning instruction in teacher preparation programs.

Results

Participants

Preservice teachers completed paper versions of the pre- and postassessment questionnaires during class time. Scores were not tied to course grades, and codes names were used to match the pre- and postassessment data only. Participants were pursuing teacher certification in elementary grades (27), elementary grades with dual certification in special education (48), middle school grades (13), secondary grades (15), or K–12 certification in fine arts education, family and consumer science, or world languages (45). In 2011, 82 preservice teachers participated. In order to increase sample size to support conclusions, the study was repeated with 66 participating in the fall of 2013, bringing the total sample size to 148.

Scale Quality for Preservice Teachers

The overall scale worked essentially the same with preservice teachers as it did with in-service teachers with slight variations in the way some subscales functioned.

Overall Scale Quality

Results provide validation of the previously evaluated scale. Over half the variance is explained by only three components: finding and evaluating evidence-based solutions, collaboration, and monitoring interventions (Table 1). When used with preservice teachers, the MTISES worked with a very strong internal consistency. The Cronbach's alpha of .942 provides evidence that the MTISES is still measuring the construct of self-efficacy in multitiered instruction.

Components

Table 2 provides the component matrix showing how items loaded on the six components. The bold text indicates items with the highest loading on the component. These items rarely cross load on other components and have values over 0.5. Values in italic cross load on more than one component. Given the interrelatedness of the components of instructional planning and implementation, having some items related to more than one component is not surprising.

Item-Total Statistics

Table 3 provides the Cronbach's alpha achieved if any one item is deleted from the scale and the item-total correlations. Cronbach's alpha values range from .939 to .942. The goal of the scale developers was to have an alpha score above .90 for this measure of internal consistency. Homogeneity of the items is strong, with corrected item-total correlations from .410 to .711.

Important to a comparison of how the MTISES worked with the two populations of educators—in-service and preservice teachers—is the pattern of how individual items loaded in groups of like items as subscale constructs, or components. One item drifted to a different component, showing that the MTISES is functioning about the same in use with these two populations. Response patterns by preservice teachers show that they perceive question 1, about differentiating presentation of information for various learning styles, to fit more with the construct of engaging learners as opposed to the in-service teacher perception that that item fit more with the construct of differentiation for teaching and assessing learners. Three constructs perceived similarly by both

Table 1. MTISES Component Variance Explained

		Initial Eigenvalues	
Construct	Total	% of Variance	Cumulative %
Finding and evaluating evidence-based solutions	11.130	39.752	39.752
Collaboration	2.383	8.511	48.262
Monitoring interventions	1.936	6.915	55.177
Data-driven decision making	1.663	5.941	61.118
Engaging learners	1.437	5.132	66.250
Meeting needs of English language learners	1.044	3.729	69.978

Table 2. MTISES Rotated Component Matrix

	Component					
	1	*2*	*3*	*4*	*5*	*6*
Item	*Evidence-Based Practice*	*Collaboration*	*Monitor Interventions*	*Data-Driven Decision Making*	*Engage*	*English Language Learners*
1	.248	.226	.006	.162	**.699**	.030
2	.192	.112	.165	.038	**.667**	.261
3	.107	-.003	.081	.006	.280	**.865**
4	-.006	-.038	.277	.111	**.806**	.048
5	.062	.135	.139	.041	**.628**	.426
6	.154	.206	.069	.252	.090	**.834**
7	.252	.240	-.054	.566	.470	.059
8	.241	.230	.136	.461	.459	.164
9	.361	.182	.106	.238	.145	**.654**
10	**.729**	.044	-.034	.126	.299	.072
11	**.752**	.104	.109	.197	.231	.062
12	**.763**	.149	.243	.200	.035	.207
13	**.755**	.240	.240	.096	.032	.221
14	**.545**	.285	.233	.409	.138	.124
15	.252	**.741**	.080	.234	.160	.072
16	.255	**.846**	.111	.133	.133	.078
17	-.004	**.807**	.321	.041	.130	.159
18	-.138	**.790**	.368	.051	.065	.074
19	.163	.236	**.755**	.112	.190	.108
20	.168	.093	**.728**	.266	.280	.005
21	.113	.012	.153	**.661**	.149	.286
22	.352	.094	.382	**.606**	-.048	.127
23	.264	.143	.347	**.734**	.079	.001
24	.151	.200	.449	**.673**	.161	.092
25	.496	.178	**.545**	.292	-.032	.077
26	.157	.475	**.514**	.376	.059	.122
27	.232	.334	**.694**	.203	.188	.043
28	-.048	.343	**.551**	.309	.072	.222

Note. Extraction method: principal component analysis. Rotation method: varimax with Kaiser normalization. (a) Rotation converged in eight iterations.

Table 3. MTISES Item-Total Statistics

Item-Total Statistics

Item	Scale Mean if Item Deleted	Scale Variance if Item Deleted	Corrected Item-Total Correlation	Cronbach's Alpha if Item Deleted
1	61.493243	201.027	.504	.941
2	61.756757	202.063	.498	.941
3	62.169568	203.665	.396	.942
4	61.472973	203.367	.410	.942
5	61.722973	202.896	.472	.941
6	62.074324	200.668	.541	.941
7	61.358108	197.606	.589	.940
8	61.567568	197.975	.644	.940
9	62.067568	198.553	.602	.940
10	61.074324	196.899	.483	.942
11	60.817568	193.007	.591	.940
12	61.256757	193.294	.655	.939
13	61.614865	195.994	.645	.939
14	61.716216	194.300	.711	.939
15	61.500000	195.190	.615	.940
16	61.513514	195.286	.624	.940
17	61.662162	196.402	.560	.940
18	61.702703	195.897	.600	.940
19	61.763514	196.590	.625	.940
20	61.466216	195.842	.621	.940
21	62.391892	198.117	.514	.941
22	62.108108	195.907	.631	.940
23	61.689189	194.610	.656	.939
24	61.662162	193.504	.703	.939
25	61.364865	194.043	.655	.939
26	61.695946	196.213	.696	.939
27	61.506757	195.490	.696	.939
28	61.621622	198.672	.559	.940

in-service and preservice teachers were meeting the needs of English language learners, collaboration, and finding and evaluating evidence-based solutions. While in-service teachers appeared to view differentiation for teaching and assessing learners as a different teaching action than using data for solutions, preservice teachers appear to perceive those as one teaching behavior: data-driven decision making. Similarly, when used with in-service teachers, item response patterns resulted in two constructs: diagnosing and monitoring progress of students and implementing interventions. With preservice teachers, those two constructs were perceived similarly as monitoring interventions. With preservice teachers, the MTISES works with fewer subscales: six in total (Table 4).

Professional Development Needs of Preservice Teachers

All items of the MTISES used a Likert scale response option scored from 1 to 5. Responses options included (1) "I'll take anything," (2) "I'm starting to get this, but I want lots more," (3) "I do this, but I could benefit from more," (4) "I don't feel the need for more," and (5) "I feel ready to help others." For preservice teachers, a response of "I feel ready to help others" would be unexpected, especially at the preassessment of professional development needs. Because the scales have different numbers of items, mean scores were used to compare professional development needs.

Entering the fall junior semester, the preservice teachers' responses resulted in the highest self-efficacy mean scores in the area of finding and judging evidence-based solutions (2.62). Lowest areas of self-efficacy relative to other constructs were data-driven decision making (2.12) and meeting the needs of English language learners (1.82) (Table 5).

Postassessment results at the close of the semester showed higher mean scores in all constructs with somewhat consistent patterns in the constructs with highest and lowest self-efficacy. After completion of the semester, preservice teachers again indicated highest self-efficacy in finding and evaluating evidence-based solutions (3.67). Lowest reported self-efficacy was reported in data-driven decision making (3.09), with self-efficacy for meeting the needs of English language learners the next lowest (3.13). Although gains were made in mean scores, at the end of the semester, the two constructs with the highest needs for professional development remain data-driven decision making and meeting the needs of English language learners.

Gains in Self-Efficacy by Preservice Teachers

Over the semester, preservice teachers made gains in overall self-efficacy for multitiered instruction as well as for all components measured by the subscales. Gains were computed using Cohen's *d*, which is defined as the difference between two means divided by the standard deviation. Using the standards established by Cohen (1988), effect sizes of .40 or greater are

Table 4. MTISES Subscale Loading

Original Subscale Names and Items	New Subscale Names and Items
Differentiation to Engage Learners	Engaging Learners
2, 4, 5	1, 2, 4, 5
Differentiation for Teaching and Assessing Learners	Data-Driven Decision Making
1, 7, 8	7, 8, 21, 22, 23, 24
Using Data for Solutions	
21, 22, 23, 24	
Meeting Needs of English Language Learners	Meeting Needs of English Language Learners
3, 6, 9	3, 6, 9
Collaboration	Collaboration
15, 16, 17, 18	15, 16, 17, 18
Finding and Evaluating Evidence-Based Solutions	Finding and Evaluating Evidence-Based Solutions
10, 11, 12, 13, 14	10, 11, 12, 13, 14
Diagnosing and Monitoring Progress of Students	Monitoring Interventions
19, 20	19, 20, 25, 26, 27, 28
Implementing Interventions	
25, 26, 27, 28	

considered significant, while effect sizes of .80 or higher are considered very strong. However, according to the What Works Clearinghouse (2011), reporting effect sizes as "small, medium, and large" can be misleading because the context is not considered. When reporting effect sizes, it is always good practice to include context information. Another suggestion is to provide graphic representations to help the reader understand the differences between the means being compared. Figures 1 through 6 provide graphic representations of the gains that preservice teachers made in these areas.

Table 5. Needs and Gains of Preservice Teachers in Multitiered Instruction

Subscale	Pre-test Mean (SD)	Posttest Mean (SD)	Gain (Change in Mean)	Cohen's d
Overall Self-Efficacy in Multi-Tiered Instruction	2.28 (.52)	3.31 (.61)	.67	1.82
Finding and Evaluating Evidence-Based Solutions	2.62 (.76)	3.67 (.74)	.57	1.39
Collaboration	2.32 (.78)	3.29 (.90)	.50	1.15
Monitoring Interventions	2.35 (.65)	3.25 (.65)	.57	1.39
Data-Driven Decision Making	2.12 (.64)	3.09 (.71)	.58	0.29
Engaging Learners	2.31 (.52)	3.43 (.74)	.6	1.76
Meeting Needs of English Language Learners	1.82 (.62)	3.13 (.80)	.72	1.84

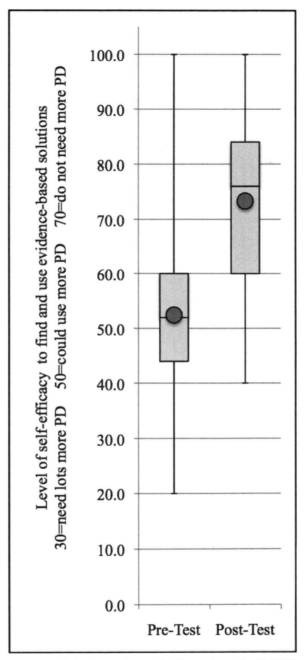

Figure 1. Gains in student self-efficacy from the MTISES, Evidenced-Based Solutions subscale. The difference between the pre- and posttest scores (20.9%) was statistically significant using a two-tailed paired t test: $t(147) = 16.65$, $p < 0.001$. The magnitude of this difference has a very large effect size (Cohen's $d = 1.39$). The whiskers represent the range of the upper and lower 25% of all scores. Average scores are indicated with dots. Boxes make up the second and third quartiles. $n = 148$.

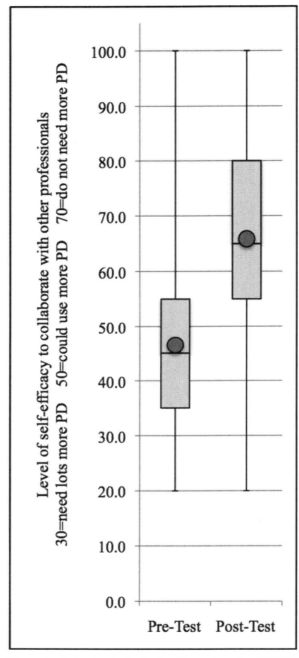

Figure 2. Gains in student self-efficacy from the MTISES, Collaboration subscale. The difference between the pre- and posttest scores (19.4%) was statistically significant using a two-tailed paired t test: $t(147) = 12.48$, $p < 0.001$. The magnitude of this difference has a large effect size (Cohen's $d = 1.15$). The whiskers represent the range of the upper and lower 25% of all scores. Average scores are indicated with dots. Boxes make up the second and third quartiles. $n = 148$.

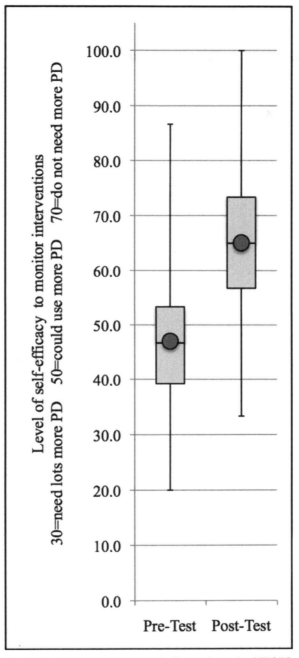

Figure 3.   Gains in student self-efficacy from the MTISES, Monitoring Interventions subscale. The difference between the pre- and posttest scores (18.1%) was statistically significant using a two-tailed paired t test: $t(147) = 15.87$, $p < 0.001$. The magnitude of this difference has a very large effect size (Cohen's $d = 1.39$). The whiskers represent the range of the upper and lower 25% of all scores. Average scores are indicated with dots. Boxes make up the second and third quartiles. $n = 148$.

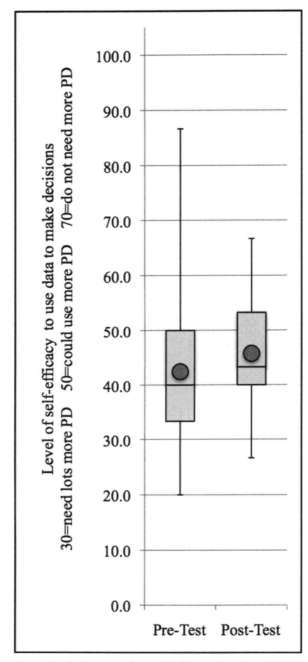

Figure 4. Gains in student self-efficacy from the MTISES, Data-Driven Decision Making subscale. The difference between the pre and posttest scores (3.3%) was statistically significant using a two-tailed paired t test: $t(147) = 2.85$, $p < 0.0005$. The magnitude of this difference has a small effect size (Cohen's $d = 0.29$). The whiskers represent the range of the upper and lower 25% of all scores. Average scores are indicated with dots. Boxes make up the second and third quartiles. $n = 148$.

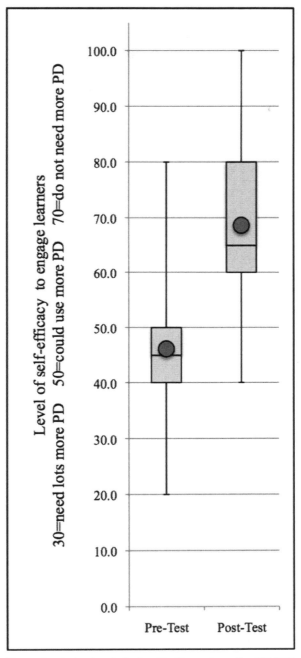

Figure 5. Gains in student self-efficacy from the MTISES, Engaging Learners subscale. The difference between the pre- and posttest scores (22.5%) was statistically significant using a two-tailed paired t test: $t(147) = 18.28$, $p < 0.0001$. The magnitude of this difference has a very large effect size (Cohen's $d = 1.76$). The whiskers represent the range of the upper and lower 25% of all scores. Average scores are indicated with dots. Boxes make up the second and third quartiles. $n = 148$.

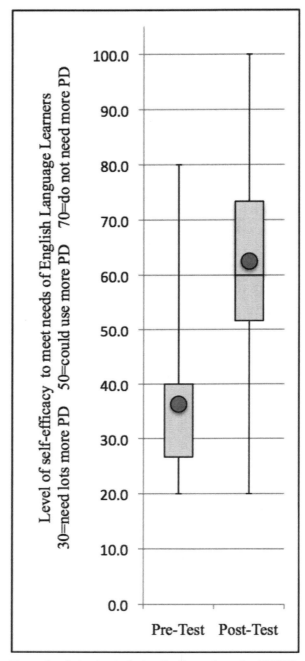

Figure 6.　Gains in student self-efficacy from the MTISES, Meeting Needs of English Language Learners subscale. The difference between the pre- and posttest scores (26.2%) was statistically significant using a two-tailed paired *t* test: $t(147) = 18.6$, $p < 0.001$. The magnitude of this difference has a very large effect size (Cohen's *d* = 1.84). The whiskers represent the range of the upper and lower 25% of all scores. Average scores are indicated with dots. Boxes make up the second and third quartiles. *n* = 148.

Two-tailed paired t tests were used to compare the pre- and posttest scores. Over one semester of teacher preparation instruction and field experiences, the preservice teachers showed growth in self-efficacy for multitiered instruction. As illustrated in Figure 7, the difference between the pre- and posttest scores (20.5%) was statistically significant using a two-tailed paired t test: $t(147) = 22.66$, $p < 0.001$. The magnitude of this difference has a very large effect size (Cohen's $d = 1.82$). Differences in subscale scores were significant as well. All the differences could be interpreted as large, except for the Data-Driven Decision Making subscale, where the effect size was significant but small.

On the Evidence-Based Practices subscale, the difference between the pre- and posttest scores (20.9%) was statistically significant using a two-tailed paired t test: $t(147) = 16.65$, $p < 0.001$ (Cohen's $d = 1.39$).

On the Collaboration subscale, the difference between the pre- and posttest scores (19.4%) was statistically significant using a two-tailed paired t test: $t(147)= 12.48$, $p < 0.001$ (Cohen's $d = 1.15$).

On the Monitoring Interventions subscale, the difference between the pre- and posttest scores (18.1%) was statistically significant using a two-tailed paired t test: $t(147) = 15.87$, $p < 0.001$ (Cohen's $d = 1.39$).

On the Data-Driven Decision Making subscale, the difference between the pre- and posttest scores (3.3%) was statistically significant using a two-tailed paired t test: $t(147) = 2.85$, $p < 0.0005$. The magnitude of this difference has a small effect size (Cohen's $d = 0.29$).

On the Engaging Learners subscale, the difference between the pre- and posttest scores (22.5%) was statistically significant using a two-tailed paired t test: $t(147) = 18.28$, $p < 0.0001$ (Cohen's $d = 1.76$).

On the Meeting Needs of English Language Learners subscale, the difference between the pre- and posttest scores (26.2%) was statistically significant using a two-tailed paired t test: $t(147) = 18.6$, $p < 0.001$ (Cohen's $d = 1.84$).

Another way to interpret gain scores is to look at effect size as the difference between the pre- and posttest means. Using this approach, the gain in self-efficacy using multitiered instruction has effect size (ES) of .67. Moderate growth occurred in collaboration (ES = .50), finding and evaluating evidence-based solutions (ES = .57), monitoring interventions (ES = .57), data-driven decision making (ES = .58), and engaging learners (ES = .66). The most growth occurred in meeting the needs of English language learners (ES = .72).

Interpreting the Significance of Gains

For the paired-sample t tests to be considered valid, the differences between the paired values of the pre- and the posttests (gain scores) should be approximately normally distributed. The normal distribution of values of the difference scores can be checked by examining the histogram of the gain scores or by doing a simple one-sample Kolmogorov–Smirnov test on the values of the difference. The histogram of the distribution of the gain scores

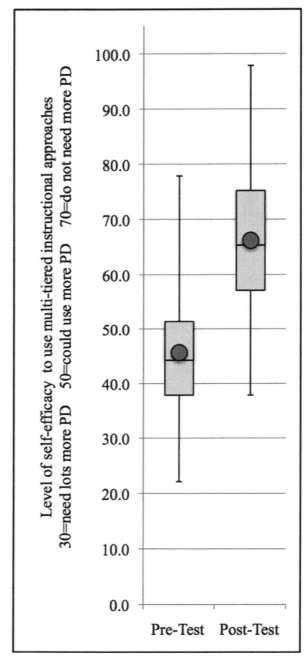

Figure 7. Gains in student self-efficacy from the MTISES. The difference between the pre- and posttest scores (20.5%) was statistically significant using a two-tailed paired t test: $t(147) = 22.66$, $p < 0.001$. The magnitude of this difference has a very large effect size (Cohen's $d = 1.82$). The whiskers represent the range of the upper and lower 25% of all scores. Average scores are indicated with dots. Boxes make up the second and third quartiles. $n = 148$.

for the total scale was fairly easy to interpret. The position of the normal distribution curve on the histogram indicates that the gain scores were approximately normally distributed (Figure 8).

Histograms for the six subscale gain scores were less straightforward. Normal distributions of the gain scores of the subscales were then checked by doing one-sample Kolmogorov–Smirnov tests. The results are mixed. Gain scores appear to be normally distributed on four of the five subscales, thus meeting the normality assumptions. It is unlikely that the gain scores for the Engaging Learners subscale and the English Language Learners subscale are normally distributed. This result makes interpretation of the *t* test of significance of gains on these scales less clear because those *t* tests have not clearly met the assumption of normal distribution of values. Table 6 provides a summary of the results of the hypothesis tests for each of the subscale gain scores. The null hypothesis is that the distribution of gain scores is normal. The decision is to either to retain or to reject this hypothesis.

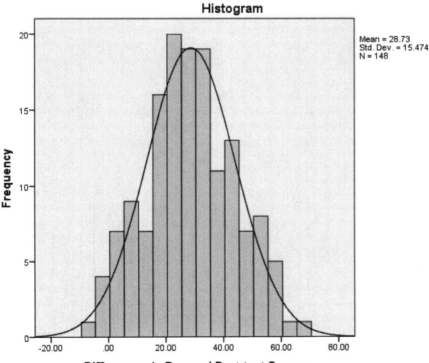

Figure 8. The histogram of differences between pre- and posttest scores (gain scores) with the normal distribution curve. Difference scores are approximately normally distributed.

Table 6. One-Sample Kolmogorov–Smirnov Test of Normal Distribution of Gain Scores on Subscales

Subscale	Gain Score Mean	Gain Score SD	Significance	Decision
Finding and Evaluating Evidence-Based Solutions	5.22	3.82	.390	Retain
Collaboration	3.87	3.78	.095	Retain
Monitoring Interventions	5.42	4.16	.523	Retain
Data-Driven Decision Making	5.79	4.59	.319	Retain
Engaging Learners	4.50	3.00	.006	**Reject**
Meeting Needs of English Language Learners	3.93	4.59	.319	**Reject**

Note. Asymptotic significances are displayed. The significance level is .05.

Discussion

Teaching to meet the needs of all learners within a context of multiple tiers of instruction is a reality for today's teachers. Preparing for the requisite competencies of multitiered teaching is important for preservice teachers and thus for teacher preparation programs. This study demonstrated the quality and utility of the MTISES in measuring both the professional development needs of preservice teachers and their short-term gains over time. Furthermore, this study demonstrated that preservice teachers are responsive to programming, combining course instruction in and field experience to practice component skills of multitiered instruction.

The way the MTISES works to measure separate constructs of multitiered instruction aligns with the theoretical expectations in its initial development (Barnes & Burchard, 2010). Perhaps this alignment is indicative of perspectives of scale designers who teach preservice teachers. The slight difference in the way the scale functions for the two groups may also be explained by differing perspectives of preservice teachers and in-service teachers toward multitiered practices. When the study of the MTISES was conducted with in-service teachers a couple of years ago, in-service teachers may have perceived Response to Intervention–mandated practices as "one more thing we have to do," while future teachers may perceive these same practices as "the way we do business." Because over 50% of the variance is explained by the three subscales (Finding and Evaluating Evidence-Based Solutions, Collaboration, and Monitoring Interventions), when using the MTISES to assess needs and gains of preservice teachers, teacher educators should likely view results for those three constructs as important measures of professional development needs and priorities in programming and course content.

Entering their junior year of a teacher preparation program, the participants of this study completed required prerequisite course work, including three writing-intensive courses requiring information literacy skills and one math course including training in standard deviations. That combined background could explain the higher preassessment score in finding and evaluating evidence-based solutions. At the time of this study, the first course about teaching English language learners occurred during this same semester. Instruction in data-driven decision making typically started near the end of this semester, continuing into the senior year. Prior to this semester of study, the field experience was observation only, with first experiences teaching occurring during this semester. Therefore, the lower preassessment scores in data-driven decision making and meeting the needs of English language learners may be indicative of limited opportunity and exposure at this point.

Measures of gains show that self-efficacy improved for multitiered teaching over just one semester, one in which preservice teachers were applying pedagogy learned in the classroom to their field experience requirements. Although meeting the needs of English language learners remains one area of greatest need for professional development at the end of that semester, gains in that construct were most impressive, indicating encouraging response to the instruction and experiences offered through the program. Considering both the gains and the trajectory of growth, opportunities for students to practice data-driven decision making are important for continued development of self-efficacy for these two cohorts of preservice teachers.

One limitation of this study is that it was conducted with participants of one teacher preparation program. While states do mandate inclusion of specific content, how that content is delivered, emphasized, or practiced can vary from program to program. Therefore, teacher educators cannot assume that all preservice teachers would make such gains over one semester in a teacher preparation program. Another limitation of this study is that gains were assessed over one semester only. Future research should assess gains in self-efficacy for multitiered instruction across participation in an entire teacher preparation program. **TEP**

Appendix

Multi-Tiered Instruction Self-Efficacy Scale (MTISES)

Directions: Please indicate the level of professional development you feel you need for each educational practice.

Each question uses the following response options:

I'll take anything	I'm starting to get it, but I want lots more	I do this, but I could benefit from more	I don't feel the need for more	I feel ready to help others
○	○	○	○	○

1. How much professional development do you need about differentiating presentation of information for various *learning styles* (listening, seeing, manipulating, etc.)?
2. How much professional development do you need about differentiating presentation of information for various *ability levels* (gifted, students with disabilities, etc.)?
3. How much professional development do you need about differentiating presentation of information for varied levels of English language proficiency?
4. How much professional development do you need about adapting learning activities to engage students of varied *learning styles* (listening, seeing, manipulating, etc.)?
5. How much professional development do you need about adapting learning activities to engage students of various *ability levels* (gifted, students with disabilities, etc.)?
6. How much professional development do you need about adapting learning activities to engage students of varied levels of English language proficiency?
7. How much professional development do you need about allowing students to demonstrate learning in ways that accommodate varied learning styles (seeing, listening, manipulating, etc.)?
8. How much professional development do you need about allowing students to demonstrate learning in ways that accommodate varied *ability levels* (gifted, students with disabilities, etc.)?
9. How much professional development do you need about allowing students to demonstrate learning in ways that accommodate varied levels of English language proficiency?
10. How much professional development do you need to find research-based articles and/or books on practices relevant to specific educational needs of students?
11. How much professional development do you need to judge the trustworthiness of research-based articles or books about effectiveness of educational practices?
12. How much professional development do you need to evaluate whether the research-based practices are worthwhile for my specific students and purposes?

13. How much professional development do you need to compare effectiveness of research-based educational practices for the best fit for my particular student population?

14. How much professional development do you need about changing educational practice to incorporate new instructional practices found in a research-based article or book?

15. How much professional development do you need to work with a team(s) of grade-level or content-specific educators to assess specific learning needs?

16. How much professional development do you need to work with a team(s) of grade-level or content-specific educators to solve specific learning needs?

17. How much professional development do you need to collaborate with professionals outside my own field of specialty to assess specific learning needs (for example, teachers working with school psychologists or guidance counselors)?

18. How much professional development do you need to collaborate with professionals outside my own field of specialty to solve specific learning needs (for example, teachers working with school psychologists or guidance counselors)?

19. How much professional development do you need to use data from appropriate assessment tools to clarify the specific problem for a struggling student?

20. How much professional development do you need to use specific assessments to measure student progress on specific learning objectives?

21. How much professional development do you need to use results of universal screening instruments (like PALS, DIAL-R, or DIBELS) to determine which students may be at risk of specific learning needs?

22. How much professional development do you need to use results of published curriculum-based assessments for instructional planning (like textbook assessments, PALS quick checks, etc.)?

23. How much professional development do you need to make decisions about academic instruction for individual students based upon data?

24. How much professional development do you need to use data on student progress to improve instructional practice?

25. How much professional development do you need to use teaching techniques described in a research-based article or book?

26. How much professional development do you need to use interventions to address specific learning objectives of specific students?

27. How much professional development do you need to implement plans as designed to solve problems for individual students or small groups of students?

28. How much professional development do you need to respond to a learning need when first evident?

References

Barnes, S. K., & Burchard, M. S. (2010). Developing a scale to assess self-efficacy for Response to Intervention practices in schools. *Conference Papers of the 2009 Northeastern Educational Research Association.* http://digitalcommons.uconn.edu/nera_2009/14

Barnes, S. K., & Burchard, M. S. (2011). Quality and utility of the Multi-Tiered Instruction Self-Efficacy Scale. *Research and Practice in Assessment, 5.* http://www.virginiaassessment.org/rpa/5_wntr2011/RPA_winter2011.pdf

Cohen, J. (1988). *Statistical power analysis for the behavioral sciences* (2nd ed.). London: Lawrence Erlbaum Associates.

Messiah College Offices of Institutional Research and Marketing and Communications. (2011–2012). Messiah College Distinctives. http://www.messiah.edu/offices/research/research/documents/at_a_glance11-12.pdf

Messiah College Offices of Institutional Research and Marketing and Communications. (2013–2014). Messiah College Distinctives. http://www.messiah.edu/offices/research/research/documents/at_a_glance13-14.pdf

No Child Left Behind Act. (2002). Public Law 107-110, § 115, Stat. 1425.

What Works Clearinghouse. (2011). *Procedures and standards handbook* (Ver. 2.1). Washington, DC: U.S. Department of Education, Institute of Education Sciences. http://ies.ed.gov/ncee/wwc/pdf/reference_resources/wwc_procedures_v2_1_standards_handbook.pdf

Susan Barnes has over 22 years of experience in education, assessment, and evaluation. She is an associate professor in the College of Education at James Madison University (JMU). Before joining the faculty at JMU, she taught preschool and elementary education in both public and private schools. Her research interests are scale development to measure unique learning outcomes and program evaluation. She has a master's degree in educational studies (concentrations in language arts and social studies) from the University of Michigan, Ann Arbor, and a PhD in assessment and measurement from JMU. She may be reached via e-mail at barnessk@jmu.edu.

Melinda S. Burchard is an assistant professor of special education at Messiah College. Before joining the faculty at Messiah College, she taught special education and math education at James Madison University (JMU), coordinated a college learning strategies program, taught special education, and trained parents of children with disabilities. Her research interests are interventions for struggling students and professional development for multitiered instruction. She holds a master's degree in special education from JMU and a PhD in special education and teacher education from George Mason University. She may be reached via e-mail at mburchard@messiah.edu.

Preparation Programs for Alternate-Route Teachers

Teacher Satisfaction With Instruction Aligned to Clinical Practice

A. Chris Torres and Elizabeth Chu

ABSTRACT: Alternate-route teachers who work to obtain certification while teaching full-time are far less satisfied with graduate-level instruction compared to teachers choosing traditional routes. Previous work shows that this discrepancy exists because some alternate-route candidates, particularly Teach for America (TFA) teachers, desire knowledge and skills that address immediate needs for their classrooms. This study analyzes perceptions of instruction in a clinically based teacher education program that serves a variety of full-time alternate-route teachers. Satisfaction with instruction is high across teachers, though TFA teachers view instruction more favorably than non-TFA teachers after controlling for confounding factors. Most teachers prefer instruction that allows them to practice and receive feedback on pedagogical techniques that are applicable to their own teaching context. A larger proportion of non-TFA teachers desired observation and feedback on their teaching compared to TFA teachers. These results underscore the important role of clinical practice for supporting alternate-route teachers.

As a first-year teacher struggling to line up 23 first graders, Otis Kriegel was frustrated. In a recent *Education Week* article, he wondered, "Why, during two years of graduate school, including a year of student teaching, didn't anyone tell me how to avoid a problem like this?" (Kriegel, 2013, p. 40). His question characterizes a long-standing debate about the content and structure of teacher education programs. What is the right mix of theory, content, and clinical practice necessary to prepare new teachers to be effective and feel successful? Some traditional, university-based teacher education programs have been criticized for their inability to integrate course work with clinical practice[1] in spite of its importance for teacher effectiveness (Fraser, 2007; Grossman & McDonald, 2008; National Council for Accreditation of Teacher Education [NCATE], 2010) and graduate students' preferences or needs (Kriegel, 2013). NCATE (2010) has noted, "Teacher education has too often been segmented with subject-matter preparation, theory, and pedagogy taught in isolated intervals and too far removed from clinical practice. But teaching, like medicine, is a profession of practice" (p. 2).

Over the past decade, scholars have advocated for a model of professional teacher education that is grounded in the core practices of teaching (Ball &

Cohen, 1999; Grossman & McDonald, 2008; McDonald, Kazemi, & Kavanagh, 2013). Grossman and McDonald (2008) observed that the field of teacher education was generally missing "opportunities to practice elements of interactive teaching" (p. 190) and that teachers must be able to "rehearse and develop discrete components of complex practice in settings of reduced complexity" (p. 190). For example, teachers may experiment explaining important concepts to their peers and then receive immediate feedback on their performance. This type of practice and feedback, backed by rigorous, connected course work and opportunities for reflection, is essential for preparing strong teachers (McDonald et al., 2013; Zeichner, 2012). In general, clinically based education programs aim to integrate course work, lab experiences (e.g., case studies of teaching situations and video examples of teaching), and embedded school experiences that offer guided practice and feedback in real-life situations (NCATE, 2010, p. 10). While traditional routes to teaching ideally offer this through well-supervised student teaching experiences, many alternate-route[2] teachers pursuing certification must learn and be supported while teaching full-time. This context presents its own set of challenges for teacher preparation programs responsible for supporting the learning of a growing number of alternate-route teachers.

A previous study found that Teach for America (TFA) candidates are far less satisfied with graduate instruction than traditional route candidates because of a strong preference for "just-in-time" knowledge to support them in their real-time classrooms (Carter, Amrein-Beardsley, & Hansen, 2011). Our study extends this by examining how the satisfaction and preferences of TFA teachers compares to other alternate-route candidates who are also enrolled in graduate school while teaching full-time. We focus on the following questions:

1. Are there differences in satisfaction with instruction in a clinically based graduate program between TFA and non-TFA teachers?
2. What are teachers' self-reported preferences for instruction, and how may these preferences explain teacher satisfaction?

Literature Review

The proportion of teachers who enter the profession through alternative certification (AC) routes is significant and growing. Between 2005 and 2010, 40% of first-year teachers entered the classroom through AC routes, compared to 23% between 2000 and 2004 (Feistritzer, Griffin, & Linnajarvi, 2011). Alternative routes to teaching emerged in response to the need to attract diverse and academically talented recruits into the profession and into hard-to-staff schools, largely because traditional university-based pathways into teaching proved inadequate at providing competent staff to work in these schools (Darling-Hammond, 2010). As such, part of the growth of alternate routes may be linked to an increasing proportion of high-poverty schools: in 2011, one in five U.S. public schools was considered high poverty compared to one in eight in 2000 (Aud et al., 2013). Alternate routes vary in quality (Darling-Hammond, 2010) and in requirements for teachers to earn certification, with some states simply requiring teachers to pass an exam and others requiring teachers to be concurrently enrolled in a graduate preparation program while teaching (Baines, 2010). Critics argue that because of limited time and training (e.g., a few weeks of summer training before entering full-time teaching), alternate routes do an inadequate job preparing teachers with the knowledge and skills necessary for the rigors of teaching (Albina, 2012; Darling-Hammond, 1994; National Commission on Teaching and America's Future, 2003; Stoddart & Floden, 1995). Others have noted that alternate routes have become a permanent feature of the U.S. education landscape (Fraser, 2007), so the debate about their merits and drawbacks should extend to how to best support and train AC teachers (Carter et al., 2011). Finding ways to balance teaching and learning and explicitly teaching practical skills are two of the most critical considerations for optimizing preparation program structures for first-year, alternate-route TFA teachers (Carter et al., 2011). In a study examining seven AC programs, the authors suggest that effective programs are characterized by timely course work tailored to individuals' backgrounds and school context as well as mentors who share curricula, demonstrate lessons, and provide feedback after frequent classroom observations (Humphrey, Wechsler, & Hough, 2008).

Increasing teachers' feelings of satisfaction, preparation, and support in alternative routes is necessary. In a nationally representative sample of 1,076 teachers surveyed in 2011, 18% of alternate-route teachers said their preparation programs were just "okay" or "poor" compared with 9% of teachers who entered the profession through college campus–based teacher education programs (Feistritzer et al., 2011). In a study of nearly 3,000 beginning New York City teachers, researchers showed that alternate-route teachers were less satisfied with their preparation programs than were those teachers from traditional routes and that these perceptions strongly correlated with teacher efficacy and commitment (Darling-Hammond, Chung, & Frelow, 2002). Because perceptions of the quality of training or course work can influence a teachers' sense of motivation, efficacy, and commitment to teaching (Darling-Hammond, 2010; Humphrey et al., 2008), it is critical to be responsive to how these teachers experience graduate course work and instruction. In particular, studies on clinical practice in teacher education demonstrate its central role in teachers' sense of preparedness and efficacy.

For example, features of clinical practice such as student teaching demonstrate a strong and positive relationship with student teacher outcomes and perceptions (National research Council, 2010; Ronfeldt, 2012). A recent study showed that the perceived quality rather than the quantity of student teaching was positively associated with self-perceived preparedness, efficacy, and planned persistence (Ronfeldt & Reininger, 2012). In a study that used pre– and post–student teaching surveys of more than 1,000 prospective teachers in a large urban district, cooperating teacher quality and the amount of autonomy student teachers had over instructional decisions were the two program-level features of clinical practice that stood out as significant and positive predictors of self-perceived preparedness and teacher efficacy (Ronfeldt, Reininger, & Kwok, 2013).

These findings are promising in terms of meeting the needs of alternate-route teachers, who, in theory, have autonomy over instructional decisions but often need guidance and oversight from their school and/or graduate program. And while some have argued that forcing teachers to "sink or swim" in alternate routes is detrimental to students and teachers because they are forced to learn on the job, Gabriel (2011) argued that experiencing the job firsthand as the teacher of record can be understood as a positive manifestation of Ball and Cohen's (1999) idea that teaching as a profession must be learned "in and from practice . . . to propose otherwise would be like expecting someone to learn to swim on a sidewalk" (p. 12). In this sense, one potential solution to improving preparation and support for alternate-route teachers is to adjust and align graduate school structures to meet their needs while in the field (Carter et al., 2011; Heineke, Carter, Desimone, & Cameron, 2010).

Indeed, alternate-route teachers, especially those who learn to teach while teaching full-time, may be particularly inclined to favor an emphasis on practical skills and clinical practice in their teacher education programs precisely because they need this knowledge to help them feel successful. Carter et al. (2011) found that first-year TFA corps members rated their courses and instructors in a traditional, university-based teacher education program significantly lower as compared with non-TFA students who were not teaching full-time and were pursuing traditional certification. TFA teachers were more critical because they desired just-in-time knowledge matched to their immediate classroom needs. For example, they wanted instructors to model practical teaching techniques. They also felt that course work and instruction lacked rigor and that its misalignment with their classroom teaching made them feel more overwhelmed by their demanding schedule. The authors recommended improving teacher education such that support more closely matches the demands of these alternate-route teachers who are working in some of the highest-need schools in the country.

The study by Carter et al. (2011) positioned differences in satisfaction as an effect of TFA teacher versus traditional graduate student, yet the reasons TFA teachers gave for low satisfaction are as likely to matter to other alternate-route teachers. As Carter et al. (2011) noted, it is unclear "whether these [differences] emerged because TFA students are simply dissimilar from their peers enrolled in traditional teacher programs (e.g., by educational backgrounds, capabilities, and expectations) or because TFA students have substantially different expectations as practicing teachers of record has yet to be determined" (p. 884).

The present study builds on their work in three important ways. First, we investigate teachers' satisfaction with instruction in a clinically focused teacher preparation program for alternate-route teachers rather than a traditional graduate school education program. Second, we consider whether satisfaction reports differ between TFA and non-TFA teachers in this clinical program. Doing so allows us to see whether TFA teachers are simply more critical than other teachers or whether they and other alternate-route candidates are equally likely to view instruction positively if it is in a program tailored to the type of support that TFA teachers desired. While the relevance of the preparation program to teachers' full-time jobs is likely to be important to other alternate-route candidates, there may be reasons to expect differences in satisfaction due to the varying level of support provided outside the graduate program and differences in the characteristics of teachers selected/recruited by programs.

Alternate routes and programs can be quite different in terms of their mission and purpose, the type of schools in which teachers are placed, the teachers recruited or selected, and supplemental programmatic support (or lack thereof) provided outside of graduate course work. Like other alternate-route programs, TFA helps certify teachers by recruiting them to work in high-need schools and partnering with universities or other teacher education programs to fulfill state credentialing requirements (Mader, 2013). However, TFA also has high admissions standards and independently provides ongoing observation, feedback, mentoring, and professional development to corps members during the 2-year commitment (Harding, 2012). Because of TFA's supplemental support and/or teacher selection effects, there may still be differences in terms of how TFA and non-TFA alternate-route teachers perceive graduate course work and instruction. If TFA teachers feel supported by TFA *and* graduate school, they may be more satisfied than teachers who do not receive TFA's supplemental supports.

Third, we control for confounding teacher characteristics—in particular undergraduate grade-point average (GPA)—that contribute to how teachers perceive instruction or course work. TFA recruits individuals who possess strong academic records and leadership capabilities due in part to the fact that these characteristics are associated with improved student outcomes (Dobbie, 2011). These same characteristics could also be associated with being more critical of traditional graduate instruction and course work. For example, TFA teachers reported being more particular than traditional students because they felt they were collectively more intelligent and graduated from top universities and therefore were conditioned in these institutions to be outspoken, critical thinkers (Carter et al., 2011).

Method

Site of Study and Participants

Our study focuses on students in one graduate school of education that confers master's degrees in teaching (MAT) to students who teach full-time in mainly low-income, urban schools and work toward their MAT on a part-time basis for a period of 2 years. The state in which this study takes place allows teachers to work full-time to earn their AC as long as they pass an exam and are enrolled part-time in a master's degree program. Students are enrolled in elementary or middle school generalist or middle school content area programs of study.

Course work focuses primarily on general pedagogy and content knowledge and is delivered through a mix of online and in-person instruction. Online instruction is flexible to a teachers' schedule, in-person general pedagogy courses meet twice a month, and in-person content area instruction (specific to grade/subject) occurs once a month on a weekend. Teachers are paired with one general pedagogy professor each year. This professor also observes teachers in their classroom several times a year and provides verbal or written feedback on instruction. This structure enables instructors to develop meaningful relationships with teachers and gain in-depth knowledge about their school and classroom context.

Course content and delivery is similar across instructors. Professors are given the course syllabus as well as lesson plans and materials, including handouts and PowerPoint presentations, that are designed by the graduate school's curriculum design team. Instructors also receive training on how to best implement the sessions and are encouraged to rehearse session delivery with their fellow instructors before presenting the material to graduate students. Variation in implementation and course content remains, however, as professors are encouraged to modify their instruction based on their expertise and to best meet their graduate students' needs. Classes consistently maintain a clinical focus: instructors model K–12 teaching techniques for their students and ask students to practice these techniques in groups to receive peer and instructor feedback; instructors show videos of highly effective teachers, and students share videos of their own teaching; and instructors ask teachers to demonstrate their understanding of course content in performance-based assessments.

Course assessments are also determined by the design team and by the program administration and are largely performance based. For example, teachers often use video of their own teaching to demonstrate proficiency. Performance-based assessments such as these underscore a general programmatic focus on practical techniques, clinical training, modeling, observation, and feedback given by professors who were or are currently teachers in urban schools. This attention to clinical practice, job-embedded training, and performance-based assessments reflects important teacher education standards that experts have emphasized for decades (Holmes Group, 1986; Darling-Hammond, Hammerness, Grossman, Rust, & Shulman, 2005) as well as recent current program accreditation standards (NCATE, 2010).

Data

We employed data from a 2012–2013 midyear survey administered online to first- and second-year students enrolled in this clinical teacher preparation program to explore differences in professor and program satisfaction by TFA status. Participation in the survey was optional and confidential. On this survey, students were asked 6-point Likert scale and open-ended questions about their satisfaction with the program curricula and their professors. Professor satisfaction measures were collected for students' general pedagogy and content area professors. The survey response rate was 87%, yielding an overall sample size of 530 students. We eliminated students enrolled in the 1-year teaching certificate program and restricted our analytic sample to students enrolled in the 2-year MAT program, yielding a sample of 467 students.

Quantitative Indicators of Professor Satisfaction

We utilized eight indicators of instructional satisfaction for both general pedagogy and content area professors. To determine whether there are differences in perceptions of professors' discrete instructional skills by one's affiliation with TFA, we employed measures indicating the degree to which students agree that the professor (1) displays knowledge of the material, (2) delivers instruction with confidence, (3) communicates ideas and presents material in a clear way, (4) holds the student's attention and makes the material interesting, (5) appropriately models K–12 techniques for the needs of adult learners, (6) establishes a positive class culture, and (7) makes the student feel comfortable going to the professor with questions about or help with their class material. These seven measures represent instructional dimensions aligned with a clinically focused graduate program. Instructors serve as models of strong pedagogy, meaning that they should exhibit expertise in the course material and in K–12 pedagogy, appear confident, communicate clearly, be engaging, and demonstrate pedagogical techniques. Establishing a positive class culture and developing relationships with students relate to clinical practice as well, as students need to feel comfortable participating in practice and feedback sessions with their peers and seeking feedback from their professors on the clinically aligned course work and assessments. Furthermore, items 6 and 7 connect to one of the themes of clinical practice on which teachers focus in this MAT program: classroom culture.

The eighth measure of satisfaction we included is a summary question that asked students about the degree to which they agree, that overall, the professor is an effective instructor who helps them become better teachers. This question provides the clearest insight into students' perception of the *overall* impact of the clinically focused instruction on their own pedagogy and is the question most suitable for providing insight into satisfaction with a clinical MAT program. All responses are measured on 1–6 scales, with 1 indicating strongly disagree and 6 indicating strongly agree. These questions were administered separately for general pedagogy and content area professors.

Student Characteristics

To examine whether professor satisfaction differs according to TFA status, we employed an indicator of whether a student is a current TFA corps member (1 = TFA; 0 = non-TFA). Because differences in professor satisfaction may not be due to TFA status but rather may be a result of student characteristics associated with TFA participation, we controlled for student sociodemographic and academic background characteristics in our analytic models. We hold constant undergraduate GPA, as TFA has drawn attention for recruiting candidates into urban teaching who come from more prestigious educational backgrounds and have higher academic qualifications than the average teacher working in high-needs schools (Maier, 2012).

Because TFA considers race in their recruitment process, explicitly attempting to recruit black and Latino teachers (TFA, 2013), we accounted for race with a categorical variable indicating whether the student is black or Latino; white, Asian, or other race/ethnicity; or an undisclosed race, with white, Asian, and other students serving as the comparison group in our analytic models. We focused on black or Latino teachers since these groups are underrepresented among urban teachers, especially considering the urban student population. We also held constant gender (1 = female; 0 = male).

Additionally, we accounted for students' teaching characteristics. We included a school sector variable that indicates whether students teach in traditional public schools, in charter schools affiliated with regional or national charter management organizations (CMOs), or in charter schools affiliated with local CMOs or charter schools unaffiliated with CMOs. CMOs selectively hire teachers (Lake, Dusseault, Bowen, Demeritt, & Hill, 2010; Merseth, 2009), and recent studies have shown that certain CMOs are associated with higher-than-average student achievement compared to other schools serving similar student populations (Woodworth & Raymond, 2013). High-performing CMOs may also have much more teacher coaching compared to other types of schools (Dobbie & Fryer, 2012; Lake et al., 2012).

Finally, we held constant whether students teach elementary or secondary school in general pedagogy analytic models.[3] TFA teachers in the studied program are not distributed equally across elementary and secondary placements. It is possible that these distinctions are also related to teachers' program perceptions, as research suggests that middle school positions are less desirable placements for prospective teachers due to increased discipline concerns (Carter & Carter, 2000). Furthermore, secondary teachers report lower levels of commitment to the teaching profession (Ingersoll & Alsalam, 1997), and middle school teachers may be more likely than elementary school teachers to view their position as a stepping-stone to a different job (Marinell, 2011).

Qualitative Measures of Professor Satisfaction

To gain insight into our quantitative results, we also coded and analyzed four open-ended survey responses. After answering the set of eight Likert scale questions regarding professor satisfaction, students were asked to complete the following two statements: (1) "[This professor] helps me become a better teacher by . . ." and (2) [This professor] could improve his/her ability to help me become a better teacher by . . ." Students answered these questions separately for general pedagogy and content area instructors. Since qualitative responses are not specifically worded to answer "why" teachers rated instructors the way that they did, the purpose of the qualitative analysis is to describe and compare teachers' self-reported *general preferences*.

Methodological Approach

We used a "triangulation design: validating quantitative data model" mixed-methods approach (Creswell & Clark, 2007, p. 63). In this design, quantitative and qualitative data are collected concurrently, analyzed separately, and merged through interpretation of results. Quantitative results are compared and contrasted with qualitative data to "validate or expand quantitative results with qualitative data" (Creswell & Clark, 2007, p. 62). This follow-up qualitative analysis allows us to identify possible reasons that explain the levels of satisfaction within and between groups of teachers in the quantitative data.

We began with our quantitative analysis. First, we identified differences in student background and teaching placement characteristics by TFA status using t tests and chi-square analyses. We then examined the measures of instructional satisfaction, both by quantifying correlations between satisfaction measures and by describing mean differences in professor satisfaction using t tests.

Finally, we employed professor fixed-effects models to estimate the relationship between TFA participation and professor satisfaction. We estimated 16 models in total, utilizing each of the eight satisfaction variables as outcomes for general pedagogy and content area professors. In each model, fixed effects were included for the appropriate professor, and we controlled for gender, school sector, race, GPA, and, in general pedagogy models, elementary placement. This approach allowed us to remove unmeasured differences between professors that may account for differential approval ratings between TFA and non-TFA students. Doing so is critical given that TFA and non-TFA students are not distributed equally across professors. Furthermore, this technique enabled us to account for student characteristics that may be associated with both TFA status and professor satisfaction, such as undergraduate GPA and teaching placement school sector.

For our qualitative analysis, we used an approach detailed by Groves et al. (2004) that entails coding open-ended survey comments for the purpose of describing the frequency and content of responses. Following their procedures, we assigned a unique number to categories of responses (e.g., see Table 5 in the Appendix). Each category has a text label designed to describe all the answers assigned to a category. Additionally, each response was mutually exclusive such that no single response is assignable to more than one category. We generated, discussed, and refined a list of codes and categories with text labels until categories were unique and mutually exclusive; *t* tests showed that nonresponders and responders within each of the four open-ended survey questions were equally satisfied with the eight indicators of professor satisfaction, suggesting that the likelihood of responding to open-ended questions was not related to teacher satisfaction.

To present the data, we report the proportion/percentage of respondents within particular coding categories (e.g., 20% of TFA respondents wanted more "modeling of effective instruction.") As relevant to the explanation of quantitative results, representative quotes from categories are presented in the analysis.

Results

Quantitative Results

First, we looked at differences between TFA and non-TFA students to establish the need for controlling for teacher characteristics in our analytic models. Table 1 presents sample and subgroup means in student sociodemographic and academic background characteristics by TFA status. Our results suggest that, on average, TFA students have somewhat higher undergraduate GPAs than their non-TFA peers. They are also more likely to teach at charter schools affiliated with local CMOs or unaffiliated with CMOs and are more likely to teach elementary school. We find no TFA differences in gender or race.

Table 2 displays sample means as well as mean differences in professor satisfaction by TFA participation. Importantly, across all metrics, students demonstrate high levels of satisfaction with their professors, with the majority of average ratings lying between "agree" and "strongly agree" on the Likert scale. Whereas there are no differences in students' approval ratings of their content area professors by TFA status, our results suggest that TFA students are slightly more satisfied with certain qualities of their general pedagogy professors than are their non-TFA peers. In particular, TFA students believe that their professors are better at establishing a positive culture than do their

Table 1. Student Characteristics for the Sample and by TFA Status

	Sample n = 467	TFA n = 257	Non-TFA n = 210
Teacher characteristics			
Female (%)	71.52	72.37	70.48
Race (%)			
Black or Latino	28.05	26.46	30.00
White, Asian, or other	63.38	65.37	60.95
Undisclosed race	8.57	8.17	9.05
GPA	3.50	3.56*	3.42
	(.32)	(.27)	(.36)
School sector (%)*			
Large CMO charter school	40.47	29.96	53.33
Local CMO charter school	38.97	52.53	22.38
Traditional public school	20.56	17.51	24.29
Grade level (%)*			
Elementary	47.54	59.14	33.33
Secondary	52.46	40.86	66.67

Note. Significance indicates difference between TFA and non-TFA.
* $p < .001$.

non-TFA peers. They also feel more comfortable approaching their professors with questions about or for help with their course content, and they more strongly believe that their professors are effective instructors who will help them become better teachers.

With this context, we turn to a more sophisticated analysis of the relationship between TFA status and satisfaction using professor fixed-effects modeling. As shown in Table 3, after controlling for unmeasured professor effects and student characteristics, our analytic models reveal slightly different results than our descriptive models. We no longer observe a relationship between TFA status and general pedagogy professors' creation of a positive culture or approachability. In addition, we continue to observe no differences between TFA and non-TFA students with regard to impressions of their general pedagogy professors' level of knowledge, confidence, and clarity or with modeling of K–12 instructional techniques. These more sophisticated models do uncover two interesting relationships. First, TFA students believe that their professors are slightly more engaging than do non-TFA students (model 4). Second, our results continue to suggest that TFA participants feel that their professors are somewhat more effective, overall, than do their non-TFA peers (model 8).

Our professor fixed-effects results for content area professor satisfaction, which are shown in Table 4, are consistent with the descriptive results presented in Table 2. The TFA differences in professor satisfaction that we observe for general pedagogy professors do not exist with content area professors. In

Table 2. Professor Satisfaction for the Sample and by TFA Status

	Sample n = 467	TFA n = 257	Non-TFA n = 210
General pedagogy			
Knowledgeable	5.39	5.43	5.34
	(.67)	(.68)	(.66)
Confident	5.32	5.37	5.25
	(.82)	(.81)	(.83)
Clear	5.16	5.21	5.10
	(.91)	(.06)	(.90)
Engaging	4.85	4.93	4.75
	(1.14)	(1.10)	(1.19)
Models K–12 techniques	4.76	4.85	4.64
	(1.18)	(1.12)	(1.24)
Establishes a positive culture	5.04	5.14*	4.91
	(1.08)	(1.03)	(1.12)
Approachable	5.14	5.26**	4.98
	(1.12)	(1.01)	(1.23)
Overall satisfaction	5.14	5.25**	4.99
	(.94)	(.88)	(1.00)
Content area			
Knowledgeable	5.46	5.49	5.43
	(.84)	(.89)	(.77)
Confident	5.40	5.47	5.31
	(.94)	(.93)	(.94)
Clear	5.30	5.35	5.23
	(1.03)	(1.04)	(1.00)
Engaging	5.16	5.23	5.07
	(1.17)	(1.22)	(1.09)
Models K–12 techniques	5.23	5.26	5.19
	(1.11)	(1.14)	(1.07)
Establishes a positive culture	5.39	5.38	5.39
	(.96)	(1.06)	(.81)
Approachable	5.34	5.34	5.34
	(1.02)	(1.10)	(.92)
Overall satisfaction	5.33	5.34	5.30
	(1.00)	(1.06)	(.92)

Note. Significance indicates difference between TFA and non-TFA.
* $p < .05$.

Table 3. Relationship Between TFA Status and General Pedagogy Professor Satisfaction

	Model 1: Knowledge	Model 2: Confidence	Model 3: Clarity	Model 4: Engagement	Model 5: Modeling	Model 6: Positive Culture	Model 7: Approachability	Model 8: Overall
Teach for America	0.01	0.09	0.05	0.27*	0.18	0.16	0.17	0.26*
	(.08)	(.09)	(.10)	(.13)	(.14)	(.12)	(.13)	(.10)
Female	-0.03	0.01	0.02	0.04	-0.09	0.04	-0.19	0.03
	(.07)	(.08)	(.09)	(.11)	(.12)	(.11)	(.11)	(.09)
School sector[a]								
Local CMO charter	0.05	0.090	0.36	.45*	0.28	0.14	0.05	0.10
	(.13)	(.15)	(.17)	(.21)	(.23)	(.20)	(.22)	(.17)
Noncharter public	0.05	0.05	0.25	0.47	0.47	0.28	0.14	-0.06
	(.17)	(.21)	(.24)	(.29)	(.32)	(.28)	(.30)	(.24)
Race[b]								
Black or Latino	-0.12	-0.06	-0.21	-0.30*	-0.19	-0.18	-0.31	-0.23*
	(.08)	(.09)	(.11)	(.13)	(.14)	(.12)	(.13)	(.11)
Undisclosed	-0.15	-0.130	-0.15	-0.15	-0.30	-0.05	-0.35	-0.23
	(.11)	(.14)	(.16)	(.19)	(.21)	(.18)	(.19)	(.16)
Elementary	0.02	0.06	0.08	0.01	0.12	0.08	0.05	0.08
	(.08)	(.10)	(.11)	(.13)	(.15)	(.13)	(.14)	(.11)
GPA	-0.12	-0.19	-0.34*	-0.66***	-0.64**	-0.41*	-0.20	-0.39**
	(.11)	(.13)	(.15)	(.18)	(.19)	(.17)	(.18)	(.15)
Constant	5.84***	5.85***	6.14***	6.78***	6.77***	6.26***	5.92***	6.33***
	(.37)	(.45)	(.51)	(.63)	(.69)	(.60)	(.64)	(.52)

[a] School sectors compared to charter schools associated with large, national CMOs.

[b] All races compared to students who self-identified as white, Asian, or other race/ethnicity.

* $p < .05$, ** $p < .001$, *** $p < .001$.

Table 4. Relationship Between TFA Status and Content Area Professor Satisfaction

	Model 1: Knowledge	Model 2: Confidence	Model 3: Clarity	Model 4: Engagement	Model 5: Modeling	Model 6: Positive Culture	Model 7: Approachability	Model 8: Overall
Teach for America	0.02	0.14	0.07	0.08	0.08	-0.03	-0.06	0.06
	(.09)	(.11)	(.12)	(.13)	(.13)	(.11)	(.12)	(.11)
Female	0.02	-0.06	-0.10	-0.04	-0.18	-0.15	-0.20	-0.12
	(.09)	(.10)	(.11)	(.13)	(.12)	(.10)	(.11)	(.11)
School sector[a]								
Local CMO charter	0.15	0.17	0.15	0.39**	0.23	0.34**	0.19	0.18
	(.10)	(.11)	(.12)	(.14)	(.13)	(.11)	(.12)	(.12)
Noncharter public	-0.13	-0.04	-0.02	0.22	0.06	0.110	-0.14	-0.06
	(.13)	(.15)	(.17)	(.19)	(.19)	(.16)	(.17)	(.17)
Race[b]								
Black or Latino	0.18	0.18	0.15	0.21	0.25	0.254*	0.08	0.120
	(.10)	(.11)	(.13)	(.14)	(.14)	(.12)	(.13)	(.12)
Undisclosed	0.20	0.190	0.15	0.16	-0.03	0.27	0.31	0.20
	(.15)	(.17)	(.19)	(.21)	(.20)	(.17)	(.19)	(.18)
GPA	0.01	0.02	-0.03	-0.10	-0.10	0.00	0.06	-0.01
	(.14)	(.15)	(.17)	(.20)	(.19)	(.16)	(.17)	(.17)
Constant	5.32***	5.17***	5.35***	5.22***	5.51***	5.28***	5.21***	5.30***
	(.49)	(.55)	(.62)	(.70)	(.67)	(.57)	(.62)	(.60)

[a] School sectors compared charter schools affiliated with large, national CMOs.

[b] All races compared to students who self-identified as white, Asian, or other race/ethnicity.

* $p < .05$, ** $p < .001$, *** $p < .001$.

other words, TFA and non-TFA students believe their content area professors to be equally knowledgeable, confident, clear, engaging, approachable, and effective as well as similarly capable of building a positive culture and modeling K–12 teaching techniques for adult learners.

Qualitative Results

How General Pedagogy Instructors Helped Teachers

To better understand these quantitative results, we examined the open-ended survey comments. First, we analyzed the open-ended survey comments about how general pedagogy instruction/instructors made them better teachers to describe why teachers were generally satisfied with and to see if there were clear differences between TFA and non-TFA teachers. Similar proportions of TFA (25.6%) and non-TFA (21.4%) teachers did not respond to the question about how general pedagogy instructors helped them become better teachers. Our results suggest that there were no substantive differences in the content of what TFA and non-TFA teachers said they liked about their general pedagogy instruction: there was less than a 3% difference within each coding category when comparing TFA with non-TFA teachers. For example, within the "focus on practical techniques" category, 8% of non-TFA respondents cited this category compared to 10% of TFA teachers (i.e., about a 2% difference between the groups).

Most of the responses and categories about how instructors made them better teachers were a reflection of the quantitative survey questions, such as the instructor's ability to model effective instruction, their ability to engage students, the quality of instructional delivery, and their approachability (see Table 5 in the Appendix). Other categories did not reflect these survey questions, for example, teachers appreciating receiving high-quality feedback on their instruction or course work and being held to rigorous or high expectations and the general focus on practical techniques that they could use in their classroom.

The largest category of responses highlighted the personal support, availability, and individualization that teachers received from their instructors (31.9% of responses). In comments that were representative of most teachers' comments in this category, one teacher said, "[The instructor] is always engaging with students with warmth and offering meaningful support when needed." Others noted, "[They are] always willing to put time aside to answer questions" and "[They are] very accessible and open to discussions and questions. She goes above and beyond to meet one on one and help." In another large category of responses, teachers praised the general quality of their instructors' delivery and course (e.g., engaging and clear instruction, being an inspirational role model, and preparation and credibility of instructor; 27.2% of responses). For example, one teacher said, "[She] delivers the course content backed by serious professional experience," while another noted, "[She makes me better by] being a positive and engaging instructor and building strong culture. She is also very responsive to feedback." Within this category, teachers often viewed instructors as credible, valuable sources of information because they had successfully navigated similar experiences when teaching in high-needs schools. For example, one teacher said, "I think it's really powerful that he continues to teach and can share current experiences from his classroom," while another noted, "[She shows] how her [instruction] relates to her own experiences as a teacher and [uses] herself as a model."

In comparison with the more general statements teachers made about the quality of instructors and instruction, teachers were also much more specific about types of instruction they found useful. They cited modeling effective instruction (12.0%), feedback on their classroom instruction (e.g., "giving me accurate and constructive feedback in a timely manner; 13%), and focusing on practical techniques (e.g., "giving practical advice for dealing with real-life classroom situations" and "giving us the opportunity to practice with other students"; 9%) as the most prevalent examples of helpful instruction (see Table 5 in the Appendix for representative quotes).

In terms of modeling effective instruction, teachers appreciated how professors modeled *specific* strategies, saying things such as "demonstrating classroom management techniques during sessions" and "modeling the strategies we are learning during the class." They also appreciated what they considered more general modeling. As one teacher put it, "[They] consistently model outstanding teaching" and "[They model] what an effective teacher is like." Finally, a small subset of respondents valued the way instructors held them to high expectations for their work generally (e.g., "expecting me to perform at a very high level"; 5.6%). Thus, while teachers valued learning specific strategies and receiving accurate and timely feedback, they also noted an underlying cultural atmosphere of instructors holding themselves and teachers to high standards and expectations for teaching.

Both TFA *and* non-TFA teachers appeared to prefer exactly what Carter et al.'s (2011) study suggested: just-in-time knowledge and techniques aligned to the real needs of their classrooms and an understanding, available, knowledgeable instructor willing to differentiate support for them. Some teachers pointed out that their instructors had credibility since they were able to share useful examples, experiences, and strategies through their expertise as a teacher in a high-needs school.

How General Pedagogy Instructors Can Improve

Next, we examined the open-ended items asking teachers to provide constructive criticism of their general pedagogy professors. We first compared improvements that TFA and non-TFA teachers desired from general pedagogy instructors to see why TFA teachers might be slightly more satisfied, looking specifically for categories that had notable differences between the two groups. We found that non-TFA teachers had a stronger preference for direct supports (such as more observations), while TFA teachers more frequently gave instructional suggestions. TFA teachers had a similar proportion of nonresponses to the question (44.6%) as non-TFA teachers (43%). These nonresponse rates for critical comments about general pedagogy instructors are about twice as large compared to the nonresponse rate asking teachers to make positive comments, which could reinforce the generally high levels of satisfaction for both groups in the quantitative data since teachers more frequently opted to leave a positive comment rather than a critical one.

Non-TFA teachers wanted more observation and feedback on their instruction (e.g., "more in-class observations" and "more specific feedback with clear action steps;" 16.5%) compared to TFA teachers (9.3%). Non-TFA teachers also desired more practical techniques, modeling of instruction, and practice (18%) compared to TFA teachers (13%). By contrast, TFA teachers more often suggested instructional improvements (26%) compared to non-TFA teachers (17%). For example, most teachers in this category gave suggestions about pacing (e.g., "working on pacing of instruction" and "getting through everything on time"), and clarity (e.g., "being more clear with assignments and expectations regarding these"). TFA teachers also wanted more differentiation of instruction (17%) than did non-TFA teachers (10%). For example, they wanted instruction that was tailored to their specific grade level or school. As one TFA teacher explained, "[She could] provide more opportunities to show model examples for different grade levels during [our] in-person sessions." A non-TFA teacher added that it would be helpful if instructors "[understood] the differences between schools that [we] are teaching at and adjusting instruction to cater to these differences." Non-TFA teachers asked for *more* of what they felt would directly support them (i.e., feedback, observations, and modeling), while TFA teachers tended to have more technical advice for instructors to improve their sessions. We propose possible reasons why these trends account for differences in satisfaction ratings in the "Discussion" section.

Satisfaction With Content Area Instruction

Next, we looked for qualitative evidence to better understand why teachers appeared to be more satisfied overall with content area instructors compared to general pedagogy instructors and why there were no differences in overall satisfaction with content area instructors between TFA and non-TFA teachers. First, we compared comments and categories about content area instructors with general pedagogy instructors. In general, teachers were more frequently positive about their content area instructors. For example, when asked how their instructor could *improve*, there were twice as many positive comments (*n* = 40) for content area instructors compared to general pedagogy instructors. Twenty percent of teachers who responded to the question (53% of all teachers) had something *overwhelmingly positive* to say about their content area instructor such as "I can't think of anything I'd want to change," "She's been the best professor I've ever had," and "She is awesome!" compared to 7.5% of teachers who responded as positively with respect to how their general pedagogy instructor could improve.

Why were teachers so positive? The majority of teachers' responses to how content area instructors made them better teachers highlighted engaging, inspirational teaching (33%); deep knowledge of content or passion for it (15%); and the relevance of examples and resources provided to teachers' specific content areas or grade levels (23%). In terms of engaging, inspirational teaching, teachers said things such as "[They are] a strong, positive role model [who shows] me how to infuse fun with science!," "She inspires me with her intelligence and gusto!," and "[She is] extremely effective and clear in her instruction." They also praised the relevance of examples and resources (e.g., "[The instructor provides] good examples of how to deliver English language arts content from [their] own experience") and the instructor's content expertise (e.g., "[The instructor] is very knowledgeable about the content matter").

In general, teachers appeared to appreciate the applicability of content area instruction because it was aligned to their grade level and/or content area. For example, teachers thought they were becoming better teachers because instructors were "teaching me *grade appropriate* [emphasis added] techniques that complement what we've learned online" and because they "clearly model what these techniques look like in my *content classroom* [emphasis added]." In other words, teachers generally looked up to their content area instructors as very knowledgeable individuals who had highly relevant pedagogical expertise aligned to their content or grade-level needs.

There was some evidence that content area instructors might be better than general pedagogy instructors at aligning their instruction to the preferences of teachers. For example, 8% of respondents appreciated how instructors facilitated discussion between content area or grade-level colleagues, saying things such as "[She allows] time for discussion in content sessions and fields questions/issues that come up in those conversations. She makes me feel accountable for being a part of this profession." In this way, teachers may be slightly more satisfied with content area instructors because it is easier to facilitate discussions and learn the material in homogeneous peer groups (e.g., groups of middle school science or math teachers). In contrast, a subset of teachers wanted more substantive discussion in their general pedagogy groups. As one teacher explained, "[She could improve by] diversifying her instruction, explicitly modeling strategies for a portion of the session, then engaging in open exploration/inquiry about the strategies and practices that are delivered. This seems necessary to our growth." Furthermore, teachers did not note peer discussion as a helpful feature of general pedagogy instruction.

Finally, there were no discernible differences between TFA and non-TFA teachers within each coding category explaining how content area instructors could improve, although a slightly higher percentage of TFA teachers (55%) did not respond to this question compared to non-TFA teachers (51.5%). This contrasts with noted differences between TFA and non-TFA perceptions of how general pedagogy instructors could improve. There was less than a 4% difference within each coding category[4] when comparing TFA and non-TFA teachers, with the exception of non-TFA teachers giving general instructional suggestions (e.g., "slowing down on tricky content" or "being more engaging") more often (35%) compared to TFA teachers (25%). In this sense, TFA *and* non-TFA teachers gave similar suggestions for their content instructors, supporting the roughly equivalent levels of satisfaction in the quantitative results.

Discussion

This study extends the literature on graduate-level education instructional preferences of AC teachers by comparing TFA teachers' preferences to those of other alternate-route teachers. We examine the views of students attending a clinical MAT program that provides AC students with the practical knowledge in which TFA teachers previously expressed interest (Carter et al., 2011). In our quantitative analysis, we controlled for confounding factors that may relate both to TFA status and to teacher preferences in a professor fixed-effects framework, thereby eliminating unmeasured differences between professors and sections and providing less biased estimates. Finally, our qualitative analysis enables us to delve into potential reasons for observed quantitative differences.

Notably, we discovered that both TFA teachers and their non-TFA peers are highly satisfied with the instruction in this clinical program. Although TFA and non-TFA teachers are equally pleased with their content area instruction, TFA teachers are more satisfied with their general pedagogy instructors' overall efficacy than are non-TFA teachers. Interestingly, this difference exists even though TFA and non-TFA teachers believe their general pedagogy instructors to be similarly knowledgeable, confident, and clear as well as successful at modeling K–12 teaching techniques and establishing a positive classroom culture.

Our qualitative analysis suggests two main reasons why there may be overall differences in general pedagogy satisfaction but not in content area. First, non-TFA teachers expressed a desire for more feedback on and modeling of instruction. In other words, non-TFA teachers want even more support of this type from general pedagogy instructors. Feedback from mentors and support tailored to individual and school contexts are important features of effective AC programs (Humphrey et al., 2008). It is possible that TFA teachers feel that the support they receive from general pedagogy professors is sufficient given the TFA coaching and professional development of which they are also a part. All TFA corps members are assigned a manager of teacher leadership and development (MTLD). Each MTLD supports a group of TFA teachers by observing them at least four times per year and by providing individualized feedback and additional resources to help teachers with their areas of growth (TFA, 2013). TFA's Teaching as Leadership framework provides structure for these observation cycles, as MTLDs use a Teaching as Leadership rubric to evaluate teachers and gather data about trends in the types of supports corps members need (Gabriel, 2011). Furthermore, TFA groups corps members by subject and grade level into learning teams that are focused on discussing best practices and sharing resources for particular ages and content areas (Gabriel, 2011; TFA, 2013).

Second, preference gaps may exist only for general pedagogy because TFA and non-TFA teachers alike demonstrated higher levels of satisfaction with their content area instructors. Twenty percent of respondents chose to provide positive feedback rather than criticism about their content area instructors when asked to comment on their professors' areas of growth. One reason these content area reviews may be more favorable is because of a more homogeneous grouping that allows for content and grade-level differentiation.

Our work also reveals differences in satisfaction based on students' undergraduate GPAs. Although not the focus of this article, highlighting this relationship is critical, as it underscores the need to control for student characteristics that may be related to selection into AC routes and satisfaction with graduate-level course work. Descriptively, we note that TFA teachers, on average, have higher GPAs than do their non-TFA peers. When the relationship between GPA and professor satisfaction is explored in the professor fixed-effects framework, we observe that higher GPAs are associated with somewhat lower levels of satisfaction with general pedagogy professors' clarity, engagement, modeling techniques, and ability to establish a positive culture as well as their overall efficacy. These differences may be a result of the fact that students with higher levels of prior academic success may have generally higher expectations of graduate school and may therefore be more critical of their graduate course work. In addition, these students may be more inclined toward theoretical course work rather than practice-based clinical programming. However, as was the case with TFA status, these differences do not exist in content area satisfaction. This discrepancy is beyond the scope of this article but may be investigated in future work.

Taken together, these findings provide a number of insights into AC teachers' preferences for instruction. Determining how to best train and support AC teachers is of great interest to education policymakers, researchers, and institutes of higher education, as the proportion of teachers who enter the profession through AC routes is significant and growing. One consideration for MAT programs is providing appropriate differentiation for AC teachers given that differing routes and teaching placements afford students varying levels of teacher support. Teachers who are in programs or schools that provide fewer supports may desire additional observation, feedback, and instruction on practical techniques, whereas those who receive this assistance from their alternative-route programs may prefer to have faster-paced instruction that moves beyond foundational techniques toward their more specific content, ability, and grade-level needs.

Similarly, AC programs may want to consider tailoring their professional development and support models to the needs of their participants depending on how much additional clinical support their teachers receive from respective MAT programs. These considerations suggest that increasing collaboration between AC programs and graduate schools of education may enable the two institutions to more effectively develop their teachers and subsequently achieve even higher levels of satisfaction. Communication and coordination with school, district, or CMO professional development also may lead to better differentiation and streamlining of supports provided to AC first- and second-year teachers. While this study did not explicitly examine the relationship between program (e.g., TFA), K–12 school placement, and graduate-level supports, it suggests the need for future studies to focus on this topic.

On a related note, our work raises questions about how to best group teachers in their MAT classes to provide the highest levels of satisfaction and efficacy of instruction. Two possibilities, in particular, seem to warrant additional investigation: grouping students by content area or grade level, regardless of whether the course specializes in content-specific knowledge, or grouping students by level of support provided by the students' AC route or school placement. Although we cannot directly answer either question based on the analysis presented here, we speculate that purposeful grouping based on either of these two criteria, especially content area and grade level, may lead to increased satisfaction.

Additionally, our findings draw attention to instructional practices in clinical programs that AC teachers find particularly useful. Teachers perceive timely feedback on course work, observations, and footage of their teaching to be beneficial in their development. They also appreciate focusing on authentic classroom situations and practicing pedagogical techniques that are immediately applicable to their own teaching. Third, our results underscore the degree to which teachers value being taught by professors who can model good teaching and the implementation of best practices and who have successfully taught in comparable contexts. Indeed, Darling-Hammond (2010) observes, "Many universities still struggle with constraints that have not been fully resolved in the 50 years since normal schools were brought into universities . . . [including] the loss of tight connections to the field . . . [and]

problems with the qualifications of those who teach in teacher education—in particular their knowledge of how disciplinary principles translate into good teaching" (p. 29). Within this program, teachers cited their professors' relevant teaching experience as proof of their expertise and highlighted how useful it is to be taught by instructors concurrently teaching in high-needs urban environments.

This valuation suggests another reason why teachers may express higher levels of satisfaction on average for content area instructors: almost all content area instructors presently work in K–12 schools, whereas the majority of general pedagogy professors work full-time in higher education and no longer regularly teach in K–12 classrooms. The experience and expertise of instructors does matter: TFA teachers in other studies have expressed dissatisfaction at being trained by second-year "novices" (Veltri, 2012, p. 65). Instructors in this study appear to have demonstrable expertise and credibility as evidenced by teachers' expressions of high satisfaction.

Future research that investigates these considerations is crucial, as our work highlights the degree to which AC teachers share similar preferences about graduate-level instruction. Full-time alternative-route teachers as a group, not *only* TFA corps members, express high levels of satisfaction when provided with clinically rich, practical instruction taught by instructors who have meaningful teaching experience in high-needs schools. These high levels of satisfaction contribute to the growing evidence base on the importance of clinical practice for teacher efficacy and preparedness, and our investigation of teachers' self-reported preferences highlights aspects of clinically rich programming that AC teachers desire and find especially helpful. Achieving and increasing the degree to which AC teachers value their MAT experience promises to positively relate to teachers' early career success by impacting teachers' sense of self-efficacy, preparedness, and job satisfaction. The fact that these teachers make up a growing segment of the new-teacher population underscores the import of this research and of further investigating how to learn from and improve on existing MAT programs and their partnerships with AC providers. **TEP**

Appendix

Table 5. Categories and Examples for "How General Pedagogy Instructors Help" Comments

Coding Category	% Responses	Representative Quotes
Personal support, availability, approachability, individualization	31.9%	• "Always engaging with students with warmth and offering support when needed." • "Always willing to put time aside to answer questions." • "Being very accessible and open to discussions and questions. She goes above and beyond to meet one on one and help." • "Believing that I really can accomplish everything on my plate and supporting me." • "Putting things into perspective and acknowledging my struggles."
General quality of instructional delivery or courses	27.2%	• "Delivering the course content backed by serious professional experience." • "Being a positive and engaging instructor and building strong culture. She is also very responsive to feedback." • "Coaching and teaching [our general pedagogy] classes in a way that makes me believe I can do this and be a great teacher." • "Describing her own experiences in the classroom."
Feedback on instruction or course work	12.9%	• "Providing insightful feedback on the work I turn in." • "Giving me constructive and accurate feedback in a timely manner." • "Giving me immediate feedback [in sessions], tailoring feedback for each teacher, giving helpful in-person feedback after observations." • "Giving constructive feedback one-on-one by viewing our videos together."

(continued)

Table 5. (Continued)

Coding Category	% Responses	Representative Quotes
Modeling effective instruction	12.0%	• "Demonstrating classroom management techniques during sessions." • "Consistently modeling outstanding teaching." • "Modeling the strategies we are learning during the class." • "Modeling what an effective teacher is like."
Teaching and general focus on practical techniques	9.0%	• "Detailing effective teaching methods and strategies." • "Giving practical advice for dealing with real life classroom situations." • "Teaching me specific, implementable teaching strategies." • "Being awesome at real-world examples and applications of exactly what we are doing." • "Giving us the opportunity to practice with other students."
High expectations and rigor	5.6%	• "Holding me accountable and having high expectations." • "Expecting me to perform at a very high level." • "Always asking me to push my thinking a little further."
Negative comment	1.4%	• "I'm not sure [he or she] actually helps me be a better teacher." • "Unfortunately, in no way at all."

Notes

1. Broadly defined as "well supervised field experiences that are congruent with candidates' eventual teaching, and that feature a capstone project" (NCATE, 2010, p. 2).
2. "Alternative routes to certification are state-defined routes through which an individual who already has at least a bachelor's degree can obtain certification to teach without necessarily having to go back to college and complete a college, campus-based teacher education program" (National Center for Alternative Certification, 2010, p. 1).
3. Students are grouped by grade level for content instruction, making this measure irrelevant in those models.
4. The coding categories were similar in number and content to those reported in Table 5 in the Appendix.

References

Albina, G. (2012). Which is better? Alternative or traditional. *Educational Leadership, 69*(8), 70–72.

Aud, S., Wilkinson-Flicker, S., Kristapovich, P., Rathbun, A., Wang, X., & Zhang, J. (2013). *The condition of education 2013* (NCES 2013-037). Washington, DC: U.S. Department of Education, National Center for Education Statistics. http://nces. ed.gov/pubsearch

Ball, D., & Cohen, D. (1999). Developing practice, developing practitioners. In L. Darling-Hammond & G. Sykes (Eds.), *Teaching as the learning profession: Handbook for policy and practice* (pp. 3–32). San Francisco: Jossey-Bass.

Blaines, L. (2010). The disintegration of teacher preparation. *Education Horizons, 80*(1), 32–37.

Carter, H., Amrein-Beardsley, A., & Hansen, C. C. (2011). So not amazing! Teach for America Corps members' evaluation of the first semester of their teacher preparation program. *Teachers College Record, 113*(5), 861–894.

Carter, M., & Carter, C. (2000). How principals can attract teachers to the middle grades. *Schools in the Middle, 9*(8), 22–25.

Creswell, J., & Clark, V. L. (2007). *Designing and conducting mixed methods research.* Thousand Oaks, CA: Sage.

Darling-Hammond, L. (1994). Who will speak for the children? How "Teach for America" hurts urban school children. *Phi Delta Kappan, 76*, 21–34.

Darling-Hammond, L. (2010). Teacher education and the American future. *Journal of Teacher Education, 61*(1–2), 35–47.

Darling-Hammond, L., Chung, R., & Frelow, F. (2002). Variation in teacher preparation: How well do different pathways prepare teachers to teach? *Journal of Teacher Education, 53*, 286–302.

Darling-Hammond, L., Hammerness, K., Grossman, P., Rust, F., & Shulman, L. (2005). In L. Darling-Hammond & J. Bransford (Eds.), *The design of teacher education programs* (pp. 390–441). San Francisco: Jossey-Bass.

Dobbie, W. (2011). Teacher characteristics and student achievement: Evidence from Teach for America. http://www.people.fas.harvard.edu/~dobbie/research/Teacher-Characteristics_July2011.pdf

Dobbie, W., & Fryer, R. (2012). Getting beneath the veil of effective schools: Evidence from New York City. NBER Working Paper No. 17632. http://www.nber.org/papers/w17632.pdf

Feistritzer, E. C., Griffin, S., & Linnajarvi, A. (2011). Profile of teachers in the U.S: 2011. http://www.ncei.com/Profile_Teachers_US_2011.pdf

Fraser, J. W. (2007). *Preparing America's teachers: A history*. New York: Teachers College Press.

Gabriel, R. (2011). A practice-based theory of professional education: Teach for America's professional development model. *Urban Education, 46*(5), 975–986.

Grossman, P., & McDonald, M. (2008). Back to the future: Directions for research in teaching and teacher education. *American Educational Research Journal, 45*(1), 184–205.

Groves, R. M., Fowler, F. J., Couper, M. P., Lepkowski, J. M., Singer, E., & Tourangeau, R. (2004). *Survey methodology*. Hoboken, NJ: Wiley.

Harding, H. (2012). Teach for America: Leading for change. *Educational Leadership, 69*(8), 58–61.

Heineke, H., Carter, H., Desimone, M., & Cameron, Q. (2010). Working together in urban schools: How a university teacher education program and Teach for America partner to support alternatively certified teachers. *Teacher Education Quarterly, 37*, 123–136.

Holmes Group. (1986). *Tomorrow's teachers: A report of the Holmes Group*. East Lansing, MI: Author.

Humphrey, D. C., Wechsler, M. E., & Hough, H. J. (2008). Characteristics of effective alternative teacher certification programs. *Teachers College Record, 110*(1), 1–63.

Ingersoll, R., & Alsalam, N. (1997). *Teacher professionalization and teacher commitment: A multilevel analysis* (NCES 97-069). Washington, DC: National Center for Education Statistics.

Kriegel, O. (2013). What teacher education programs don't tell you. *Education Week, 32*(35), 40–44.

Lake, R., Bowen, M., Demeritt, A., McCullough, M., Haimson, J., & Gill, B. (2012). *Learning from charter school management organizations: Strategies for student behavior and teacher coaching*. http://www.crpe.org/cs/crpe/download/csr_files/pub_CMO_Strategies_mar12.pdf

Lake, R., Dusseault, B., Bowen, M. Demeritt, A., & Hill, P. (2010, June). *The national study of charter management organization (CMO) effectiveness: Report on interim findings*. Seattle: Center on Reinventing Public Education.

Mader, J. (2013). Alternative routes to teaching become more popular despite lack of evidence. http://hechingerreport.org/content/alternative-routes-to-teaching-become-more-popular-despite-lack-of-evidence_12059

Maier, A. (2012). Doing good and doing well: Credentialism and Teach for America. *Journal of Teacher Education, 63*(1), 10–22.

Marinell, W. (2011). The Middle School Teacher Turnover Project: A descriptive analysis of teacher turnover in New York City's middle schools. http://steinhardt.nyu.edu/scmsAdmin/media/users/jnw216/RANYCS/WebDocs/TTP_FULL-REPORT-FINAL.pdf

McDonald, M., Kazemi, E., & Kavanagh, S. S., (2013). Core practices and pedagogies of teacher education: A call for common language and collective activity. *Journal of Teacher Education, 64*(5), 1–9.

Merseth, K. (2009). *Inside urban charter schools: Promising practices and strategies in five high-performing schools.* Cambridge, MA: Harvard Education Press.

National Center for Alternative Certification. (2010). Alternative teacher certification: A state-by-state analysis. http://www.teach-now.org/intro.cfm

National Commission on Teaching and America's Future. (2003). *No dream denied: A pledge to America's children.* http://nctaf.org/wp-content/uploads/2012/01/no-dream-denied_summary_report.pdf

National Council for Accreditation of Teacher Education. (2010). *Transforming teaching education through clinical practice: A national strategy to prepare effective teachers.* Washington, DC: Author.

National Research Council. (2010). *Preparing teachers: Building evidence for sound policy* (Report by the Committee on the Study of Teacher Preparation Programs in the United States). Washington, DC: National Academies Press.

Ronfeldt, M. (2012). Where should student teachers learn to teach? Effects of field placement school characteristics on teacher retention and effectiveness. *Educational Evaluation and Policy Analysis, 34,* 3–26.

Ronfeldt, M., & Reininger, M. (2012). More or better student teaching? *Teaching and Teacher Education, 28*(8), 1091–1106.

Ronfeldt, M., Reininger, M., & Kwok, A. (2013). Recruitment or preparation? Investigating the effects of teacher characteristics and student teaching. *Journal of Teacher Education, 64*(4), 319–337.

Stoddart, T., & Floden, R.E. (1995). *Traditional and alternative routes to teacher certification: Issues, assumptions, and misconceptions* (Issue Paper 95-2). East Lansing, MI: National Center for Research on Teacher Learning.

Teach for America. (2013). Teach for America: Coaching. http://www.teachforamerica.org/why-teach-for-america/training-and-support/coaching

Veltri, B. T. (2012). Teach for America: It's more about leading than teaching. *Educational Leadership, 69*(8), 62–65.

Woodworth, J. L., & Raymond, M. E. (2013). Charter school growth and replication: Volume II. http://credo.stanford.edu/pdfs/CGAR%20Growth%20Volume%20II.pdf

Zeichner, K. (2012). The turn once again toward practice-based teacher education. *Journal of Teacher Education, 63*(5), 376–382.

A. Chris Torres is currently an assistant professor of educational leadership at Montclair State University's College of Education and Human Services and will be joining the faculty at Michigan State University as an assistant professor of K–12 educational administration in the Department of Educational Administration in the fall of 2016. His research currently focuses on teacher turnover, teacher education, and how market-based reforms and charter schools shape the careers and development of urban teachers and leaders. He teaches MA and PhD courses that focus on charter school policy and leadership, policy perspectives on teacher education and teacher development, leadership for curriculum development and to foster effective teacher collaboration, and the use of data in professional learning communities. He may be reached via e-mail at torresch@mail.montclair.edu.

Elizabeth Chu is the senior director of research, content, and curriculum at Columbia University's Center for Public Research and Leadership (CPRL) and a lecturer in law at Columbia Law School. At CPRL, she teaches research methods and problem-solving skills and leads research and consulting projects on building organizational learning capacity. Before joining CPRL, she was an assistant professor of practice at Relay Graduate School of Education. She began her career as a middle and high school English teacher in the South Bronx. She earned her BA from Yale University, her MA in teaching from Pace University, and her PhD in education policy from Columbia University. She may be reached via e-mail at lchu@relay.edu.

Call for Book Reviews

Teacher Education and Practice is interested in receiving high-quality book reviews for upcoming issues. Individuals interested in reviewing a book or providing a review essay that examines one to three books focused on a common issue, topic, or theme should submit a proposal to the editor. The proposal should not exceed one page and should identify the book or books, along with a rationale supporting the appropriateness of the book review or review essay for *Teacher Education and Practice*.

Books selected for review should demonstrate a clear alignment with teacher preparation and practice. Book reviews and review essays should provide a critical examination of the books under review. High-quality reviews offer readers thoughtful critiques of the books, juxtaposing select and salient points in relation to other important contributions in the field of teacher preparation and practice. Reviewers may offer reviews or review essays that align with a special issue or an open-theme issue. *Teacher Education and Practice* is interested in receiving manuscripts that address social practice, teacher preparation, pedagogy, curriculum, standards and accountability, teacher learning, issues of diversity, teacher as researcher, alternative certification programs, and other germane topics. Submissions should follow manuscript guidelines for *Teacher Education and Practice* and should be approximately five to seven double-spaced pages, depending on whether the review is for a single book or an essay covering multiple books. In addition, the submission should include a separate page listing, for each book, the book title, publisher, year published, ISBN, price of book (paperback and/or hardback, depending on format reviewed), and number of pages.

Timeline for Submissions

The timeline for receipt of submissions for inclusion in an upcoming issue is 3 months in advance. All submissions should adhere to the manuscript preparation guidelines set for *Teacher Education and Practice*.

Upcoming Issues

Volume (Issue)	Theme	Timeline for Submissions
30(1)	Open Theme	August 1, 2016
30(2)	Examining the Neoliberal	December 1, 2016
30(3)	Social Imaginary in Teacher Education	January 1, 2017
30(4)	Wither Democratic Accountability in Teacher Education	March 1, 2017

Calls for Reviewers

Editors of *Teacher Education and Practice* seek individuals to serve as Editorial Reviewers. Reviewers will serve a minimum of two years. Responsibilities include the following:

- ➤ Review manuscripts for publication in *Teacher Education and Practice*.
- ➤ Stay current in issues in teacher education.
- ➤ Communicate effectively with editors and/or authors about the manuscript(s).
- ➤ Meet deadlines to ensure prompt responses to authors.

If interested, please send via regular mail or e-mail a letter of interest and a current vita (attached file in Microsoft Word, PC or Mac) to Editor, Dr. Patrick M. Jenlink, Stephen F. Austin State University, PO Box 13018, SFA Station, Nacogdoches, TX 75962-3018; e-mail: pjenlink@sfasu.edu; phone: (936) 468-2908.

Reengagement

Bringing Students Back to America's Schools

Andrew O. Moore

978-1-4758-2674-6 • $60.00 Cloth
978-1-4758-2675-3 • $30.00 Paper
978-1-4758-2676-0 • $20.99 eBook
April 2016 • 202 pages

"This extraordinary book provides communities the evidence and tools they need to help millions of America's youth get back on track to a better life. Such work is urgent to fulfill the potential of our young people, strengthen our fraying communities, and restore a fundamental belief in equal access to the American dream."—**John M. Bridgeland, CEO, Civic Enterprises and former director, White House Domestic Policy Council**

"The recent rise in the nation's high school graduation rates has been no accident. It has resulted from smart and dedicated work on the ground, including the invention of new strategies to provide students who have dropped out second and third chances to succeed. Central to this has been the realization that for reengagement to occur we need to be able to provide students who have dropped out with supported pathways back in. This highly informative volume shows the art and science of how that can be done."—**Robert Balfanz, Everyone Graduates Center, Johns Hopkins University**

"This book provides important insights into different ways in which the nation could respond to re-engage teens and young adults and increase their chances for a life of opportunity and fulfillment."—**Paul Harrington, director and professor of education, Center for Labor Markets and Policy, Drexel University**

ROWMAN &
LITTLEFIELD   www.rowman.com | 800-462-6420

The Laughing Guide to Well-Being

Using Humor and Science to Become Happier and Healthier

Isaac Prilleltensky

978-1-4758-2573-2 • $70.00 Cloth
978-1-4758-2574-9 • $35.00 Paper
978-1-4758-2575-6 • $34.99 eBook
May 2016 • 168 pages

"This book is hilarious. It is so funny that you will be tempted to race through abstract advice about well-being and happiness to get to the next funny story and have another belly laugh. Do not race. You will miss the wisdom for the wit."—**Martin E. P. Seligman, professor, University of Pennsylvania, and author, *Flourish: A Visionary New Understanding of Happiness and Well-Being***

"This is a disarmingly clever and humorous book that offers a rich array of wise advice on how to live a happier, healthier, more meaningful life in a topical and relevant way that makes you want more and more! The best part? The author shares many personal amusing stories from his own fascinating life! A brilliant and useful tool for everyone!"—**S. Leonard Syme, professor emeritus, University of California Berkeley, and co-editor, *Promoting Health: Intervention Strategies from Social and Behavioral Research***

"This book is extremely funny and informative at the same time. If you want to improve your well-being while laughing out loud, read this book. Prilleltensky shows that you can do both!"—**Talma Lobel, professor, Tel Aviv University, and author, *Sensation: The New Science of Physical Intelligence***

ROWMAN & LITTLEFIELD

www.rowman.com | 800-462-6420

The Newcomer Student

An Educator's Guide to Aid Transitions

Louise H. Kreuzer

THE NEWCOMER
STUDENT

—

AN EDUCATOR'S GUIDE
TO AID TRANSITIONS

LOUISE H. KREUZER

978-1-4758-2558-9 • $60.00 Cloth
978-1-4758-2559-6 • $30.00 Paper
978-1-4758-2560-2 • $29.99 eBook
May 2016 • 212 pages

"*T*he Newcomer Student deeply honors the talents and skills of refugee children and their families and also the teachers who are the key to their success. Each detail of *The Newcomer Student,* such as chapter epigraphs in the languages of new arrivals, reveals Louise H. Kreuzer's student focus. I loved this book for its deep research, but also for Kreuzer's heart as an ambassador for students as they find their voices in their new language and culture."—**Terry Farish, author, Either the Beginning or the End of the World and The Good Braider, and writing teacher, Manchester (NH) Community College**

"*The Newcomer Student* offers an insightful exploration into the incredible challenges of refugee and immigrant students and families. From the process that brings them to our country, coupled with their fears and daily challenges, to instructional specifics on how to help both parent and child integrate as strong contributing members of a new society, Louise H. Kreuzer's book inspires compassion and stimulates new thinking. This is a must-read, not only for aspiring and practicing educators at all levels, but also for anyone who wishes to enhance their understandings, thoughtful reflection, and ability to meaningfully interface with this population. As a seasoned educator who has worked with many non-English-speaking families, I wish that I had had access to such a comprehensive scope of information and insights long ago!"—**Judith Husbands Damas, Westminster Colorado School District, former director, Learning Services**

ROWMAN & LITTLEFIELD

www.rowman.com | 800-462-6420

Manuscript Preparation and Submission

Teacher Education and Practice uses a blind peer-reviewed process to review submissions. All submissions will be reviewed by the editorial staff prior to an external blind review and a contact person assigned from the staff to work with each contributing author. Authors should submit manuscripts that focus on a topic or theme set for the journal that makes a contribution to the understanding and advancement of teacher preparation, practice, and policy. *TE&P* serial publication includes both open-theme and/or special-theme issues. Submissions may include reports of research, expository pieces, pedagogical and/or methodological issues, scholarly practice, epistemological considerations, innovative ideas or approaches, etc. *TE&P* welcomes contributions that address teacher preparation, practice, and policy issues from experienced and novice scholars, teacher educators, teacher practitioners, researchers, policy developers and analysts, etc.

Authors are selected based on an expertise and/or scholarship they have contributed to and therefore should interact with the *TE&P* editorial staff to clarify the specific contribution to be made to a special issue or for consideration in an open-theme issue. Authors should review the following guidelines prior to preparation and submission of a manuscript. Authors submitting manuscripts to the journal should not simultaneously submit them to another journal, nor should manuscripts have been published elsewhere in substantially similar form or with substantially similar content. Authors in doubt of what constitutes prior publication should consult the editor.

Manuscript submission. Manuscripts should be submitted in hard copy (3 copies) and soft copy on disk in Microsoft Word (6.0 or more recent version, Mac or PC) (including text files and files for tables and figures). All files, including cover page, title page, abstract, manuscript, tables, figures, etc., should be included on the disk. Submit all materials to Patrick M. Jenlink, Editor, *Teacher Education and Practice*, Department of Secondary Education and Educational Leadership, McKibben 404j, Stephen F. Austin State University, 1936 North Street, PO Box 13018-SFA, Nacogdoches, TX 75962-3018.

Commitment to publish. Submission of a manuscript implies commitment to publish in the journal. *TE&P* editorial policy requires that submissions received have not been previously published and are not under simultaneous consideration elsewhere.

Manuscript. Manuscripts should be submitted on 8½" × 11" white paper, entirely double-spaced. Use a standard font style/size of Times New Roman 12 or Times 12. Margins should be one (1) inch and header/footer half (.5) inch. All manuscripts should be a maximum of 20 double-spaced pages in length and follow the style of the *Publication Manual of the American Psychological Association* (APA), 5th edition. Manuscripts (including hard copies and disk copy) submitted to *TE&P* for consideration will not be returned to the contributing author(s).

Transmittal page. A separate page for transmittal purposes, with all authors' names and affiliations, current addresses, phone numbers, fax numbers, and e-mail addresses should accompany the manuscript materials submitted.

Title page. A separate title page should accompany the manuscript. The title of the manuscript should be concise and reflect the topic/contents of the manuscript. The title page should include the title of the manuscript as well as the contributing author(s) name, affiliations, and highest professional degrees.

Abstract. A separate abstract page should follow the title page. The abstract page should include the title of the manuscript, followed by an abstract (75–125 words) that clearly summarizes the salient points of the article.

Citations and references. All citations in text should conform to APA 5th edition guidelines and contain relevant and required information. All references should appear at the end of the manuscript, with complete information including volume/issue numbers, page numbers (articles, chapters, etc.), URL addresses, etc., as designated by APA. All author reference should be deleted from the paper as required for a blind review. In the event that the manuscript author cites her/his own work, then "author" should be substituted for the name of the actual author name. A separate list of author references should be included with the submission.

Figures, tables, graphics. Figures and tables should conform to APA 5th edition. Number each in sequence, using Arabic numerals, and supply a heading. Provide a list for each on a separate page(s). All figures and tables must be in black and white only (no grayscale) and should fit within the published margins of the journal page. No photographs will be accepted. A soft file for each should be provided. When and where a software application is different from the word-processing software for the manuscript, designate the application by name, version, and type of platform used.

Endnotes. Authors should use endnotes only when essential. Endnotes should be placed at the end of the manuscript, following the final paragraph of text but preceding the reference list.

Headings. Headings should be structured throughout the text. Normally no more than two to three subheadings are used. A brief running head with pagination should be placed in upper right corner of the manuscript within the header.

Varicose Veins...
A Patient's Reference

James A. Heinz, M.A.H.A.

E-BookTime, LLC
Montgomery, Alabama

Varicose Veins... A Patient's Reference

Library of Congress Control Number: 2010940776

ISBN: 978-1-60862-234-4

First Edition
Published December 2010
E-BookTime, LLC
6598 Pumpkin Road
Montgomery, AL 36108
www.e-booktime.com

Varicose Veins...
A Patient's Reference

Dedication and Appreciation

This book is dedicated to my wife Elizabeth, and my children Bailey and Joshua. I want to thank my parents, Arthur and Doris Heinz for their encouragement and recognizing my entrepreneurial skill set at an early age. Above all, I want to thank GOD for the wisdom, life experiences, opportunities, setbacks, and success that have been granted to me and my family.

Special thanks and appreciation to Dr. Thomas Pester, Dr. Joseph Smith, Dr. David Smith, and Dr. Michael Herion. They are all Medical Directors of a Center for Venous Disease office. They are my friends, business partners, and confidants. They are experts in the field of Phlebology.

Thank you to the early vein care luminaries in Europe and the U.S. Most of the names of the early investigative surgeons, professors, and clinicians are listed below and in the reference area of this book. Special acknowledgement to:

Jose I. Almeida – Miami, FL
Alan Dietzek – Danbury, CT
Peter Gloviczki – Rochester, MN
Lowell Kabnick – Morristown, NJ
Robert B. McLafferty – Springfield, IL
Robert Merchant – Reno, NV
Nick Morrison – Scottsdale, AZ
Oliver Pichot – France
Neil Sadick – New York, NY
Steven E. Zimmet – Austin, TX.

John J. Bergan – La Jolla, CA
Steve Elias – Englewood, NJ
Mitch P. Goldman – La Jolla, CA
Robert L. Kistner – Honolulu, HI
Paul McNeil – Frederick, MD
Robert J. Min – New York, NY
Peter J Pappas – UK
Thomas M. Proebstle – Germany
Margaret and Robert A. Weiss
Baltimore, MD

The preceding were early adopters of the technology and have written many of the early clinical papers related to endovenous ablation and the treatment of venous disease. Most of them continue to collect data, provide educational opportunities, and support Phlebology as a specialty around the world.

Thank you to The American College of Phlebology and the American College of Phlebology Foundation Boards as they have been focused on Phlebology and driving educational programs in our specialty (ABPh Board Certification).

Special appreciation to The American Venous Forum for their focus on patient screening programs across the U.S.

Additionally, I want to thank all the ultrasound sonographers. The giant leap in minimally invasive venous treatment has a great deal to do with ultrasound technology, image quality, and the professional sonographers who are responsible for doing the venous ultrasound studies.

To Terry Egan (Former Sr., V.P. Zimmer Patient Care Division, Bristol Myers-Squibb), and Scott Cramer (Former, V.P. of Sales, VNUS Medical Technologies) for your mentoring and friendship over the years.

I especially want to thank the staff at every Center for Venous Disease® or JoshuaBay™ medical office who work tirelessly to help our patients with their problems. Without you, we're just another vein clinic or medical spa. Please accept my highest regards for your efforts in implementing our core value and mission statement:

"We'll treat your symptoms and touch your Heart."

Finally, thank you to Michelle Parciak, Patty Smith, R.N., and Joseph M. Smith, M.D., R.V.T., for your editing expertise and support of this project.

The Center for Venous Disease

Patient Testimonials

"I wanted to send a note telling my feelings towards the staff at the Center for Venous Disease. It was fate that brought me to their office. It was ever since the first moment that I had walked into their office that I felt warmth, care and concern for my well-being. I was treated like a person that needed help and not just someone that was an insurance number."
CVD-Glendale, AZ

"I have been meaning to write to you for several weeks and thank you Dr. Smith and your terrific staff for the wonderful care that I received and for the great results of the various procedures that were performed."
CVD-Glendale, AZ

"Dr. Herion & his staff were great to work with. Very Professional, good "bed side manner" and great professionals."
CVD-Glendale/Paradise Valley, AZ

"I have given your number (Dr. David Smith) out to several of my friends with the same problem."
CVD-Glendale, AZ

"It is hard to believe that the very painful and unsightly ulcer is gone from my right ankle, that the pain is gone from my legs and that huge rope vein is no more. Thank you Dr. Smith."
Joseph M. Smith, M.D., R.V.T.
CVD-Santa Fe, NM

"I believe (Dr. Pester) that you saved my friend's life by finding a blood clot in her leg."
CVD-El Paso, TX

"Dr. Pester did an excellent job! My legs feel great."
CVD-El Paso, TX

Contents

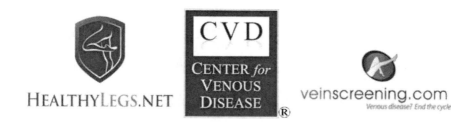

HEALTHYLEGS.NET

CVD
CENTER *for*
VENOUS
DISEASE ®

veinscreening.com
Venous disease? End the cycle.

About the Author

Company Affiliations and Honors:

Founder/Center for Venous Disease®

Founder/JoshuaBay™ Aesthetics Centers

Founder/Heinz Nutraceuticals™

Co-Founder/A²CE™ – Advanced Aesthetic Center for Excellence

Active Member / American College of Phlebology

Founder's Circle Donor / American College of Phlebology Foundation

Board Member / American College of Phlebology Foundation

VNUS™ Medical Technologies / Former Certified Clinical Trainer, Sr. Manager

USCGAux / Flotilla Staff Officer / Desert Eagles – Phoenix, AZ

Cambridge "Who's Who" / Lifetime Member

Education:

Master of Arts – Healthcare Administration

Bachelor of Science – Marketing

Associates Applied Science – Management

Charities Supported:

World Vision International – WorldVision.org

Hope for Kids International – HopeforKidsInternational.org

Compassion International – Compassion.com

Feed our Starving Children – FMSC.org

Fellowship of Christian Athletes – FCA.org

Streetlight PHX Safe House – StreetlightPhx.com

Susan G. Komen Breast Cancer 3 Day – the3day.org

James is no stranger to the medical field. For over 26 years, he has worked in the healthcare industry as a sales specialist, associate product manager, product manager, clinical sales management, regional sales management, and corporate account management for various medical device companies. His experience extends to healthcare insurance issues, standard of care for the patient, and clinical outcome data collection. He has a Masters Degree in Healthcare Administration.

Before he started the Center for Venous Disease® (CVD™), he worked with VNUS® Medical Technologies. VNUS designed the first endovenous catheter system for ablating veins. During his career, James brought new technology to many doctors, hospitals, and surgery centers. Most importantly, he brought new vein care technology to the Southwest region of the U.S. through VNUS. Over his career, he has attended thousands of surgical procedures in an operating room, surgery center, or office-based setting. These operations included orthopedic trauma, sports medicine, total joint replacement, spinal surgery, general surgery, plastic surgery, vascular surgery, and even heart transplants.

Although the title of the book is "Varicose Veins... A Patient's Reference," the content encompasses all treatments of venous disease in various stages with a variety of medical interventions. A very small percentage of venous disease patients are "cosmetic" in nature, regardless of what you may have heard or read. This book offers patients with venous disease an insight into newer treatments available with commentary from an industry insider.

In March of 1999, The Food and Drug Administration cleared the way with approval to VNUS Medical Technologies, allowing the introduction of the VNUS Closure™ procedure to U.S. doctors. The doctors were trained by a small group of VNUS Certified Clinical Trainers and by VNUS sponsored Medical Education Courses. This minimally invasive procedure offered treatment options for patients around the world suffering from varicose vein issues who did not want vein stripping surgery.

James was employed by VNUS Medical Technologies as Sr. Territory Manager and Certified Clinical Trainer. In 2003, he was "Rookie" Manager of the Year at VNUS; and in 2004, he became "Territory" Manager of the Year. James has helped train doctors in northwest Texas, New Mexico, and Arizona on the VNUS Closure® procedure (www.VNUS.com) and other related vein techniques. Over 35 new surgeon sites have been supported by James and his expertise on this procedure. In addition, as a Certified Clinical Trainer, James helped train new VNUS sales people, company personnel, and new clinical specialists hired by the company. He was also in attendance to help support medical educational meetings and workshops that VNUS offered the doctors who were interested in performing this procedure. In addition, James attended conferences, medical trade shows, and conventions associated with venous disease. In 2005, he created the website veinscreening.com to help educate patients before "no charge" vein screenings were offered by anyone in the country. In 2007, additions were made to our website highlighting the expertise of the doctors working with the Center for Venous Disease. CVD is focused on a Total Vein Care philosophy, with its emphasis on the patient. CVD is a certified training site for the VNUS Closure Procedure. The mission statement for the company, "We'll treat your symptoms and touch your Heart" is the cornerstone of their patient-driven programs.

The stated goal of veinscreening.com is to "End the Cycle" of venous disease through effective patient screenings. This is also a stated goal for the American Venous Forum (www.veinforum.org), and a former Surgeon General of The United States, to help reduce or diagnose Deep Vein Thrombosis (DVT) in its earliest stages. DVT, or blood clots, are caused by a blockage of the vein, which is usually acute and very painful. Founded in 1988, the written mission statement of the American Venous Forum is "To promote venous and lymphatic health through innovative research, education, and technology." Venous disease is progressive and tends to move from one generation to another. Oftentimes, the disease remains untreated, due to the lack of education of the patient or healthcare provider. Veinscreening.com offers patients educational insight as related to venous disease. In 2010, www.healthylegs.net was launched as an additional patient reference focusing on the expertise of the CVD doctors in Arizona, New Mexico, and Texas. One of the key components of this website and the advertising is information related to how a patient should choose their doctor.

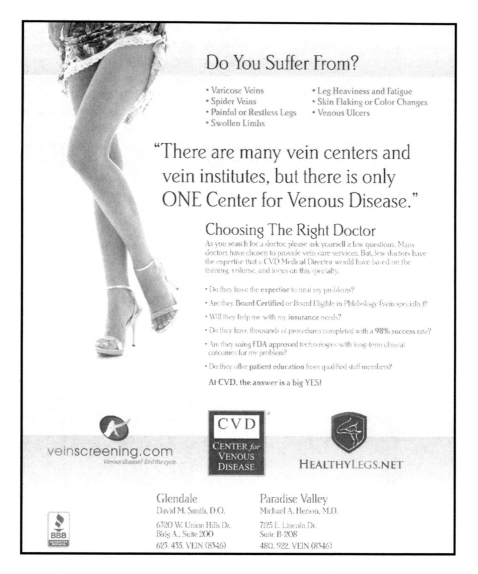
* Locations in Albuquerque, Santa Fe, Glendale, Gilbert, Phoenix, Paradise Valley, and El Paso.

James is the Founder of The Center for Venous Disease, one of the premier vein treatment centers in North America. CVD offers patients the opportunity to be treated and cared for by professionals with expertise in Chronic Venous Disease treatment. Under the guidance and direction of Cofounders, Thomas L. Pester, M.D. and Joseph M. Smith, M.D., R.V.T., the Center for Venous Disease incorporates "best practice" methods with FDA approved drugs or FDA cleared medical devices, to insure quality patient outcomes. Their nurse practitioners, medical assistants, ultrasound sonographers, and medical aestheticians help support the company's vision and values as related to patient care.

Dr. Pester and Dr. Smith are ABPh Diplomates: American College of Phlebology, a Board Certification related to venous disease. Dr. Tom Pester is the Medical Director for CVD in El Paso, TX. Dr. Joseph Smith is the Medical Director for the CVD Santa Fe and Albuquerque centers. Dr. David Smith and Dr. Michael Herion are the Medical Directors responsible for the CVD Glendale, AZ center and Paradise Valley, AZ JoshuaBay™ Aesthetics programs respectively. All CVD Medical Directors are Board Certified in Phlebology (vein specialty). This is along with any other Board Certifications they have earned like Vascular Surgery, General Surgery, General Vascular Surgery, etc... This ABPh Board Certification for CVD doctors is a mandate as agreed upon by the founding partners of CVD. We feel that this additional training leads to a better understanding of venous disease, its treatment, and better outcomes. In addition, many of our doctors have extensive training and credentials in ultrasound.

The Center for Venous Disease also offers additional training opportunities for other doctors, physician assistants, nurse practitioners, ultrasound technicians, nurses, office personnel, medical assistants, etc., to help them learn current techniques in venous disease treatment. Part of this training is accredited and offers medical personnel an opportunity to earn credit hours towards their educational requirements needed to keep their certification or licensing. CVD training programs include live case observation and ultrasound training, as well as business insight, and reimbursement training to help the practice with their insurance issues. For information related to training opportunities, please email cvd@veinscreening.com.

The doctors associated with veinscreening.com, healthylegs.net, and The Center for Venous Disease have numerous years of experience with venous disease, its root cause, and treatment options. The treatment of varicose veins by doctors in the U.S. is growing at over 30% a year. This is a great sign that patients are finally seeking treatment for a progressive disease.

AUTHOR'S GOALS

At the conclusion of this book you'll understand where to be treated, by whom based on education and experience, and with what technology. You should be able to select a doctor, the technology you desire to treat your problem, and where to have the procedure done. I've also included information related to your cosmetic issues, and information on newer treatment options. The information is historical, accurate, and up-to-date at the date of publication.

I made a decision not to publish a group of ugly "before" and post-treatment "after" photos. I have a couple of issues with this. 1) Patient privacy, 2) the "before" photos are a turn off for most people, 3) the "after" photos are subject to interpretation as it relates to success. In saying this, please understand that "cosmetic" outcomes take months. We usually photograph patients (post-procedure) at three months, six months, one year and do follow up ultrasound studies at the same time. You will see examples of photographed legs that have advanced venous disease. Something you'll want to avoid.

What better place to start than the Hippocratic Oath... I think patients should understand the core values of the people treating them. I wrote the mission statement for CVD to reflect our professionalism, expertise, and empathy for our patients. With this said, I think the wisdom of Hippocrates is brilliant. Hippocrates was also the first physician to recognize and treat varicose veins.

Hippocratic Oath

"To consider dear to me, as my parents, him who taught me this art; to live in common with him and, if necessary, to share my goods with him; To look upon his children as my own brothers, to teach them this art.

I will prescribe regimens for the good of my patients according to my ability and my judgment and never do harm to anyone.

I will not give a lethal drug to anyone if I am asked, nor will I advise such a plan; and similarly I will not give a woman a pessary to cause an abortion.

But I will preserve the purity of my life and my arts.

I will not cut for stone, even for patients in whom the disease is manifest; I will leave this operation to be performed by practitioners, specialists in this art.

In every house where I come I will enter only for the good of my patients, keeping myself far from all intentional ill-doing and all seduction and especially from the pleasures of love with women or with men, be they free or slaves.

All that may come to my knowledge in the exercise of my profession or in daily commerce with men, which ought not to be spread abroad, I will keep secret and will never reveal.

If I keep this oath faithfully, may I enjoy my life and practice my art, respected by all men and in all times; but if I swerve from it or violate it, may the reverse be my lot."

Hippocrates (460 BC - 370 BC)
Greek Physician, Father of Western Medicine

The prevailing theme is to "do no harm" and that doctor "specialists" in the art should do the work!

Like Hippocrates, the doctors at The Center for Venous Disease strongly agree that a "specialist" in Phlebology should do the work without doing harm to the patient. Every decision we make is tied to this philosophy, our mission statement, and the Total Vein Care concept.

"This patient reference book is the first of its kind. It is written for potential vein patients in a language they can understand and insight that they can apply on their first visit with the doctor of their choice. I sincerely hope you enjoy the book and share it with others."

~ James A. Heinz, M.A.H.A.

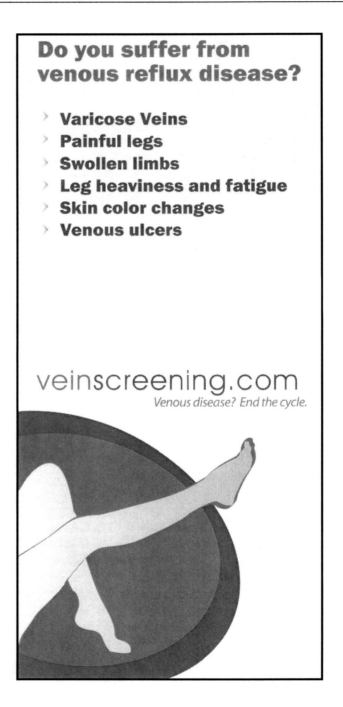

End the cycle!

If you have any of the symptoms listed you are at risk. Venous disease is a progressive disease that will only worsen if left untreated. Our mission is to help you "end the cycle of Venous Disease" through effective patient screening techniques. Our goal is to identify your problem areas and help you seek treatment. Healthy legs can be yours again!

Who's at risk?

Conditions contributing to varicose veins include genetics, obesity, pregnancy, hormonal changes or menopause, work or hobbies requiring extended standing, and past vein diseases such as thrombophlebitis (i.e. inflammation of a vein as a blood clot forms.) Women suffer from varicose veins more than men, and the incidence increases to 50% of people over age 50.

What can be done?

The first step in treatment is to identify the source of venous reflux. This can be done by a simple screening process based on family history and physical exam. Both legs will need to be evaluated and both legs should receive a complete duplex ultrasound exam. The ultrasound exam can identify problem areas related to valve damage, direction of blood flow, and velocity of blood flow in the leg. Identification of the source of reflux is very important as your doctor will then weigh and discuss your treatment options with you. The entire limb must be evaluated to help with a successful treatment. The first step is the screening process!

veinscreening.com
Venous disease? End the cycle.

Disclaimer and Financial Disclosure

This book should not be a substitute for an in-depth conversation with your doctor related to venous disease, its treatment, complications, or outcomes. This book is not a medical opinion. It is simply a summary of some of the public information that is available to you as a patient. It should serve to help you discuss your treatment options with the doctor of your choice. It is a great reference to review certain information that you might find helpful before, during, and after your treatment. The ultimate decision and responsibility for the type of treatment you receive is yours! Please discuss all your options with your doctor, and be aggressive with your questions to find out all you can about your problems and concerns related to venous disease. I am not a doctor "but.....I did stay in a Holiday Inn Express™ last night." I love their commercials. I have been involved with vein care since 2003. So, this book is a testament to what I've learned and what I would like to share with you, the patient.

All kidding aside, you need to be diligent and informed as a patient and as a consumer of care. A doctor specializing in Phlebology is a great start. You can visit www.phlebology.org for information on a Board Certified Phlebologist (ABPh-American Board of Phlebology) near your home. You can use some of the information provided in this book to decide on which ablative technique (VNUS vs. laser) that you're comfortable with. So, choose your doctor, choose the treatment technology, choose which point-of-service, and have a better outcome.

Not every doctor listed on the site is Board Certified, so you'll want to review the information carefully. Other available references are the Medical Board or Osteopathic Medical Board websites provided by your state government. These sites will disclose any pending action by the board against a doctor in your area which relate to complaints from patients, other healthcare providers, or court ordered postings. This is good information to have before you decide on a doctor or a procedure.

A word of caution! Due to the downward trend of reimbursement fees for doctors, increasing overhead expenses, and technology changes (by medical specialty) that might make a particular doctor's expertise obsolete, many doctors have gravitated towards vein care and aesthetic medicine or Medical Spa Directorships.

It also appears that some doctors, who have had numerous hospital-based disciplinary actions, are transitioning themselves to office-based procedures due to the loss of privileges in the hospitals and reduced peer review oversight. Just because a doctor hangs a sign on a door stating that he is a vein doctor doesn't make it true. He may or may not have the training you would expect or accept as the standard in these fields. In addition, just because he has "Medical Director" behind his name doesn't mean he is an expert in aesthetic medicine. Medical Spas have popped up everywhere and have opened at the same rate as they closed. This is a disturbing trend where investors have hired a nurse or a Medical Director to oversee (based on State law) midlevel estheticians, other nurses, or medical assistants to perform the treatments. I would rather have an onsite doctor overseeing the work or doing the work.

Do your homework! It is your body and your decision about which doctor treats your symptoms. As a medical insider, let me offer you a question that I often think about myself when seeking care from any doctor. Would I send my wife, mother, sister, or children to that office? If I feel comfortable with the answer, then I'll usually feel at ease that I've done my background check, reviewed the credentials, and asked around for a referral. This advice is coming from someone who has spent the last 26 years working with doctors in various specialties at multiple points of service locations (hospitals, surgery centers, offices, etc...).

At the end of the book there are pages of references that will help you. Use your favorite search engine to retrieve and review the information related to vein care treatment and technology choices. These clinical papers can help you decide which technology you're comfortable with and help you with a list of questions for your provider. The more you know, the more comfortable you'll be when you seek treatment. My opinions are based on my experience with the training, technology, observations, doctor collaboration, clinical papers, workshops, medical education meetings, American College of Phlebology interaction, American Venous Forum educational materials, attendance in over 5,000 Endovenous Ablation procedures, and from self study. I've tried to be open and honest about what I see as the Administrative Partner and Founder of the Center for Venous Disease.

I have no financial interest in any company or technology discussed with the exceptions of the companies I have ownership in listed below:

Center for Venous Disease® (CVD™)

JoshuaBay™ Aesthetics

Advanced Aesthetic Center for Excellence – A²CE™

Preface

Venous disease is a medical condition that affects nearly 50-80 million Americans. This condition touches the lives of nearly 25-40% of every given community in the United States based on gender statistics in the population base. Estimates of the U.S. prevalence of venous reflux disease is broken into smaller demographics. There are over 20-30 million people with varicose veins. Six million with swelling of the lower legs. Over one million people have skin damage of the lower legs. There are over 500,000 people with venous ulcers near the ankle area. These numbers are very low estimates in my opinion. Because of these issues, pain increases, greatly reducing quality of life. Despite this, venous disease is a relatively low priority for medical practitioners and insurance providers who pay for the services. Without proper training, venous disease can be hard to diagnose and in many cases left untreated. In order to provide the best care for the patient, doctors advance their education related to venous disease by attending medical education courses in venous disease and diagnostic vascular / venous ultrasound. Doctors who specialize in this area are dedicated to helping solve issues related to venous disease, and are called Phlebologists (vein specialty).

The goal of this patient reference is to educate you with the knowledge of venous disease so that you can make informed decisions related to your care. It will also guide you through a conversation with a doctor who specializes in the care of venous disorders by giving you suggested discussion points to review with him or her. By using the information in this book you will be able to "weed out" doctors who don't have the expertise to treat your symptoms. I will help you with the questions that you need to ask before agreeing to treatment. My motives are pretty simple. You deserve to be informed and to receive the best treatment, with the best technology, by a doctor who is an expert in this field, at the lowest cost. Don't you agree?

This book will also be a great resource for primary care physicians, obstetricians, nurse practitioners, physician assistants, dermatologists, podiatrists, and any medical director that works for an insurance company that is responsible for vein care policy. This book will give them more information than they currently have unless they have been to a course focused on venous disease or Phlebology. This should not alarm you, as the treatment of advanced venous disease with more modern techniques is known to very few doctors across the country. In addition, many patients in the past were asked to live with it (venous disease), wear compression stockings forever, or were told there was nothing that could be done. These are comments from our patients who finally decide to come in after being told by another doctor the wrong information. Some patients were told that vein stripping was an alternative. However, when the procedure was described, the patients opted for no treatment vs. vein stripping as an option. Vein stripping is "barbaric" in my opinion, and performed in a hospital setting where other, more life threatening, issues can arise. This option is not a viable solution for most patients vs. the more minimally invasive Radio-Frequency or Laser technologies that I'm going to describe. There are a few doctors in the country that do vein stripping in an office setting with more minimally invasive stripping techniques. Since we are dealing with a progressive disease that could lead to loss of work, continued pain and swelling, or even a venous ulcer, a better treatment modality is needed. It is now available to you through minimally invasive procedures in an office setting.

I also hope that this book will become required reading for the policy makers and the insurance providers before they write medical policy for their respective insurance companies. It has been our experience that doctors who have had no training in venous disease are writing the policies that affect you. As an active member of the American College of Phlebology, I'm very concerned that we may not be able to provide Total Vein Care to patients if we can't get paid for the work we do. Often, insurance companies hide behind words like, preexisting, experimental, or non-covered benefit. If the technology is good enough for the FDA to approve the drugs or clear the devices, supported by clinical data, then it should be good enough for the insurance industry to pay for the services. The approval process for drugs can take years and cost millions of dollars.

Cleared medical devices, can take from 90 days to 2-3 years depending on the FDA classification and application process. Last time I checked we were all paying a premium to take advantage of healthcare options. Last time I checked, it was cheaper to be proactive than to be reactive related to disease. Last time I checked, it was more advantageous from a complication and cost base to treat someone in an office setting vs. a hospital O.R. (lab work, pre-op care, x-rays, anesthesia, and post-op recovery), or surgery center setting.

Finally, the insurance companies are there to manage risks, and offer a profit to the shareholders. That's fine with me. I own four companies and sit on the board of two others. I'm all about the Return on Investment, but not at the sacrifice of others. Especially when it comes to your health. So, the insurance industry should manage risk. Don't limit healthcare options for the patients that are your customers. You can do both. The sooner something is treated with the least invasive modality, the cheaper it is for everyone. This simple idea eludes the insurance industry. That is why we don't have a more progressive healthcare industry when it comes to preventive care. The idea of preventive care only applies to OB where a woman has regular appointments or "well visits" as a part of the delivery process for the new baby. This same process is followed by pediatricians after the birth. Why can't we adopt the same type of protocols for men, women, and children and be proactive instead of reactive with people's healthcare? Let's do things responsibly, using common sense to guide everyone who pays for or treats a patient.

Back to the subject at hand... A positive medical policy from the insurance company establishes the "ground rules" for treatment of certain diseases or procedures. There is nothing wrong with this. While some of them have written positive medical policy for vein care, they often fall short of understanding the underlying causes and treatments available to their patients. I have found the insurance companies and the Medical Directors associated with them to be quite open-minded when they have the facts. They look at clinical data, patient "quality of life" scores, cost associated with the technology, and other parameters.

As a Founder's Level Donor to American College of Phlebology Foundation (www.phlebologyFoundation.org) we have a passion for the Total Vein Care concept that has to be achieved for every patient. This means that we need positive medical coverage on the entire leg, for every

29

refluxing system, and not parts of this complex web of veins. Organizations like the Foundation are vital in raising the bar, by providing education to all parties interested in the treatment of venous disease or Phlebology. Your contribution is encouraged. Please let them know I sent you!

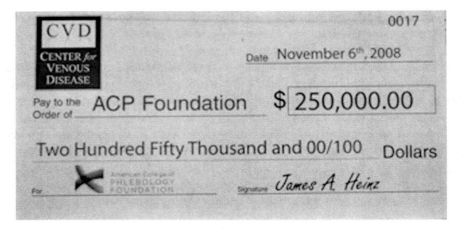

ACPF commitment of $250,000 over 5 years funded by CVD offices

Through corporate and individual donors like doctors, nurses, ultrasound sonographers, and others, the ACP Foundation continues their charter to help provide education to patients and the providers who treat them. The commitment from CVD doctors is obvious and visible.

The ACPF drives educational programs for doctors, ultrasound sonographers, and staff members that treat venous disease. The ACPF does this through the American College of Phlebology courses related to vein care, ultrasound, anatomy, treatment options, and case studies. They also offer a doctor the opportunity to become Board Certified in Phlebology through The American Board of Phlebology Organization. For more information please go to: www.americanboardofphlebology.org. Our doctors support the ACPF and the ACP as donors and active members. All of our CVD Medical Directors are ABPh Board Certified. This designation is a requirement to treat patients at the Center for Venous Disease.

The goals of the ABPh designation are listed below:

The American Board of Phlebology is an independent, non-profit organization founded in 2007 for the purpose of certifying physicians who have met a defined standard of education, training and knowledge in the field of phlebology. The American Board of Phlebology (ABPh) was established to:

1. Improve the standards of medical practitioners and the quality of patient care related to the treatment of venous disorders and all aspects of venous disease

2. Serve the public and the medical profession by establishing initial and continuing qualifications for certification and maintenance of certification as physician specialists in the practice of phlebology

3. Examine physician candidates for certification and maintenance of certification in the practice of phlebology

4. Establish educational standards for teaching and training programs in phlebology

5. Maintain a registry of individuals who hold certificates issued by the Board

For more information, visit http://www.americanboardofphlebology.org.

I hope this book serves the patients, doctors, and the insurance providers with the facts. As a patient, it is your responsibility to be informed and to understand that you are a customer of your insurance company. Too many times, patients look to the staff of doctors' offices to solve insurance issues. The insurance providers are paid by you. The best way to handle insurance issues is to deal with them as their customer and not direct anger or blame toward your doctor for issues beyond their control. I hope this book gives you the information and insight to ask the right questions of your doctor and insurance providers. They are all there to help you!

As the creator of veinscreening.com and www.healthylegs.net, and someone who has intimate knowledge of venous disease, I am excited to share this information with you as a starting point to your treatment options. Thank you for taking responsibility for your own healthcare related to your legs. "Healthy Legs are your Foundation for life."

Chapter 1

My Unsightly Legs?

Do you suffer from venous reflux disease? It's a great question. If you have varicose veins, spider veins, painful or restless legs, swollen limbs, leg heaviness and fatigue, skin color changes, or venous ulcerations, the answer is probably yes! If you have any of the symptoms listed above, you are at risk for further discomfort, a lower quality of life, possible loss of work, and lower self-esteem. Venous disease is progressive in nature and will only worsen if left untreated.

The first step in treatment is to identify the source of venous reflux or retrograde blood flow. The second step is to understand what the newest, minimally invasive procedures can do to improve the quality of your life. It is estimated that in 2008, there were over 20,000 vein stripping surgeries, over 100,000 laser ablation procedures, and over 100,000 radio-frequency procedures performed in the U.S. (VNUS Medical Technologies, San Jose, CA). That's over 220,000 operations or procedures done to correct venous reflux. Shouldn't you have the information you need to make a good decision about your treatment options? Current estimates on total procedures are more than 250,000 per year and growing.

For many of you, the first conversation you have will be with your primary care physician or your OBGYN. Unfortunately, you might know more about the treatment of venous disease after reading this book than the person that is looking at your legs. This might be considered an inflammatory statement, but it is the truth. Until they make a decision to treat venous disease, most doctors just don't understand its underlying causes. Your signs may be cosmetic to untrained eyes, and you may be told that insurance companies won't pay for treatment. However, this is not true based on the underlying medical issue or problem that can be diagnosed, documented, and treated effectively. Blue Cross, United Healthcare, Beech Street, Aetna, Cigna, Kaiser, Humana, Health Net, PacifiCare, and Coventry all have coverage for the treatment of venous reflux disease. In addition, Medicare covers these treatments when 'Medical Necessity' requirements are met. Over 220 million people are covered by the top ten insurers related to vein care coverage.

Word of caution! Each insurance company has their own rules and regulations related to treatment. This is contained in your policy and provided to the doctors as Medical Policy to be followed. Ultimately, the patient is the customer of the providing insurance company. Be responsible and read your policy, and if you have questions or concerns, please speak with your personnel department and your insurance company directly.

We will discuss medical policy issues and "red flags" to avoid when seeking out a doctor who specializes in the treatment of varicose veins later in the book.

The following will give you an idea of other vascular surgery procedures and the annual U.S. volume.

PROCEDURE	ESTIMATED ANNUAL PROCEDURES
Stab Micro - Micro-Phlebectomy	160,000
Vein Stripping (Operating Room)	100,000
Endovenous Ablation (Office Setting)	80,000 (+30%)
Carotid Endarterectomy & Stenting	150,000
AV Access for Hemodialysis	79,500
Revision of AV Access	45,000
Peripheral Bypass	115,000
Open repair of AAA	66,000
Stent Graft repair of AAA	19,000
Thrombectomy	130,000

As you can see, if you combine the Micro-Ambulatory Phlebectomy, Vein Stripping, and Endovenous Ablation numbers together, you have over 340,000 operations or procedures done in the U.S. related to vein treatments. Don't get too caught up in the numbers other than understanding that the treatment of venous disease is a relevant specialty (Phlebology) in the U.S., and it should be recognized.

The ultimate goal of treatment is to get pain relief and return to a normal or higher quality of life in the safest environment for the patient. Too often people don't seek treatment, with men being the worst when it comes to this disease. By the time most men come in to be seen, they often have advanced disease and will end up needing to have multiple procedures. In comparison, if the water pump or radiator on their car needed repair due to a rupture or stuck thermostat, the car would be in the shop the same day. In many ways, the water flowing through the engine of a car is similar to the venous system we will discuss in the next chapter. Please don't wait to be treated. As with a car, if you don't have water circulating through the entire engine, it will overheat and the repair cost with mount. There is no difference in the human body. Blood flowing away from the heart should return to the heart. It should complete the cycle to keep the efficient circulation of blood. Remember this as you read the next chapter.

Chapter 2

Venous Anatomy

In order to understand what you have and why, you need to understand a little bit about how veins work. Think of venous anatomy as an interstate highway system. You have highways coming and going, twisting and turning, and these routes or tributaries serve different destinations. These destinations fulfill our need to arrive at work on time. They fuel our passion for exploration or relaxation. They allow us to move freely across vast regions. Our highways and roads lead over bridges, through tunnels, and often are unfamiliar territory to us. When something is unfamiliar to us, we get nervous, uptight, or discount help from others. That is why men don't ask for directions. My goal is to get you familiar with the twisting and turning of the interstate that lies within your venous and vascular system and help offer solutions and directions.

In the body, veins carry oxygen-depleted blood back to the heart through healthy veins. The arteries carry oxygen-rich blood away from the heart to all of your major organs and extremities. By treating the veins, no harm should come to the arteries. Veins return blood to the heart by way of the heart pump and the calf muscle pump that occurs when you walk or exercise. This leads to normal circulation of blood flow throughout your body. Venous disease occurs when the blood that is supposed to be flowing back to the heart doesn't reach the heart efficiently. The blood that doesn't reach the heart often "pools" in the lower leg region usually in the thigh, calf level or lower to the ankle. This excessive "pooling" of blood causes leg fatigue, swelling, skin color changes (due to the iron content in the blood) and "pop outs" or "blow outs" present on your legs as varicose veins. Left alone, the varicose vein issues will worsen, and the skin color changes will become more apparent. The thickening of skin or a leather-like look and feel will be the next visible signs, followed by a venous ulceration or skin sore. Not only is the ulcer problematic but it is very costly. The estimated cost to treat a venous stasis ulcer is over $40,000.

Once you're at this point, you are in the worst possible shape. You'll be treated for the venous ulcer and for the underlying cause of the venous disease. You have substantially increased healing and recovery times, and your quality of life has been extremely diminished. The lesson here is to seek treatment early! As demonstrated later, the longer you wait, the worse it is going to get. The poster which can be found in most doctor's offices using the VNUS catheter is a great teaching tool for patients. The most important part of this poster in my opinion is the visual progression of venous disease (lower left corner). I can guarantee that if you do not address your issues, your skin will flake, itch, break down, discolor, and split open. Then you have to treat the source of venous disease and the open wound.

So, why do most people wait or ignore the obvious signs? Some people have a higher tolerance to pain. Some people don't care if others stare or point at the clusters of varicose veins. Some are in denial. Some fear the treatment. Some people have the wrong information about treatment options. Others just decide to live with it for reasons not stated. Some don't have insurance. Some think insurance companies won't pay for it. Some patients think it's "cosmetic." I think it's ugly and treatable without much pain, discomfort, restriction, or complications. As you read through the book, your fears should fade as your education related to venous disease increases.

As you look at the legs (from left to right) at the lower left side of the poster you'll see the progression of venous disease. Treatment(s) of the underlying medical problem to stop the retrograde blood flow yields the possibility of the ulcer healing more quickly. Ulcers often take months, if not years, to heal and are often misdiagnosed by healthcare providers. This degradation of the skin is all due to pressure buildup on the system. There is no cure for this; however, it can be diagnosed and treated very successfully by a trained doctor that understands the need to treat the entire leg with a multifaceted approach. We will discuss this in depth later in the book.

Just like our highways, there are different routes to take and different reasons we take the road we're on. In our legs, there are a few main veins mentioned. They are:

Common Femoral Vein

Femoral Vein

Great Saphenous Vein (GSV)

Small Saphenous Vein (SSV)

Sural Veins

Mid Thigh Perforators (PERFs)

Paratibial Perforators

Posterior Tibial Perforators

Intergemellar Perforators

The GSV, SSV, and Perforator Veins are the most common veins for ablation procedures for treatment of Varicose Veins. You'll be more familiar with them as we get further into the book.

Where your Common Femoral Artery, Common Femoral Vein, and Great Saphenous Vein come together in the groin is generally known as the

Saphenofemoral Junction. A photo of this image on ultrasound is below. We often refer to this as the "Mickey Mouse" view with patients because it kind of looks like Mickey's ears in this view. This junction is an area of the body where high volumes of blood move down the legs and then returns to the heart. The junction lies in the crease of the groin in the pelvic area.

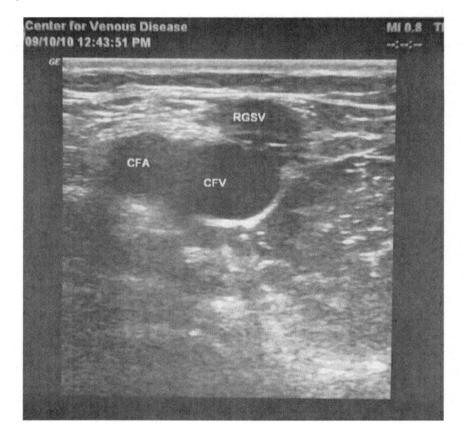

Ultrasound Photo courtesy of The Center for Venous Disease, Glendale, AZ

The superficial vein located behind the leg below knee level and in the calf region running down towards the back of your foot is the Small Saphenous Vein (SSV). The superficial system (GSV, SSV) usually lie between .05-1.0 cm from your skin, making its location close to the surface of your skin. The Femoral Vein is down farther from the skin and runs down the leg from your groin to the ankle area and connects to the GSV. Communicating veins between the Femoral Vein and the Great Saphenous Vein or Small Saphenous Vein are called Perforator Veins. Perforator Veins, or PERFS, run up and down the entire leg and act as bridges between the GSV and the deep system. The above mentioned veins are all part of the highway, and all have to work together in order to work efficiently. Please feel free to review the VNUS Patient Exam Poster or the photos provided to familiarize yourself with the anatomy.

Your doctor should be able to diagnose and treat all of these areas. You cannot treat one part of the system; the entire limb has to be evaluated and treated based on the findings. We often refer to this as Total Vein Care which includes diagnostic ultrasound, vein ablation methods, micro-ambulatory phlebectomy, sclerotherapy, and the possible use of surface laser, or radio wave technology to cosmetically "clean up" the leg post-procedure. We'll discuss surface laser devices later in the book.

Word of caution! You cannot effectively treat the cosmetic appearance of varicose or spider veins until you rule out venous reflux. Some doctor's offices are known for doing sclerotherapy injections/treatments before reflux disease is ruled out. They simply don't have the expertise or the diagnostic equipment to evaluate this. If you have numerous spider veins or varicose veins, and you are receiving injections without a duplex ultrasound, then you are wasting your money.

All healthy leg veins contain valves along the vein segment, which open and close with respiration from the lungs and a pump from the heart. Along with the heart pump, the calf muscle pump (from walking) also helps to return blood to the heart when there is normal valve operation. This describes what is supposed to happen; but with venous reflux disease, the valves do not work as described. These diseased or damaged valves reduce the normal blood return to the heart, and cause the symptoms that we have already described. These damaged valves or over dilated valves are the primary causes of your problem areas. They allow blood to flow back down the leg (retrograde flow), adding pressure to the next valve. The next valve may fail and then another and another. Like a dam breaking on a river, the pressure begins to build until a large outward burst occurs. In the leg, these are called "pop outs" or "blow outs." This "pop out" is usually a good sign (bad sign), that you have venous disease, and you need to seek treatment. The "pop outs" are the varicose veins that you see on your legs. The chosen treatment has to be able to reroute or detour the blood flow to other healthy veins so the blood return to the heart is reestablished. The treatment will take the pressure off the system. By normalizing the pressure, varicose veins diminish in appearance, swelling goes down, and your legs will feel better. The goal is to relieve pain, which occurs when the pressure is reduced in the lower legs. Healthy legs are your Foundation for life!

A good illustration of normal valve operation and a damaged vein valve is diagramed below:

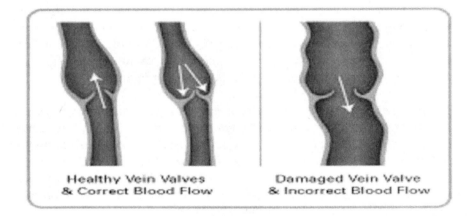

Healthy Vein Valves
& Correct Blood Flow

Damaged Vein Valve
& Incorrect Blood Flow

Diagram courtesy of VNUS Medical Technologies, San Jose, CA

The left-hand diagram shows normal blood flow in one direction with the tiny valve closing and stopping the downward flow. The damaged valve on the right shows the valve staying open causing the blood to flow downward. This is venous reflux, referred to as an incompetent valve, which is the start of something worse. As the pressure builds, other valves fail, and the "pop outs" occur. These "pop outs" or varicose areas are a direct result of valve damage in your legs. Unless treated, the pressure will continue to increase, and more damage will occur down the leg.

By now, you probably understand that everything you feel in your legs is based upon pressure on the nerve(s). The heavy feeling or crawling feeling or cramps can be caused by pressure on the system due to failed valves above. A healthy vein will restore normal venous flow to the area, while a damaged vein will allow blood to flow retrograde, or downward, causing blood to "pool" in an area of your lower legs and ankles. If left untreated, serious problems can occur including skin breakdown, a venous ulcer, flaking skin, a blood clot, or all of the above. If you look at the diagram below, you will see the overall complexity of the entire system that needs to be diagnosed using comprehensive ultrasound imaging.

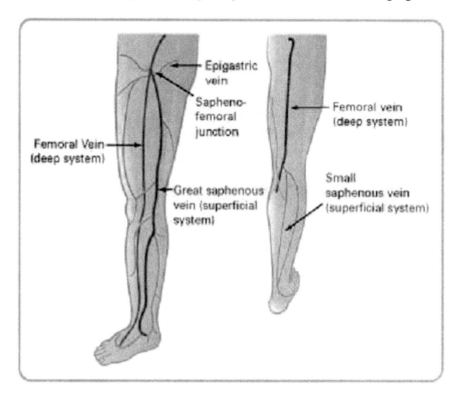

Diagram courtesy of VNUS Medical Technologies, San Jose, CA

With the use of sensitive diagnostic ultrasound equipment that includes color wave Doppler, we can evaluate blood flow direction, flow rates, valve damage, and vein diameters. This helps us to evaluate whether the system is healthy or diseased and helps us to "map" the leg to determine the next step. Considering the findings, you may not need any treatment, or you may need treatment in multiple areas of the system. The ultrasound equipment gives us a great tool to use to diagnose and treat your particular problems. The information from the ultrasound sonographer is then given to your doctor. Your doctor will review this information with the sonographer and again with you on your next visit. At this time, treatment discussions can occur and decisions made.

The last vein we will discuss in the superficial system is the Perforator Vein. The Perforator Veins, or the "communicator veins" offer a connection between the deep system and the superficial system. There are over 100 Perforator Veins in the lower leg. These veins are also a source of venous reflux and need to be addressed. They are usually a problem below the knee and are often responsible for "feeding" blood to venous ulcers located below the knee or near the inside part of the leg near the ankle. Perforator Veins are an area of medicine that is often ignored. This is due to the lack of complete understanding of the system and the skill set needed to treat these with more modern techniques. However, they have to be addressed if you are to have a good outcome. This is especially true when you have Perforator Veins that are causing or contributing to a venous ulcer. Here is a very good illustration of Perforator Veins:

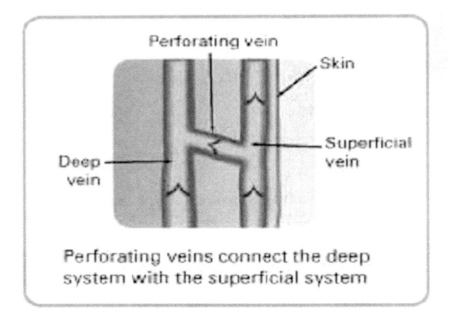

Diagram courtesy of VNUS Medical Technologies, San Jose, CA

The basic ideal as a treating physician is to understand what is going on with you and your legs as it relates to these systems. This is determined by a complete examination that includes your history and physical exam, a complete bilateral (both legs) ultrasound examination to determine valve damage and blood flow direction, and discussion of your treatment options with your doctor. With the proper training and education, your doctor can diagnose these issues, and have a plan to treat this disorder effectively.

Now that you have an understanding of the anatomy, let me take a moment to drive a couple of points home.

- Your symptoms and the complete diagnosis of your superficial and deep venous systems are the key to a successful outcome. This is provided by ultrasound and your physical exam.

- There is no cure for this progressive disease, although it can be managed very effectively, along with a good cosmetic outcome as a result. You have to have realistic expectations.

- Your understanding of venous disease is the first step and will help you to self-evaluate your symptoms and concerns. It will also help you with any future discussions you have with your doctor related to treatment options.

- You should only see a doctor that specializes in this disease (ABPh Board Certified). I would not recommend anyone who just decided that treating veins was a nice addition to their practice and a new revenue stream or profit center.

- I would avoid treatment from anyone that tells you that you just need sclerotherapy injections to solve your vein issues before an ultrasound examination.

- Openly seek out opinions from people who have been treated with the newer technology. This might include friends, family members or even nurses or other healthcare providers that you know.

- Then you can schedule your office visit.

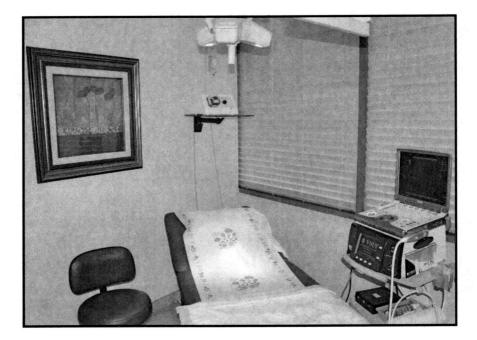

Photo courtesy of the Center for Venous Disease, Glendale, AZ
CVD Patient Treatment Room

During your exam, you can expect to have a full History and Physical, Review of current illness, Review of Systems (head to toe) assessment, allergy and medications review, social history, family history, and a vein exam on both legs. If the doctor feels based on the exam that you may have venous disease, your doctor will order an ultrasound on both legs. Wear shorts to your exam or you might have to change into the ugliest disposable shorts you've ever seen. During your exam notes will be taken and forms filled out to document the physical exam. One of the modern "instruments" to document the serious nature of your condition is the use of the C.E.A.P. classification system. The worse your physical symptoms are, the higher the C.E.A.P. classification from a scale from C0-C6.

Clinical – Etiologic – Anatomic – Pathophysiologic C.E.A.P. Classification(s)

C0:   No visible signs of venous disease
C1:   Telangiectasias or reticular veins
C2:   Varicose veins
C3:   Edema
C4a: Pigmentation and/or eczema
C4b: Lipodermatosclerosis and/or atrophie blanche
C5:   Healed venous ulcer
C6:   Active venous ulcer

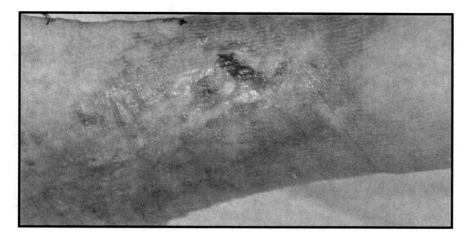

**Venous ulcer photo courtesy of Joseph M. Smith, M.D., R.V.T.
Center for Venous Disease, Santa Fe, NM**

Another useful "instrument" to document venous disease in your medical chart is The Venous Clinical Severity Score. This information documents Varicose Veins (VV), Edema, Pigmentation, Pain, Inflammation, Induration, Acute Ulcers, Duration of Ulcers, Diameter of Ulcers, Compression stocking compliance. Each category receives a score from 0-3; (0) Absent, (1) Mild, (2) Moderate, or (3) Severe. The score is added up and documented in our CVD Electronic Medical Report. Obviously you should have a worse score before your treatment. So, for example, you may be a 20+ score before treatment and a 9 after. This information helps us track our outcomes. Good documentation is key to receiving payment from your insurance company. More on this later. The exam is very important to the patient and we take the time to explain our treatment decisions with the patients in great detail. This is important for any vein center. If you feel you are not receiving this type of care or feel that your questions are not being answered then I would recommend going to another office.

Photo courtesy of Center for Venous Disease, Glendale, AZ

At CVD, patient comfort and patient education is paramount. In each room you'll find comfortable seating, artwork, educational posters, brochures, flip charts, and a CVD designed Electronic Medical Record system. The chairs were designed as well to recline for patient comfort after a procedure. We wanted to make our environment less institutional and more patient friendly. We succeeded.

Chapter 3

Understanding Venous Ultrasound

I would like to now explain the bilateral ultrasound study, or venous scan, mentioned earlier. The use of ultrasound across many specialties has helped diagnose problems with patients related to venous disease, cardiovascular disease, obstetrics, vascular disease, and more. If you were ever pregnant, you probably remember seeing the ultrasound machine. The ultrasound machine has a probe, monitor, and many dials for many different functions.

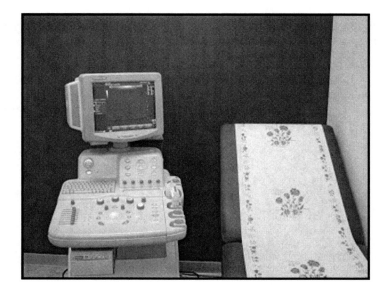

**Photo courtesy of Joseph M. Smith, M.D., R.V.T.,
Center for Venous Disease, Santa Fe, NM**

Most modern ultrasound equipment for vascular examinations uses many different ultrasound modes to look inside the body.

- B mode uses sound waves to create gray scale images and is primarily used to study anatomy.

- Duplex ultrasound is a mode of ultrasound that can display an anatomical image and blood flow information at the same time.

- Pulse Wave Doppler calculates blood velocity.

- Spectral Doppler displays blood velocity as it appears in time, duration, and flow direction.

- Color Flow Doppler superimposes color on gray scale images (red or blue) and provides more information on the presence of blood flow, velocity, and direction of blood flow in the segment under review.

Common ultrasound terms that you might hear related to your symptoms and the ultrasound exams include:

- Transverse – cross section view

- Patency – usually refers to the vessel being open where blood flow is present

- Antegrade flow – refers to blood that is flowing towards the heart

- Retrograde flow – refers to blood that is flowing away from the heart or downward

- Echogenic/Hyperechoic images – very bright echoes that reflect white reflectors on grayscale images

- Hypo-echoic – light shades of gray echoes on grayscale images

- Echolucent/Anechoic – without echoes, the black reflectors of the grayscale image

- Compression – pressure that is applied to the transducer that collapses the vessel upon itself

- Augmentation – compressive maneuver that moves blood towards the transducer

- Valsalva – patient assisted maneuver whereby the patient uses abdominal muscles to "bare down" and release when directed. This is used to test for valve incompetence at the Saphenofemoral Junction.

- Longitudinal Access – long view of area of interest

These are just some of the terms used in your ultrasound exam, and most of them are used in conversations between the sonographer and your doctor. This may help you to understand what is being said should you hear a discussion between the two.

The ultrasound probes are dedicated by procedure use and are sensitive to looking at different parts of our anatomy for different reasons. For our purpose in venous disease of the lower limbs, we use ultrasound to view the veins in the leg. We use it to locate the vein, determine the size of the vein diameter, to measure blood flow and direction, and to view any obstructions or abnormal anatomy, such as an aneurismal segment of a vein. We can view the opening and closing of the vein valves. We can identify how fast or slow the valve closes. We can also rule out deep vein thrombosis, or a blood clot. All these things are done with the help of a good ultrasound device and a good ultrasound technician. Good sonographers are usually highly trained and paid well. They bring a level of expertise to any venous scan or venous procedure. This is done by charting information on your lower extremities that can be reviewed by your doctor.

At this point, your doctor can plan a course of treatment. Documents are submitted to the insurance company, including your health questionnaire, the doctor's history and physical, and the ultrasound report. This is done to obtain the insurance pre-authorization or predetermination often needed before you can seek procedural treatment. Not all insurance carriers require this authorization. This report from the sonographer is very important to you as a patient, and it is very important to your doctor for many reasons previously discussed.

Word of caution! If a doctor or staff member at a vein clinic tells you that they can't or won't file insurance or ask you to file the forms yourself, this is a "red flag" and often puts the burden of payment directly on your shoulders. Most U.S. insurance companies will provide coverage of vein procedures as long as medical policy is followed. Most credible medical offices will file insurance forms on your behalf. Remember, insurance companies cover over 220 million people related to vein care. In addition, the documentation by your doctor has to be complete and fulfill the requirements of the insurance companies' medical policy. CVD has a very complete Electronic Medical Record that is filed on your behalf. Without proper documentation, the claim may be denied.

The ultrasound sonographer should be trained in the superficial venous system, and might have credentials as a Registered Vascular Technician or RVT. The RVT credential designates greater academic study in vascular ultrasound by the sonographer. Some doctors may also have this designation. Again, this is a credential that sets this particular doctor apart as an expert on venous disease treatment.

The actual venous insufficiency ultrasound exam will rule out deep vein thrombosis (blood clot) and document reflux in the deep and superficial venous systems. The exam usually requires a patient to remove their clothing below the waist excluding the underwear. We recommend that a person come in with loose fitting shorts. The area in the groin will need to be evaluated as this is the location of the Saphenofemoral Junction (SFJ). The ultrasound probe needs to reach this area without interference from clothing. The location of the SFJ lies high in the pelvic area and is the key to the entire exam in most cases. This anatomy is crucial to the exam, so if you're asked to remove your clothing below the waist, don't be surprised. The exam will be used by your doctor to establish treatment options. You may have to revisit the anatomy section to follow the steps in the exam.

The actual exam for venous insufficiency takes about 30-45 minutes and will include:

1. The Saphenofemoral Junction is studied, which includes the Deep Femoral Vein, Femoral Artery, and the Great Saphenous Vein, and any refluxing tributary or branches off the SFJ. DVT is then ruled out.

2. A Valsalva maneuver is performed at the Saphenofemoral Junction to determine reflux at SFJ. Valsalva will be explained to you at the time of your exam.

3. Distal augmentation for Great Saphenous Vein below the junction is performed along the vein track, reflux is documented, and the Deep Vein is examined along the vein track.

4. Small Saphenous Vein is examined with augmentation to determine reflux levels and DVT is ruled out at the Saphenopopliteal Junction (behind the knee crease). SSV is scanned down to the foot.

5. Perforator Veins (communication veins) are examined and measured, and reflux studies are performed.

6. Reflux is noted and charted and sent to the doctor for review.

7. Deep Vein Thrombosis is noted and charted if present and doctor is notified as soon as possible. This is a very serious situation that needs immediate attention.

8. Any abnormality that includes greater than +0.5 seconds of reflux or retrograde blood flow is charted and discussed with the doctor.

Ultrasound is a key component to successful treatment in any minimally invasive procedure related to venous disease. It is used before the treatment, during the treatment and post-procedure to document success and rule out any complications. You will have several ultrasound exams as part of the standard of care and follow up needed to track your results and the success of any treatment you may receive. Having a trained and credentialed sonographer and a doctor who understands the findings can really make the difference for a successful treatment and outcome for the patient. It is also important that the doctor you are seeing has invested in a high quality ultrasound system.

Once the ultrasound exam is completed, your ultrasound sonographer or doctor will use the photos taken from the ultrasound machine and "chart" them on forms that will likely be sent to your insurance carrier. The form that we use follows. This form, as well as the doctors "findings or impression" will be dictated through an Electronic Medical Charting system or EMR. The visual chart will list all areas of reflux for both legs in RED, at multiple levels, from a frontal view and a posterior view. We chart reflux greater than .5 seconds or as required by the insurance companies, vein size, and any issues related to blood clots in your superficial veins, deep veins, or issues with an artery if detected. This exam usually will take 30-45 minutes and must be accurate. This, again, is where the training comes in and the credentials.

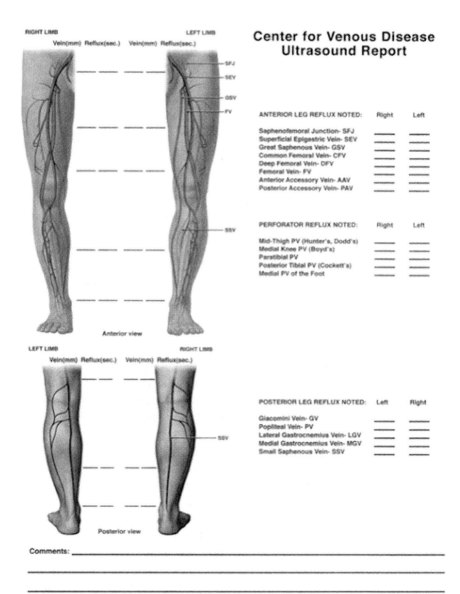

RIGHT LIMB   LEFT LIMB
Vein(mm) Reflux(sec.)   Vein(mm) Reflux(sec.)

SFJ
SEV
GSV
FV

SSV

Anterior view

LEFT LIMB   RIGHT LIMB
Vein(mm) Reflux(sec.)   Vein(mm) Reflux(sec.)

SSV

Posterior view

Center for Venous Disease
Ultrasound Report

ANTERIOR LEG REFLUX NOTED:	Right	Left
Saphenofemoral Junction- SFJ		
Superficial Epigastric Vein- SEV		
Great Saphenous Vein- GSV		
Common Femoral Vein- CFV		
Deep Femoral Vein- DFV		
Femoral Vein- FV		
Anterior Accessory Vein- AAV		
Posterior Accessory Vein- PAV		

PERFORATOR REFLUX NOTED:	Right	Left
Mid-Thigh PV (Hunter's, Dodd's)		
Medial Knee PV (Boyd's)		
Paratibial PV		
Posterior Tibial PV (Cockett's)		
Medial PV of the Foot		

POSTERIOR LEG REFLUX NOTED:	Left	Right
Giacomini Vein- GV		
Popliteal Vein- PV		
Lateral Gastrocnemius Vein- LGV		
Medial Gastrocnemius Vein- MGV		
Small Saphenous Vein- SSV		

Comments: _____

_____

_____

Signature: _____

CVD Ultrasound Report
©2010, Center for Venous Disease, James A. Heinz

Chapter 4

Why Me?

There are many reasons for this disease, some of which are related to: age, gender, family history, multiple pregnancies, obesity, and professions that require long periods of standing or sitting. Symptoms often include: pain, swelling, skin breakdown, heaviness, fatigue, aching, burning, restless legs, edema, throbbing, cramping, tingling.

Word of caution! If you come into a doctor's office and don't disclose, discuss, or document pain, swelling, symptoms, and how it affects your quality of life, shame on you. Your doctor cannot help you with insurance issues if all we can document is a "cosmetic" situation.

Within these descriptions, we can think of many reasons for our painful and somewhat ugly appearance to our legs. Some experts estimate the prevalence of venous insufficiency at 50-80 million. Conservative estimates include 25 million Americans with varicose veins. Approximately 40% of the population will experience some form of venous disease, and 50% will experience pain associated with the symptoms. It is estimated that 20-30% of women will have significant life altering consequences related to venous disease, while 15-20% of men will have clinical significance. The loss of worker productivity related to this disease cannot even be measured, as it is in the billions of dollars. This disease is costly to American companies. These companies are the ones providing insurance coverage for their employees. In saying this, it is important for human resource managers to make sure they have coverage for their employees for the treatment of this disease. I have seen waitresses, single moms, working moms, fire fighters, police officers, nurses, doctors, pilots, flight attendants, factory workers, and the like affected by some sort of issue related to venous disease. There is no pill you can take, and you can't wear compression hose forever. There are no special vein creams that are proven to work on the underlying cause. However, the Center for Venous Disease endorses the Total Vein Care Kit, consisting of three products, for post-procedure (RF or laser ablation; Sclerotherapy or surface laser) pain and/or bruising. This kit includes: a Post-Procedure Anti-inflammatory Gel, Vitamin K Spritz, and Vein Strengthening Moisture Whip loaded with natural antioxidants. This kit is not a substitute for treatment. It is a product formulated to help reduce swelling, bruising, and pain after the VNUS Closure, Endovenous Laser, cosmetic laser or sclerotherapy injections. It would be more effective for laser ablation, as it is documented that laser causes more post procedure pain and bruising. This custom kit is sold through our website, CVD and JoshuaBay™ offices, and other approved medical offices. Ordering information is available at veinscreening.com or healthylegs.net and includes the three products, zippered bag, and instructions.

Total Vein Care Kit

Formulated for use with post-procedure protocols to reduce post-procedure tenderness, bruising, or swelling associated with vein ablation, sclerotherapy treatments, or cosmetic laser.

It is not feasible for any patient to take pain medication or anti-inflammatory medicines forever. Putting your feet up or placing cold or warm compresses won't work either. Wearing compression hose will help reduce swelling, but will not cure venous disease. All of these are temporary "fixes" to the underlying problem. As an employee, you cannot give 100% to your employer if you have problems with your legs. As mentioned earlier, if you're the employer, you need to make sure that the insurance you provide for your employees covers vein care. By being proactive, both the employee and the employer benefit due to increased productivity achieved by a pain-free, active employee. I've included a patient photo that delayed treatment of the underlying problem and ended up with a venous ulcer. The slide presentation was developed by VNUS and provided to clinics to educate patients on wound care challenges.

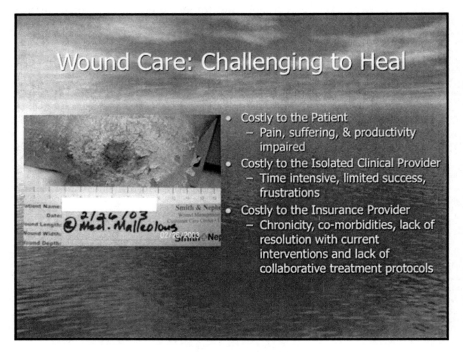

Photo courtesy of VNUS Medical Technologies
Wound Care Presentation - 2003

Chapter 5

Next Steps?

First, you should visit veinscreening.com or healthylegs.net and review the patient information provided and then register on the site. Again, if you have varicose veins, painful legs, swollen limbs, leg heaviness and fatigue, skin color changes, or venous ulcers at the ankles, you should seek medical treatment. However, many of the primary care physicians, plastic surgeons, dermatologists, and obstetricians don't understand the underlying problem, even though they see patients with these symptoms every day of the week. You may or may not get the referral you need to see a trained doctor that treats this disease. You may need a referral, with some insurance policies, to see a specialist "in network" or not at all. Therefore, my advice would be for you to be persistent in your request if you are required to have a referral to see an expert. In case you were wondering, the insurance companies don't pay the "expert" any more than any other physician. You simply get the best in your area at the same cost to you and your insurance provider.

You may also need to seek treatment "out-of-network" to get the help you need. This is going to be more expensive than your co-pay, but you'll at least get to someone who understands what is going on with you and knows how to treat it. The "out-of-network" option may be more affordable than you think, based on point-of-service. For example, if you decide to seek treatment from a doctor who is hospital-based, a hospital will charge you over $10,000 for this procedure. You'll also pay the anesthesiologist and the surgeon fee. If you have an 80% coverage policy, you'll pay more than $2,000-$7,000 to do this. However, in our facility (office setting), you would pay about $1,000-$3,000 and see doctors who do more procedures than anyone in the Southwest U.S. even if you were out-of-network. You may even opt for paying cash for your treatment. This is not a bad option if your "deductible" for the calendar year has not been met, and you have a high yearly deductible. You might just prefer to take control of your own treatment options without all the bureaucracy or restrictions related to vein treatment. You may be told to "live with it." You may also be asked to take over-the-counter anti-inflammatory medicines or wear compression hose for life. In Arizona, where I live, wearing compression hose could kill you due to the heat. Well, not really, but compression hose and desert heat don't deserve to be used in the same sentence together! You know what I mean if you have ever worn them.

In all fairness, compression stockings have come a long way, and there are companies out there that have great products that are more comfortable and breathable than in the past. You may also have to wear them to comply with your insurance company's medical policy related to "conservative therapy" for vein care patients. Just so you know, there is no documented medical study or data to suggest that wearing compression stockings cures valve damage or venous disease. It puzzles the medical community why compression stockings have to be worn as part of "conservative therapy." There is absolutely no scientific data to support the theory that compression hose cures varicose veins, or the valve damage that causes venous disease. Compression stockings do, however, provide temporary relief and post-procedure benefits as part of the post-procedure protocol that has been adopted as the standard of care. The amount of time you are required to wear them is up to your doctor. Again, there is no consensus on this. Our CVD centers recommend two weeks post-procedure compliance during the day depending on a few variables related to the patient.

So, how do you get help? You need to be informed, which was my reason for writing the book. Then you need to find a doctor. If you can go directly to a doctor who treats this disease, that is great. If not, call your primary care or OBGYN and ask him or her who you can go to that they trust. As a note to our OBGYN, primary care, doctors, NP-C, or PA's who might be reading this; you can fit the patient with compression hose at your office and start the conservative treatment plan, thus expediting the insurance approval for the patient. Conservative treatment will help reduce edema, blood pooling, venous stasis, vessel thrombosis, leg fatigue, and may help with pain reduction. Stockings are not a cure for venous disease!

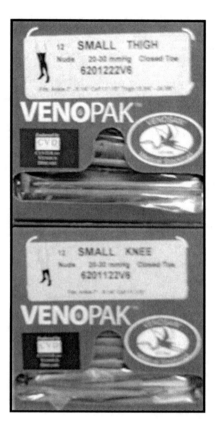

Venosan VENOPAK™

The Venosan compression stocking is endorsed by CVD due to its quality, cost savings, single stocking dispenser pack, and inventory convenience! If you need one stocking, you simply pull it from the dispenser pack. If you need two, you pull two. We carry an assortment of knee high, thigh high, and panty hose in our offices in black and nude color. They easily stack on a shelf without all the bulging packaging from other vendors. The patient only pays for what they need vs. companies who sell by the pair.

The stockings require a Physician's Rx and ready-to-wear stockings are usually ordered for Therapeutic (15-20mmHg) or Medical applications (20-30mmHg, 30-40mmHg, 40-50mmHg). They can also be measured and custom-made. Ordering these off the internet is not a good idea. You need medical grade compression hose in a compression rating that a doctor recommends that are measured and fitted properly.

The range of compression states 100% of compression at the ankle, 70% at mid-calf, and 40% at mid-thigh. So, as you apply a 20-30mmHg stocking, you now understand the word "gradient" compression. More compression at the ankle than thigh. This helps return pooling blood to the heart. There are devices, or "Leg Butlers" to help you get these on. Compliance is always an issue with stockings. The more you wear them, the better you'll feel.

Types of Compression

Calf
Thigh high
Thigh high with waist strap
Maternity panty hose
Men's leotard

CVD Compression Recommendations
Before or After Treatment

Type of Vein Treatment	Compression	Duration
Telangiectasias - Spider V	15-20mmHg	1-2 weeks
Reticular Veins < 1-2mm	20-30mmHg	2 weeks
Reticular Veins > 2mm	30-40mmHg	2-3 weeks
Varicose Veins > 3mm*

Pre treatment | 30-40mmHg | Per Insurance Medical Policy, 3-6 months. |
| Varicose Veins > 3mm

Post treatment | 30-40mmHg | 2-3 weeks after treatment of the refluxing vein(s) as directed. |
| Pregnancy related Varicose Veins* | 20-30mmHg or 30-40mmHg | Per Doctor's orders for duration of pregnancy, then treat source of refluxing vein(s) to eliminate source of problem. |

* Conservative therapy insurance requirement before treatment of refluxing veins can be approved for payment.

For providers that are reading this, early fitting of stockings by a doctor starts the documentation for "Conservative Therapy" insurance requirements for the patient. This simple step can help the patient get treated sooner than if you simply refer them out. The patient can get a copy of the records, and we can include your notes in our charts that we submit to the insurance companies. You can also charge for the stockings in your office with a fair mark-up, which is less expensive to the patient than sending them to a medical supply house that charges over $100 per pair. It is better patient care, more economical for the patient, and you have a viable product to sell from your office. As far as referring patients out to other doctors, many times doctors work together to work through the insurance issues with their patients and refer them to people they know and trust.

Word of caution! Doctors help other doctors whom they call friends. This is no surprise. Just make sure you understand the motivation behind the referral. If the referral doesn't make sense to you after researching their training, ask your doctor to refer you to a ABPh Board Certified Doctor in Phlebology (www.phlebology.org).

So, how do you find a doctor who treats venous disease? We receive a great number of calls at The Center for Venous Disease because we put venous disease right in our name. This was no accident as we want people to know we're the experts in our markets. The CVD name is a Registered Trademark.

There are multiple ways you can find a doctor. You can ask your friends, other doctors you know, or you can ask the referral service at hospitals and clinics. You can phone any general or vascular surgeon and they will probably have a name for you, or they will treat you themselves. I would not rely on print advertising or fancy ads to lure you in. Just because someone advertises a great deal doesn't make them a vein expert. It just means they have money to advertise. This being said, please make sure that the doctor you see is focused on venous disease and knows how to treat it.

So, you find a doctor, what is next? An appointment will be scheduled to evaluate your condition. A health questionnaire, patient history and physical exam will be done. The doctor will look at your legs and listen to your concerns. It is very important for your doctor and for you to document all signs, symptoms, pain, swelling, medications, and compression therapy for your insurance company. They should photograph your legs as well for visual proof of your symptoms. The CVD documentation is very extensive and meets or exceeds the insurance policy requirements. It usually takes a patient 15-20 minutes to fill out the Patient Intake Form. Some examples of our patient forms are included in a later chapter. The answers selected by your doctor drives a written record into your Electronic Medical Chart. These records are often forwarded to the insurance company, and if applicable, to the referring physician. So, complete every question.

Once this information is reviewed and your exam completed, your doctor will, if warranted, schedule a duplex ultrasound exam of your legs. That means both legs should be looked at and evaluated. Remember, the earlier you catch the problem, the earlier it can be treated. The test results will give your doctor the information needed to discuss your treatment options. A treatment option will be agreed upon and scheduled. You might have to decide if you want the procedure to be done at the hospital, office, surgery center, or other point-of-service. Some of this will depend on your insurance.

Please note: From a complication point of view, the preference is the office treatment setting for many doctors now doing these procedures. Modern treatments are safe, quick, efficient, and you're out walking, generally, in less than an 15-30 minutes with minimal discomfort.

The advantage is that you are ambulatory right after the procedure, thus reducing post-procedure complications. There is a reason they call it "surgery" when it is done at the hospital and a "procedure" when it is done in an office setting. One involves general anesthesia, lab work, x-rays, etc... and a typical procedure doesn't require it. This is the single biggest concern that you should have when seeking treatment for varicose veins. Where to be treated?

Post-procedure, you'll be asked to walk frequently and refrain from any heavy lifting for a period of time. Physical activities beyond walking will need to be discussed with your doctor. This isn't because you aren't able to walk, but rather because we don't want large volumes of blood pumping through the treated vein segments. The faster your heart pumps, the more blood volume has to return to the heart. We want to keep your heart rate down. You'll leave with your leg wrapped from ankle to groin or be in compression stockings with an elastic bandage wrapped over the stocking. This provides additional compression on the treated vein segment. You'll need to come back for a follow-up ultrasound scan to rule out any complications. If you don't receive this follow-up from your doctor, they are not following the established protocol that was established by the industry. Follow-up visits will be discussed and scheduled as recommended. Your doctor will answer any questions related to the treatment you receive and your post-procedure instructions. CVD office protocol will have you followed out 12 months post-procedure. This involves multiple ultrasound scans at intervals of one week, three months, six and 12 months. We collect data and work with the industry to troubleshoot any issues we come across. Following is a sample of our post-procedure instructions for our RF Ablation (VNUS Closure) patients.

Post Radio-Frequency Ablation Procedure Instructions

1. Most Important: Walk every hour 10-15 minutes for the remainder of the day to prevent any complications. It is not necessary to get up during the night. The groin area is the hardest area to compress post procedure. If the groin area is tender or sore, apply an ice pack. However, if it becomes abnormally swollen and/or severely painful, hot and reddened, call 911 or go to the emergency room for evaluation. You will have an ultrasound exam to rule out DVT.

2. Post procedure discomfort is usually minimal. The vein tract has been numbed. However, if soreness develops Tylenol®, Advil® (Ibuprofen) or Aleve® are recommended.

3. You will leave the office with compression stockings with an elastic bandage wrap over the top. This is to remain over the area treated night and day for 48 hrs. If the elastic bandage wrap loosens, please reapply by using the hook and loop closure at the end of the bandage.

4. After the initial 48 hrs, the stocking/elastic bandage may be removed and a shower may be taken. No tub baths or Jacuzzis. Then reapply the stocking/elastic wrap combo and only wear it during daytime hours for 3 more days.

5. On day 5, the elastic bandage wrap may be discarded and continue to wear the stockings during the day (when you are upright) for a total of 2-3 weeks from the day of your procedure or as indicated by your doctor.

6. Remember, no heavy lifting or strenuous exercise for 3-4 weeks or as discussed with the doctor or NP-C. This would include anything that elevates the heart rate beyond a normal range and no lifting over 25-30 pounds.

If you have any questions, please call our office. Thank you!

Chapter 6

Treatment Options?

The primary goal of any new technology or procedure is to restore quality of life to the patient in the most minimally invasive fashion. New technology should also provide for treatment with minimal pain and downtime for the patient. The use of postoperative narcotics should also be minimized. You can't take care of your family or work if you're under the influence of narcotics. With certain technologies and procedures, postoperative narcotics are the only alternative, due to the pain and bruising they inflict. Newer technology offers treatments that are fast, efficient, and cost effective for everyone involved. There are experts located near you that can help you explore your treatment options. Let's explore some of the current treatment methods for treating venous disorders so that you are more informed.

There are three methods to treating the superficial venous system that have damaged valves. You can "strip" the vein from the body, you can apply radio-frequency heat to ablate and seal the vein shut, or you can use a laser fiber to induce a thrombus in the vein. All three of these techniques are being used today and are described below in some general detail. They all have complications associated with them that should be discussed with your doctor. Vein stripping has the highest complication rate due to the method and operating room requirement. Endovenous Laser is commonly known for mild to moderate post-op pain and bruising as reported by the medical journals and publications. Pain medication is usually prescribed for one to two weeks after the Endovenous Laser procedure, with lasers using a lower wavelength than 1319nm. The laser procedure is fast and inexpensive for the doctor's office. However, the cost to the patient is similar to RF Ablation due to established reimbursement guidelines that are published each year. These rates are tied to Medicare reimbursement rates by most insurance carriers. RF Ablation has the fewest complications and the most published clinical data. Multi-center data is usually accepted as more accurate and more credible than single-center studies. Single-center studies, as suggested, involve one doctor. Commonalities of vein stripping, RF Ablation, and Laser Ablation require a good ultrasound exam preoperative or pre-procedure. Both RF Ablation and Laser Ablation can be performed in the operating room, hospital outpatient, or office setting. Vein stripping can only be performed in an operating room setting. The O.R. setting and outpatient setting will require some form of general anesthetic or sedation leading to a higher complication rate and risk situation for the patient.

Word of caution! As a rule, you do not want to be given anesthesia or sedation unless absolutely necessary. The risks of complications are higher in the hospital or outpatient setting when anesthesia is in use. That is why CVD doctors do all the procedures in the office setting without general anesthesia. Local anesthesia along the treated vein is all you need. Most of our patients will leave within 15 minutes of the procedure.

Treatment options are usually directly related to vein size, location, and treatment tolerance by the patient. The color, size, and shape will usually dictate a treatment modality with your doctor.

Vein Stripping

For years, the "gold standard" was vein stripping surgery in an operating room setting. The "gold standard" was black and blue, and green and purple. This describes the look of the treated leg for weeks. This is an Operating Room surgery. There are a few doctors doing this in an office setting, but not too many of them. The reason it has been done in the O.R. was that it is very painful and the patients couldn't tolerate the procedure in an office setting. The procedure is very intrusive. A groin incision is made where the Common Femoral Artery, the Common Femoral Vein, and the Great Saphenous Vein come together. As a review, this junction is called the Saphenofemoral Junction. At this intersection, the vein(s) is/are cut or ligated, tied off with suture, and stripped out of the body using a pin stripper or acorn vein stripper. An ankle or knee incision is made to pull it from one incision to the other incision. In the groin, any other veins that can be seen are also cut and tied off. The patient usually has pain for two to three weeks and is prescribed pain medication. Quality of life is low, and the pain is usually high. Post-op thigh bruising and tenderness is seen and may not go away for 30-60 days. There are still about 100,000-120,000 vein stripping surgeries done each year. Go figure! There are less invasive treatments with fewer complications available to the patient. Vein stripping surgery is a low reimbursement item for the surgeon with little advantage to the patient. I would not recommend a vein stripping unless all other options are off the table.

As a reminder, 25 million of you need treatment for varicose veins. In addition, studies have shown a 52% recurrence rate at 24 months with vein stripping surgery. It is not only a painful procedure, but it is not all that successful. For years, this procedure was thought to work well. However, few patients were followed out for two to three years, as is currently done with more minimally invasive techniques. There are a variety of clinical studies that your doctor can explore that validate this statement. After hearing the details of vein stripping, most patients won't have the surgery done due to the "nightmare" stories from friends and family members who have experienced it themselves. For more information, please do an internet search for "vein stripping surgery" and you'll see the horrific photos that I'm describing. In the United States, vein stripping surgery should be a thing of the past. Each year thousands are still performed in the operating room by doctors who are not informed or trained on the minimally invasive techniques. Across Europe, vein stripping and injections of sclerotherapy are the norm.

In saying this, the newer techniques are more successful, and can be done in the office setting. The patients are walking within the hour with minimal to moderate pain and minimal to moderate bruising depending on the technology.

Minimally Invasive Ablative Techniques

The newest techniques and most discussed methods of treating venous disease consist of Endovenous Ablation techniques. They are minimally invasive to a point and offer the patient greater comfort and recuperation time than vein stripping. Within this new frontier of medical treatment for venous disease lie two technologies that address venous insufficiency with two different energy sources and two different methods of action – RF Ablation, using an electrode-based catheter and generator system, and Laser Ablation, using a round laser fiber connected to a laser unit. As we compare both technologies, you'll have enough information to decide the right procedure for you. Both of these technologies offer advantages over vein stripping procedures. Both have been proven to "close" the problem vein (GSV, SSV, etc...) over 90% of the time. Endovenous Ablation was developed by VNUS Medical Technologies located in San Jose, CA and is referred to as the Closure® Procedure. The stated goal was to replace vein stripping and move this from a surgical operation to a treatment procedure. In 1999, the FDA cleared the way for a new technology to be born related to the treatment of venous disease. Before this technology, vein stripping surgery was the only other choice for patients with chronic venous insufficiency. VNUS was the first to introduce this technology. The first generation VNUS Closure Catheter system included a small catheter-based system with electrodes that are passed up the vein through an introducer sheath up to the Saphenofemoral Junction. The placement of the catheter is guided and placed at the SFJ using ultrasound imaging. The first generation product was used primarily in the hospital setting, had a large white handle and stiff catheter which led to vein navigation issues.

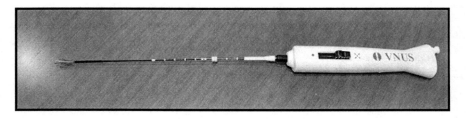

Original 1st Generation VNUS Demo Catheter

The catheter was attached to the RF Generator/computer. The electrodes were deployed and the RF Generator was turned on. The vein is then sealed shut internally using controlled heat with the deployed electrodes against the vein wall. All of this was done in 45-60 minutes from the time the RF Generator is turned on. The electrodes direct heating of the vein wall is the primary method of action. This primary method of action causes a collagen contraction and vein coagulation, which in turn seals the vein shut in six to eight weeks. At one year, 90% of the GSV's that were treated were not visible in the body under ultrasound examination. The durability of this method of action is well documented over a five year period. The first generation product had about a 89-90% published success rate, was more complicated for the doctor to perform, and was mostly hospital based. The second generation product had a new RF Generator and an improved, more flexible catheter with a smaller handle. This led to better vein navigation, easier treatment for the doctor, and improved outcomes. The new generator was also more user friendly with less "fiddle" factor than the first generation. More of these procedures began to be performed in the office setting without the use of general anesthesia. Guess what? Patients had less post-procedure complications.

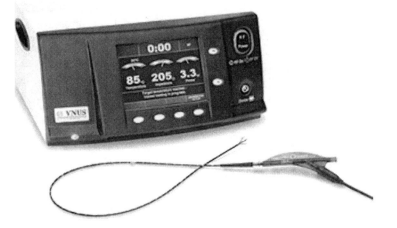

VNUS Radio-Frequency Generator with the
VNUS Closure Plus Catheter - 2nd Generation
VNUS Medical Technologies, San Jose, CA

During the procedure, the RF Generator/computer monitors response inside the vein to control and monitor temperature, time, and vein wall contact. This technology is proven to have five year longevity in multi-center randomized trials vs. vein stripping. The term multi-center refers to the studies being conducted with multiple site locations, with many surgeons contributing to the study. These studies are seen by peer review groups to be more scientific in nature than single-center studies. Single-center studies have also been completed with success ranging from 90% to 99%. In another study, 98% of patients who received this treatment would recommend it to a friend or family member.

As compared to vein stripping, the Closure Procedure has improved the quality of life for many patients with good clinical success and low complication rates. The complication rates are published and can be discussed with your doctor.

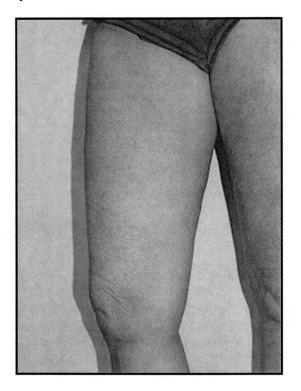

48 hour post procedure photograph of a VNUS Closure Patient

The newer or third generation catheter system from VNUS is ClosureFast™.

This catheter treats 6.5 cm of vein in cycles of 20 second intervals. Each vein segment of 6.5 cm in length is treated over its entire length in 20 seconds then moved to the next untreated segment under ultrasound guidance. The RF Generator was updated with a new software package to accommodate the new catheter. CVD centers have used the new technology for over two years and had great results with over 98.8% of treated GSV, and SSV closed. Complication rates were less than .2% on over 1,500 legs. This doesn't happen by accident. Your doctor must have a working knowledge of venous anatomy, diagnostics, treatment options, technology advances, and results that can be validated. A photo of the new catheter is below:

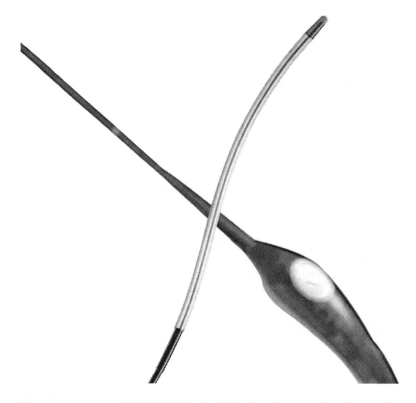

Photo courtesy of VNUS Medical Technologies, San Jose, CA

In the Endovenous Ablation market, VNUS Medical Technologies is the clear leader in this field if you compare RF to a specific laser offering. It is estimated that VNUS Medical Technologies has 55%-59% of the market share as compared to all laser companies combined. There have been over 500,000 VNUS procedures performed. This catheter-based system is seen as more expensive than vein stripping surgery. However, based on medical trials, 85% of patients return to normal activity within 24 hours. This is a huge benefit of this technology, which is driven by data and patient outcome.

A summary of VNUS Medical Technologies "highlights" related to the Closure Procedure is as follows:

- 220,000,000 covered (insured) lives in the U.S.

- 500,000+ total treated patients

- 98% of treated patients would recommend Closure to a friend

- 97.4% vein closure at 1 year

- 34+ published papers on the Closure procedure

- Five year multi-center registry follow-up data

- Three positive randomized trials of Closure vs. vein stripping

- Five year follow-up on multi-center randomized trial

- 89.1% of patients return to normal activity vs. 69.8% for endovenous laser patients in 24 hours

- Post-procedure bruising is 4% vs. 38% for endovenous laser patients.

The information provided is related to the ClosurePlus, RF device (second generation). With the arrival of the new ClosureFast third generation product, VNUS solved a couple of issues for the doctor and the staff. As its name implies, the new system is more efficient, faster, less technician-driven, and provides more information to the doctor based on the improved software for the RF Generator. These enhancements have improved the clinical outcome for The Center for Venous Disease from 97% vein occlusion rates and a 1% complication rate with ClosurePlus Catheters to 98.8% vein occlusion rates and less than .2% complication rates with ClosureFast catheters in our hands. The complications occurred within the first 5-10 patients treated during the learning curve on the device. There is also less treatment time involved for the doctor and the patient, thus reducing cost and overhead expense. This technology is a home run, which is very good news for the doctor and the patient! The Center for Venous Disease was the first vein center in Arizona and New Mexico to evaluate the new ClosureFast Catheter from VNUS Medical Technologies. In the Glendale, Arizona location Mr. Brian Farley, former VNUS CEO and President, personally released this product to our doctors. We continue to work closely with the industry innovators to develop new technology for our patients.

Another option for patients, Endovenous Laser Ablation using a laser fiber and laser unit, was approved by the FDA in 2002. From 2002 until now, there have been numerous fiber designs, manufacturers, treatment suggestions, and doctor champions emerge. The first item of business is to differentiate Endovenous Laser Ablation of the superficial venous system with surface lasers used primarily for spider veins, photo facials, hair removal, or tattoo removal. The term "laser" is often advertised for these sorts of treatments and is positioned to the public as high tech and innovative. This is not the same type of laser, as lasers are not created equal. The surface lasers are generally "job" specific and work on many different light wavelengths and wattage outputs. Most State agencies have begun to mandate training requirements and credentialing of these lasers due to poor outcomes, patient complaints, complications or all three. Lasers in the wrong hands can be very dangerous to the patient and to the staff who are using them. The lasers used in large vein applications are not the same as the above mentioned, but can be as dangerous in untrained hands.

There are several types of Endovenous lasers and several companies that manufacture them. Please feel free to research "endovenous laser ablation" on the internet. Each company has its own website, clinical data, and doctor champions promoting the technology.

Most of these lasers operate in a 810nm to 1470nm light range. The number behind the name is the laser light wavelength that this device performs under. The other important number for most lasers is the wattage that is delivered at treatment. It varies from 5 to 30 watts based on current published studies. With all of these systems, wavelength and wattage work together to deliver the damage to the vein wall using heat as high as 1300 degrees Fahrenheit.

This commentary applies to industry information as it relates to treating venous disease, and may not be accurate for all the different technologies or manufacturers. I have not specified the manufacturers, as the treatment parameters are different for almost every one of them. There is no standard of treatment regarding laser technology. Each manufacturer, based on consulting surgeon input, has initiated a different treatment parameter or modality. Most of them operate on different light wavelengths and wattage output during treatment. You also have the many doctors who are trying to modify the settings so they have fewer complications as well. There have been over 40 gyrations related to wattage, wavelength, and pulsed vs. continuous pullback deviations since inception.

Of the patients seeking treatment, it is estimated that 45% of treatments related to venous disease are now completed with the help of a laser fiber and laser unit as compared to 52% to 55% for RF Ablation or the VNUS Closure Procedure. Multiple companies compete in this market. Laser is often marketed to the doctors and patients as innovative, sexy, fast, and cheap. By cheap, I am referring to the supply cost of the laser fiber. The patient charges have nothing to do with the supply cost. The lower supply cost may provide the doctor a higher profit margin than the VNUS RF catheter. Currently, there are about five or six laser companies that compete with different units that deliver different wattage and wavelengths to treat venous disease. Of these companies, many have filed chapter 11 or reorganized, merged, or folded. The primary reason behind this in my opinion is that they competed as a commodity and made their money primarily on the laser unit itself while under cutting each other on the price of the fibers. This along with different laser companies filing litigation against each other lead to a very tough economic model to sustain. In addition, VNUS Medical Technologies initiated its own lawsuits against most of the laser companies for patent infringement related to "vein ablation." VNUS had 31 original patents on this technology in the vein ablation market. Had it not been for VNUS and the early doctor pioneers, vein ablative techniques in a minimally invasive environment would not have occurred. Last time I checked, litigation from VNUS was continuing against the laser companies. Some of the companies have already settled with VNUS rather than go into a court room and defend the suit. While this does not affect your treatment of choice as a patient, I thought you might enjoy the historical significance of the early VNUS efforts, the R&D group, the clinical trainers, medical education department, customer service, and sales group that brought this technology to the patient.

The technology differences are often referred to as the ablative Method of Action. In other words, how does this thing work? The primary Method of Action for most lasers and laser fibers is the boiling of the patient's blood in the vein to reach a temperature that will destroy the vein wall and form a thrombotic occlusion of the treated vein. This has been proven in medical trials. There have been presentations from different doctors and laser manufacturers arguing this point. It is common knowledge that this is what occurs with laser technology.

There is a company who suggests that the hemoglobin is targeted and somehow this changes everything. Last time I checked, hemoglobin was made up of mostly water. Water boils. So, back to the boiling blood theory. This indirect heating method damages the vein wall through the boiling of blood at high temperatures. Some patients have reported a "burnt broccoli" taste in their mouths during treatment as a result of laser ablation of the vein. This is a result of the boiling of blood, the high heat, and steam bubble formation that travels through various vein branches (tributaries). The laser fiber fires a burst of energy that is delivered based on wattage and wavelength of the designated system. In an animal study completed by Dr. Robert Weiss (2002 by the American Society for Dermatologic Surgery, Inc.), peak temperatures in the vein averaged 729 degrees Celsius. 100% of the treated veins showed laser perforations and blood leakage to the soft tissue. This dissection of the vein due to the laser fiber causes pain, discomfort, and visible signs such as bruising and discoloration along the vein track. So, if you've had laser ablation of a vein and experienced this, you now know what caused it.

This dissection or perforation of the vein causes pain and bruising along the vein track that is treated due to the laser penetration of the vein wall into soft tissue. At the higher laser wavelengths (CoolTouch® 1320nm), the bruising and pain are reduced. A lower light wavelengths with higher wattages, you see more bruising. Therefore, the balance of laser light wavelength and wattage are critical in the reduction of pain and bruising. The CoolTouch 1320nm laser comes the closest to achieving VNUS RF results from a post-procedure pain and bruising standpoint.

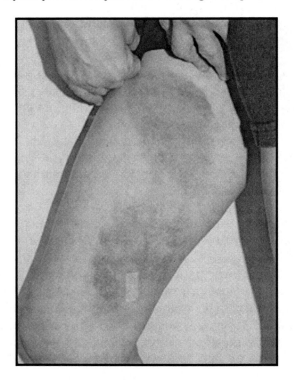

48 hour post procedure Endovenous Laser (810nm laser)

Laser treatment over the years has changed and the technique modified to try to decrease patient complications related to post-procedure laser pain and bruising. It has been reported that post-op bruising can occur with some of these systems at a rate as high as 40% with lower wavelength laser fibers. After the bruising occurs, pain follows, then the need for pain management in the form of narcotics. Narcotics reduce your ability to return to normal activity in a timely fashion. The pain and bruising comes from vein wall perforations and the subsequent leaking of blood from the damaged area. The visible signs of laser ablation for some patients will be the black and blue discoloration along the vein that was treated. Pain, tenderness, and slight inflammation may also be present, but not always. Perforation of the vein wall is the weak link in some of these systems. The complications related to Endovenous Ablation can be discussed with your doctor. They will share with you the complications that they see with the laser unit they may use.

Laser wattage outputs in treatment range from five watts in these systems to 30 watts with wavelengths ranging from 810nm to 1470nm.

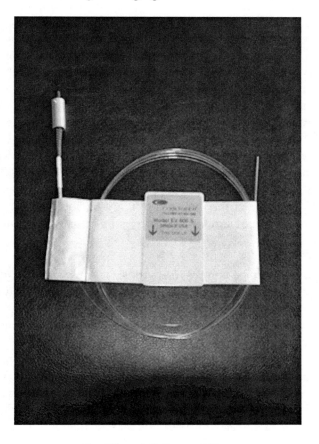

CoolTouch® Laser Fiber

Generally, the lower the wavelength, the more bruising and pain based on a 10-18 watt power output. The higher wavelengths have less bruising as reported by the manufacturers at 5-12 watts of power. The long-term multi-center data (as compared to VNUS 5 year) on endovenous laser are not available from the manufacturers at this time. I'm not sure why this is, since this all started in 2002-2005. Most laser companies submitted no more than one year of data to the insurance industry that now allows payment for laser ablation. There is some discussion that at 5-10 watts, the vein will not remain closed. However, the data collection is still underway. Promising technology in the 1319nm, 1320nm, and 1470nm laser light ranges may have the durability that most doctors would be looking for as well as the reduction of pain for the patient. We'll have to see what is published in the coming years. In an evaluation completed by The Center for Venous Disease, we found that the 1320nm laser from CoolTouch compared favorably with the VNUS ClosurePlus (2nd generation) catheter immediately post-procedure (one week), as far as patient pain and bruising scores were concerned. Vein occlusion rates were similar to ClosurePlus™ catheters at one month, but were not as favorable as the third generation VNUS ClosureFast product. We do not have any long-term data on the CoolTouch device. Of all the lasers sold in the U.S. for Endovenous Ablation, this one had more of a VNUS RF like post-procedure result than we had seen with other lasers. CVD doctors would like to see multi-center data on this device rather than the single-center data available at the time of printing this book. The patient should find out what brand of laser a doctor uses and make a decision based on the information provided.

Along with the wattage and wavelength wars, there are still differences in medical opinions related to "pulse" vs. "continuous" pullback of the laser fiber down the vein. Pulsed methods were originally used to try to keep the heat at a minimum for patient comfort in an office setting. Basically, the differences are a continuous pullback of the laser fiber vs. a pulsed method or "on and off" method. Continuous pullback methods with an increased pullback speed seem to be gaining popularity in most circles. However, you have to keep the fiber moving or you will "slice" or "perforate" the vein. Single-center surgeon studies have reported 92-99% success rates at one year with both pullback techniques. Two-year data is in the same range depending on the single-center study and surgeon author. The primary author on laser technology is Dr. Robert Min (Journal of Vascular Interventional Radiology 2003). Dr. Min has been a strong advocate of this technology and has presented single-center data at numerous medical conferences and meetings. Dr. Min received royalties for the development of this technology. He is an Interventional Radiologist and is respected for his work related to laser ablative techniques with his colleagues.

Long-term (3-5 year) multi-center results have not been published as of the printing of this book for laser ablation. No clinical comparison to vein stripping surgery has ever been studied or published for laser. There were, however, multiple parameter changes in Endovenous Laser Ablation treatment parameters between the years 2001-2004 that were published in various medical journals. This validates my earlier comments that there is not a standard of care related to treatment with laser ablation. It keeps changing due to the post-procedure issues related to patient pain and bruising. As mentioned before, the lower the wavelength of the laser the more pain and bruising. So, if you're a patient doing your homework, I would not recommend any laser below the 1319nm wavelength based on the pain and bruising issue.

Successful laser treatment is based on the amount of energy delivered to the vein segment during pullback. Without feedback to the doctor from the laser device unit to the laser tip, it is almost impossible to achieve. Even with the development of pullback devices that achieve pullback speed assistance for the operator (CoolTouch 1320nm); there is no way to achieve the recommended dosage of energy based on the anatomy of a vein. The vein shapes, diameters, and length are almost always different patient-to-patient. In theory, a pullback device would help. It's better than nothing.

It was recommended in a published study by Dr. Paul E. Timperman, (October 2004 – Society for Interventional Radiology), that a higher concentration of energy be delivered to the treated vein segment. The study indicates a higher success rate with EVLT™ (laser) when the energy concentration was 80 J/cm or higher with 10-12 watts of power. Similar results were seen with 810nm and 940nm wavelengths. When treated with 80 J/cm, higher success rates were documented. The other highlight of this study was the 77.5% success rates stated as an average energy delivery of 63.4 J/cm. 77.5% is not acceptable to any doctor for any procedure that I have met with over the years. Thus the higher 80 J/cm recommendation was made.

Oddly enough, there are laser manufacturers advertising that they are delivering 40-55 J/cm, way below Dr. Timperman's recommendations. It was a great new study for laser doctors. However, this variation of the vein anatomy and pullback times makes the recommended energy level almost impossible to achieve with the laser units that were described. There is no feedback to the surgeon from the current laser devices to insure the energy delivery to the patient's vein segment at the recommended level of energy. They have wattage windows, treatment times, fiber use (some are reusable), etc... But, they don't have feedback for energy delivered at a particular time or treatment segment. Therefore, the success rates may not be as good as the manufacturers and lead clinicians are stating. In the hands of the "community" doctors, the success rates have never been as good as what have been published by the thought leaders on laser technology. Three to four year follow up data may be needed to validate this statement; however, Dr. Timperman opens the door for this to be discussed in the future. I thought his insight was very timely as the community doctors were not getting the results reported by the "experts" who wrote the original studies.

The manufacturers challenge is to find a way to offer feedback to the doctor so they know how much energy they are delivering along the vein segment they are treating as they are treating it. In some circles, this is a hit or miss situation based on the training of the doctor involved and the case volume they have completed. I'm not sure what the learning curve would be to deliver the energy levels that have been recently recommended to the laser user. However, in recent studies, the energy levels could not be controlled even with experienced users. I have included numerous pages of references in the back of this book that you can look up and review for yourself. I think it is important to understand that my opinions are generally formed as a result of firsthand experience and the references listed at the back of this book.

If you look at the history of VNUS, Diomed Inc., Dornier MedTech, and AngioDynamics, you'll understand who came first, second, third, etc... Once you understand that VNUS started the industry with multi-center data and numerous meetings with the FDA, insurance medical directors, and hundreds of Vascular and General surgeons, you can understand the hostility between VNUS and the laser companies. VNUS set the stage with the upfront work, and with a simple 510K FDA application (cleared in 90-180 days), and a 1-year study from an Interventional Radiologist, laser ablation was born in the United States.

Despite everything I stated previously related to the history, pain and bruising issues, Laser Ablation is still a better alternative than vein stripping surgery. However, as discussed, a laser vs. vein stripping study has never been completed. In addition, we are now seeing two and three, and four year data on single-center results. Therefore, laser data at this point as compared to vein stripping or the VNUS Closure RF Procedure is viewed by some insurance companies as "experimental" even today. However, the laser technology is often promoted and positioned to the doctor as "faster" and "cheaper" than RF Ablation. Therefore, while the data is seen by many as weaker, laser technology has an economic appeal to doctors, office managers, and administrators. This economic advantage may or may not translate to a lower bill for the patient. All lasers are not created equal and not all lasers for Endovenous Laser Ablation of the superficial system lead to all the things previously discussed. However, it is valid to bring these items up as topics of discussion between you and your doctor for specific laser systems. There is nothing wrong with asking a doctor what type of device they use for vein ablation. If it's a lower wavelength, prepare yourself for more pain and bruising.

The following chart will give you an idea of what the post procedure pain and bruising would be like for the first 5-10 days. This chart is not absolute or scientific. It is an opinion based on published literature that is available. The references on laser pain and bruising are numerous from various clinical authors. They all have clinical results showing the occlusion of the treated veins between 90%-99% depending on what you read.

Diode Lasers	Pain or Bruising	Manufacturer	Wavelength**
EVLT™ / 2002*	High	Diomed (Angiodynamics)	810nm
Medilas D / 2003*	High	Dornier MedTec	810nm
ELVes™ / 2002*	High to Moderate	Biolitec, Inc.	810nm-980nm
VenaCure™/ 2002*	High to Moderate	Angiodynamics	810nm-980nm
Vari-Lase®/ 2003*	High to Moderate	Vascular Solutions	810nm-980nm
CoolTouch CTEV™/ 2005*	Low	CoolTouch	1320nm

* FDA cleared for sales and marketing in the United States.

** Pain and bruising go hand-in-hand based on wavelength and wattage, and expertise related to tumescent infiltration of the vein. Pain, tenderness, and bruising are reduced by lower wattage and higher wavelength lasers (1319, 1320, 1470).

If you can find out the manufacturer or name of the laser, and you'll know the wavelength from the above information. The wavelength for laser is the direct cause for the pain and bruising associated with lower wavelength laser systems. Newer 1319nm, 1320nm, and 1470nm wavelengths may offer the best result to reduce pain and bruising with laser. However, I'm skeptical that the 1470nm will close the vein long-term based on the energy per centimeter (40-50 J/cm) delivery they are advertising and the 3-5 watts of power that they are recommending. It's not 80 J/cm or the 10-15 watts that are recommended. VNUS continues to lead in data, patient pain scores, medical durability, and patient satisfaction. The Center for Venous Disease uses VNUS 100% of the time for all ablative treatments. The CVD Medical Directors trained on VNUS and have had great success with this technology. In saying this, they are always open to looking at newer technology that has proven data, is cost effective, and offers great service from the manufacturer.

Endovenous Ablation(s) Procedure

The steps of the procedures are similar for both RF and Laser Ablations. While some steps may vary from doctor to doctor based on preference or office flow, this is generally what would happen on the day of your procedure.

1. Patient would check in and pay for their copay, coinsurance amounts, and/or unmet yearly deductible (insurance requirement). Patient may pay cash for procedures.

2. Procedure patient consent form signed or reviewed. Questions answered.

3. Patient would be transferred to procedure suite.

4. Patient would be positioned on the procedure table in disposable underwear or shorts.

5. Patient would be tilted so that the feet were lower than the heart. This fills up the treated vein.

6. Pre-procedure ultrasound mapping of the leg may be done by drawing on the leg to determine entry site, vein size, perforator locations, or navigation issues.

7. The leg would be cleaned, leg draped, and all sterile set up completed.

8. The doctor would come in and start the procedure using sterile technique.

9. The entry site would be numbed with local anesthesia.

10. A small needle would be used to gain access to the vein and a small guide wire would be inserted under ultrasound guidance.

11. An introducer sheath would be advanced into the vein under ultrasound guidance to allow passage of the catheter or laser fiber over the small guide wire.

12. The catheter or laser fiber (laser procedures require safety glasses for everyone in the room) would be inserted and positioned under ultrasound guidance.

13. The vein track would be injected with local anesthesia (Tumescent Anesthesia) to accomplish three things. 1) Numb the identified vein along the vein track. 2) Drive the vein downward, away from the skin by at least 1 cm. 3) Reduce the vein size by collapsing the vein against the catheter or fiber to gain apposition with the heat source and the vein wall thus ablating the vein.

14. The patient would be tilted so that the head was lower than the legs to drain the blood from the vein being treated.

15. The RF generator or Laser Unit would be turned on and the vein ablation would begin. You will probably hear an audible beep or other noise while the unit is on.

16. Upon completion of vein ablation, ultrasound would verify that the vein wall is thickened and blood flow is reduced or eliminated.

17. Post-procedure instructions would be given and compression stockings or wrap would be applied.

VNUS ClosureFast RF Ablation Procedure

Through the cooperation of one of our patients, we photographed each step for you. As you look at the photos, realize our patient is wide awake and watching the ultrasound monitor while the steps are being explained. Her music selection is playing in the background. The patient is a female in her 30's with two children. Her symptoms were related to pain, swelling, cramping, and restless legs.

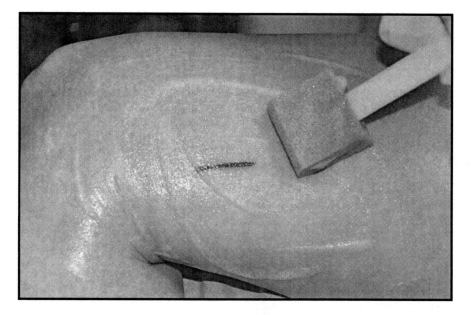

The leg is prepared by marking the vein access site and cleaning the leg. Please tell your doctor if you have an allergy to iodine as Betadine is used 90% of the time. We used Hibiclens® on this patient due to the sensitivity to iodine.

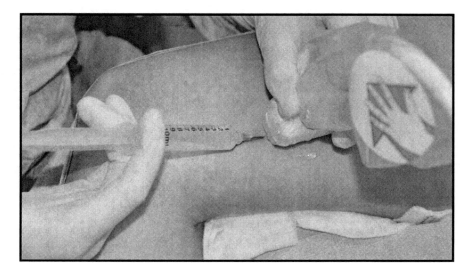

Local anesthesia is used to numb the access site. The needle is very small.

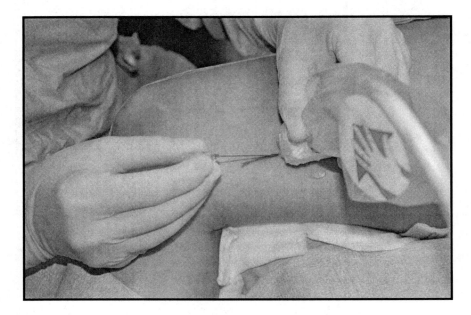

An access needle is used to access the GSV. The needle is longer to reach the veins that are deeper away from the skin. But, it is also a small diameter needle.

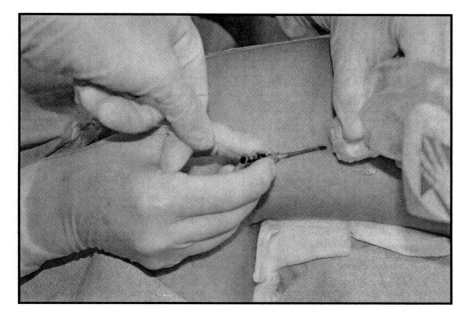

When we see blood "flash" coming back, a small guide wire is inserted into the vein under ultrasound guidance. You should not feel the passing of this wire. CVD uses a micro-introducer set that has a "mini" wire and a smaller access needle.

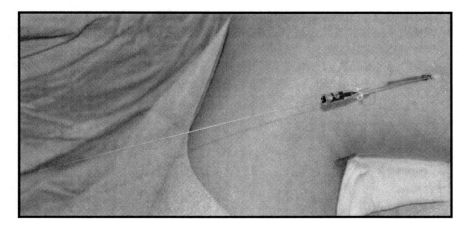

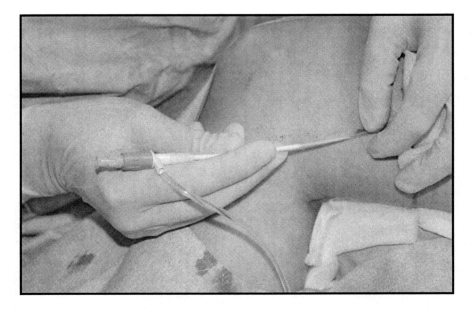

The introducer sheath is placed over the wire and allows for the catheter to be placed into your vein. All of this is done under ultrasound imaging. If our patients feel anything, it will be a pressure sensation, not pain. We involve our patients in the treatment of their veins. It is nice to receive comments from them during the procedures. In our centers, patients select their own music or music video that they watch or listen to during the procedures. Some patients bring in their own MP3 players, read a book or magazine, or just talk to our staff. For years I have assisted with the procedure, and I have made many new friendships due to my interaction with "wide" awake patients. With over 5,000 procedures completed when I stopped counting, I had 5,000 opportunities to meet new people. It's been a great experience for me and our staff.

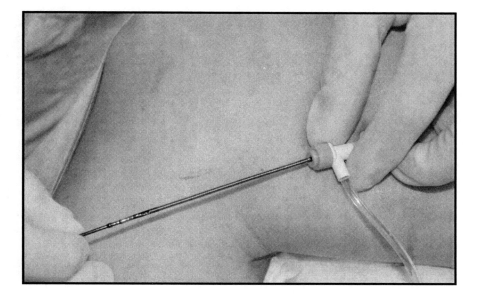

**Photos courtesy of Dr. Michael Herion and James A. Heinz
Center for Venous Disease, Paradise Valley, AZ**

The catheter is now placed into the vein through the introducer sheath. This catheter has a 6.5 cm heating element and will treat 6.5 cm of vein in 20 seconds. Once the catheter is in place, the vein track is "numbed" with local anesthesia (Tumescent) from the inserter sheath up to the groin. The catheter will be moved down your leg from the groin (SFJ), down to the introducer sheath in 6.5 cm segments. This is all done with the visual aid of ultrasound. The computer monitors the heat source and the temperature inside the vein giving the doctor visual feedback of the entire procedure.

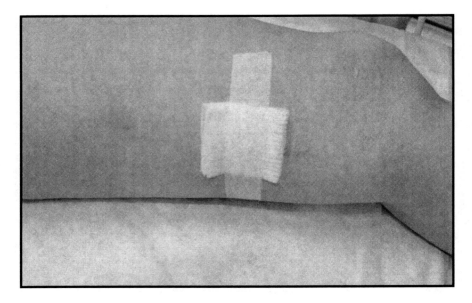

This is what the leg looks like at 24 hours. Minimal bruising from the needle and introducer site. NO pain or bruising from the technology. This is the patient's left leg. The right leg was photographed for the procedure steps that we've included above. We did not do both legs at the same time due to the amount of lidocaine used as a calculation of patient's body weight. This is per the drug package insert. Another consideration is patient preference and insurance issues or restrictions. Just left of the bandage, you'll see one of the injection sites. By using a "pump" device and tilting the head down, the pressure behind the pump and the position of the table decrease the amount of injection sites for the patient. On this patient there were four injection sites from the entry site to the groin. With a hand held syringe, there would have been at least 8-10 injection sites.

Close up photo of where the introducer was placed in the vein on the 24 hour post-procedure photo. The line is from the marker we use to "map" the vein access site. This will wash off in a couple of days. If you look at the photo the pressure from the 2" x 2" bandage and tape caused more skin irritation than the procedure access.

In most cases the procedure would take less than an hour and you would leave 15-20 minutes later or sooner. At CVD, vein access is about a 1-3 minute exercise. This is important because you don't want to feel like a pin cushion. Just another area of expertise that pays off for our patients. Positioning the catheter, applying the local, and treating the vein takes about 30 minutes on average. Set up time may take 10-15 minutes. Now that you know what to expect, your hesitation to get treated may be greatly reduced.

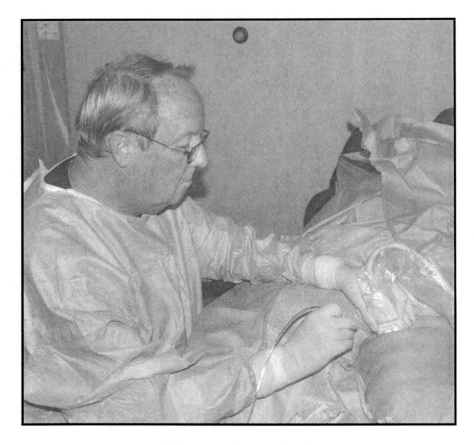

Thomas L. Pester, M.D.
Center for Venous Disease, El Paso, TX

In this photo, Dr. Pester is applying tumescent anesthesia to the vein along the "mapped" segment during a Great Saphenous Vein Ablation using a tumescent pump device manufactured by VNUS. The tubing is connected to a pump and a foot pedal is applied to place the fluid around the vein. A small needle is attached to the pump tubing. The doctor controls the flow and placement of the fluid that numbs your vein track. Good tumescent placement is an absolute necessity!

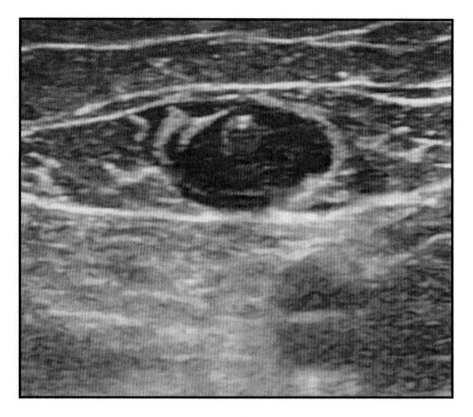

**Ultrasound image courtesy of Michael A. Herion, M.D.,
Center for Venous Disease, Paradise Valley, AZ**

In this image, the white glowing tip of the catheter can be seen around the GSV in a cross section view or transverse view. The catheter inside the vein is surrounded by local anesthesia delivered by our tumescent pump and a small needle. The black area around the vein is the local anesthesia. This fluid numbs the vein and the nerve bundle so you don't feel the heat of the catheter. It also moves the catheter down away from the skin by at least 1 cm. The fluid reduces the diameter size of the vein and brings the vein wall and the catheter closer together. This provides vein wall contact of the heating element.

Once the vein track is numbed by the local anesthesia, the control of when the VNUS RF Generator is turned on and off against the treatment protocol is in the hands of the doctor by way of the circular button on the handle. The 60 cm portion of the catheter contains the heating element which is located at the end or tip of the catheter. The cap on the end of the handle accepts "flushing" of fluids or the passing of a guide wire to help with vein navigation. The design of the VNUS catheter incorporates all the function of the first two generations with added benefits for the doctor and staff without the "fiddle factor" of previous designs. In saying this, the first and second generation catheters worked well as documented in the journals. The new design is just easier for the doctor and staff with a better overall outcome for the patients.

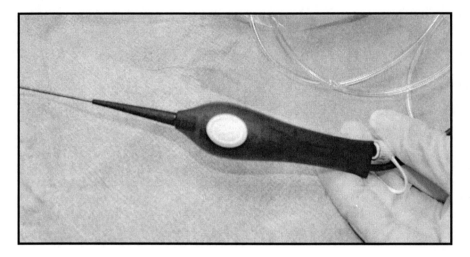

VNUS ClosureFast™ Catheter

Vein ablation as earlier mentioned can be used on the Great Saphenous Vein, Small Saphenous Vein(s), or Perforator veins. VNUS has the only FDA cleared device for Perforator vein(s) at the publishing of this book. Some doctors are using sclerotherapy or laser "off label." The VNUS Radio-Frequency Stylet (RFS™) allows a physician to treat perforators with an FDA cleared device in an office setting using only local anesthesia. In contrast, the SEPS™ procedure is done in an operating room only. SEPS™ stands for Sub-facial Endoscopic Perforator Surgery and replaced the out-dated open Linton procedure. If you've had a Linton procedure, then you probably have a nice surgical scar on the inside of your leg from ankle to mid-calf. The VNUS RFS perforator device is a stylet that connects to the RF generator. The software recognizes the device and programs the treatment algorithms.

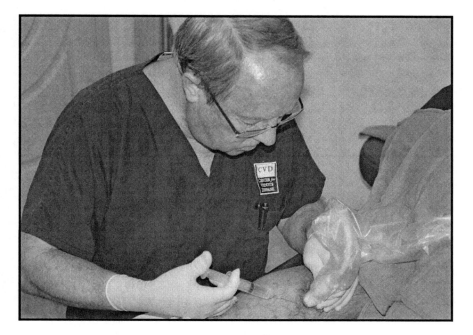

Thomas L. Pester, M.D.
Center for Venous Disease, Glendale, AZ

Dr. Thomas L. Pester and Dr. Joseph M. Smith are experts in RF ablation of refluxing perforators. They teach this technique to other doctors in cooperation with VNUS Medical Technologies. Perforator courses are offered in El Paso, TX, Santa Fe, NM, and Glendale, AZ.

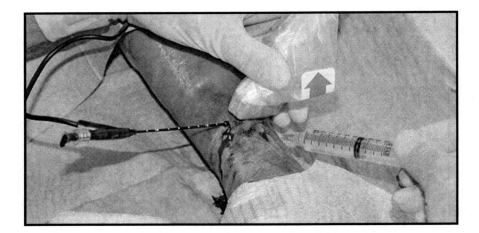

Joseph Smith, M.D., R.V.T.
Center for Venous Disease, Albuquerque, NM

This perforator location is above the ankle bone and feeding a venous ulcer. The skin has been prepped with Betadine. Lidocaine is being applied over the tip of the stylet to numb the area before the RF generator is turned on. We've had great success treating the refluxing perforator veins that are "feeding" the venous ulcer. Now, we need the insurance companies to STOP denying us payment for fixing the issue in a more minimally invasive fashion. It's better to do this in an office setting than to take someone to the OR for SEPS™. This operation entails an endoscope, harmonic scalpel, monitor, carbon dioxide insufflator, a 10mm incision for the camera, and a 5mm incision for the instruments. A tourniquet must be on the leg for the duration of the operation. You'll need the O.R. staff and anesthesiologist as well to support the operation. With the FDA approved VNUS RFS device, you need a wide awake patient, a #11 blade, a 1mm incision, no tourniquet, a small needle with a 10cc syringe, and a VNUS generator and about 45 minutes of your time. You'll leave with a 2" x 2" bandage and stockings on.

This is something again that the insurance industry is challenging payment on. So, should they send the patient to the OR for $10,000-$15,000 worth of charges or the office setting for $2,000? Hold on, let me ask my 8 year old son. He said, "Take the two grand." There are no endovenous lasers cleared by the FDA for the treatment of refluxing perforators. So, if the insurance industry is going to say, "no" it should apply to laser fibers and not the VNUS RFS perforator stylet. RF and Laser should never be "lumped" together as far as technologies, data, or outcomes to decide payment from the insurance industry. They have consistently done this as if there were no differences in the method of action, data collection, patient post-procedure pain scores, FDA clearance, or other crucial information.

While laser is "off label" for this procedure (as of the writing of this book), some doctors are using laser in the office setting to treat perforators. I've mentioned "off label" use a couple of times. Here is what the FDA says related to off label indications:

"Off-Label" and Investigational Use of Marketed Drugs, Biologics and Medical Devices

"Off-Label" Use of Marketed Drugs, Biologics and Medical Devices

Good medical practice and the best interests of the patient require that physicians use legally available drugs, biologics and devices according to their best knowledge and judgment. If physicians use a product for an indication not in the approved labeling, they have the responsibility to be well informed about the product, to base its use on firm scientific rationale and on sound medical evidence, and to maintain records of the product's use and effects. Use of a marketed product in this manner when the intent is the "practice of medicine" does not require the submission of an Investigational New Drug Application (IND), Investigational Device Exemption (IDE) or review by an Institutional Review Board (IRB). However, the institution at which the product will be used may, under its own authority, require IRB review or other institutional oversight.

Source: Food and Drug Administration

It is up to the laser industry to submit the 510K applications to the FDA to gain approval for laser ablation of perforator veins. The insurance industry is justified in my opinion to deny payment on laser for this procedure because they have not gained FDA clearance on the fibers they sell for perforator ablation. However, the VNUS device is on its 2nd generation product and CVD has treated thousands of perforators at over 96% success. For the most part, we find a direct correlation between venous ulcers and refluxing perforators.

Remember, an active venous ulcer is a C.E.A.P. classification of C6. So, I really have a problem with an insurance company denying approval to treat an ulcer. As a side-note, I was one of the early VNUS Clinical Managers that used the first generation product in clinical trials with three doctors in the Southwest. The success rate increased from the high 88% to high 96% occlusion rates when our patients were more compliant to the post-procedure compression instructions. The alternative to both VNUS and laser is the use of sclerotherapy which in my opinion is the wrong option due to the proximity of the deep system. The perforators, as a review, are the bridge between the superficial and deep system. There are over 150 communicating veins or perforator veins of the lower leg. We only treat the clinically significant ones.

Chapter 7

Questions? What Questions?

So far I have given you some useful information related to the disease, treatment options, accurate documentation, technology summary, and prevalence in society. Now I think it is time you selected a doctor. I have listed below some of the questions that our patients at CVD offices ask us. I have added questions that are valid from a patient perspective as well. Obviously, you're not going to be able to ask your doctor all of these questions. You can get a few things answered from the staff, literature provided, diplomas on the walls, or from the doctors themselves.

Questions for your prospective Phlebology doctor:

1. How long have you been treating venous disease?

2. Did you ever do vein stripping?

3. What does your history and physical and exam consist of?

4. Will my insurance company pay for it based on your findings?

5. What is your preferred method for treating venous disease? RF or Laser? Who is the manufacturer of the device? Wavelength? (The lower the wavelength the more pain and bruising).

6. How many ablation cases have you performed in an office setting?

7. What specific training have you completed for treating venous disease?

8. Are you board certified in Phlebology?

9. Are you a Registered Vascular Technician?

10. What are the complications and risks associated with the procedure?

11. Are you a consultant or financially involved with the RF or Laser companies? If so, what capacity?

12. After the procedure, what can I expect related to pain? Bruising? Medications?

13. What is the post-op routine that you follow? Does it meet with the standard of care in the industry?

14. Will I have a follow up ultrasound? What intervals?

15. Will the treated vein disappear? What timeframe?

16. Is this a cure? (If anyone tells you yes, then they are mistaken.)

You can get a feel of the questions based on what you have already read. With any of the treatment methods and surgical techniques, there are complications and risks involved. These procedures are currently being performed in office settings, outpatient centers, hospitals, and surgery centers. There are risks associated with general anesthesia, local blocks, epidurals and spinals, which are eliminated in the office setting. It can be done safely and comfortably for the patient in the office setting by a trained staff. The patients usually leave within 15 minutes of the procedure and they do very well.

As a former VNUS Certified Clinical Trainer, I feel that VNUS delivers the best treatment option at this point. Laser has good potential and the two and three year data is promising. However, at this time, I do not feel that the pain and bruising issues have been addressed by laser technology. I also am concerned that most of the available data comes from single-center clinicians who are usually (not always) compensated by the laser manufacturers for their results. While there are some good independent single-center studies, they are usually one to two year studies with minimal new information for us to digest or think about.

I think that Dr. Timperman (JVIR, October 2004) has the most valid study on laser related to energy delivery by vein segment. His study suggests a higher energy delivery (80 J/cm) for a higher success in the treatment of the venous reflux disease with endovenous laser. To achieve this, feedback to the surgeon from the laser unit must be developed to monitor the delivery of this energy, which currently does not exist. Due to this issue, CoolTouch developed a fiber pullback device that keeps the pullback of the fiber at a consistent pace against the settings preferred by the doctor. VNUS uses software to give the doctor feedback on a constant basis while performing the procedure and indicates when the vein is under treated by visual displays.

As a partner in multiple vein centers, I am very interested in cost savings and profit. If the laser companies could duplicate the longevity of VNUS data with the immediate post procedure patient advantages, at a lower cost, we would evaluate that technology in our centers. Please take the time to ask your doctor the tough questions. If they won't take the time to answer them, or don't know the answers, then chances are you are seeing the wrong doctor! There are many good doctors who treat venous disease. You now are equipped with more information than most primary care physicians or your OBGYN. Please use this information wisely to make your own decisions as related to venous disease and the treatment you are offered. Below are frequently asked questions related to venous disease and provided by VNUS Medical Technologies.

Frequently Asked Questions

What is superficial venous reflux?
Superficial venous reflux is a condition that develops when the valves that usually keep blood flowing out of your legs become damaged or diseased. This causes blood to pool in your legs. Common symptoms of superficial venous reflux include pain, swelling, leg heaviness and fatigue, as well as varicose veins in your legs.

How is the Closure procedure different from vein stripping?
During a stripping procedure, the surgeon makes an incision in your groin and ties off the vein, after which a stripper tool is threaded through the saphenous vein and used to pull the vein out of your leg through a second incision just above your calf.

In the Closure procedure, there is no need for groin surgery. Instead, the vein remains in place and is closed using a special (Closure) catheter inserted through a small puncture. This may eliminate the bruising and pain often associated with vein stripping (i.e., that may result from the tearing of side branch veins while the saphenous vein is pulled out). Vein stripping is usually performed in an operating room, under a general anesthetic, while the Closure procedure is performed on an outpatient basis, typically using local or regional anesthesia.

Three randomized trials of the Closure procedure vs. vein stripping, including the most recent multi-center comparative trial, show very similar results. In the multi-center comparative trial, the Closure procedure was superior to vein stripping in every statistically significant outcome. In the study, 80.5% of patients treated with the Closure procedure returned to normal activities within one day, versus 46.9% of patients who underwent vein stripping. Also, Closure patients returned to work 7.7 days sooner than surgical patients. Patients treated with the Closure procedure had less postoperative pain, less bruising, faster recovery and fewer overall adverse events.[1]

Is the Closure procedure painful?
Patients report feeling little, if any, pain during the Closure procedure. Your physician will give you a local or regional anesthetic to numb the treatment area.

How quickly after treatment can I return to normal activities?
Many patients can resume normal activities immediately.[2] For a few weeks following the treatment, your doctor may recommend a regular walking regimen and suggest you refrain from very strenuous activities (heavy lifting, for example) or prolonged periods of standing.

How soon after treatment will my symptoms improve?
Most patients report a noticeable improvement in their symptoms within 1-2 weeks following the procedure.

Is there any scarring, bruising, or swelling after the Closure procedure?
Patients report minimal to no scarring, bruising, or swelling following the Closure procedure.

Is the Closure treatment covered by my insurance?
Many insurance companies are paying for the Closure procedure in part or in full. Most insurance companies determine coverage for all treatments, including the Closure procedure, based on medical necessity. The VNUS Closure procedure has positive coverage policies with most major health insurers. Your physician can discuss your insurance coverage further at the time of consultation.

How effective is the Closure procedure?
Data from a prospective multicenter study have shown 97.4% vein occlusion 1 year post-treatment.[3]

What are patients saying about the Closure procedure?
98% of patients who have undergone the Closure procedure are willing to recommend it to a friend or family member with similar leg vein problems.

1 Lurie F, Creton D, Eklof B, Kabnick LS, Kistner RL, Pichot O, et al. Prospective randomized study of endovenous radiofrequency obliteration (Closure) versus ligation and stripping in a selected patient population (EVOLVES study). J Vasc Surg 2003;38:207-14.
2 Goldman, H. Closure of the greater saphenous vein with endo radiofrequency thermal heating of the vein wall in combination with ambulatory phlebectomy: preliminary 6-month follow-up. Dermatol Surg 2000; 26:452-456.
3 Dietzek A, Two-Year Follow-Up Data From A Prospective, Multicenter Study Of The Efficacy Of The ClosureFAST Catheter, 35th Annual Veith Symposium. November 19, 2008. New York.

* CVD has a 98.8% vein occlusion rate with the new ClosureFast Catheter from VNUS.

Chapter 8

Cosmetic Treatments

Often with venous disease, the actual treatment may involve more than one method. I have already touched on Endovenous Ablation. This treatment or procedure seals the vein that is refluxing so that healthy veins can take over. This takes care of the major problem. Think of it like a tree. The tree has roots, a trunk, limbs, and branches coming out of it. In the venous system, the varicosities are the branches, and the Great Saphenous Vein or Small Saphenous Vein is the tree trunk. These branches empty after venous ablation and will be begin to shrink in appearance because the "feeder" vein has been ablated or sealed. You can also think of the GSV or SSV as the "garden hose" that when turned off, begins to empty and flatten out. This flattening may not occur for a while; it may take a few months to get the cosmetic result you're looking for. However, be patient! Remember, the primary reason we did the procedure was for pain relief or to reduce the ankle swelling at the end of the day. We also did it to "end the cycle" of venous disease. Remember it is progressive in nature. It is also important to manage the patient's expectations, which is what I'm trying to do with you now. With adjunctive or complimentary treatments at the time of vein ablation, the cosmetic results may come quicker. With certain patients, the need for adjunctive or secondary treatment sessions is needed to get the desired effect and to reduce the visible signs of vein issues. They may include sclerotherapy injections, surface laser treatments, or micro-phlebectomy. Your treatment might include any combination or possibly all three. It depends on the severity of your legs and your desire as the patient to have the treatments done. These treatments may be staged depending on a variety of reasons. You'll need to discuss this with your doctor, but it is your decision to make.

Sclerotherapy injections may be necessary to reduce the appearance of some of the smaller veins that you would like to see disappear. These injections usually fall into one of these descriptions; 1) saline, 2) detergents, or 3) chemical. Each one causes damage to the vein wall in different ways. The effectiveness of each one comes with some success and complications. This is not unusual in the medical environment. Your treatment may include injections that contain hypertonic saline, hypertonic glucose/saline, sodium tetradecyl sulfate (STS), Polidocanol (PolyD), sodium morrhuate, ethanolamine oleate, or chromated glycerin. Your doctor should explain what they will be using and why. They should also discuss the complication and success rates with you.

Common classifications of veins that are treated fall into one or more of these categories:

- Telangiectasia (spider veins): 01.-1mm in diameter and may appear red in color

- Venulectasia: 1-2mm and may appear red and or green

- Reticular Veins (feeder veins): 2-4mm and may appear blue-green

- Varicose Veins: > 3 mm and may appear to be blue or blue-green

- Saphenous Veins: > 5 mm or larger and blue to blue-green in appearance

Your doctor will be able to decide what you need to have done based on the size, shape, and location of your problem areas. Sclerosing agents are commonly used for veins from 0.1 to 3 mm that are not saphenous or near the Saphenofemoral Junction. Before anything is done, you will have a history and physical exam to determine what you need, usually followed by some patient education and an informed consent form to sign. Photographs should be taken so that you can review the before and after pictures with your doctor. The actual treatments are then discussed and prepared according to the doctor's instructions. A 30 gauge needle that is 1/2" long with 1 ml to 3 ml syringes are used during the treatment. The higher the gauge needle, the smaller they are. Compression pads or cotton balls will be used over the injection sites. Your doctor will need magnification glasses to see the veins due to their smaller size. A polarizing headlamp or VeinLite® may also be used to help see the veins that need treatment. The more advanced doctors or staff will also use ultrasound to help position the fluid in the vein. This is often referred to as Ultrasound Guided Sclerotherapy or UGS using foam sclerotherapy. The foam mixture can easily been seen on ultrasound, and it tends to contact the vein wall better. Post-procedure compression is strongly recommended by most doctors. This involves wrapping the leg or putting patients in 15-20 mm hg compression stockings immediately after the treatment session. Because multiple sessions are usually involved, I believe stockings are a better way to go. This keeps the vein compressed, empty and flat which is what we want.

Various solutions are used to decrease the appearance of veins up to 3 mm in diameter if needed. Keep in mind that a good result won't last if the primary source of reflux flow is not dealt with. It is for this reason that many of you have been unsatisfied with injections of your veins. These injections are usually performed by a family practice doctor, dermatologist, plastic surgeon, or nurse at a Medical Spa, which can have a higher failure or recurrence rate. Some of the recurrence has to do with the solution that is used and with the "feeder" veins that are left untreated. As stated earlier, without an ultrasound exam and the proper training, the source of the problem usually lies undetected by non-trained personnel. These solutions are usually injected after Endovenous Ablation.

A word of caution! Many facilities offer injections for "spider veins" and other cosmetic vein treatments. These injections may work, but they may not work long-term. They do not solve the underlying source of reflux and should not be a substitute for the treatments suggested above. These injections are advertised very aggressively, and most patients are disappointed with the results over time due to untrained providers. The trend in insurance coverage for cosmetic clean up is that it is NOT paid for by the payers.

The most common sclerotherapy solutions in the United States are Sotradecol (STS) and Polidocanol. PolyD was recently approved by the Food and Drug Administration in the United States. Throughout the world, the drug has had great success. However, it had not gone through the FDA protocols in the U.S. until recently. This drug is distributed in the U.S. by BioForm Medical Incorporated under the name Asclera™.

Despite this, some doctors used the drug before FDA approval and obtained it through compounding pharmacies or ordered the solutions from outside the country. You may or may not have been informed of this. However, PolyD is the best product for sclerotherapy in my opinion based on millions of injections worldwide and the reduced side effects vs. STS. Patient satisfaction with PolyD also trumps STS in a multi-center, double-blind, placebo based study by a margin of 87% favorable to 64% after 12 weeks. As a patient, you should know what is in the syringe. The placebo received a 14% "satisfied" or "very satisfied" rating. Sclerotherapy complications related to telangiectatic matting, hyper-pigmentation, and phlebitis are rare. Injection site hematoma, irritation, discoloration, site pain, site pruritus, injection site warmth, neovascularization, injection site thrombus, ulceration, cutaneous necrosis, and infection are also possible. In saying this, your legs will look worse before they look better. This is due to the injection agent doing its job on the vein(s) that were injected. Also, you should know that it will take most patients 3-5 sessions before the average person is comfortable with the result. One of the worst things that can happen is to have an artery injected instead of the vein. It has happened. This warning is in the package inserts for the drugs. The caution includes "seek treatment from a vascular surgeon immediately."

Therefore, while the procedure is relatively easy to do, the outcome may be less than desirable and could be quite dangerous. The informed consent that you sign with your doctor should give you the information above. Feel free to ask questions related to outcomes and complications. A simple injection by a medical professional is nothing new. Be careful who you choose. Finding a trained doctor and staff is crucial for these types of treatments.

There are basically three ways to inject sclerotherapy. 1) free hand without visual aids, 2) with the use of visual lamps, lights, etc..., 3) Ultrasound Guided Sclerotherapy (1989). CVD utilizes mostly #2 in order to see slightly below the injected vein to see what is feeding the visual vein, and #3 based on size and location. I like UGS because you can see the treated vein while the injection is being made. The visual feedback from the monitor is important to know where it went, how far it traveled, and to protect anatomy that can be damaged by the injection. We have an issue with some insurance companies denying payment for UGS. As a patient please understand that your doctors office is constantly fighting insurance battles on your behalf. More on this later!

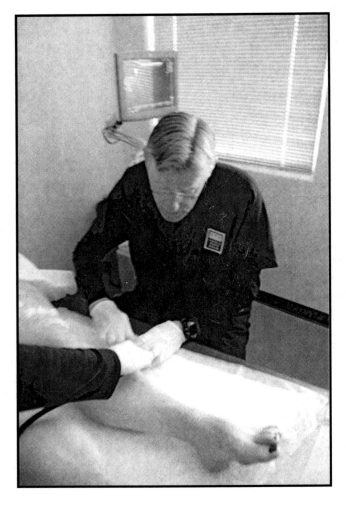

Joseph M. Smith, M.D., R.V.T.
Center for Venous Disease, Albuquerque, NM

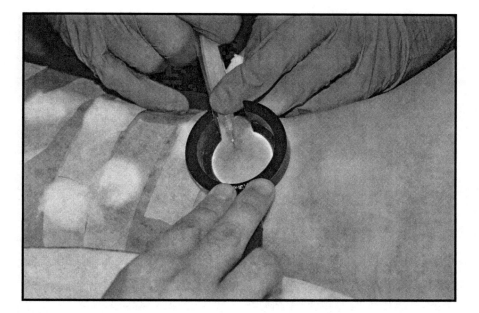

Joseph M. Smith, M.D., R.V.T.
Center for Venous Disease, Santa Fe, NM

Dr. Smith is using a VeinLite™ to increase the visibility of the underlying vein. This allows the doctor to see below the skin and to see what is "feeding" the spider vein. By using the light source, the doctor can visualize the vein they are injecting and see how far the fluid travels. Doctors who "free hand" these solutions are at risk of getting the sclerosant outside the vein, causing damage to skin, or other crucial anatomy in the area of the injection.

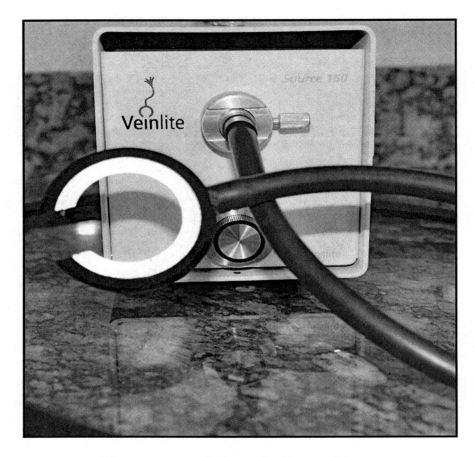

Photo courtesy of Center for Venous Disease
VeinLite® Illuminator

As seen in the patient photo, cotton balls or folder 2" x 2" gauze pads are taped over the injection site to add compression after the injection. This patient will also be fitted and wear compression knee high stockings as directed by the doctor. The injection will help the vein scar down and disappear. Several injections may be needed to get the cosmetic outcome the patient is looking for. Sclerotherapy is the last step in treating venous disease. Possible complications of using sclerotherapy may include ulceration at the injection site, skin breakdown, clotting, redness, or allergic reaction, dizziness after injection, or burning sensation during the injection. Most patients feel a burning sensation when injected, but tolerate them without any complications.

I have included a few slides from a presentation that Dr. Michael Herion uses in his training courses on sclerotherapy. While some of the information is a duplicate of what has already been presented, Dr. Herion's slides are a helpful reinforcement. Also, we may have doctors or nurses reading this book who are seeking more training on venous disease, ablative techniques, or cosmetic clean up courses.

A²CE™ (AACE, LLC) provides training to doctors in Glendale, Arizona under the direct supervision of Board Certified doctors in Phlebology. I've included our pricing structure on our certification courses. If you're a healthcare provider needing more training, please call us at 623-234-2542.

A²CE CERTIFICATIONS

BOTOX® & Dermal Filler Certification (Juvederm®, Radiesse®, Cosmoplast® & Cosmoderm®)
>2-day full package - $3900

BOTOX® & Dermal Filler Theory & Sales Techniques
>1-day course - $1100

Arizona Radiation Regulatory Agency endorsed Cosmetic Laser Certification
>10-day full package - $7500

Physician Fast-Track Cosmetic Laser Review
>1-day full package - $1900

Laser Safety Officer Certification
>Price included in Cosmetic Laser Certification Course

Cosmetic Sclerotherapy Certification
>1-day course - $1350

Aesthetic Medical Director Orientation
>1-day course - $1350

A²CE CERTIFICATIONS OFFERED

Hair Reduction
Pigment Lesion Reduction
Vascular Lesion Reduction
Thermage® Skin Tightening
Thermage® Collagen Synthesis
Thermage® Cellulite Reduction
Thermage® Body Sculpting
Intense Pulsed Light (IPL) Photofacial
Blu-U® Acne treatment
Photodynamic Therapy Theory and Demonstration
Laser Safety Officer Certification
CPR and AED (Automated External Defibrillator)
   Certification
BOTOX®
Dermal Fillers
Sclerotherapy

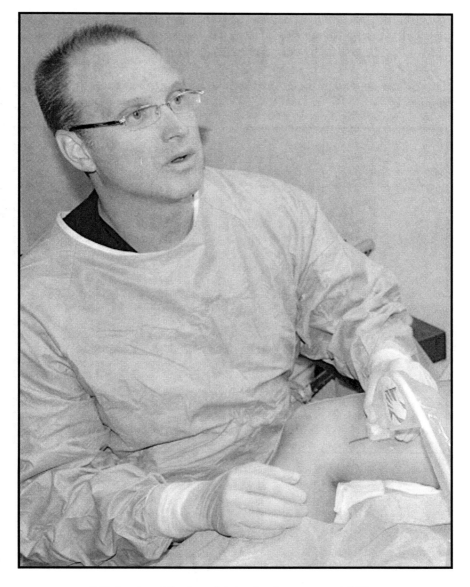

**Michael A. Herion, M.D. Co-Founder A²CE™
Center for Venous Disease, Paradise Valley, AZ**

The training presentation below is composed of hundreds of slides. I selected a few of them. The content has not been edited or modified for this book. The content is provided by Dr. Herion with his permission.

The following slides focus on types of veins, treatment solutions, and technology.

Table of Contents

- Venous Anatomy
- Venous Insufficiency
- Epidemiology
- Sclerotherapy
- Sclerosing Solutions
- Injection Techniques
- Compression

Spider Veins (Venulectasia & Telangiectasia)

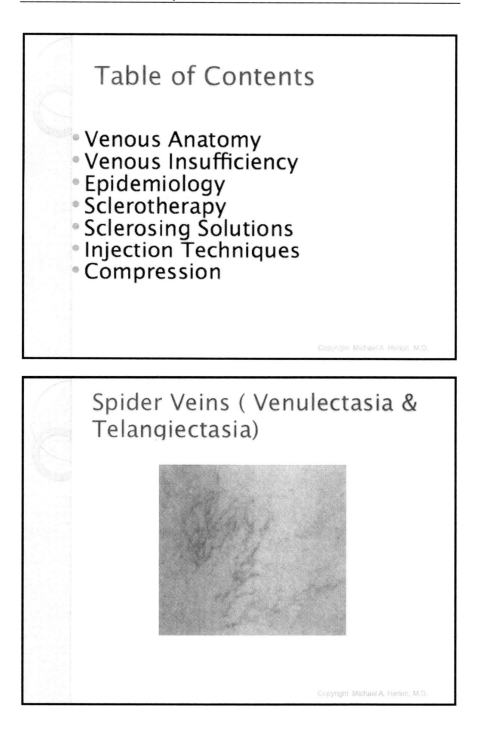

Spider Veins (Reticular

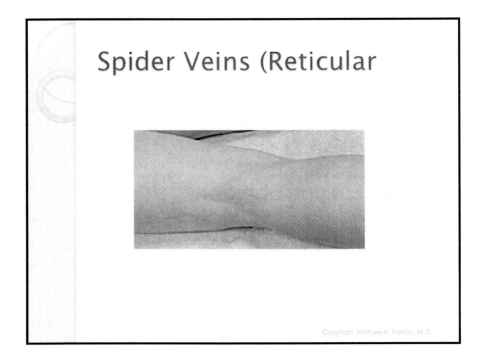

Copyright Michael A. Herion, M.D.

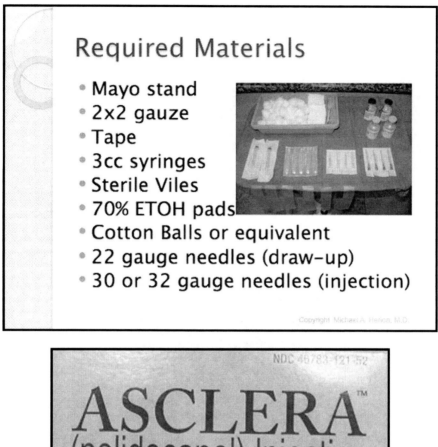

Required Materials

- Mayo stand
- 2x2 gauze
- Tape
- 3cc syringes
- Sterile Viles
- 70% ETOH pads
- Cotton Balls or equivalent
- 22 gauge needles (draw-up)
- 30 or 32 gauge needles (injection)

Copyright Michael A. Henon, M.D.

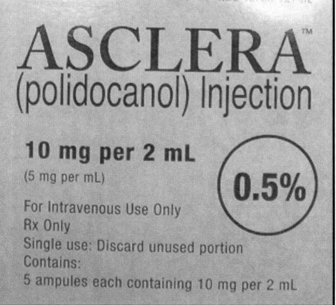

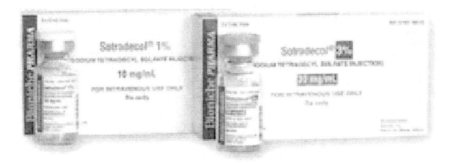

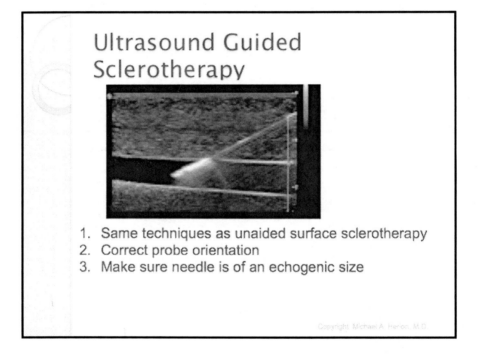

Ultrasound Guided Sclerotherapy

1. Same techniques as unaided surface sclerotherapy
2. Correct probe orientation
3. Make sure needle is of an echogenic size

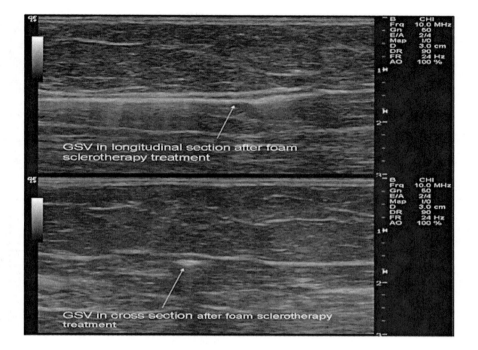

Ultrasound photo courtesy of Dr. Herion
Paradise Valley, AZ

This photo demonstrates what Ultrasound Guided Sclerotherapy looks like after the injection. You can see the white thickened section (arrows) where the sclerotherapy solution affixed itself to the vein wall. The vein wall will scar down and the vein visually disappears. The injected vein will look worse before it looks better. This is normal. The treatment is a process and it may take more than one session to get the cosmetic effect you're looking for. In some cases 5-10 sclerotherapy sessions may be needed between both legs. The selection of the sclerotherapy solution, and the expertise of the doctor will limit the sessions as compared to a "weaker" or less effective solution and an inexperienced provider.

Common solutions for sclerotherapy include:

Name	Type of Sclerotherapy	FDA Approval
Polidocinol Asclera™	Detergent	YES
Sodium Tetradecyl Sulfate (STS)	Detergent	YES
Sodium Morrhuate	Detergent	YES
Glycerin	Chemical	NO
Hypertonic Solution	Saline	NO

As you review the chart, please note that most of the agents have been injected since the 1930's and offer different benefits and have different side effects. We receive the most negative comments on saline injections that were done by other doctors. This hurts. It's ineffective. Causes skin staining. It's a waste of money. My opinion! You get what you pay for related to the cost of the product and the expertise of your doctor. This is not usually paid for by insurance due to its cosmetic nature.

A special thanks to Dr. Herion for letting me include a few slides from his training course as additional information on the types of veins treated, technology, injection techniques, and available injectable solutions. Sclerotherapy should be done by a trained doctor or nurse. Practice and understanding the adverse reactions is key to avoiding them. As reinforcement, venous reflux should be ruled out before any sclerotherapy is done. This observation has been validated by CVD doctors seeing patients after months or years of sclerotherapy whereby the root cause was never addressed. We also see patients with complications from other vein clinics, where an ultrasound was never performed. So, save your money and seek a professional.

Surface Laser or High-Intensity Pulsed Light (IPL) may be used to "clean up" smaller veins and blemishes that you would like removed. As stated before, lasers come in all shapes and sizes and are dedicated to do certain things. Most of these types of lasers or IPL's are expensive to buy and the treatments can be expensive for the patient as well. Most insurance companies will not pay for these treatments, as they view the procedure as cosmetic. Dermatologists usually do the best jobs with these types of devices.

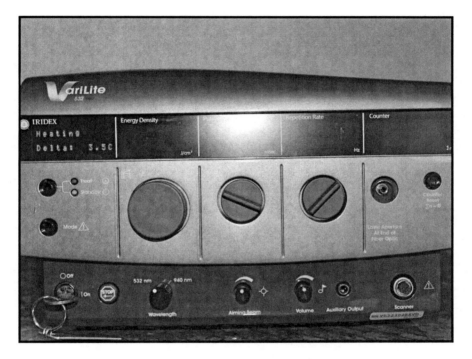

IRIDEX® laser

They have been well-trained and have multiple lasers in their offices for different applications. This, however, may be costly, and sometimes the sclerotherapy injections alone take care of the problem, with less out of pocket cost to the patient. The most important thing to consider related to these devices is the expertise of the operator. Complications can include skin blanching, thermal damage to the skin, and skin pigmentation, leading to a very unsatisfied patient. In my opinion, a laser in untrained hands is the most dangerous piece of equipment that can be used on a patient in an office or medical spa setting. At CVD, Michael Herion, M.D., Aesthetic Medical Director, oversees all certification of laser technicians in our company. He is a podium speaker at major aesthetic and vein conferences and Cofounder of AACE, LLC, a company focused on physician and medical staff training related to injectables, energy based devices (laser certification), and the basic scientific foundation you need to be successful without causing harm to the patient or hurting a staff member.

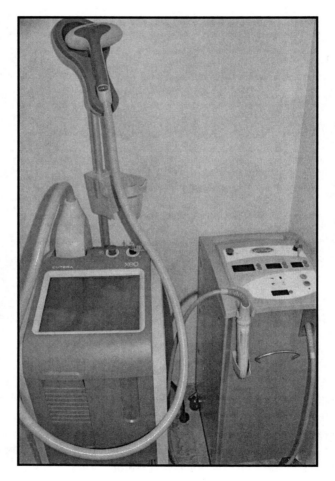

**Aesthetic Laser Certification available through
AACE, LLC, Glendale, AZ**

Micro Ambulatory Phlebectomy is often used at the time of surgery to "pluck" out the veins that are larger in diameter or in a cluster. The most popular technique is called micro-ambulatory phlebectomy. This procedure is done with a very small 1-2 mm incision near the vein segment that is to be removed. A small blade might be used "free hand" or placed on an instrument to poke through the skin with an even smaller opening than the incision method. Despite which method is used, a small opening is usually enough to remove the vein in segments. Special hook type instruments are used to gently pull the vein up to the surface and remove them in a minimally invasive method. The patients can easily tolerate this procedure in an office or outpatient-setting due to the use of local anesthetics. Usually a small dose of 1% lidocaine, with or without epinephrine, is used at the treated area. The technique that we like injects the solution under the vein, pushing it up against the skin, providing a local pressure on the vein. The vein turns white due to the epinephrine which reduces the amount of blood leakage. In areas of vein clusters, some pain due to the overlapping of veins can be uncomfortable when removed. But, again, much is gained by not going to the operating room. The small incisions will heal rather quickly, and the bulging veins will diminish over time. This complements the Endovenous Ablation techniques already discussed. As you can see, the set up uses just a few instruments and can be nearly pain-free in an office setting.

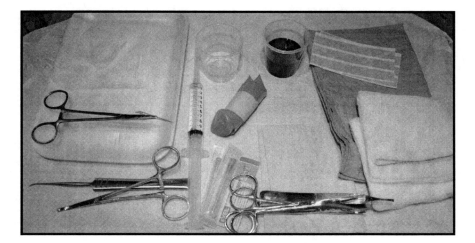

Basic set up Micro-A/P includes: 4" x 4" gauze pads, A/P instruments, Betadine, curved forceps, steri-strip type bandages, small needles, and a syringe. The first step is to have the patient stand up and the veins marked (purple markings on the skin). This marking is a guide for the doctor for when the patient is lying down and having the procedure. The patient included in these photographs was a male patient in his late 50's who has had issues with his legs for years. Another validation of a patient who waited too long to be treated.

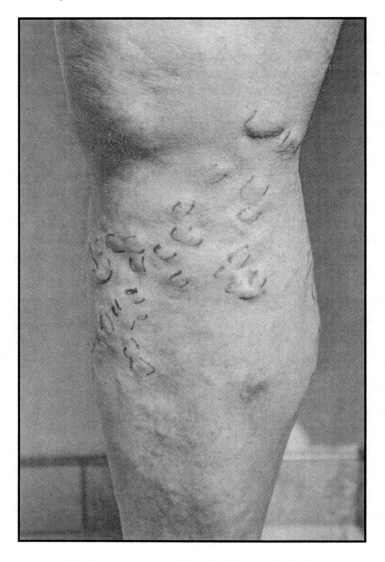

Photos courtesy of David M. Smith, D.O.
Center for Venous Disease, Glendale, AZ

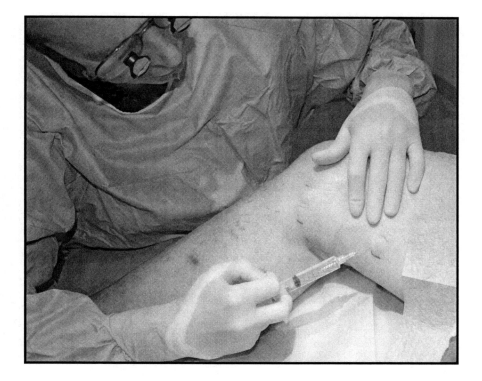

Once the leg is prepped and draped, Dr. Smith will use a small needle to inject lidocaine on the surface of the skin and under the vein to push the vein up to the skin. A small skin incision (1-2mm) is made to allow the passing of the A/P hooks discussed. Dr. Smith does a great job with A/P. I think this is due to his experience as a "surgeon." I think this is a distinction that patients and insurance medical directors should take into account when deciding "who" should perform these procedures. If you can find an ABPh Board Certified physician who has surgery experience, you'll probably have a winning situation and a better outcome.

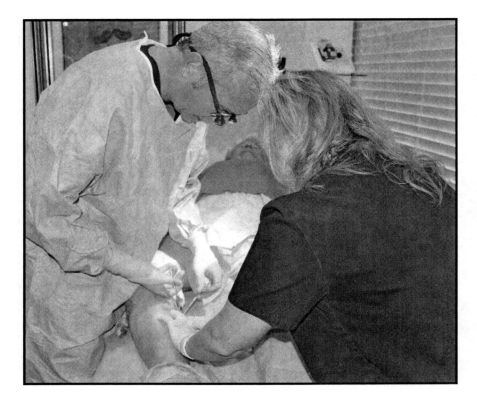

In this photo, a small hook has pulled a vein up from below the skin and held in place with a curved hemostat. Dr. Smith will gently remove the vein by pulling and pushing down on the skin. This is a procedure that needs an extra set of hands. If you look closely at the next photo, the vein almost appears "white." This is due to the injection of the local anesthesia, and the position of the table that is tilted slightly so that the patient is head down.

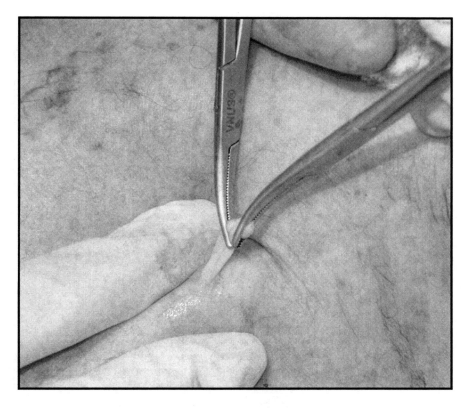

There is little blood coming out of these tiny puncture sites and as described, the vein looks more white than red. That is not what you would have expected based on the original photo. I think most patients would think that there would be a great deal of blood. There is not! Please let your doctor know if you are taking a blood thinner or daily aspirin. It's nice to have a "heads up" before we start a procedure such as micro-ambulatory phlebectomy.

Safety is important to the patient. In each CVD office, a STAT kit, oxygen, and an AED is within arm's reach. Since we do not sedate our patients, the risk of anything happening is very rare. These are procedures and protocols that can be safely done in an office setting with trained doctors and staff members.

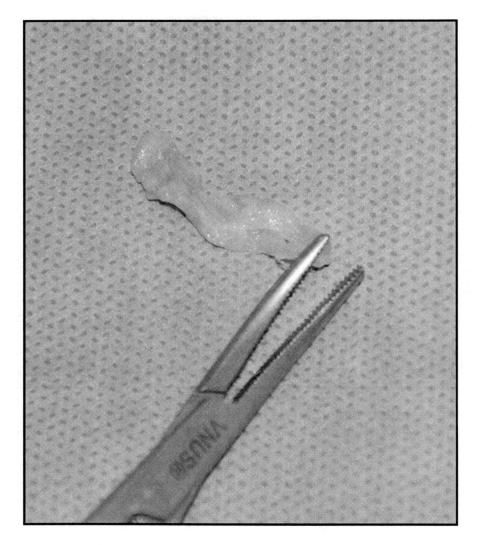

The process is continued until the desired results are obtained. The photo above shows a small segment of vein that was removed. This vein segment when filled with blood was unsightly, painful, tender, and uncomfortable for the patient. Within minutes, the bulging veins are gone! As a reminder, we would not do micro-A/P without ablating the GSV above. We have to shut down the source of the problem and let the healthy veins return the blood to the heart. A/P is done secondary to the ablation in most cases.

In summary:

After the refluxing veins are treated to reduce or eliminate the refluxing condition, Micro A/P can be used to remove bulging varicose veins. The process is simple:

Step 1   The patient's leg is marked while the patient is standing.

Step 2   The patient's leg is cleaned and draped.

Step 3   Local anesthesia is applied under the vein and at skin level.

Step 4   The A/P Hook is inserted into the opening, and the vein is gently removed.

Step 5   Repeat as necessary.

Step 6   "Butterfly" type bandages are applied if needed and then the treated leg is wrapped with compression bandages.

Step 7   The patient is provided with post-procedure instructions and will return to the office in 24 hours.

This patient received this treatment without sedation and without an Rx for narcotics afterwards. He was seen back in the office within 24 hours, and the compression wraps were removed. Micro A/P can be done with a simple procedure tray, A/P instruments, and without a great deal of discomfort to the patient. Doing this well takes some training and years of experience to master.

Another option for A/P point-of-service is the operating room with the above mentioned technique or powered phlebectomy or commonly referred to a TriVex™. The system was originally developed by Greg Spitz, M.D., from Aurora, Illinois. The system is comprised of a small rotating shaving device used in arthroscopic procedures, an irrigator for tumescent, and a light source. Transillumination and powered resection were born. As with most first generation medical devices, improvements were made and TriVex II was introduced. Regardless of which system a doctor has, this is an operating room procedure for most doctors. There is no way a patient would tolerate this procedure in an office setting without at least intravenous sedation. With sedation comes patient monitoring, and depending on the State, may require additional licensing and equipment in the procedure room. The procedure has a moderated learning curve with 10-30 cases being required before a doctor is comfortable with the device. I like the device which is currently marketed by Smith+Nephew and manufactured by Dionics®, a Smith+Nephew company focused on arthroscopic and endoscopic medical devices.

Chapter 9

Navigating Your Insurance Questions

There are many questions to understand related to your insurance policy. There are also vein care policy statements that doctors have to follow in order for payment to be processed to them. This chapter will help you understand all of this. Before I attempt to take you through the maze of insurance issues, let me say in love: ***You need to find an office that understands insurance issues related to vein care.***

As a patient you are ultimately responsible for payment no matter what! Some patients are under the impression that if United Healthcare, BCBS, or Aetna refuse payment, then; "I'm off the hook." Not true. You're completely on the hook for all monies due the doctor.

In saying this, there are many reasons why your claim may be denied or only partially paid. Among them:

- Claim had been filed with the wrong insurance card.

- Claim had been filed with expired insurance card or in transition with another provider.

- Claim had been filed with the wrong patient's name (Smith, Gonzales, Gomez, Johnson, etc...). If the SS#, patient demographics, DL#, etc... don't match, the claim may be reviewed, delaying payment or refusing payment altogether.

- Address was wrong for the patient.

- Conservative treatment policy or therapy was not followed by your doctor.

- Yearly deductible was not met by patient. So, the patient is shocked when they get the bill.

- No coverage for the treatment you had (Vein Care).

- Doctor was not on your insurance program or plan.

- Insurance company doesn't provide out-of-network benefits.

The list goes on and on. In the wake of our healthcare crisis, strict medical policy and new mandates on "who" can treat you are now being introduced. So, in addition to Vein Care Policy, insurance companies are now limiting which doctors can treat you for the disease. You'll be surprised by the decisions that BCBS in Massachusetts and Aetna in Arizona decided to do.

Word of caution! Last year in Massachusetts Blue Cross Blue Shield made a decision to limit who could do your vein treatment by restricting certain doctor specialties to the procedure. On the surface this sounds pretty good. Except they didn't include ABPh Board Certified Doctors.

The article below was reprinted by permission from the Editor of VEIN Magazine and written by Sarah Spataro. Sarah Spataro is a freelance writer in Los Angeles, California. She can be reached at: sarahspataro@gmail.com.

I highlighted this specific part of the article for your review. The entire article is included for your reference.

The Medical Director of BCBS commenting on their decision to contract with Vascular Surgeons, Interventional Radiologist, and General Surgeon specialties.

"To remedy their lack of understanding, BCBSMA looked to the American Board of Medical Specialties (ABMS) to create new privileging criteria. Says Dr. Cook, "Like other insurers we use the

ABMS as our gold standard. In that world, these specialties [VS, IR, GS] are the ones who specialize in venous diseases. We need to ensure that our members have the benefit of seeing professionals who can offer them a wide range of treatment options for symptomatic venous disease."

VEIN asked Dr. Cook (BCBSMA Medical Director) if the company consulted with physicians, vein specialists, or either of the two main vein societies in the U.S., the American Venus Forum (AVF) or the American College of Phlebology (ACP). She responded that BCBSMA "consulted with a variety of people in our network."

To answer more directly, the AVF and ACP were not consulted by BCBSMA. As described earlier in the book, an ABPh Board Certified doctor is more educated than a non-ABPh doctor regardless of their specialty. Our offices were perfect examples of this. We had Vascular Surgeons, General Vascular Surgeons, and General Surgeons who at first, were surprised by my recommendation to become ABPh Board Certified because they already treated veins for years. They thought they knew everything about Total Vein Care. They didn't!

They received their ABPh Board Certification and each one of them confided in me that they learned a great deal from the American College of Phlebology Boards even though they had a good foundation related to vein care.

The ACP and AVF committees are available to help insurance companies write medical policies that are fair, consistent, and provide expertise in vein care for their customers. Just for the record, I think insurance companies should limit who can treat venous disease.

My recommendation is to include the ABPh Board Certified Doctors. As a healthcare consultant, I'm always available to help the insurance industry solve problems!

On a positive note, BCBS was the first private pay insurance company to endorse Radio-Frequency Ablation (VNUS) and pay for the services based on multi-center data, outcomes, and direct RF to vein stripping clinical trials. Aetna was not far behind. So, while I understand why BCBS and Aetna are looking at these issues, I think they need help in making the decisions. It appears that both companies confided locally with doctors who had their own interest in mind during the conversations which led to the decisions earlier discussed.

My recommendations (if followed) related to "who" treats vein patients in the future will insure a better outcome for the patient, more profit for the insurance company due to the training of the doctors, and limit doctors who may have attended a weekend course sponsored by the technology industry, then decided to hang a sign on the door saying that they are a "vein specialists."

I truly feel that a ABPh doctor who has a procedure background is going to do a better job than a non-ABPh. I also feel that a ABPh doctor in conjunction with any other Board Certification is going to do a better job than a non-ABPh doctor, regardless of specialty.

Remember, I helped train doctors in three states, at workshops, and educational meetings on this technology. It was easy for me to see who had the best set of hands and the education to back up the skill set.

The BCBSMA article that I referenced follows. It, of course, was a "warning shot" across the bow for Phlebologists across the country. If insurance people start looking at medical specialties instead of education, experience, and expertise, then we're all in trouble.

Years ago, the idea of medical "Centers of Excellence" came and went. I thought this was a great idea. CVD is that type of institution. I'm sure there are other doctors as well across the country who have the experience, the credentials, and have multiple Board Certifications including ABPh. Why not get the best doctors you can for your insurance customers?

The Blue Cross/Blue Shield Memo that Vein Care Specialists Can't Afford to Ignore

From Issue 2 of Volume 2 / 2009
4/1/2009

December 15th was a normal day at The Vein & Aesthetic Center of Boston. Doctors Elizabeth Foley and Judith Hondo bustled from room to room, caring for patients and doing procedures. Their office staff made sure everything was running smoothly. Little did they know, as they settled into the comfortable, daily groove of a well-established vein care practice, that their thriving business was about to be threatened—threatened by a memo that slipped into the office like a stealth bomb.

The memo was from Blue Cross Blue Shield of Massachusetts (BCBSMA). Ironically, for the gravity of the news that it contained, it was written with the seemingly casual heading, "F.Y.I."

For your information: Effective on April 15th, 2009, there will be "new privileging requirements" for the treatment of varicose veins. Specifically, varicosities treated with radio frequency ablation (RFA) and endovenous laser ablation (EVLT). In order to continue to get reimbursed for these procedures, physicians must meet one of the following criteria:
• Board-certified in vascular surgery (VS)
• Board-certified in radiology with interventional training (IR)
• Board-certified in general surgery prior to the establishment of the vascular boards (GS)

In addition, all sites of service must be accredited by the American College of Radiology (ACR) or the Intersocietal Commission for the Accreditation of Vascular Laboratories (ICAVL). Claims for procedures performed at unaccredited sites will be denied, regardless of the performing physician's privileging status.

BCBSMA: "Quality is the focus of this initiative."

The memo cites "safety" and "the rapid adoption of these procedures by physicians" as the reason for the new requirements. Dr. Jan Cook, Regional Medical Director for BCBSMA, said, "Over the last five years, an increasing number of people have been receiving this procedure with a wide variety of physicians performing it. We became concerned about the quality of the training. We don't understand the quality of the training of the physicians that are rendering this service."

To remedy their lack of understanding, BCBSMA looked to the American Board of Medical Specialties (ABMS) to create new privileging criteria. Says Dr. Cook, "Like other insurers we use the ABMS as our gold standard. In that world, these specialties [VS, IR, GS] are the ones who specialize in venous diseases. We need to ensure that our members have the benefit of seeing professionals who can offer them a wide range of treatment options for symptomatic venous disease."

VEIN asked Dr. Cook if the company consulted with physicians, vein specialists, or either of the two main vein societies in the U.S., the American Venus Forum (AVF) or the American College of Phlebology (ACP). She responded that BCBSMA "consulted with a variety of people in our network."

In modern vein care, quality not necessarily tied to specialty

The ABMS is of course a good place to find specialties with the skill set to treat venous disease. But by adhering exclusively to the ABMS, BCBSMA has overlooked the "contemporary world" of vein care, where skilled physicians across many specialties have been providing quality care for years—and have been getting reimbursed for it. Doctors Foley and Hondo, from The Vein & Aesthetic Center of Boston, are a prime example.

Both board-certified in OB/GYN, Dr. Foley and Dr. Hondo dedicated their practice exclusively to vein treatment in 2002. BCBSMA has been reimbursing them for RFA and EVLT since 2004, when the treatments were approved for coverage. In addition to handling thousands of cases and having innumerable hours of experience, both doctors have earned their credentials as registered vascular technicians (RVT) and registered physicians in vascular interpretation (RPVI). Both doctors became board certified Phlebologists in May of 2008, having met the rigorous standards set by the American Board of Phlebology (ABPh). Prior to receiving this memo, the doctors had initiated the process for ICAVL accreditation.

And yet, as of April 15th, after five years of coverage, their practice will be denied payment from BCBSMA, which represents approximately 40% of their patients.

By comparison, an IR, VS or GS who has potentially never performed RFA or EVLT will be eligible for reimbursement—provided their site of treatment is ACR or ICAVL accredited. There is no specific requirement for the study or treatment of superficial venous disease in general surgery, vascular surgery, or interventional radiology fellowships.

It is worth mentioning that there is no division between medical specialties on this issue. To the contrary, concerned physicians and societies are uniting en masse to address it. Significantly, one of the doctors heading a special task force on the issue, Dr. Julie Stoughton, is a general surgeon who operates an ACR accredited facility in Massachusetts. Another key committee member, Dr. Robert Min, is a prominent interventional radiologist and past president of the ACP. In addition to the ACP, societies that have pledged their support include the Society of Interventional Radiology (SIR), the Society of Vascular Surgery (SVS), the American Venous Forum (AVF), the Society for Vascular Ultrasound, (SVU) and the American Society of Dermatologic Surgery (ASDS).

Quality of care: A defensible argument?

Nobody will argue that the patient comes first: high quality care is—or should be—of paramount importance to physicians and insurers alike. However, looking at the facts, it is difficult to give BCBSMA the benefit of the doubt when they say that patient care is the focus of this initiative.

Dr. Nick Morrison, President of the ACP, calls the BCBSMA reasoning "disingenuous and indefensible... it's a blatant attempt to restrict access to patients under the guise of providing them with high quality care."

In addition to missing the mark by excluding many highly skilled vein care specialists from their privileging criteria, technological advancements and low rates of serious complication also argue against their claim that this directive is quality-driven.

EVLT and RFA are minimally invasive, ultrasound-guided procedures most commonly performed on an outpatient basis, using local anesthesia.

The most common risk of complication is deep vein thrombosis (DVT). The occurrence of DVT in RFA/EVLT treatments is around 1%. In the majority of cases, these procedures have replaced the older practice of vein stripping. Vein stripping is commonly performed in operating rooms under general anesthesia. In addition to the higher risks associated with general anesthesia, DVT occurrence in vein stripping is closer to 5%. And in simple terms of patient comfort and recovery, there is no comparison: EVLT/RFA patients can usually resume normal activities within hours or days, whereas vein stripping recovery can take weeks, with substantial discomfort.

Varicose veins have been estimated to occur in 15-20% of people. An aging population and enduring obesity epidemic will likely keep those percentages on the rise. It is easy to see how patient access to safe, affordable treatment has driven rapid growth in the field of vein care, particularly over the last five years.

It is also easy to deduce that this phenomenon has caused a rapid and substantial increase in claims to insurance carriers. BCBSMA does not mention this in their memo.

Why all vein specialists should be concerned

The memo that has Massachusetts on edge could be the snowstorm before an avalanche. Asked if this is a matter of national concern, Dr. Morrison of the ACP responded, "for now it's Massachusetts, but there is a well-founded intuition that if they go ahead with this, similar policies will be adopted nationwide. That would have terrible consequences for patients in terms of accessibility, and for the venous disease industry across the board, from physicians to equipment manufacturers. It is critically important that we stop this or get them to be more reasonable. Everybody except the insurance companies will suffer."

At the time of this writing, a special ACP appointed committee is attempting to talk with BCBSMA. First and foremost, the committee hopes to delay the implementation of the directive and to open discussions. One critical topic is the importance of continued patient access to treatment. Another is rethinking privileging criteria to include a broader range of specialists. Physicians who can prove their competency should have the opportunity to do so, and to be considered for continued payment privileges.

Dr. Cook of BCBSMA says the insurer is "always open to talking with network physicians," and that they are "having ongoing conversations with [the ABPh] and their members on this topic."

Nonetheless, she said the program is still set to go live on April 15th.

Back at The Vein & Aesthetic Center of Boston, things are on hold. A large investment in new ultrasound equipment has been shelved, and the ICAVL accreditation process has been frozen. Says Dr. Foley, "My initial reaction [to the memo] was that this issue would be easily rectified. I thought we'd just call and explain that they'd forgotten to include phlebology in their privileging criteria. I never thought it would turn into the nightmare it's become."

For more information, please contact the American College of Phlebology at (510) 346-6800.

Sarah Spataro is a freelance writer in Los Angeles, California. She can be reached at sarahspataro@gmail.com.

Vein Industry News VEIN Magazine, Volume 2, Issue 2, 2009 reprinted by permission. www.veindirectory.org.

* * * * *

In Arizona, Aetna just recently made a similar decision. Of the 26 doctors approved to treat varicose veins in Arizona, only two of them were ABPh Board Certified. Aetna removed one of our CVD doctors from the approved list of doctors who can now treat veins in Arizona. Dr. Thomas L. Pester, M.D., has done over 4,000 procedures, is double-board certified (General Surgery-Phlebology), is a Certified Trainer for ablative techniques, and has 30 years of ultrasound experience. We've appealed this decision and, as of the writing of this book, there has been no response from Aetna even acknowledging our correspondence. We wrote the appeal letter in August, 2010. The book was published in November, 2010.

This disturbing trend of making decisions on who can treat you regardless of experience should be reviewed closely. To restrict or limit the scope of a doctor based on specialty rather than training or Board Certification is irresponsible and short-sighted. The medical director who made the decision for Aetna knew nothing about The Center for Venous Disease or Dr. Pester's vast experience in treating vein patients.

In the Arizona Aetna example, you could have a Vascular Surgeon (Specialty accepted by Aetna) who has not completed a course, not completed a single endovenous procedure, with little or no ultrasound experience, and receive a contract with Aetna to treat veins over Dr. Pester who has 30 years of experience and 4,000 procedures under his belt. Aetna and Blue Cross Blue Shield need to reevaluate these decisions.

These decisions do not help the patient and they are not good decisions for the insurance companies either. Training = better outcomes = lower costs = higher profits for the insurance carrier.

As a member of the ACP's Reimbursement Committee, our committee can help with and have made recommendations to the insurance industry that are fair and balanced and benefit their "customers." One of the key concerns for every patient related to treatment cost is, will my insurance company pay for the treatment? The answer is "YES" if you meet the requirements of the insurance companies. These requirements are usually addressed as Medical Policy requirements or directives. These are the ground rules for the physicians to follow if payment is to be made to the doctor. That's the good news. The bad news is that if the insurance company finds that their policies were not followed, the doctor's fees will not be paid and the entire amount will be owed by the patient.

As I already mentioned earlier, over 220 million people have access to insurance coverage for venous disease as long as the policy is followed. The policy for veins might include; wearing stockings for 3-6 months, taking products like Tylenol, Advil, Motrine, etc..., elevating your legs, applying cold or heat to the area, etc.... In addition, many insurance companies require documentation of the progression of the disease over the same time period. To clarify this, let me walk you through a six-month conservative therapy regiment for a major insurance carrier.

1. You make your appointment (wait 3-4 weeks) with a Phlebologist (ABPh).

2. You walk into the office, give the front office person your drivers license and insurance card, pay your copay, fill out the patient intake form (history, present illness, review of systems, and chief complaint), and wait.

3. You are then taken back to an exam room, the medical assistant takes your vitals, reviews the forms, and then enters your information into the Electronic Medical Record (chart).

4. The doctor comes in and does a physical exam and enters his notes in the EMR.

5. Your doctor, due to your history, physical exam, C.E.A.P. classification, and CVSS orders an ultrasound.

6. You schedule a visit for ultrasound with your doctor (R.V.T.) or sonographer (R.V.T.) and more information is gathered to chart into the EMR.

7. An office visit is scheduled to discuss the findings of your ultrasound.

8. In the office visit, you're told what the issues are and what treatment options you have. Then you're told that because your insurance company is so-in-so, you have to wait six months to be treated, wear compression hose, elevate your legs, exercise, take over-the-counter pain medication, and schedule follow up appointments to see if any of this works. I've already told you that these measures will not take care of diseased vein valves in your legs.

9. You're now frustrated, angry, and upset with the doctor's office.

10. You come back every other month for follow up visits and maybe one or two more ultrasounds, and guess what, you're worse. The disease is progressive!

11. Now you're really upset because you've waited six months, we now have to process your pre-authorization or predetermination to get approval to treat you so that the insurance company will pay for it. The approval is relying on all the documentation that we will file on your behalf. This documentation better be complete and follow every requested piece of information or they will deny the treatment. Oh, and to really make your day, this approval still doesn't guarantee payment to your doctor. It's in your doctors contracts with the insurance companies.

12. So, assume we get the approval, you find out that you need $10,000 worth of treatment and you have to pay $1,500 to meet your yearly deductible, $2,000 (20%) for your coinsurance, and your copay amount for each visit, on top of the monies paid already for the doctors appointments and ultrasounds (which were a waste of time and money for you).

13. Disgusted, you make your appointments for your procedures. At this time, you've invested almost 7-8 months for something that can be treated in the office in 45 minutes, and while you're happy that you had it done, you're worn thin due to the process mandated by the insurance companies.

14. If you have multiple procedures to do, there is a time limit of 30 days to complete your treatment or we have to go back to the insurance company and extend the authorization.

You've been through the process once and it was agonizing. Not the treatment, or procedures, but the time spent trying to get resolution.

Think about our staff for a moment, and the volume of patients we treat and the cycle of delaying treatment and payment when everyone that knows anything about the disease knows it is progressive and will only get worse. This is all a delaying tactic by the insurance industry. They know conservative treatment does not cure venous disease!

Here's the really bad news. There are a few doctors in your area that will ignore this mandated policy by the insurance companies, and if caught, will be refused payment. That means you pay for all of it! If your medical chart is audited by Medicare and they have a vein care policy and the chart is "doctored" to meet the policy, its fraud. If your chart is audited by private pay providers (BCBS, Aetna, United, etc...) payment will be refused for not following the stated vein care policy. The doctor could also lose their contract with the insurance company. So, you have to see someone who has your best interest at heart and who will follow the rules or you are exposed financially.

Word of caution! If you go to a doctor and they tell you that you can be treated immediately for a vein problem, you need to proceed very carefully. Call your provider and ask your insurance representative about their vein care policy BEFORE you get treated. There are dishonest doctors treating veins. If they don't follow the policy and they get caught, you will pay for it because the insurance company will deny payment.

Many of our patients out of pure frustration with the insurance companies are starting to pay for the procedure. We've packaged a plan for cash pay patients whether they live near us or want to fly to one of our CVD offices located in:

Arizona
Glendale
Paradise Valley
Gilbert
Phoenix

New Mexico
Albuquerque
Santa Fe

Texas
El Paso, East-West

GRAB YOUR LEGS....IT'S ON!

**Original notes for the creation of The Center for Venous Disease
and CVDJBA, LLC Management Group on a
Southwest Airlines® cocktail napkin!**

Colleen Barrett, the former President of Southwest Airlines and I corresponded early in the development of the CVD Business Plan and her encouragement was, and is, appreciated. I just happened to attend a conference where Colleen was a guest speaker. I wrote to her thanking her for comments during the meeting and she wrote me back. That's how it all started.

Keep sending those drink coupons Colleen!

While the plan for our vein centers has evolved, the basic organization has remained consistent, reproducible from one CVD center to another, with focus on quality, and great patient outcomes. Colleen has worked with Southwest Airlines since 1971. Colleen has a long history with Southwest Airlines working in the capacity of Corporate Secretary, Vice President of Administration, Executive Vice President, and President. Colleen is most known for her "Servant Attitude" which was incorporated into our companies mission statement from day one; "We'll treat your symptoms and touch your Heart." Thanks Colleen for your thoughtfulness. I do appreciate all that you do for Southwest Airlines and for the big heart you've shared with so many.

A sample ad from Phoenix. FLY IN & OUT, or if you're in town drop by.

* Visit www.healthylegs.net for an office near you.

If you call any of our offices, in any State, we'll honor this advertisement regardless of this advertising being a local promotion in the Phoenix market. Keep in mind the expertise you're getting with a Board Certified Doctor, the best technology, in the right setting, and at a cost you can afford. For just a little more, you can participate in our FLY in & FLY out program. If you have any questions, just call me. My information is on our websites; veinscreening.com and healthylegs.net.

The insurance dilemma! It is the doctor's responsibility to understand each policy and effectively document against the requirements as stated. The challenge is that there is no standardized policy across payers. I would like to help change this. We should have one vein care policy across all payers. It's not that hard to accomplish, and it would help save millions of dollars worth of wasted time, appeals, paperwork, E-Filings, and unnecessary communication between doctors and insurance medical directors related to payment and policy.

We spend more than 40% of our time chasing down insurance issues for our patients. As a side note, I sent the White House "points of light" to reform healthcare and to my surprise didn't receive a response. I sent the same list to Bill O'Reilly at FOX News and they didn't respond either. Shame on you Bill! Just for that, I'm sending you my book!

My plan would create a level playing field for doctors, insurance companies, attorneys, patients, etc…at a cost reduction while saving Medicare. No one responded. Go figure! HEINZ-care makes too much sense!

At the end of the day, it is the patient who is responsible for payment for services related to a visit with your doctor. It is part of the forms packet you fill out at every doctor you visit.

A couple of chapters back, I emphasized the need for great documentation, photos of the legs, and good ultrasound diagnostics. I have examples of our Electronic Medical Record forms that drive the dictated reports for your electronic chart shown below.

CVD New Patient (HPI, ROS, Exam)		
Lower Extremity Leg Pain or Discomfort:	⊙ Y	○ N ○ N/A

Onset

○ 1-3 months	○ > 1 year
○ 4-6 months	○ > 2 years
○ 6-12 months	○ > 3 years

Frequency

daily	⊙ N/A	○ Y	○ N	several times per month	⊙ N/A	○ Y ○ N
a few times per week	⊙ N/A	○ Y	○ N	with increasing frequency	⊙ N/A	○ Y ○ N
about once a week	⊙ N/A	○ Y	○ N	with decreasing frequency	⊙ N/A	○ Y ○ N
about every other week	⊙ N/A	○ Y	○ N	ongoing	⊙ N/A	○ Y ○ N

Timing

mostly during the day	⊙ N/A	○ Y	○ N	mostly at night	⊙ N/A	○ Y ○ N
mostly in the evening	⊙ N/A	○ Y	○ N			

Severity

○ mild	○ stable
○ moderate	○ improving
○ severe	○ fluctuates in severity
○ worsening	

Location

Left thigh	⊙ N/A	Y	○ N	Right thigh	⊙ N/A	○ Y ○ N
Left knee	⊙ N/A	Y	○ N	Right knee	⊙ N/A	○ Y ○ N
Left calf	⊙ N/A	Y	○ N	Right calf	⊙ N/A	○ Y ○ N
Left ankle	⊙ N/A	Y	○ N	Right ankle	⊙ N/A	○ Y ○ N

Quality/Description

pain or discomfort	⊙ N/A	○ Y	○ N	swelling	⊙ N/A	○ Y ○ N
ants crawling/ pins and needles	⊙ N/A	○ Y	○ N	cramping	⊙ N/A	○ Y ○ N
burning or itching	⊙ N/A	○ Y	○ N	aching	⊙ N/A	○ Y ○ N
shock-like	⊙ N/A	○ Y	○ N			

Exacerbating Factors

painful leg movements	⊙ N/A	○ Y	○ N	skin breakdown	⊙ N/A	○ Y ○ N
interrupted sleep	⊙ N/A	○ Y	○ N	swelling limits movement without pain	⊙ N/A	○ Y ○ N
fatigue	⊙ N/A	○ Y	○ N	pain limits mobility or limits standing or sitting	⊙ N/A	○ Y ○ N

Remitting Factors

wearing compression wraps or stockings	⊙ N/A	○ Y	○ N	warm or cold compress	⊙ N/A	○ Y ○ N
taking over-the-counter anti-inflammatory medications	⊙ N/A	○ Y	○ N	elevation of legs	⊙ N/A	○ Y ○ N
rubbing the legs/ massage	⊙ N/A	○ Y	○ N	other-	⊙ N/A	○ Y ○ N

Notes:	⊙ Y	○ N ○ N/A

Quality/Description

Past Vein Treatments

Patient prior vein treatments

Sclerotherapy	● N/A	Y	N	phlebactomy	● N/A	Y	N
vein stripping/ligation	● N/A	Y	N	surface laser (skin)	● N/A	Y	N
vein ablation	● N/A	Y	N				

Notes:

Quality of Life

The symptoms affect and/or limits quality of life:	● Y	N	N/A
The symptoms affect performance on the job and/or limits advancement:	● Y	N	N/A
Condition affects patient sleeping through the night:	● Y	N	N/A
Condition limits patients choices when getting dressed for work, recreation, or social activities:	● Y	N	N/A
Condition is embarrasing for patient:	● Y	N	N/A

CVD New Patient (HPI, ROS, Exam)			
ROS - Constitutional			
Unremarkable (Normal)	● Y	○ N	○ N/A
Headache	○ Y	○ N	● N/A
Fever	○ Y	○ N	● N/A
Weight loss	○ Y	○ N	● N/A
Weight gain	○ Y	○ N	● N/A
Fatigue	○ Y	○ N	● N/A
Increased appetite	○ Y	○ N	● N/A
Decreased appetite	○ Y	○ N	● N/A
Skin			
Unremarkable (Normal)	● Y	○ N	○ N/A
Rash	○ Y	○ N	● N/A
Skin changes	○ Y	○ N	● N/A
Dry skin	○ Y	○ N	● N/A
Pigmentation	○ Y	○ N	● N/A
Moles	○ Y	○ N	● N/A
ROS - Cardiovascular			
Unremarkable (Normal)	● Y	○ N	○ N/A
chest pain/pressure	○ Y	○ N	● N/A
palpitations	○ Y	○ N	● N/A
dyspnea	○ Y	○ N	● N/A
syncope	○ Y	○ N	● N/A
edema	○ Y	○ N	● N/A
leg cramps/calf pain	○ Y	○ N	● N/A
Respiratory			
Unremarkable (Normal)	● Y	○ N	○ N/A
Cough	○ Y	○ N	● N/A
Hemoptysis	○ Y	○ N	● N/A
Pleuritic chest pain	○ Y	○ N	● N/A
Wheezing	○ Y	○ N	● N/A
Dyspnea	○ Y	○ N	● N/A
Gastrointestinal			
Unremarkable (Normal)	● Y	○ N	○ N/A
Frequent heartburn	○ Y	○ N	● N/A
Abdominal pain	○ Y	○ N	● N/A
Jaundice	○ Y	○ N	● N/A
Blood in stool	○ Y	○ N	● N/A
Black tarry stools	○ Y	○ N	● N/A

Painful bowel movements	○ Y	○ N	◉ N/A
Constipation	○ Y	○ N	◉ N/A
Diarrhea	○ Y	○ N	◉ N/A
Musculoskeletal			
Unremarkable (Normal)	◉ Y	○ N	○ N/A
Joint pain	○ Y	○ N	◉ N/A
Joint stiffness	○ Y	○ N	◉ N/A
Joint swelling	○ Y	○ N	◉ N/A
Muscle pain	○ Y	○ N	◉ N/A
Muscle weakness	○ Y	○ N	◉ N/A
Back pain	○ Y	○ N	◉ N/A
Neck pain	○ Y	○ N	◉ N/A
Neurological			
Unremarkable (Normal)	◉ Y	○ N	○ N/A
Headaches	○ Y	○ N	◉ N/A
Dizziness	○ Y	○ N	◉ N/A
Syncope	○ Y	○ N	◉ N/A
Vertigo	○ Y	○ N	◉ N/A
Seizures	○ Y	○ N	◉ N/A
Numbness	○ Y	○ N	◉ N/A
Tingling	○ Y	○ N	◉ N/A
Weakness	○ Y	○ N	◉ N/A
Difficulty walking	○ Y	○ N	◉ N/A
Memory disturbance	○ Y	○ N	◉ N/A
Speech changes	○ Y	○ N	◉ N/A
Tremor	○ Y	○ N	◉ N/A
Hematology/Lymphatic			
Unremarkable (Normal)	◉ Y	○ N	○ N/A
Anemia	○ Y	○ N	◉ N/A
Easy bruising/bleeding	○ Y	○ N	◉ N/A
Lymphonode enlargement	○ Y	○ N	◉ N/A
Endocrine			
Unremarkable (Normal)	◉ Y	○ N	○ N/A
Polyuria	○ Y	○ N	◉ N/A
Polydypsia	○ Y	○ N	◉ N/A
Cold/heat intolerance	○ Y	○ N	◉ N/A
Weight changes	○ Y	○ N	◉ N/A
Difficulty or delayed healing	○ Y	○ N	◉ N/A
Psychological			

CVD New Patient (HPI, ROS, Exam)			
Constitutional	NE	Ex	⦿ Norm (Well appearing, well nourished, well groomed. A&O x 3. Ambulatory)
Skin	NE	Ex	⦿ Norm (Intact, no rash, no ulcers, no lesions, no jaundice)
Head	NE	Ex	⦿ Norm (Normocephalic, symetrical. No facial tenderness)
Neck	NE	Ex	⦿ Norm (Supple, trachea midline. No lymphadenopathy, no masses, no thyromegaly, no tenderness.)
Lymphatics	NE	Ex	⦿ Norm (No tenderness, no swelling.)
Cardiovascular	NE	Ex	⦿ Norm (Regular rate. Regular rhythm. No murmers or extra sounds.)
Chest	NE	Ex	⦿ Norm (Clear to auscultation, good air exchange. No rales, wheezing or rhonchi)
Musculoskeletal	NE	Ex	⦿ Norm (Full ROM of joints. No swelling, redness, tenderness or increased warmth of joints. Full ROM of lumbar spine. No muscle or bony tenderness of spine)
Neurological	NE	Ex	⦿ Norm (Normal gait and motor function. Sensory function normal. Cranial nerves II-XII intact.)
Edema - Vascular	NE	Ex	⦿ Norm (No edema, JVD or hepatojugular reflux. Carotid pulses 2+. Lower extremity pulses 4+)
EXAM: LEFT LEG	NE	⦿ Ex	Norm (none present)

Past vein treatment(s):

Left sclerotherapy	⦿ N/A	Y	N	Right sclerotherapy	⦿ N/A	Y	N
Left laser ablation	⦿ N/A	Y	N	Right laser ablation	⦿ N/A	Y	N
Left RF ablation (VNUS)	⦿ N/A	Y	N	Right RF ablation	⦿ N/A	Y	N
Left vein stripping/ligation	⦿ N/A	Y	N	Right vein stripping/ligation	⦿ N/A	Y	N
Left phlebectomy	⦿ N/A	Y	N	Left phlebectomy	⦿ N/A	Y	N

Vein(s):

palpable	⦿ N/A	Y	N	linear in size	⦿ N/A	Y	N
inflamed	⦿ N/A	Y	N	vein cluster present that is twisted	⦿ N/A	Y	N
tender	⦿ N/A	Y	N				

Vein(s) - Type:

Telangectasias (<1mm)	⦿ N/A	Y	N	Reticular veins (>2mm-3mm)	⦿ N/A	Y	N
Venulectasias (1-2mm)	⦿ N/A	Y	N	Bulging Varicose Veins (>3mm)	⦿ N/A	Y	N

Vein Locations:

thigh	⦿ N/A	Y	N	calf	⦿ N/A	Y	N
above knee	⦿ N/A	Y	N	ankle	⦿ N/A	Y	N
below Knee	⦿ N/A	Y	N				

CLINICAL CLASSIFICATION: CEAP- Varicose Veins:

C0- No visible signs of venous disease	⦿ N/A	Y	N	C4a- Pigmentation or exzema	⦿ N/A	Y	N
C1- Telangiectasias or reticular veins	⦿ N/A	Y	N	C4b- Lipodermatosclerosis and or atrophie blanche	⦿ N/A	Y	N
C2- Varicose Veins	⦿ N/A	Y	N	C5- Healed venous ulcer	⦿ N/A	Y	N
C3- Edema	⦿ N/A	Y	N	C6- Active venous ulcer	⦿ N/A	Y	N

VENOUS CLINICAL SEVERITY SCORE (VCSS): _____ Total VCSS Score

**The VCSS represents for each limb, a

Venous Ulcer, location:

Notes:

EXAM: RIGHT LEG		NE	☉ Ex	Norm (none present)			
Past vein treatment(s):							
Left Sclerotherapy	☉ N/A	Y	N	Right Sclerotherapy	☉ N/A	Y	N
Left laser ablation	☉ N/A	Y	N	Right laser ablation	☉ N/A	Y	N
Left RF ablation(VNUS)	☉ N/A	Y	N	Right RF ablation(VNUS)	☉ N/A	Y	N
Left vein stripping/ligation	☉ N/A	Y	N	Right vein stripping/ligation	☉ N/A	Y	N
Left phlebectomy	☉ N/A	Y	N	Right Phlebectomy	☉ N/A	Y	N
Vein(s):							
palpable	☉ N/A	Y	N	linear in size	☉ N/A	Y	N
inflamed	☉ N/A	Y	N	vein cluster present that is twisted	☉ N/A	Y	N
tender	☉ N/A	Y	N				
Vein(s) - Type:							
Telangiectasias (<1mm)	☉ N/A	Y	N	Reticular veins (>2mm)	☉ N/A	Y	N
Venulectasias (1-2mm)	☉ N/A	Y	N	Bulging Varicose Veins (>3mm)	☉ N/A	Y	N
Locations:							
thigh	☉ N/A	Y	N	calf	☉ N/A	Y	N
above knee	☉ N/A	Y	N	ankle	☉ N/A	Y	N
below knee	☉ N/A	Y	N				
CLINICAL CLASSIFICATION: CEAP- Varicose Veins;							
C0- No visible signs of venous disease	☉ N/A	Y	N	C4a- Pigmentation or exzema	☉ N/A	Y	N
C1- Telangiectasias or reticular veins	☉ N/A	Y	N	C4b- Lipodermatosclerosis and or atrophie blanche	☉ N/A	Y	N
C2- Varicose Veins	☉ N/A	Y	N	C5- Healed venous ulcer	☉ N/A	Y	N
C3- Edema	☉ N/A	Y	N	C6- Active venous ulcer	☉ N/A	Y	N

VENOUS CLINICAL SEVERITY SCORE (VCSS):   Total VCSS Score

**The VCSS represents for each limb, a

Venous Ulcer, location:

Notes:

Conservative Therapy		NE	☉ Ex	Norm (Conservative Therapy Started:)			
Compliance per medical policy:							
Compression stockings measured, fitted, and patient instructions for use and care provided.	N/A	☉ Y	N	Patient instructed to take over-the-counter anti-inflammatory medications for pain, discomfort, or swelling.	N/A	☉ Y	N
Photos taken of limbs, in an anterior, posterior, or lateral position as needed.	N/A	☉ Y	N	Recommend leg elevation, cold wraps, or heat as tolerated for pain or discomfort.	N/A	☉ Y	N

CVD Patient Exam Templates
© 2010 Center for Venous Disease, James A. Heinz

The new patient exam is very important to demonstrate the need for treatment based on the information gathered. Most insurance companies will not pay for cosmetic vein issues. Therefore, the doctor must establish from your medical intake form, the physical exam, and ultrasound whether you meet the requirements of your insurance policy on vein care. To simplify, varicose veins are defined as veins larger than 3 mm in size along the vein track. Good documentation of pain or discomfort that impedes your quality of life is necessary to meet the requirements. This may be job related as most people who suffer have jobs requiring them to stand or sit for long periods of time. Photographs must be submitted to validate varicose veins and skin condition. The ultrasound report documenting venous reflux greater than .5 second (valve Closure time), size of the vein, and locations of problem areas are required as well. The paperwork submitted from your doctor on your behalf has to be very complete and accurate. Payment depends on this!

The different forms that we use have been developed to answer all the pertinent information for the insurance Medical Directors if your chart gets requested or audited for review. As you can see our forms give the insurance company most of the information they are looking for and treatment intervals that are determined by the contract between the doctor's office and your insurance company. In reading this book, I bet you had no idea that all of this was going on behind the scenes. It costs us hundreds of thousands of dollars a year just to comply with requests. Like the exam form, the ultrasound report has to be as detailed. The form identifies the type of equipment, the sonographer who performed the study, the position of the patient, and whether there is a clot or obstruction. It also measures the vein size along the vein track, and gives us validated reflux time and duration. All of this is documented on the form.

CVD Ultrasound(s)			
ULTRASOUND TECHNIQUE	⦿ Y	○ N	○ N/A

Quality/Description

⦿ Technique: The ultrasound study was performed on-site by a certified sonographer under the supervision of the physician using a General Electric ultrasound machine with linear transducer frequencies of 8-12 MHz. The attached ultrasound schematic demonstrates retrograde flow as indicated, DVT, or SVT by location or level. The deep venous system including the Common Femoral (CFV), Femoral (FV), Popliteal (POP), Posterior Tibial (PTV), Anterior (ATV), and Peroneal (PERO) veins and the superficial system including the Great Saphenous Vein (GSV), Level 1 @ the Terminal Valve, Level 2 @ the Sub-terminal Valve, Level 3 @ mid-thigh, Level 4 @ AK, Level 5 @ BK, Level 6 @ mid-calf, Level 7 @ ankle, Small Saphenous Vein (SSV) Level A @ SPJ, Level B @ mid-calf, Level C @ ankle, perforators or communicating veins, and large tributaries. Valve closure times of > + 0.5 seconds were identified, as were vein diameters at various levels as noted. Pulse wave spectral Doppler was utilized.

Study- Lower Extremity Venous Duplex

Patient's name:

Sonographer's Name:

Chief Complaint:

Patient Position:

Standing facing the sonographer with the patients weight on the opposite leg or in steep reverse (30-45 degrees) Trendelenburg, or as directed by insurance medical policy and as adopted by The American College of Phlebology

○ N/A ⦿ Y ○ N

Scanned Leg:

Left	⦿ N/A	○ Y	○ N	Bilateral	⦿ N/A	○ Y	○ N
Right	⦿ N/A	○ Y	○ N				

Deep Vein Thrombosis is:

positive	⦿ N/A	○ Y	○ N	acute	⦿ N/A	○ Y	○ N
negative	⦿ N/A	○ Y	○ N	sub acute	⦿ N/A	○ Y	○ N
non-compressable	⦿ N/A	○ Y	○ N	chronic	⦿ N/A	○ Y	○ N
partially compressable	⦿ N/A	○ Y	○ N				

Patient presents with DVT at the following location(s):

Deep System Obstructed:

Popliteal	⦿ N/A	○ Y	○ N	Saphenofemoral Junction	⦿ N/A	○ Y	○ N
Common Femoral	⦿ N/A	○ Y	○ N	Peroneal Vein	⦿ N/A	○ Y	○ N
Superficial Femoral	⦿ N/A	○ Y	○ N	Anterior Tibial	⦿ N/A	○ Y	○ N
Posterior Tibial	⦿ N/A	○ Y	○ N	Gastrocnemius	⦿ N/A	○ Y	○ N

Patient presents with SVT at the following location(s):

Patient presents with Deep Vein Reflux in the following location(s):

Varicose Veins >3mm, and > +.5 seconds reflux noted at (see diagram):

L GSV Terminal Valve (L1)	● N/A	○ Y	○ N	R GSV Terminal Valve (L1)	● N/A ○ Y ○ N
L GSV Sub-Terminal Valve(L2)	● N/A	○ Y	○ N	R GSV Sub-Terminal Valve(L2)	● N/A ○ Y ○ N
L GSV Mid-Thigh (L3)	● N/A	○ Y	○ N	R GSV Mid-Thigh (L3)	● N/A ○ Y ○ N
L GSV @ Knee (L4)	● N/A	○ Y	○ N	R GSV @ Knee (L4)	● N/A ○ Y ○ N
L GSV below Knee (L5)	● N/A	○ Y	○ N	R GSV below knee (L5)	● N/A ○ Y ○ N
L GSV mid-calf (L6)	● N/A	○ Y	○ N	R GSV mid-calf (L6)	● N/A ○ Y ○ N
L GSV ankle (L7)	● N/A	○ Y	○ N	R GSV ankle (L7)	● N/A ○ Y ○ N

Anterior Branch Vein Reflux > .5 noted (see diagram):

Left Leg	● N/A	○ Y	○ N	Right Leg	● N/A ○ Y ○ N

SSV Reflux > .5 seconds noted at (see diagram):

L SSV @ Level A	● N/A	○ Y	○ N	R SSV @ Level A	● N/A ○ Y ○ N
L SSV @ Level B	● N/A	○ Y	○ N	R SSV @ Level B	● N/A ○ Y ○ N
L SSV @ Level C	● N/A	○ Y	○ N	R SSV @ Level C	● N/A ○ Y ○ N

Medial Perforator Reflux noted at:

Left Hunters	● N/A	○ Y	○ N	Right Hunters	● N/A ○ Y ○ N
Left Dodd	● N/A	○ Y	○ N	Right Dodd	● N/A ○ Y ○ N
Left Boyd	● N/A	○ Y	○ N	Right Boyd	● N/A ○ Y ○ N
Left Cockett I	● N/A	○ Y	○ N	Right Cockett I	● N/A ○ Y ○ N
Left Cockett II	● N/A	○ Y	○ N	Right Cockett II	● N/A ○ Y ○ N
Left Cockett III	● N/A	○ Y	○ N	Right Cockett III	● N/A ○ Y ○ N

Other Perforator Reflux noted at (see drawing):

Left Paratibial	● N/A	○ Y	○ N	Right Paratibial	● N/A ○ Y ○ N
Left Posterior Tibial	● N/A	○ Y	○ N	Right Posterior Tibial	● N/A ○ Y ○ N
Left Lateral Gastrocnemius	● N/A	○ Y	○ N	Right Lateral Gastrocnemius	● N/A ○ Y ○ N
Left Medial Gastrocnemius	● N/A	○ Y	○ N	Right Medial Gastrocnemius	● N/A ○ Y ○ N
Left Lateral Ankle	● N/A	○ Y	○ N	Right Lateral Ankle	● N/A ○ Y ○ N
Left Lateral Lower Leg	● N/A	○ Y	○ N	Right Lateral Lower Leg	● N/A ○ Y ○ N

Other Observations:

IMPRESSION/FINDINGS: ● Y   ○ N   ○ N/A

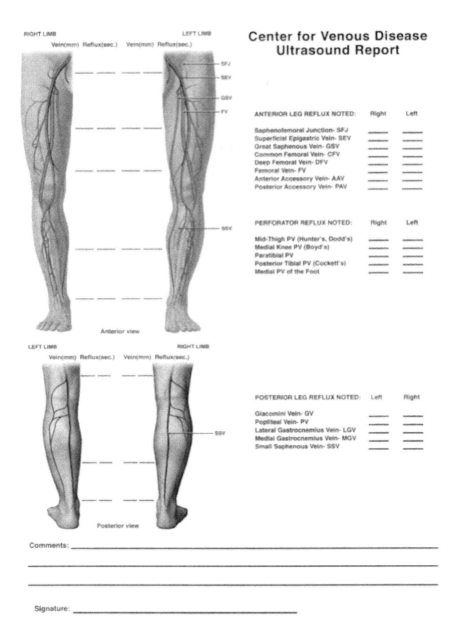

CVD Ultrasound Report
© 2010 Center for Venous Disease, James A. Heinz

As you can see, our forms are an important part of the process in making sure we document your issues against the insurance requirements. These are not the only forms we use to document and record our findings. They are just examples of template options that are specific to the patient. Once the diagnostics are completed, we can then review your treatment options and costs associated with the procedures.

At CVD we put together a slide presentation in English and Spanish which is reviewed with every patient with examples. The following presentation is an example of a person with varicose vein coverage. Not all policies include vein care. So, that is the first question that needs to be determined. Does your policy include veins? Once you understand your policy, then you can seek treatment from a qualified doctor. Once you're at the office, a co-payment is due at almost every visit according to your policy. Coinsurance is the amount that is your responsibility (90-10%, 80-20%, 70-30%, etc…). The first number is the insurance responsibility. For example, a 90-10 policy states that 90% will be paid by the insurance company and 10% by the patient for approved procedures. You'll also have to meet your annual deductible before they pay anything. My annual deductible is $1,500.00 per calendar year. In this example, I would be responsible for the first $1,500.00 + 10% + my co-pay for that visit. The deductible is a one-time charge if you have not made your deductible for the year. Patient education and staff training are key to any successful conversation with a patient related to insurance issues, billing, statements, or the Explanation of Benefits (EOB) you receive from your insurance company. The EOB is a summary of what the insurance company is going to pay for and what you owe. In this economy, a doctor has no choice but to aggressively collect any debts owed by patients.

Every year the doctors do more work, make less or the same from Medicare and the insurance companies, and have a 15-20% increase in overhead. The mandated Electronic Medical Record that was passed in the new Healthcare Bill will cost each practice between $45,000 and $120,000 just for the software. Training cost, learning curve, EDI payment set up, template builds, and staff implementation will be costly along with the upfront purchase price. In total, I believe that the cost to implement in each office may top $200,000 - $250,000. So, if you owe CVD or any other doctor money be prepared to pay the amount due. With the decreasing payments to doctors, the added overhead due to mandates from Washington D.C., increasing malpractice insurance rates, an environment that lacks the will to limit or cap lawsuits, and attorneys who advertise and encourage lawsuits based on a percentage of award, then doctors are doomed to be upside down in their practices in the coming years. Be prepared for doctors from all specialties to leave medicine if these things are not addressed soon.

In saying this, we do whatever we can to educate our patients related to their insurance policies and questions. The CVD Insurance Policy flip charts I mentioned follow:

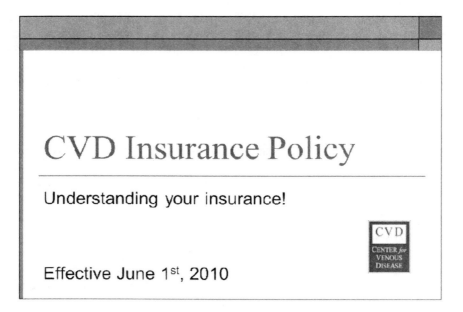

CVD Insurance Advocacy

- ☐ Since our opening, we have taken great pride in our ability to work with the insurance companies to provide you with payment approval based on medical necessity to "Treat your symptoms and touch your Heart." Our commitment has not changed. CVD will continue to aggressively provide this service for you. Our staff spends about 40% of our time on insurance issues.

Disclosure

- ☐ CVD offices are obligated under Federal or State Insurance guidelines based on your insurance carrier or Medicare mandates.
- ☐ We are directed to collect any co-pay amounts, co-insurance, or unmet deductibles at the time of service.
- ☐ We have to follow your policies guidelines or risk being audited or refused payment altogether.
- ☐ Ultimately, you are responsible for all costs associated with your treatment.

Office Visits

- Co-pays are to be paid at check in for all patients for all appointments.
- NO EXCEPTIONS!
- We accept Cash, Checks, Credit Cards, and offer GE Care Credit as an option.

- Co-Pay amounts can vary from $10.00-$65.00 based on policy. Phlebology is a specialty and SPECIALIST co-pay amounts apply to this office.

Procedure Cost Estimates

- On the day of your procedure(s), CVD will collect a co-pay, co-insurance amount (10-30% of contracted amount), and any un-met deductible you have per your insurance policy!
- Cost estimate(s) will be supplied to you by the Office Manager.

- Procedure example:
- $25.00 Co-Pay
- $440.00 Co-Insurance (20% of RF ablation charge)
- $1000.00 Un-met deductible
- Total = $1465.00 paid on the day of your procedure.

Patient Responsibility

- Payments are made on a "pay as you go" basis. If you have multiple procedures, you will have a co-pay and co-insurance payment at the time of each procedure. This must be paid upon check in at the front desk. Remember, our front office people are doing their jobs. Please be courteous related to this policy.
- If you cannot make your payment, your procedure or office visit will need to be re-scheduled!
- Please keep in mind, we are usually booked out for 2-3 months at a time.

Financial Form

- Each patient will have a copy of our financial policy and sign as an acknowledgement of receiving a copy. You will also receive a worksheet that explains the charges for your procedure appointments.
- Payment is due at time of service.

Patient Statements

☐ Patients will receive statements monthly from CVDJBA, LLC our management company. Statements are mailed from Arizona and payment is due upon receipt. Unpaid balances will be sent to collections after 2 statements.

☐ Once a patient is sent to collections, future appointments cannot be made at our office until the bill is paid in full.

Policy Statement

☐ Our policy is based on your insurance requirements. Please do not take out your frustration related to this policy on our staff. We offer our patients Board Certified Specialist, state-of-the art treatment modalities, and great outcomes. This could not be possible without a positive cash flow.

☐ Thank you for your understanding!

James A. Heinz-CVD Founder

The best advice I can give you related to insurance issues for your treatment of venous disease is to know your policy, or pay cash for your services. Cash pay programs are not as bad of an idea as you think. If you have a high deductible, a 70-30% or 80-20% policy, and large co-pay, a cash pay program might make more sense. We have payment options and use GE CareCredit™ with many of our patients to pay for their services, interest free for one year.

Navigating insurance issues occupy my staff's time by about 40-55% based on the State and policies we're dealing with. It was a core value of CVD partners to help our patients with many of these issues. With that said, it is not our fault if you have problems with your insurance company. You are the customer. You are more able to solve issues related to your coverage, problems, or EOB than we are. We are contracted with them and have specific "hoops" to jump through to help you as the patient. So, we're under their control when it comes to how we can communicate with them and in what time frames.

So, don't call us up or your doctor's office and scream and yell because you don't have the coverage you wanted or that your employer purchased on your behalf. If your company selects a company that does not include vein care then I would suggest that you get some of your coworkers together (women between 25-55 who have had children) and request it be added.

Your personnel department is a good place to start. They can amend the policy working with the insurance carrier, or change carriers. It was estimated in a published study that work related losses cost the employers $1.2 billion. This was a few years ago, so it is probably more now. Can employers really afford to have this type of loss in productivity because of venous disease? I hope this information has helped you with your insurance questions.

Chapter 10

Conclusion and Summary

From the beginning of this book, my goal was to help answer your questions related to venous disease. With more than 50-80 million Americans affected by this disease and with the loss of productivity, it is important to diagnose and treat promptly. This book is a reference source and not a substitute for an evaluation by your doctor or specialist. It was never my intent to replace a good conversation between you and your doctor. The doctor is the only one who can review your symptoms and advise you on how to continue. However, it was my intent to equip you with key information so that when you have the conversation, you will be well informed. The education gained through this book will guide you through your treatment and help manage your expectations of the procedures themselves. It is often a mistake to go into any medical treatment with sky-high expectations, leaving you to feel let down and unfulfilled. Our primary focus is on chronic venous insufficiency.

In summary, there are three treatment options for venous insufficiency: 1) Vein stripping and ligation, 2) RF Ablation, and 3) Laser ablation.

A new and promising technology that we will evaluate for GSV and SSV vein ablation is the ClariVein® product (vascularinsights.com). This device utilizes a mechanical ablative method coupled with sclerotherapy solutions to roughen and scar down the vein. CVD doctors are looking forward to evaluating this product and comparing ClariVein to ClosureFast results based on 1 week, 3 month, 6 month, and 12 month results. If the product gives us a reproducible and successful outcome for our patients, then we will look at the cost and make a decision based on our overall evaluation of this product.

As you can imagine with the volume of CVD, many vendors want to do business with our group. We put the clinical results first, then look at cost. As stated earlier, if we get the clinical results were looking for without pain or bruising, 98% vein occlusion rates, with low complications, and can save some money, we'll convert our business to that technology.

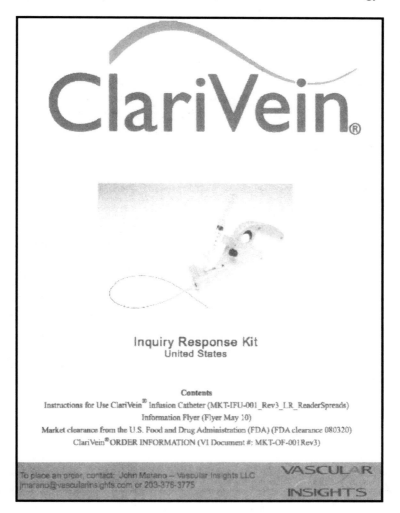

ClariVein® – courtesy of Vascular Insights LLC

The biggest advantage I see for this device is that it doesn't require local anesthesia. So, no shots for the patients along the vein track to numb the vein and protect it from a heat source. This device is in the approval process with the FDA. It will also have to have studies comparing technologies in order for doctors to use it. Doctors don't change from technology they are comfortable with very easily. There are also insurance issues to solve related to receiving payment and being a covered benefit for patients. All of these considerations have to have a positive result for the product to be successful.

Another new technology that is emerging in the vein marketplace is a product called Veinwave™. Veinwave utilizes radio-frequency energy to thermocoagulate spider veins safely and effectively without an injection. This energy is delivered only to the target veins with no thermal damage to any of the surrounding tissue. The entire process is extremely gentle and quick, and will cause limited side effects to the patient.

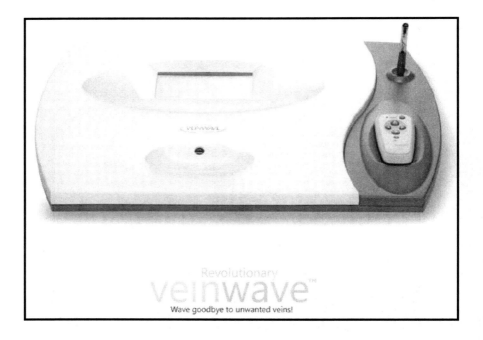

VEINGOGH™

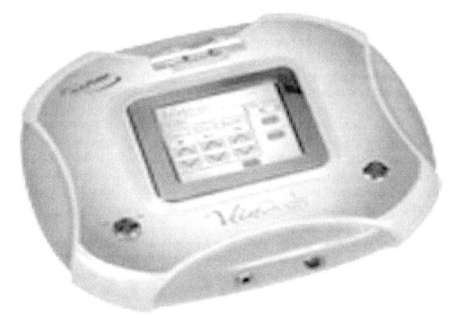

Another promising technology for small veins of the face and legs is the VEINGOGH. At this time, FDA clearance is pending for leg veins. However, this is another good alternative to IPL lasers. As mentioned earlier in the book, technology should allow you to treat what you want, and accomplish great results without pain, tenderness, or bruising, while limiting side effects. These newer technologies work to shrink spider veins by using a spectrum of radio waves, and can effectively treat smaller veins without thermal damage to the skin, or other complications related to sclerotherapy injections.

The Center for Venous Disease treatment preference at the current time for varicose vein treatment is VNUS RF Ablation due to the long-term clinical data, and immediate patient post-procedure benefits. Adjunctive procedures such as sclerotherapy, surface laser treatments, and micro-phlebectomy may be needed as well. As I stated, if any of the laser companies can prove to us that they have clinical longevity, without the pain and bruising, our centers will evaluate the technology. The lower cost of the laser fiber is only one consideration for us, as the patient comes first.

We are driven by long-term data and patient outcome. Currently we have better than 98.8% vein occlusion rates with this technology on thousands of patients. Based on the success and the hundreds of thousands of dollars in investment for the RF Generator, it would be hard for us to convert to another technology. We also desire that our patients leave our centers with positive experiences they will share with others. This is a key referral source for CVD. The largest patient demographic that brings us the most pride, is the patient who is also a healthcare provider or married to one. We treat more nurses, medical assistants, PA's, NP's, doctors, doctor's wives, relatives, etc... than any other offices in our markets. We treat friends of ours, working moms, teachers, landscapers, roofers, construction workers, factor workers, police officers, waitresses, investors, bankers, attorneys, celebrities, and even my wife!

I hope that you're delighted with what you just learned about your issues and concerns. It is hoped that you can use the knowledge to get the best treatment possible by a trained doctor in your area. As stated, finding a doctor and staff offering total vein care is crucial. You deserve "Healthy Legs," and the only way to get them is to have them treated by people who understand the entire venous system and can treat you as an individual with integrity, compassion, and respect.

We're happy to file your insurance for you or offer you payment terms to get treated today. The Center for Venous Disease offers a Fly-in & Fly-out program as well for those patients who live elsewhere. I would recommend getting your primary care doctor or OBGYN to order a venous insufficiency ultrasound exam and then send us the report. Once we receive this, we can help you understand the treatment options and cost. Our fax number is 623-234-2543. We can make all the arrangements including flights, hotel, and transportation. Please call 623-234-2542 for more information on this program.

To the primary care providers who bought this book for themselves or to give to their patients, I congratulate you! I also want to thank the doctors, physician's assistants, nurses, ultrasound technicians, and medical assistants that encourage patients and help educate them on venous disease. If you're a medical director for an insurance company, thanks for keeping an open mind. There is an expertise to treating venous disease, and the patient deserves the very best. You are a part of the solution for many of these patients! I would encourage patients and health providers to visit veinscreening.com, healthylegs.net, phlebology.org, VNUS.com, or one of the laser websites for more patient information. If you're a provider (doctor, nurse practitioner, physicians assistant, sonographer, primary care, or OBGYN) it would be a good idea to join the American College of Phlebology or American Venous Forum and attend their meetings. Some educational courses include CME credits.

Patients, please remember, it is my opinion that an American College of Phlebology Board Certified doctor will have more experience than any other doctor you can visit. ABPh Board Certification takes about 9-16 months to complete. This shows additional dedication to the specialty. As mentioned before, a CVD doctor must take the Phlebology Board within 12 months of signing their contract with CVDJBA, LLC Management Group (Policy Statement). This requirement along with other credentials such as Vascular Surgery, General Vascular Surgery, or General Surgery, etc... sets the Center for Venous Disease apart as far as expertise, outcomes, and patient satisfaction.

One other point to drive home. Some doctors will advertise that they do vein ablation and explain that the technology is all the same during your exam. You now know that is not true.

While working for VNUS in Arizona, New Mexico, and Texas I observed laser ablation doctors advertising that they did "venous Closure." The VNUS and Closure names are registered trademarks of VNUS Medical Technologies, San Jose, CA, a Covidien (NYSE: COV) company. This is just more validation of the misinformation and blending of technologies by some doctors who now know they have invested in the wrong technology.

As stated, VNUS is what we use and recommend. We were very happy with the 1320nm laser from CoolTouch. The 1319nm and 1470nm lasers are relatively new and we don't have any clinical data related to this technology yet that has been validated.

The technology is not the same despite what you've been told or seen in advertising. Let's face it. Many doctors have purchased a piece of equipment and invested up to $45,000-$130,000 or more to treat venous disease with a lower wavelength laser and an ultrasound unit. As the pain and bruising subject became increasingly visible to the patient, the laser industry evolved and began introducing the higher wavelength products for a more Radio-Frequency VNUS Closure like post-procedure result. If they are all striving for a result closer to VNUS, then why should you even consider other technology as a patient?

A recent ad highlighting the newer 1470nm laser (higher wavelength) from Total Vein Solutions™ pitched the following:

- LESS BRUISING

- LESS SWELLING

- VIRTUALLY NO PAIN

So, if you're in an office with a doctor that uses a LOWER (810-920nm) wavelength laser and they say that pain, bruising, and post-procedure swelling is NOT an issue to discuss, go somewhere else. It's documented and the higher wavelength laser companies are exploiting what the clinical documentation has already validated. 810nm-920nm lasers are painful for the patient.

Point-of-service is another consideration for the patient. It is safe to do this in the office setting if the doctor you select has the proper training. Another key observation is that there are many doctors using VNUS technology in an operating room setting. This is totally unnecessary and increases the cost to the nation's healthcare system and puts the patient at a higher risk. Again, I think this point-of-service is truly due to economic forces. The hospital may have bought the equipment for a doctor or group of doctors. I have seen charges from hospitals for one leg as high as $16,000 for this procedure. This point of service only increases the cost and your risk related to complications from the anesthesia. The lack of immediate ambulation afterwards increases the risk of "blood clots" which could lead to pulmonary embolism (PE). If you don't believe me, ask for a copy of the Informed Consent that the hospital requires you to sign. To be fair, this doesn't happen very often. Why take the risk when there are offices like ours with highly skilled, better trained, Board Certified Phlebologists? They can do all of this in about 30-45 minutes,

174

and you're on your way home or back to work. At CVD, we do not sedate our patients. Local anesthesia is all you need.

Just to add another degree of validity for the office setting. Medicare rates to doctors doing these procedures in a hospital setting were slashed years ago. If Medicare felt like the procedure wasn't safe, they would not incentivize (higher reimbursement) doctors who perform these procedures in their offices. Specifically, if a doctor does this in the OR, Medicare will pay on average $300 to the doctor. The hospital bills out the rest ($8,000-$16,000) and you pay more based on your co-insurance percent. In the office setting the doctor is paid a fee of $1,800-$1,900 on average and the doctors pays all the overhead for the staff, equipment, and catheter or laser kit. This is the right setting and saves everyone money. If you have to pay 20% of the cost, do you think 20% of a hospital bill, anesthesiologist cost, labs, chest x-rays, etc... are going to be less than you walking into an office setting and walking out within 15-20 minutes of your procedure with less chance of complications?

In summary:

1. Be informed. Visit the websites for the American College of Phlebology or The American Venous Forum, VNUS Medical Technologies, the Center for Venous Disease (healthylegs.net – veinscreening.com), the different laser companies and educate yourself.

2. Do your homework related to the selection of your doctor and seek out a Board Certified (ABPh – American Board of Phlebology) doctor. Go to your State's medical board (MD or DO) and look at their backgrounds, complaints, legal action.

3. Do your homework related to the technology. Radio-Frequency and Endovenous Laser are proven to close veins. The lower wavelength lasers hurt more, cause tenderness and/or bruising along the treated vein. VNUS is our choice.

4. Do your homework related to YOUR insurance plan. It's not my plan or the doctor's plan, it is YOURS. Your complaints should be aimed at your insurance company.

5. You decide the treatment point-of-service. I recommend the office setting based on meeting the above conditions. Do not go to the operating room for surgery when a "procedure" will do! The only time you should ever go under general anesthesia is when you absolutely have to. I've been in the operating room for over 20 years, and a perfectly healthy person can have a problematic situation including death under general anesthesia. It happens!

6. Keep your expectations real. The primary reason patients seek out our help is for swelling, pain, visible varicose veins, or vein clusters. If you have advanced venous disease and you're expecting your legs to look like an 18 year old, then that is not realistic. If you want to help reduce the pain, swelling, and stop the progression before you get a venous ulcer, then we can help you. We can improve the cosmetic appearance as well. Keep it real.

If you follow these simple suggestions, you'll find yourself with a better doctor, with better technology, manageable expectations, and better outcome.

Final remarks:

1. Find a ABPh (Phlebology) Board Certified Doctor with a surgery background. They are the "specialist" and can provide you with Total Vein Care.

2. I am recommending VNUS ClosureFast from VNUS Medical Technologies (Covidien-COV / NYSE) over any endovenous laser device. As stated, CVD will evaluate new technologies as they are FDA cleared.

3. I am recommending the office setting for this procedure to reduce the complication rates without sedation. Safety is not compromised with a trained staff and the right equipment (STAT kit, AED, oxygen).

4. The office has to have integrity and understand the insurance issues related to vein care.

5. CVD offers a FLY in & FLY out program if you would like us to treat you. Our contact information is at www.healthylegs.net.

6. Manage your expectations related to your "cosmetic" expectations.

Please consider gifting this book to a friend, family member, healthcare worker, or relative. Buying a copy for them might be one of the best gifts they could ever receive. This book is available online at:

www.E-BookTime.com
www.Amazon.com
www.BarnesandNoble.com.

The book was published by E-BookTime and I couldn't be happier in working with them on this project. The book is immediately available through them.

Remember that Venous Disease is progressive and will only worsen if left untreated. Please don't wait to get treated now that you have the information you need to make a good decision.

If you would like us to treat you, please contact The Center for Venous Disease business office at 623-234-2542 (CVDJBA, LLC Management Group) and we can discuss your options.

Thank you!

James A. Heinz, M.A.H.A.
Founder, Center for Venous Disease

Appendix 1

References and Clinical Papers

Publications and abstracts related to Radio-Frequency Ablation (VNUS Closure Procedure) and Endovenous Laser Ablation as treatments for varicose veins.

Published Papers

Boros M et al. High Ligation of the Saphenofemoral Junction in Endovenous Obliteration of Varicose Veins. Vasc and Endovasc Surg;42:235-8
http://www.ncbi.nlm.nih.gov/pubmed/18230872?ordinalpos=2&itool=Ent rezSystem2.PEntrez.Pubmed.Pubmed_ResultsPanel.Pubmed_RVDocSum

Perrin M. Traitement des varices par la radiofréquence. Sang Thrombose Vaisseaux 2008; 20:166-82.

R. Bush, MD, MPH. Endovenous and Surgical Extirpation of Lower-Extremity Varicose Veins. Sem in Vasc Surg 2008;21:50-3.
http://www.ncbi.nlm.nih.gov/pubmed/18342736?ordinalpos=1&itool=Ent rezSystem2.PEntrez.Pubmed.Pubmed_ResultsPanel.Pubmed_RVDocSum

T. Proebstle, M.D. et al. Treatment of the incompetent great saphenous vein by endovenous radiofrequency powered segmental thermal ablation: First clinical experience. J Vasc Surg 2008;47:151-6.
http://www.ncbi.nlm.nih.gov/pubmed/18178468?ordinalpos=1&itool=Ent rezSystem2.PEntrez.Pubmed.Pubmed_ResultsPanel.Pubmed_RVDocSum

A. Dietzek, M.D., Endovenous radiofrequency ablation for the treatment of varicose veins. Vascular. 2007 Sep-Oct;15(5):255-61.
http://www.ncbi.nlm.nih.gov/pubmed/17976324?ordinalpos=1&itool=Ent
rezSystem2.PEntrez.Pubmed.Pubmed_ResultsPanel.Pubmed_RVDocSum

L. Roland, M.D., AM Dietzek, M.D., Radiofrequency ablation of the great saphenous vein performed in the office: tips for better patient convenience and comfort and how to perform it in less than an hour. Perspect Vasc Surg Endovasc Ther. 2007 Sep;19(3):309-14.
http://www.ncbi.nlm.nih.gov/pubmed/17911563?ordinalpos=2&itool=Ent
rezSystem2.PEntrez.Pubmed.Pubmed_ResultsPanel.Pubmed_RVDocSum

S. Roth, M.D., M.S., Endovenous Radiofrequency Ablation of Superficial and Perforator Veins. Surg Clinics of N Am 2007 87:1267-84.
http://www.ncbi.nlm.nih.gov/pubmed/17936486?ordinalpos=1&itool=Ent
rezSystem2.PEntrez.Pubmed.Pubmed_ResultsPanel.Pubmed_RVDocSum

S. Zan, L. Contessa, G. Varetto, C. Barra, M. Conforti, F. Casella, P Rispoli, Radiofrequency minimally invasive endovascular treatment of lower limbs varicose veins: clinical experience and literature review. Minerva Cardioangiol. 2007 Aug;55(4):443-58.

M. Vasquez, M.D., The utility of the Venous Clinical Severity Score in 682 limbs treated by radiofrequency saphenous vein ablation. J Vasc Surg 2007 May;45(5):1008-1014; discussion 1015.
http://www.ncbi.nlm.nih.gov/pubmed/17466795?ordinalpos=1&itool=Ent
rezSystem2.PEntrez.Pubmed.Pubmed_ResultsPanel.Pubmed_RVDocSum

H. Welch, M.D., Endovenous ablation of the great saphenous vein may avert phlebectomy for branch varicose veins. J Vasc Surg 2006;44:601-5
http://www.ncbi.nlm.nih.gov/pubmed/16950441?ordinalpos=1&itool=Ent
rezSystem2.PEntrez.Pubmed.Pubmed_ResultsPanel.Pubmed_RVDocSum

C. Dunn, M.D., L. Kabnick, M.D., R. Merchant, M.D., R. Owens, M.D., R. Weiss, M.D. Endovascular Radiofrequency Obliteration Using 90C for Treatment of Great Saphenous Vein. Ann Vasc Surg 2006;1-5
http://www.ncbi.nlm.nih.gov/pubmed/16865607?ordinalpos=3&itool=Ent
rezSystem2.PEntrez.Pubmed.Pubmed_ResultsPanel.Pubmed_RVDocSum

B. Kianifard, M.D., MS Whitely, M.D., JM Holdstock, R.V.T. Radiofrequency ablation (VNUS Closure) does not cause neo-vascularisation at the groin at one year: results of a case controlled study. Surgeon. 2006 Apr;4(2):71-4.
http://www.ncbi.nlm.nih.gov/pubmed/16623160?ordinalpos=2&itool=Ent rezSystem2.PEntrez.Pubmed.Pubmed_ResultsPanel.Pubmed_RVDocSum

P. Stone, M.D., P. Armstrong, D.O., M. Shames, M.D., M. Back, M.D., B. Johnson, M.D., S. Flarherty, B.S., D. Bandyk, M.D. Impact of Postoperative Duplex Surveillance After Radiofrequency Ablation of the Greater Saphenous Vein. J Vasc Ultrasound 2006; 30(2):65-68

R. Merchant, M.D., O. Pichot, M.D., for the Closure study group. Long-term outcomes of endovenous radiofrequency obliteration of saphenous reflux as a treatment for superficial venous insufficiency. J Vasc Surg 2005;42:502-9
http://www.ncbi.nlm.nih.gov/pubmed/16171596?ordinalpos=3&itool=Ent rezSystem2.PEntrez.Pubmed.Pubmed_ResultsPanel.Pubmed_RVDocSum

D. Monahan, M.D. Can phlebectomy be deferred in the treatment of varicose veins? J Vasc Surg Dec 2005;42:1145-9

A. Puggioni, M. Kalra, P. Gloviczki. Superficial vein surgery and SEPS for chronic venous insufficiency. Semin Vasc Surg 2005;18:41-8
http://www.ncbi.nlm.nih.gov/pubmed/15791553?ordinalpos=4&itool=Ent rezSystem2.PEntrez.Pubmed.Pubmed_ResultsPanel.Pubmed_RVDocSum

Tzilinis A, Salles-Cunha SX, Dosick SM, Gale SS, Seiwert AJ, Comerota AJ.
Chronic venous insufficiency due to great saphenous vein incompetence treated with radiofrequency ablation: an effective and safe procedure in the elderly. Vasc Endovascular Surg. 2005 Jul-Aug;39(4):341-5.
http://www.ncbi.nlm.nih.gov/pubmed/16079943?ordinalpos=1&itool=Ent rezSystem2.PEntrez.Pubmed.Pubmed_ResultsPanel.Pubmed_RVDocSum

N. Morrison. Saphenous ablation: what are the choices, laser or RF energy. Semin Vasc Surg 2005;18:15-8.
http://www.ncbi.nlm.nih.gov/pubmed/15791548?ordinalpos=4&itool=Ent rezSystem2.PEntrez.Pubmed.Pubmed_ResultsPanel.Pubmed_RVDocSum

P. Nicolini and the Closure group. Treatment of primary varicose veins by endovenous obliteration with the VNUS Closure system: Results of a prospective multicentre study. Eur J Vasc Endovasc Surg 2005;29:433-9. http://www.ncbi.nlm.nih.gov/pubmed/15776398?ordinalpos=1&itool=Ent rezSystem2.PEntrez.Pubmed.Pubmed_ResultsPanel.Pubmed_RVDocSum

R. Merchant, M.D., O. Pichot, M.D., KA Mayers, M.D. Four Years Follow-up on Endovascular Radiofrequency Obliteration of Saphenous Reflux. Derm Surg 2005;31:129-134 http://www.ncbi.nlm.nih.gov/pubmed/15762202?ordinalpos=14&itool=Ent rezSystem2.PEntrez.Pubmed.Pubmed_ResultsPanel.Pubmed_RVDocSum

T. Ogawa, S. Hoshino, H. Midorikawa H, Sato K. Clinical results of radiofrequency endovenous obliteration for varicose veins. Surg Today 2005;35:47-51. http://www.ncbi.nlm.nih.gov/pubmed/15622464?ordinalpos=9&itool=Ent rezSystem2.PEntrez.Pubmed.Pubmed_ResultsPanel.Pubmed_RVDocSum

F. Lurie, D. Creton, B. Eklof, LS. Kabnick, RL. Kistner, O. Pichot, C. Sessa, S. Schuller-Petrovic Prospective Randomised Study of Endovenous Radiofrequency Obliteration (Closure) Versus Ligation and Vein Stripping (EVOLVeS): Two-year Follow-up. Eur J Vasc Endovasc Surg 2005;29:67-73. http://www.ncbi.nlm.nih.gov/pubmed/15570274?ordinalpos=1&itool=Ent rezSystem2.PEntrez.Pubmed.Pubmed_ResultsPanel.Pubmed_RVDocSum

L. Stotter, I Schaaf, A Bockelbrink, HJ Baurecht. Radiofrequency obliteration, invaginated or cryostripping: Which is the best tolerated treatment by the patient? Phlebologie 2005;34:19-24.

S Soumian, AH Davies. Endovenous management of varicose veins. Phlebology 2004;19:163-9.

SX Salles-Cunha, AJ Comerota, A Tzilinis, SM Dosick, SS Gale, AJ Seiwert, L Jones, M Robbins. Ultrasound findings after radiofrequency ablation of the great saphenous vein: descriptive analysis. J Vasc Surg 2004;40:1166-73. http://www.ncbi.nlm.nih.gov/pubmed/15622371?ordinalpos=2&itool=Ent rezSystem2.PEntrez.Pubmed.Pubmed_ResultsPanel.Pubmed_RVDocSum

M Perrin. Endoluminal treatment of lower limb varicose veins by endovenous laser and radiofrequency techniques. Phlebology 2004;19:170-8.

SM Elias, KL Frasier. Minimally invasive vein surgery: its role in the treatment of venous stasis ulceration. Am J Surg 2004;188(1A Suppl):26-30.
http://www.ncbi.nlm.nih.gov/pubmed/15223499?ordinalpos=3&itool=Ent
rezSystem2.PEntrez.Pubmed.Pubmed_ResultsPanel.Pubmed_RVDocSum

AP Hingorani, E Ascher, N Markevich, RW Schutzer, S Kallakuri, A Hou, S Nahata, W Yorkovich, T Jacob. Deep venous thrombosis after radiofrequency ablation of greater saphenous vein: a word of caution. J Vasc Surg 2004;40:500-4.

SX Salles-Cunha, H Rajasinghe, SM Dosick, SS Gale, A Seiwert, L Jones, HG Beebe, AJ Comerota. Fate of great saphenous vein after radiofrequency ablation: detailed ultrasound imaging. Vasc Endovascular Surg 2004;38:339-44.
http://www.ncbi.nlm.nih.gov/pubmed/15306951?ordinalpos=2&itool=Ent
rezSystem2.PEntrez.Pubmed.Pubmed_ResultsPanel.Pubmed_RVDocSum

M. Perrin. Endovenous therapy for varicose veins of the lower extremities. Ann Chir. 2004 May;129(4):248-57.
http://www.ncbi.nlm.nih.gov/pubmed/15191854?ordinalpos=3&itool=Ent
rezSystem2.PEntrez.Pubmed.Pubmed_ResultsPanel.Pubmed_RVDocSum

A. Zikorus, M. Mirizzi. Evaluation of Setpoint Temperature and Pullback Speed on Vein Adventitial Temperature During Endovenous Radiofrequency Energy Delivery in an In Vitro Model. Vasc Endovasc Surg 2004;38(2):167-74.
http://www.ncbi.nlm.nih.gov/pubmed/15064848?ordinalpos=2&itool=Ent
rezSystem2.PEntrez.Pubmed.Pubmed_ResultsPanel.Pubmed_RVDocSum

M. Perrin. Varices des membres inférieurs traitées par radiofréquence (Closure). Contrôle annuel des résultats : un suivi sur 3 ans (Longitudinal assessment at yearly intervals for lower limbs followed up three years after Endovenous radiofrequency obliteration (Closure)). Phlébologie 2004; 57:69-73.

WH Wagner, M.D., PM Levin, M.D., et al. Early experience with radiofrequency ablation of the greater saphenous vein. Ann Vasc Surg 2004;39:189-95.
http://www.ncbi.nlm.nih.gov/pubmed/14727161?ordinalpos=5&itool=Ent rezSystem2.PEntrez.Pubmed.Pubmed_ResultsPanel.Pubmed_RVDocSum

O. Pichot, M.D., L. Kabnick, M.D., FACS, D. Creton, M.D., R. Merchant, M.D., FACS, J. G. Chandler, MD and S. Schuller-Petrovic, M.D., Ph.D. Duplex Ultrasound Findings Two Years After Great Saphenous Vein Radiofrequency Endovenous Obliteration. J Vasc Surg 2004;39:189-95.
http://www.ncbi.nlm.nih.gov/pubmed/14718839?ordinalpos=6&itool=Ent rezSystem2.PEntrez.Pubmed.Pubmed_ResultsPanel.Pubmed_RVDocSum

F. Lurie, M.D.,Ph,D., D. Creton, M.D., B. Eklof, M.D., Ph.D., L.S. Kabnick, M.D., et al. Prospective Randomized Study of Endovenous Radiofrequency Obliteration (Closure Procedure) versus Ligation and Stripping in Selected Patient Population (EVOLVeS Study). J Vasc Surg 2003;38:207-214.
http://www.ncbi.nlm.nih.gov/pubmed/12891099?ordinalpos=2&itool=Ent rezSystem2.PEntrez.Pubmed.Pubmed_ResultsPanel.Pubmed_RVDocSum

N. Fassiadis M.D., JM Holdstock M.D., MS Whiteley M.D. Endoluminal radiofrequency ablation of the long saphenous vein (VNUS Closure) – a minimally invasive management of varicose veins. Minim Invasive Ther Allied Technol. 2003 Mar;12(1):91-4.
http://www.ncbi.nlm.nih.gov/pubmed/16754084?ordinalpos=1&itool=Ent rezSystem2.PEntrez.Pubmed.Pubmed_ResultsPanel.Pubmed_RVDocSum

O. Pichot, MD, C. Sessa, MD, JL Bosson, MD, Duplex imaging analysis of the long saphenous vein reflux: basis for strategy of endovenous obliteration treatment. Int. Angiol 2002; 21:333-6.
http://www.ncbi.nlm.nih.gov/pubmed/12518112?ordinalpos=5&itool=Ent rezSystem2.PEntrez.Pubmed.Pubmed_ResultsPanel.Pubmed_RVDocSum

N. Fassiadis M.D., B. Kianifard M.D., JM Holdstock M.D., MS Whiteley M.D. Ultrasound changes at the saphenofemoral junction and in the long saphenous vein during the first year after VNUS Closure. Int. Angiol 2002;21:272-274.
http://www.ncbi.nlm.nih.gov/pubmed/12384650?ordinalpos=3&itool=Ent rezSystem2.PEntrez.Pubmed.Pubmed_ResultsPanel.Pubmed_RVDocSum

O. Pichot, M.D., M. Perrin, M.D. Aspects échographiques de la jonction saphéno-fémorale après oblitération de la grande veine saphène par radiofréquence (Closure). Phlébologie 2002;55:329-334.

C. Lebard M.D., F. Zuccarelli, M.D. Intérêt de l'angiographie de la jonction saphéno-fémorale au cours de la destruction de la grande veine saphène par le système (Sapheno-femoral junctions angiography during great saphenous vein obliteration with VNUS Closure). Phlébologie 2002;55:263-268.

J. E. M. Sybrandy, M.D., C. H. A. Wittens, M.D., PhD. Initial experiences in endovenous treatment of Saphenous vein reflux. J Vasc Surg 2002;36:1207-12.

R. Kistner, M.D. Endovascular Obliteration of the Greater Saphenous Vein: The Closure Procedure. Jpn J. Phlebology, 2002; 13(5); 325-333.

R. Merchant, M.D., R. DePalma, M.D., L. Kabnick, M.D. Endovascular Obliteration of Saphenous Reflux – A Multicenter Study. J Vasc Surg 2002;35:1190-6.
http://www.ncbi.nlm.nih.gov/pubmed/12042730?ordinalpos=6&itool=Ent rezSystem2.PEntrez.Pubmed.Pubmed_ResultsPanel.Pubmed_RVDocSum

T. Rautio, M.D., J. Perala, M.D., Ph. D, et al. Endovenous Obliteration with Radiofrequency – resistive Heating for Greater Saphenous Vein Insufficiency: A Feasibility Study. J Vasc Interv Radiol 2002;13:569-75.
http://www.ncbi.nlm.nih.gov/pubmed/12050296?ordinalpos=2&itool=Ent rezSystem2.PEntrez.Pubmed.Pubmed_ResultsPanel.Pubmed_RVDocSum

J. Bergan, M.D., FACS, Hon FRCS, N. Kumins, MD, E. Owens, M.D., S. Sparks, M.D. Surgical and Endovascular Treatment of Lower Extremity Venous Insufficiency. J Vasc Interv Radiol 2002;13:563-68.
http://www.ncbi.nlm.nih.gov/pubmed/12050295?ordinalpos=1&itool=Ent rezSystem2.PEntrez.Pubmed.Pubmed_ResultsPanel.Pubmed_RVDocSum

T. Rautio, M.D., A. Ohinmaa, M.D., J. Perala, M.D., et al. Endovenous obliteration versus conventional stripping operation in the treatment of primary varicose veins: A randomized controlled trial with comparison of the costs. J Vasc Surg 2002;35:958-65.
http://www.ncbi.nlm.nih.gov/pubmed/12021712?ordinalpos=3&itool=Ent rezSystem2.PEntrez.Pubmed.Pubmed_ResultsPanel.Pubmed_RVDocSum

R. Weiss, M.D., M. Weiss, M.D. Controlled Radiofrequency Endovenous Occlusion Using a Unique Radiofrequency Catheter under Duplex Guidance to Eliminate Saphenous Reflux: A 2-Year Follow-Up. Dermatol Surg 2002; 28:38 – 42.
http://www.ncbi.nlm.nih.gov/pubmed/11991268?ordinalpos=35&itool=Ent rezSystem2.PEntrez.Pubmed.Pubmed_ResultsPanel.Pubmed_RVDocSum

M. Goldman, M.D., S. Amiry. Closure of the greater saphenous vein with endoluminal radiofrequency thermal heating of the vein wall in combination with micro-phlebectomy: 50 patients with more than 6-month follow-up. Dermatol Surg. 2002;28:29-31.

R. Weiss. Comparison of endovenous radiofrequency versus 810nm diode laser occlusion of large veins in an animal model. Dermatol Surg. 2002;28:56-61.
http://www.ncbi.nlm.nih.gov/pubmed/11991272?ordinalpos=34&itool=Ent rezSystem2.PEntrez.Pubmed.Pubmed_ResultsPanel.Pubmed_RVDocSum

N. Fassiadis, M.D., B. Kianifard, M.D., JM Holdstock, M.D., MS Whiteley, M.D. A novel endoluminal technique for varicose vein management: The VNUS Closure. Phlebology 2002;16:145-8.

O. Pichot, M.D., C. Sessa, M.D. Traitement de l'insuffisance veineuse superficielle par radiofréquence: Indications et resultants à moyen terme (Radiofrequency endovenous obliteration of the long saphenous vein: Indications and mid-term results). Phlébologie 2002;55:51-8.

R. Weiss, MD Endovenous techniques for elimination of saphenous reflux: A valuable treatment modality. Dermatol Surg 2001;27:902-5.
http://www.ncbi.nlm.nih.gov/pubmed/11722532?ordinalpos=5&itool=Ent rezSystem2.PEntrez.Pubmed.Pubmed_ResultsPanel.Pubmed_RVDocSum

L. Kabnick, M.D., R. Merchant, M.D. Twelve and Twenty Four Month Follow-up After Endovascular Obliteration of Saphenous Vein Reflux – A Report from the Multi-Center Registry. J Phleb 2001; 1:17-24.

C. Lebard M.D, F. Zuccarelli M.D. Destruction de la Grande Veine Saphene par le Systeme Closure, Occlusion of Greater Saphenous Vein by Closure System. Phlebologie 2001, 54, No 3, 285-291.

T. Dauplaise, RVT, R. Weiss, M.D. Duplex Guided Endovascular Occlusion of Refluxing Saphenous Veins. J Vasc Tech 2001;25(2):79-82.

M. Perrin, M.D. Un Procédé Nouveau Dans Le Traitement Des Varices Des Memberes inférieurs: La Technique Closure. Angeiologie, 2000, vol. 52 n°, 4 pp. 23a 28.

O. Pichot, M.D., C. Sessa, M.D., J.. Chandler, M.D., M. Nuta, M.D., and M. Perrin, M.D. Role of Duplex Imaging in Endovenous Obliteration for Primary Venous Insufficiency. J Endovasc Ther 2000; 7:6 451-459.
http://www.ncbi.nlm.nih.gov/pubmed/11194816?ordinalpos=6&itool=Ent rezSystem2.PEntrez.Pubmed.Pubmed_ResultsPanel.Pubmed_RVDocSum

J.. Chandler, M.D., O. Pichot, MD, C. Sessa, M.D., S. Schuller-Petrovic, M.D., Ph.D., F. Jose Osse, M.D., J.. Bergan, M.D. Defining The Role of Extended Saphenofemoral Junction Ligation: A Prospective Comparative Study. J Vasc Surg 2000; 32:941-53.
http://www.ncbi.nlm.nih.gov/pubmed/11054226?ordinalpos=7&itool=Ent rezSystem2.PEntrez.Pubmed.Pubmed_ResultsPanel.Pubmed_RVDocSum

J.. Chandler, M.D., O. Pichot, MD, C. Sessa, M.D., S. Schuller-Petrovic, M.D., PhD, L. Kabnick, M.D., and J. Bergan, M.D. Treatment of Primary Venous Insufficiency by Endovenous Saphenous-Vein Obliteration. Vasc Surg 2000;34:201-214.

M. Goldman, M.D. Closure of the Greater Saphenous Vein with Endoluminal Radiofrequency Thermal Heating of the Vein Wall in Combination with Micro-Phlebectomy: Preliminary 6 Month Follow-up. Dermatol Surg 2000; 26:452-456.
http://www.ncbi.nlm.nih.gov/pubmed/10816234?ordinalpos=8&itool=Ent rezSystem2.PEntrez.Pubmed.Pubmed_ResultsPanel.Pubmed_RVDocSum

S. Manfrini, MD, V. Gasbarro, MD, J. Chandler, M.D., A. Nicolaides, M.D., FRCS et al, for the Endovenous Reflux Management Study Group. Endovenous Management of Saphenous-Vein Reflux. J Vasc Surg 2000;32:330-42.
http://www.ncbi.nlm.nih.gov/pubmed/10917994?ordinalpos=4&itool=Ent rezSystem2.PEntrez.Pubmed.Pubmed_ResultsPanel.Pubmed_RVDocSum

Published Book Chapters

Towards Vascular and Endovascular Consensus – Copyright 2005
Varicose veins: endovascular option. M Whiteley Pages 564-72.

The Fundamentals of Phlebology: Venous Disease for Clinicians – Copyright 2004
Radiofrequency endovenous occlusion (Closure technique). Weiss RA Pages 101-4.

Vascular and Endovascular Challenges – Copyright 2004
Percutaneous radiofrequency ablation of varicose veins (VNUS Closure), MS Whiteley, J. Holdstock, Pages 361-74.

Trends In Vascular Surgery 2003
Endovenous radiofrequency obliteration of saphenous vein reflux. R.F.Merchant, RL. Kistner, WH Pearce, JS Matsumura, JS Yao. Pages 451-463.

Encyclopedie Medico Chirurgicale – Copyright 2003
"Traitement endovasculaire des varices des members inférieurs", M. Perrin, 43-161-C, Pages 1-11.

Viguera Editores, S.L. Insuficiencia Benousa Cronica – *Epidemologia, investigacion, diagnostico y tratamiento* – Copyright 2002
"Endovascular Therapy for Varicose Veins", M. Perrin, Chapter 24: Pages 211-20

Mosby Inc. *Advances in Vascular Surgery* – Copyright 2001
"Endovenous Saphenous Vein Ablation", J. Bergan, M.D.
Volume 9; Chapter 9: Pages 123-132.

W. B. Saunders Company – April 2001
Vascular and Endovascular Surgical Techniques:
"Endovenous Vein Closure", A. Nicolaides, M.D.
Vascular and Endovascular Surgical Techniques 4th Edition

McGraw Hill Companies – Copyright 2001
Vein Diagnosis & Treatment a Comprehensive Approach
"RF Mediated Endovenous Occlusion" Editors, R. Weiss, C. Feied, M. Weiss, Chapter 23: Pages 211-222.

Quality Medical Publishing, Inc. – Copyright 1999-2000
Varicose Veins and Telangiectasias Diagnosis and Treatment
"Controlled Radiofrequency-Mediated Endovenous Shrinkage and Occlusion", Editors, M. Goldman, R. Weiss, J. Bergan, Chapter 12: Pages 217-224.

Varicose Veins....A Patient's Reference, E-BookTime.com, © 2010, James A. Heinz, M.A.H.A., Founder, Center for Venous Disease®

Appendix 2

JoshuaBay™ Aesthetics

In early 2011, The JoshuaBay™ Aesthetics brand will announce the national release of our new skin care line through licensed aestheticians. This approach is in line with our dedication to quality products with training and education at the fore front. Through A²CE™ / Advanced Aesthetics Center for Excellence, licensed aestheticians will be trained on our skin care line under the supervision of Michael A. Herion, M.D.

Can you think of a better consultant for your skin care issues, anti-aging, or corrective treatments than someone who is certified as a skin care consultant? Wouldn't it make sense to buy skin care products through someone who is educated vs. the cosmetics counter at a retail store or from someone who was recruited by Mary Kay®, Avon, or Arbonne®?

Nothing against these products. However, they are NOT formulated by healthcare insiders and they are not sold by people whose livelihood is skin care. That's what sets us apart. It's a formula that has worked for us with vein care, and we feel it will work well with skin care.

Our thought process on the development of this line was to have a tailored seven step process based on your skin type and problem areas. The product line is color-coded and easy to follow. Some of the products you'll use in the a.m. and some in the p.m. to maximize the results. Part of the product line brochure and explanation of benefits are listed below. We will also release a men's line in 2011 that helps men with their skin care needs, hair care, and body wash products, to insure healthy skin from head to toe. JBA for men will follow a similar philosophy as the current

JBA product line. I would invite you to try these products. If you're a licensed aesthetician and are interested in receiving training and/or selling this product line, please call me at 623-234-2542. Your start up kit, training, and software for success is inclusive in your contract with AACE, LLC. What are you waiting for?

SKIN CARE SYSTEM

Your daily skin care routine should be an enjoyable ritual not a time consuming chore.

JoshuaBay™ products have been developed with this in mind.

PATIENT INFORMATION

NAME: _____

SKIN CARE SPECIALIST: _____

DATE STARTED: _____

RECOMMENDED PRODUCTS:

_____

_____

_____

_____

_____

_____

CLEANSER: _____

TONER: _____

EXFOLIATOR: _____

CORRECTIVE SERUM: _____

EYE CARE: _____

MOISTURIZER: _____

SUN PROTECTION: _____

FOLLOW-UP DATE: _____

FOLLOW-UP DATE: _____

FOLLOW-UP DATE: _____

1

JBA STORY

The JoshuaBay™ Skin Care System was formulated with one goal in mind... results and patient compliance.

Our physician-lead team of aesthetic experts combined their best practice experiences in medical aesthetics to design and introduce a simple-to-follow, color-coded, step-by-step, complete Skin Care System. Our system is formulated using only the most efficacious processes and natural ingredients.

Our skin care team understands a skin care program should be based on treating the skin from the inside out, which will increase the skin's cellular replacement, greatly enhancing its health and appearance. As we age, the skin's cellular turnover decreases, leading to evidence of sun damaged skin, wrinkles, hyperpigmentation, skin laxity, and an overall unhealthy and dull-looking complexion.

Our team has identified seven essential steps that should be practiced on a daily basis to initiate and maintain a healthy cellular turnover. Our seven step focus includes:

1. Cleanse
2. Tone
3. Exfoliate
4. Correct
5. Eye Care
6. Moisturize
7. Protect

Without specific focus in these areas, your skin care program is incomplete. Since no two patients have the same skin type, products will be specifically chosen and tailored to address each client's particular skin condition. This is accomplished by any or all of the following; a detailed patient questionnaire, computer facial analysis, consultation with your doctor.

Our complete JoshuaBay™ Aesthetic Skin Care System developed by doctors, aestheticians, skin care professionals and patient input, was formulated and manufactured especially for YOU!

Your comments, suggestions, and testimonials are always welcome. Please visit our website at www.joshuabayaesthetics.com. Thank you!

2

CPSIA information can be obtained at www.ICGtesting.com
Printed in the USA
BVOW08s2204040813

327711BV00006B/21/P

9 781608 622344